UNSETTLED REMAINS

UNSETTLED

CANADIAN LITERATURE AND THE POSTCOLONIAL GOTHIC.

REMAINS

EDITED BY
CYNTHIA SUGARS AND GERRY TURCOTTE

Wilfrid Laurier University Press

[WLU]

This book has been published with the help of a grant from the Canadian Federation for the Humanities and Social Sciences, through the Aid to Scholarly Publications Programme, using funds provided by the Social Sciences and Humanities Research Council of Canada. We acknowledge the support of the Canada Council for the Arts for our publishing program. We acknowledge the financial support of the Government of Canada through the Book Publishing Industry Development Program for our publishing activities.

Canada Council for the Arts / Conseil des Arts du Canada

ONTARIO ARTS COUNCIL / CONSEIL DES ARTS DE L'ONTARIO

Library and Archives Canada Cataloguing in Publication

Unsettled remains : Canadian literature and the postcolonial gothic / Cynthia Sugars and Gerry Turcotte, editors.

Includes bibliographical references and index.
ISBN 978-1-55458-054-5

1. Gothic revival (Literature) — Canada. 2. Postcolonialism in literature.
3. History in literature. 4. Ambivalence in literature. 5. Canadian fiction (English) — 20th century — History and criticism. I. Sugars, Cynthia, [date] II. Turcotte, Gerry

PS8191.G6U57 2009   C813'.0872909054   C2009-900095-4

© 2009 Wilfrid Laurier University Press
Waterloo, Ontario, Canada
www.wlupress.wlu.ca

Cover image by Rosalie Favell, "I awoke to find my spirit had returned" (1999), from the series Plain(s) Warrior Artist.
Cover design by Blakeley Words+Pictures.
Text design by Daiva Villa, Chris Rowat Design.

This book is printed on FSC recycled paper and is certified Ecologo. It is made from 100% post-consumer fibre, processed chlorine free, and manufactured using biogas energy.

Printed in Canada

Contents

Canadian Literature and the Postcolonial Gothic

Cynthia Sugars and Gerry Turcotte

Dead bodies can talk if you know how to listen to them, and they *want* to talk.
— Margaret Atwood, *Negotiating with the Dead*

How is it we can live / with how we forget them.
— Steven Heighton, "Graveyard in the North Country"

Postcolonial and gothic discourses have for some time been paired in critical invocations of the "unhomely" or "spectral" legacies of imperialism and globalization.[1] This legacy, which appears in the form of unresolved memory traces and occluded histories resulting from the experience of colonial oppression, diasporic migration, or national consolidation, is readily figured in the form of ghosts or monsters that "haunt" the nation/subject from without and within. In *Specters of Marx,* Jacques Derrida insists that "[h]aunting belongs to the structure of every hegemony" (1994, 37), and the recognition of the always already phantom that haunts the literary, the political, the social, and the corporate has compelled writers to seek out appropriate metaphors to represent such phenomena. Homi Bhabha is perhaps the most well-known postcolonial theorist to invoke the Freudian "uncanny" as a way of articulating the ambivalence of colonial power structures, although Frantz Fanon, a practising psychiatrist, had used Freudian theory years before to elucidate the "psychology" of colonialism ([1952] 1967; [1961] 1966). Edward Said's ground-breaking study, *Orientalism* (1978), explored the ways the "Orient" emerged in colonialist documents as a discursive construct characterized by exotic and gothic fantasies of fear and desire. In 1989, this project was applied in a settler context by Terry Goldie, who used a similar approach to uncover the ways the figure of the "Indigene" in Canadian, Australian, and New Zealand literatures was disseminated through gothic tropes of savagery, sexuality, and primitivism. Contemporary critical texts such as Avery Gordon's *Ghostly Matters: Haunting and the Sociological Imagination* (1997) and Ken Gelder and Jane M. Jacobs's *Uncanny Australia* (1998) argue that the postcolonial nation is haunted by "ghost stories" and that the reappearance of these suppressed "stories" or histories produces an uncanny and haunted space in the narratives of nationhood. In the context of Canadian literary and cultural studies, such critics as Diana Brydon (1995; 2003), Justin Edwards (2005), Marlene Goldman and Joanne Saul (2006), Sneja Gunew (2004), Jonathan Kertzer (1998), Alan Lawson (1995), Roy Miki (1998), Stephen Slemon (1990), Cynthia Sugars (2003; 2004a and b; 2006a and b), and Gerry Turcotte (1998a and b; 2004) have made use of the notion of "unhomely" unsettlement to describe various engagements with, and subjections to, the "postcolonial" Canadian nation-state.[2]

This volume engages with the intersection of gothic modes of influence in a settler-invader postcolonial context. In particular, it attempts to unpack the manifestations of the Gothic in Canada as a transplanted form. Alan Lawson and Stephen Slemon describe the inherent, yet often occluded, instability of settler-invader locations, specifically their "in-between" positioning between "two origins of authority and authenticity: the originating world of Europe, the imperium ... [and] that of the First Nations, whose authority the settlers not only effaced and replaced but also desired" (Lawson 1995, 29). Both critics highlight aspects of ambivalence, liminality, mimicry, boundary dissolution, and epistemological destabilization that characterize the negotiations that occur in these locations. Viewed in this way—and, admittedly, positioned from the perspective of a White settler rather than that of an Aboriginal subject—settler locations would seem to invite gothic figuration, not only in terms of the monstrous or grotesque (as Margot Northey outlines in her study) but also in terms of subjective and national interiority and unsettlement. It is the latter categories that more typically characterize the "postcolonial Gothic" in Canadian literature, which is concerned less with overt scenes of romance and horror than with experiences of spectrality and the uncanny. In many of these works, there is an aura of unresolved and unbroachable "guilt," as though the colonial/historical foundations of the nation have not been thoroughly assimilated. If early instances of the Gothic in Canadian literature, as in John Richardson's 1832 novel *Wacousta,* were concerned with terror in the face of the unknown wilderness (see Hurley 1992; Turcotte 2009a), a more recent strain of gothic literature in Canada has been less preoccupied with an overtly externalized and alien sense of gothic otherness that is "out there" and more concerned with an interiorized psychological experience of gothic "uncanniness" and illegitimacy.

The uncanny is one among many possible manifestations of the Gothic, yet it provides a key hinging point for expressions of territorial and historical dispossession and inauthenticity. The term "uncanny," as Sigmund Freud defines it, is integrally linked to the paradox of home and "unhomeliness" — those moments when the familiarity of home (or what *should* be the familiarity of home) is infected by unhomeliness and elicits an "uncanny" or unsettling experience ([1919] 1956). Instances of this effect include scenes where the distinction between past and present, real and spectral, civilized and primitive, is tenuous and disjunctive. When the uncanny is combined with the Gothic, elements of the supernatural, the monstrous, or the paranormal are foregrounded. When these are conjoined with the postcolonial, it takes a variety of possible tacks: fears of territorial illegitimacy, anxiety about forgotten or occluded histories, resentment towards flawed or complicit ancestors, assertions of Aboriginal priority, explorations of hybrid cultural forms, and interrogations of national belonging and citizenship. All of these phenomena point to the continuing legacy of colonial history in settler-invader cultures, lingering traces that reveal "the return of the colonial moment" in the narratives through which "our ambiguously postcolonial cultures characterize themselves and their tendentious histories" (Lawson 1995, 32, 20). Even more crucial are fears that the Gothic is itself a mode that can never be indigenous to Canadian experience. For non-Indigenous subjects, the Canadian postcolonial Gothic arguably charts a largely psychological experience — haunted minds rather than a haunted wilderness (though for invaded peoples, the sense of their "wilderness" being haunted *by* Europeans would seriously texture this perception). It attests to a tentative, yet also palpably immediate, perception of overlapping realities and temporalities in the wake of settler-invader-diasporic colonial history.

The question of the postcolonial status of Canadian society and culture necessarily arises in the context of these discussions. Indeed, it might be said to haunt the very discourse of settler-invader postcolonial theory itself. Not long ago, Laura Moss published a collection of essays entitled *Is Canada Postcolonial?* (2003), inviting a series of inquiries into the tenuous postcolonial status of the Canadian nation-state. Yet if one reads the term postcolonial less as a descriptive label than as a series of questions that are enabled in the aftermath and continuance of colonialism, it becomes easier to see how a variety of authors have engaged with the legacy of colonialism in different ways and at different historical junctures. Hence, one can examine a text such as Charles De Guise's *Le Cap au diable* (1863) with an eye to an emergent gothic rendition of colonial experience following the Acadian Expulsion. Viewed from a different perspective, novels such as Sheila Watson's *The Double Hook* (1959), Joy Kogawa's *Obasan* (1981), Tomson Highway's *Kiss of the Fur Queen* (1998), Janice Kulyk Keefer's *The Green Library* (1996), and Michael Crummey's *River Thieves* (2001) take up a gothic modality in sometimes incongruent ways as they respond to historical crisis and dispossession. The subject of the postcolonial Gothic, far from being assumed in the essays gathered in this volume, is rehearsed, contested, and interrogated. Together, these essays take an approach that holds in abeyance any possibility of a uniform postcolonial status. In her introduction to *Unhomely States*, Cynthia Sugars suggests that although "[t]here may be some quibbling with the terminology itself, and much debate about how postcolonial theory is to be applied in a Canadian context (if at all), and, perhaps, little agreement on 'whose postcolonialism' we are speaking of when we invoke such a label as 'Canadian postcolonialism,'" the plethora of Canadian literary and critical texts that engage with this topic "illustrate that the postcolonial is anything but 'post'" (2004a, xx). As Helen Tiffin so clearly puts it, "[t]he term post-colonial…implies the *persistence* of colonial legacies in post-independence cultures, not their disappearance or erasure" (1996, 158). The very persistence of gothic motifs of haunting and monstrosity that invoke the colonial past testifies to the incomplete resolution of these histories.

This book addresses what is becoming a distinctive, though by no means homogeneous, subgenre—a postcolonial Gothic. Gothic tropes have emerged in Canadian literature as integral to the postcolonial interrogation of national identity constructs and dominant representational practices. Sometimes these tropes are used to convey the ways in which the Canadian national project is inherently haunted. In other cases, gothic discourse is used to mediate forgotten histories and, in some instances, initiate forms of cultural mourning (signalling a loss of cultural memory/history resulting from colonialism or migration or, alternatively, because of a perceived illegitimacy in one's tenancy of the land). In Canadian literature, the postcolonial Gothic has been put to multiple uses, above all to convey experiences of ambivalence and/or split subjectivity resulting from the inherent incommensurability of conflicted subject positions that have emerged from a colonial context and persisted into the present. In many instances, the postcolonial Gothic involves a transposition of conventional gothic and colonialist metaphors, turning gothic conventions on their head by converting the unfamiliar or ghostly into nonthreatening—even sustaining—objects of desire. Paradoxically, the haunting effect can be unsettling and enabling at the same time. As Avery Gordon puts it, "the ghost is a crucible for political mediation and historical memory" (1997, 18).

Historically, Canadian authors and critics have been compelled by the supposed tenuousness of the gothic project in the colonial settler-invader context. The inherent ambivalence of gothic discourse became magnified in this context where it was not the ontological status of gothic monsters that was in question but, rather, the very applicability of gothic tropes themselves. For many early settlers in Canada, the overwhelming epistemological question was whether an appropriated landscape could be truly *unheimlich* if it had not been previously assimilated as a *heimlich* space. Nevertheless, from the beginnings of first contact and settlement in Canada, gothic projections onto the landscape were prevalent, in part because the colonization of Canada coincided, in the late eighteenth and early nineteenth centuries, with the literary genre of the Gothic in Europe. Early European explorers' encounters with the vast and seemingly uninhabited landscapes of North America were often marked by an aggressive and resistant response to Canadian Indigenous peoples. When writers turned to the Gothic to generate terror or dread, it was frequently to textualize a form of white history that cast colonized or invaded peoples and the colonial landscape as a ghostly or monstrous threat to the civilized (white) world (Goldie 1989; van Toorn 1992–93; Turcotte 1998b and 2009b; Bergland 2000).

Gothic figurations of the Canadian landscape are evident in a good deal of Canadian literature from the nineteenth century onwards. Jennifer Andrews's contribution to this collection, "Rethinking the Canadian

Gothic," provides a useful survey of some of these approaches. Susanna Moodie responded to the backwoods surrounding her early homestead by populating the wilderness with imagined wild beasts set to attack her — a fearful response that was picked up years later by Margaret Atwood in her well-known sequence of poems, *The Journals of Susanna Moodie* (1970). John Richardson's 1832 novel *Wacousta* is a gothic text in which the British regiment during the Pontiac uprisings of 1763 is surrounded by an impenetrable wilderness and threatening Natives, and it culminates in the revelation that the British have themselves been "invaded" by the spirit of savagery in the form of the British-turned-Native Wacousta himself. Philippe Aubert de Gaspé, son and father, and William Kirby wrote novels that included numerous folk legends and superstitions in their accounts of pre-conquest Quebec, namely *L'Influence d'un livre* (1837), *Les Anciens Canadiens* (1863), and *The Golden Dog* (1877). Likewise, such texts as Julia Catherine Hart's *St Ursula's Convent* (1824), Charles Dawson Shanly's famous poem, "The Walker of the Snow" (1859), and the short stories of Duncan Campbell Scott and Charles G.D. Roberts from the late nineteenth and early twentieth centuries, like Robert Service's popular poems about the "spell" of the Yukon (1907), provide acutely gothic responses to remote Canadian settings and rural villages — a phenomenon that is epitomized in Earle Birney's 1952 poem, "Bushed," in which an isolated settler is "killed" by his feverish projections onto a hostile, personified landscape. Gothic projections onto a purportedly unsettled "wilderness" were thus often used to express the settler-invader's alienation from the New World territory that had been appropriated by illegitimate means. However, such gothic responses could also be used to legitimate the settler's presence or even, as Brian Johnson's analysis of the "northern gothic" of Farley Mowat demonstrates in this volume, to establish white settler *priority* in the New World. Northrop Frye, seeking an overarching summation of Canadian sensibility, enunciates an inherently settler-invader gothic modality that embraces a poetics of "incubus and *cauchemar*" that is rooted in the paranoia of a "garrison mentality" (1971, 141; 1965, 830). Taking her cue from Frye, in her 1972 study *Survival,* Margaret Atwood posits a plethora of Canadian monsters that a supposedly prototypical Canadian "victim" must confront and survive.

Paradoxically, given the extensive presence of gothic tropes in Canadian literature, the Gothic was also widely invoked for its purported *absence* in Canada, which was in part a colonial response arising from the perceived

secondary or inferior status of Canadian culture and society in compari- ✓
son to that in Britain and Europe. In short, the sense was that Canada was
too "new" to be sufficiently haunted. Catharine Parr Traill, in *The Backwoods of Canada,* famously proclaimed that Canada was "too matter-of-
fact a country for the supernatural" (1836, 128). Her sister Susanna
Moodie insisted that the country "was too new for ghosts" ([1852] 1991,
267). The force of this denial informed Earle Birney's famous assertion,
almost a century later, that "it's only by our lack of ghosts / we're ✓
haunted" ([1966] 1977, 49). Birney's observation articulated the widely
held sense that Canada was devoid of a meaningful (European/American)
history. Notwithstanding Margot Northey's 1976 study *The Haunted
Wilderness: The Gothic and Grotesque in Canadian Fiction,* the notion of
Canada as being too prosaic a land to be inhabited by gothic monsters
was widely taken up by numerous Canadian writers. Margaret Atwood
echoed Birney's sentiments in her essay "Canadian Monsters" by stating
that Canadian literature, by definition, had typically excluded the Gothic
and the supernatural in favour of a more "social-realistic" mode (1977,
98). Similarly, in his introduction to his 1982 collection of ghost stories,
High Spirits, Robertson Davies famously contended that Canada suffered
from an absence of ghosts: "Canada needs ghosts, as a dietary supplement, a vitamin taken to stave off that most dreadful of modern ailments,
the Rational Rickets" (1982, 2). And yet, typical of the doubled nature of
gothic discourse (at once both familiar and strange), both writers also
insisted that Canada was an inherently gothic space. In a 1986 interview
with Michael Hulse, Davies stressed the intractable gothic tenor of
Canadian life — "Gothic goings-on are to be found in every part of
Canada" (1989, 254) — while Atwood, in her two essay collections, *Strange
Things* (1995) and *Negotiating with the Dead* (2002), emphasized Canadian
literature's overwhelming fascination with gothic elements. The repeated
invocations of the prosaic nature of Canadian sensibility and the purported absence of ghosts are now as much a part of the ghosts in the
landscape as the specter of colonization itself.

    In response to the oft-proclaimed "lack of ghosts" that haunts Canadian
culture, Canadian writers have been led to conjure, and indeed channel,
the crowded landscape of ghosts and monsters that circulate above,
around, and within the parameters of the Canadian nationalist project.
Canada, it would seem, has long contained sites (and subjects) of gothic
instability, many of which have been neglected at a cost. Gothic revenants

are often used to figure the culpable history of the Canadian nation-state, founded upon "the contradictory injunction ... to remember to forget its fantasmatic and traumatic history" (Coleman 2006, 224). The construction of the Canadian nation as a homogeneous and civil society—what Northrop Frye described as the "peaceable kingdom" (1965, 848)—is belied by those peoples and cultures whose suppression made national consolidation possible and yet who remain as "haunting" presences that challenge the national imaginary. Andrea Cabajsky's discussion of the Acadian Expulsion as a haunting yet constitutive history in Charles De Guise's work and Gerry Turcotte's analysis of the ways in which Joy Kogawa's *Obasan* reveals the nation as *unheimlich* to itself, both included in this volume, are illustrative examples of this dynamic. Atef Laouyene's analysis of the haunting effect of "race" in Ann-Marie MacDonald's *Fall on Your Knees* highlights a similar instance of the return of a repressed history. Other contributors to this collection explore the ways that the illegitimate appropriation of Native lands comes back to haunt the Canadian settler-colonial state in the form of gothic tropes that are inherently ambivalent. Such a response is evident in Sheila Watson's *The Double Hook* (1959), as Marlene Goldman discusses in "Coyote's Children," and is also present in the "Beothuk Gothic" of Michael Crummey's 2001 novel *River Thieves*, as Herb Wyile delineates in his essay in this volume. Davies, in reassessing Moodie, was prescient when he observed that a "country which too vigorously asserts its normality and rationalism is like a man who declares that he is without imagination; suddenly the ghosts he has denied may overcome him" (1981, 234). In recent years, a recurrent gesture has been made towards the strange things that negotiate with the (un)dead and monstrous, by way of bringing to the fore a sense of the forgotten and unacknowledged, the repressed and the denied. These signposts of a gothic order have become frequent in contemporary criticism of the last decade, most notably in Derrida's oft-cited *Specters of Marx* (1994), which enjoins readers to learn to speak with ghosts—to acknowledge the shrouded and silent—and to move towards a collective sense of redefinition and reconciliation. The explosion of interest in the field of study that brings together the Gothic, the uncanny, the haunted, and the haunting, together with a postcolonial reassessive method, suggests that perhaps the ghosts and monsters that haunt the nation/subject (from without and within) are finally being heard. To contemplate the present, and to imagine the future, it may be necessary to revisit the past and to come to terms with the fact that, as David Punter has put it, "we live in a world peopled by ghosts, phantoms, and spectres" (1999, 1).

That the tools of the Gothic should be paired with the language of the postcolonial in order to articulate and interrogate national identity constructs and dominant representational practices is unsurprising. The Gothic, as a mode, is preoccupied with the fringes, the unspoken, the peripheral, and the cast aside. It is populated with monsters and outcasts, villains and victims, specters and the living dead. The Gothic is often located in a realm of unknown dangers and negotiates both internal and external disquiet. It is a literature of excess and imagination, but one that is used as well to reassure and compartmentalize unreason. It is therefore a literature that both enacts and thematizes ambivalence. As Maggie Kilgour puts it, the Gothic is a "puzzling contradiction, denounced and now celebrated for its radical imaginative lawlessness, feared for its encouragement of the reader to expect more from life than is realistic, and also for its inculcation of social obedience and passivity. Revolutionary or reactionary? An incoherent mess or a self-conscious critique of repressive concepts of coherence and order?" (1995, 10). In some cases, as Kilgour suggests, the Gothic—perhaps even more so the postcolonial Gothic—offers a possibility of mediation into real-world politics, since it "exposes the Gothic reality of modern identity, and by failing to represent an adequate solution it forces its readers to address them in real life, thus (ideally) using literature to encourage social change" (10). As Shelley Kulperger argues in this collection, such a possibility is especially true of the feminist postcolonial Gothic in Canada, which materializes and familiarizes haunting and trauma by merging the real world with the otherworldly. "Such refractions of the uncanny—the strange made familiar and the familiar made strange," Kulperger states, "are intricately hinged to the material world."

Lizabeth Paravisini-Gebert has noted that from its "earliest history" the Gothic has been "linked to colonial settings, characters, and realities as frequent embodiments of the forbidding and frightening" (2002, 229). The postcolonial has similarly negotiated the complex parameters of haunted spaces, where imported and local voices have vied for existence through often violent encounters. Like the Gothic, postcolonialism has had almost endless incarnations, moving from celebratory to fatalistic forms and from the local to the global, but always in the context of a sense of anxious enquiry—over its "name," its approach, its political framework, its disciplinary base, and its relevance. As Alan Lawson puts it, "postcolonialism and anxiety [are] always tied together" (2000, 24). The connection between the Gothic and the postcolonial thus brings together highly useful overlaps that afford new approaches for understanding cultural production. This is particularly apparent in contemporary Canadian writing, which, in multiple and often contending ways, reveals an obsession with the uncanny or invisible world and in which, arguably, the Gothic has taken on a dimension distinct from Old World prototypes. As Justin Edwards puts it, "Canadian conceptions of identity take place on the ground of indecipherability" (2005, xx). Gothic phantoms, captured through the figure of the ghost, the vampire, the monstrous, and the uncanny, exist at the limits of the imaginary, both troubling and constituting the stories that we write. Lawson suggests that settler-invader contexts such as Canada are the location "where the processes of colonial power as negotiation, as transactions of power, are most visible" (1995, 22). If postcolonialism is inherently unsettling, this might suggest that tropes of the Gothic and uncanny are especially useful in figuring Canadians' ambivalent relation to their past and present. As Graham Huggan has argued, "[g]hosts bring the past into our midst, that we might recognise it. But they also estrange the past: their relationship to the history that they reinstate is inherently uncertain" (1998, 128). These "histories," in other words, are familiar but hidden, and, thus, their summoning is specifically uncanny in Freud's sense, in that they "lead us back to something long known to us" ([1919] 1956, 369–70).

   This "hauntology" may well explain what Roger Luckhurst has identified as the "spectral turn" that sees the "language of ghosts and the uncanny" dominating the work of writers subjected to "political disempowerment" (2002, 536). However, Luckhurst cautions that the "generalized structure of haunting" that is emerging in current criticism may be "symptomatically blind to its generative loci" (528). He insists, following Derrida, that it is important for critics not to surrender to an aestheticized discourse that ignores historical specificity and that produces an atemporalized reading of such figurations. Instead, he urges us to recognize the way in which a situated gothic voice might function "as a grounded manifestation of communities in highly delimited locales subjected to cruel and unusual forms of political disempowerment" (536). This recognition might suggest that the geography of the spectral is most pointedly understood through more profoundly disenfranchised and fragmented communities often invoked under the aegis of the postcolonial.

Given the preponderance of colonialist accounts that demonize "otherness," it is not surprising that many writers have avoided gothic metaphors. And, yet, in recent years, many "marginalized" writers have chosen to speak through a myriad of spirits—local and foreign, self-generating and imposed, empowering and overwhelming. This is the subject of Lindy Ledohowski's compelling argument about Ukrainian-Canadian gothic texts in her essay included in this volume. These works, she argues, signal something uncanny at the level of ethnic identity by making use of gothic tropes as a way of evoking continuing anxiety about ethnicity even in a postcolonial context. This writing back to literary tradition is given an additional twist in Vincent Lam's *Bloodletting & Miraculous Cures* (2005), as Cynthia Sugars explores in her essay, where "reading for the Gothic" is used as an uncanny counterpoint to conventional, empirically driven epistemologies, as well as providing a different understanding of the postcolonial Gothic that takes us beyond direct engagements with colonialism.

This collection of essays, then, examines various ways that Canadian writers have combined a postcolonial awareness with metaphors of monstrosity and haunting in order to articulate their response to a multitude of attestably unsettling contexts within Canada. As these essays demonstrate, this approach differs radically depending on the social and cultural positioning of the author/reader in question. Historically, Canadian writers have used gothic tropes to articulate their sense of the contingency of their presence in Canada. Initially, it is fair to say, the Gothic emerged as a way of responding to the unfamiliar by demonizing and even fetishizing the "unknown"—be it human or landscape. Often this monstrous presence was figured as an Indigenous one—a danger lying just beyond the garrison but not sufficiently removed. Over time, Canadian writers began to appropriate this force, to bend it to a national purpose, and to map the parameters of an identity that might embrace what was resonantly local so that the Gothic became a way to insist on, rather than deny, a colonial history. In effect, the gothic mode was used to articulate a suitably "haunted" version of Canadian identity, one that lent the Canadian locale a "feel" of authenticity because it had been rendered "(un)homely" (that is, both familiar and unfamiliar at the same time). The much-heralded "homegrown" genre of Southern Ontario Gothic (for example, the writings of Matt Cohen, Robertson Davies, Alice Munro, Margaret Atwood, Timothy Findley, and James Reaney) or French Canadian Gothic (from Philippe Aubert de Gaspé's *Les Anciens Canadiens* to the work of *québécois* writers such as Anne Hébert and Marie-Claire Blais) exemplify this approach. In recent years, many Canadian authors have turned to the Gothic to articulate a postcolonial—sometimes transnational—revisioning of Canadian history and overarching national meta-narratives. Works such as John Steffler's *The Afterlife of George Cartwright*, Ann-Marie MacDonald's *Fall on Your Knees*, Gail Anderson-Dargatz's *The Cure for Death by Lightning*, Michael Crummey's *River Thieves*, Larissa Lai's *When Fox Is a Thousand*, Nalo Hopkinson's *Brown Girl in the Ring*, SKY Lee's *Disappearing Moon Cafe*, Joseph Boyden's *Three Day Road*, and any number of works by Margaret Atwood fall into this category. One can also speak of a Canadian Prairie Gothic tradition (including such writers as Robert Kroetsch, Rudy Wiebe, Margaret Sweatman, and Hiromi Goto), or an Atlantic-Canadian Gothic (including Wayne Johnston, Michael Crummey, Kenneth Harvey, John Steffler, Patrick Kavanagh, and Ann-Marie MacDonald), or possibly even a contemporary urban Gothic (including writers such as Tony Burgess, Andrew Pyper, Judith Thompson, and Lynn Crosbie), all of which "write back" to nationalist paradigms.

Perhaps most importantly, the postcolonial Gothic has been used to challenge dominant literary, political, and social narratives. The cover image to this collection, a photo-montage by Winnipeg Métis artist Rosalie Favell entitled *I awoke to find my spirit had returned* (1999), is an excellent example of this dynamic. The montage adapts a scene from the Hollywood movie *The Wizard of Oz* (1939) in which the character of Dorothy, a self-portrait of Favell, looks up from under a colourful Hudson's Bay trading blanket (with the recognizable Hudson's Bay Company stripes), while the family (film characters) huddled around the bed are joined by Métis leader Louis Riel looking in through the window in the spot where the wizard stands in the original scene from *The Wizard of Oz*. The caption alludes to Riel's purported statement that Native people would rise to prominence 100 years after his death. The photo has an uncanny effect as it is unclear whether the black-and-white figures are benevolent or alien. The expression on the woman's face highlights this ambiguity. The mix of colour and black-and-white plays on the overlayering of dream and reality that is prevalent in the film, making it unclear which portion of the photo, if any, is "real." Favell turns this iconic Hollywood image into a commentary on Métis history, while also ironizing it, by drawing on the parodic conjunction of the figures in "Kansas" and the Canadian prairies. Barbara Gabriel, who first used this image on the cover of her book *Tainting History: Essays in Life-Writing*, suggests that the photo "disrupt[s] the fabled machinery of nation from behind the scenes" (2006, 11). The Hudson's Bay Company blanket, she argues, "returns us to Riel's own place in the 1869 occupation of Fort Garry (over which a flag of the Metis provisional government was raised in place of the Hudson's Bay Company ensign)" (11). The photo thus highlights the ways that we are imbricated in a troubled history that refuses to let ghosts lie. The spirit of Riel, benevolent or vengeful depending on how you look at it, infuses the present context of Aboriginal-settler relations in which "a young Aboriginal girl [such as Favell] growing up in the dominant North-American culture...must reweave stories in ways that are simultaneously acts of rebellion and acts of accommodation, finding her own 'home'" (11).[3]

A related use of gothic structures is evident in much contemporary writing by Canadian Aboriginal authors. As numerous critics have noted, "the figure of the Indian ghost," signalling the supposed disappearance of Indigenous peoples, has long been prevalent in North American writing (Bergland 2000, 2). Ironically, the refusal of Indigenous peoples to disappear has been as long-standing as invader narratives proclaiming this inevitability. In recent years, many First Nations writers have invoked this notion of the "Indian ghost" for political effect. Thomas King's powerful short story, "A Seat in the Garden" (1993), is a prime example, as are King's and Tomson Highway's frequent representations of "trickster" figures as spirits and ghosts who haunt both Natives and non-Natives alike (although, admittedly, in different ways). Eden Robinson's *Monkey Beach* (2000) invokes an "Indian ghost" of a quite different sort, as Jennifer Andrews demonstrates in her essay in this collection, by overturning conventional associations of Native people with gothic "savagery" and populating her novel with spirits and monsters that guide her protagonist. This "spectral turn" reverses long-standing characterizations of some identities as "monstrous" or invisible and reveals a simultaneous connection to, and disconnection from, stories of the nation. Yet if these texts offer counter-discursive inversions of the colonial Gothic, Highway's 1998 novel *Kiss of the Fur Queen*, as Jennifer Henderson argues here, is compelling for its resistance to easy resolution as a postcolonial gothic text due to the ambiguity of the novel's linking of colonialism, homosexuality, and misogyny. Even as the novel invokes the gothic trope of Catholicism, its concurrent alignment of this tradition with both sexual abuse and same-sex desire renders its sexual politics ambivalent.

Recently, debates have arisen about the applicability of the term "gothic" to the spiritual worlds represented by Aboriginal authors (see Castricano 2006 and Jennifer Andrews's contribution to this collection). Works by Louise Bernice Halfe, Tomson Highway, Thomas King, Daniel David Moses, and Eden Robinson invite a reassessment of the association of gothic conventions with psychoanalytic motifs of repression and unsettlement since Aboriginal spirits often do not carry the same threatening aspect as conventional gothic monsters. Is there an "Aboriginal Gothic" or an "Aboriginal uncanny" and is it appropriate to use a term derived from Western European tradition (such as the term "postcolonial" itself) to describe cultural texts by Aboriginal authors? Or can one identify in some of these works a use of the Gothic to convey the return of a once "familiar" spiritual culture that was repressed by the process of colonization? Are some of these texts consciously mobilizing the Gothic for particular counter-discursive effects? Novels such as Joseph Boyden's *Three Day Road* (2005) and Tomson Highway's *Kiss of the Fur Queen* (1998), for example, chart the ways the Windigo monster of northern Cree tradition can be used to figure the voracious and implacable nature of imperial power relations. One might also ask what happens when different spiritual systems meet or even clash, as occurs in Maria Campbell and Linda Griffiths's *The Book of Jessica* (1989), a provocative study of uncanny mediation in which "half-digested theatrical gods" meet "Native spirits" and "all hell [breaks] loose" (14). Indeed, Campbell makes the point that cultural appropriation will not cease, and cultural healing will not begin, until non-Indigenous people stop fetishizing Indigenous ghosts and finally acknowledge their own (see Turcotte 2001, 187–88).

Unsettled Remains foregrounds a series of connected, but independent, readings of Canadian literary texts in order to explain the way a modern nation might stage a literary rehearsal of the past as mediated through the gothic mode. The collection demonstrates how being haunted is intimately connected to the activity of haunting and how possessing is always already a negotiation with dispossession, hence suggesting ways the colonial becomes postcolonial and, by extension, how postcolonialism is itself "haunted" by its grounding in a compromised history. The essays gathered in this volume explore the links between postcolonialism, nationalism, diaspora, and the Gothic in Canadian literature by addressing some of the following interrelated questions. What are the connections between postcoloniality and the Gothic? How are gothic conventions used or modified in a Canadian context? Are national narratives necessarily haunted by an inherently gothic subtext and how have writers attempted to gothicize the Canadian nation-state? In what ways is the Gothic used to explore questions of history, nostalgia, genealogy, memory, trauma, guilt, or mourning? How are settler/Aboriginal relations "gothicized" and how do writings by Aboriginal authors engage with gothic conventions? These essays range from treatments of early postcolonial gothic expression in Canadian literature (essays by Cabajsky and Johnson) to attempts to define a Canadian postcolonial gothic mode (essays by Andrews, Goldman, Kulperger, and Sugars). Kulperger's essay, in particular, which focuses on novels by Dionne Brand, Ann-Marie MacDonald, and Eden Robinson, opens with an explicit delineation of a feminist postcolonial Gothic as a mode that seeks to "materialize and familiarize" the inherited legacies of colonization through the construction of a "mundane supernatural." Many of these texts wrestle with Canada's colonial history and the voices and histories that were repressed in the push for national consolidation (essays by Henderson, Laouyene, Turcotte, and Wyile). In addition, some consider the ways a gothic mode enables an articulation of the "in-between" nature of identity in Canada (Ledohowski and Turcotte). Inevitably, many of these essays also investigate the ways in which the postcolonial Gothic is a necessarily complicit modality in its attempts to articulate a distinct Canadian national identity (essays by Goldman, Johnson, and Wyile).

The Canadian nation emerges as an inherently uncanny site in these narratives. As Atef Laouyene puts it in his contribution to this collection, "[h]ybrid and imagined though it is, Canadian national identity still feeds upon the chimera of an originary, mythopoeic idea of the nation, yet what that chimera usually spawns is an uncanny, spectral Otherness that keeps re-turning and haunting the nation at large." A study of the postcolonial Gothic in Canadian literature necessarily examines what has been silenced or forced to the sidelines in a national context and is therefore concerned with what emerge as uncanny reminders of that problematic history.

Notes

The editors would like to acknowledge the assistance of the Social Sciences and Humanities Research Council of Canada in the preparation of this book.

1 For consistency, the term "gothic" when used as an adjective has been written with a lower-case "g"; when used as a noun or as a description of the genre (e.g., Gothic tradition), the term has been capitalized.
2 All of these authors explore the ways haunting and gothicism are seminal metaphors in describing nation formations and postcolonial experience.
3 We would like to acknowledge Rosalie Favell for permission to use her image on the cover of this book as well as Barbara Gabriel and Penumbra Press, who first used the image on the cover of Gabriel's *Tainting History* (2006). Gabriel's introduction to the book contains an extended discussion of Favell's artwork in the context of other visual allusions to Louis Riel.

Works Cited

Anderson-Dargatz, Gail. 1996. *The Cure for Death by Lightning.* Toronto: Knopf.
Atwood, Margaret. 1970. *The Journals of Susanna Moodie.* Toronto: Oxford UP.
———. 1972. *Survival: A Thematic Guide to Canadian Literature.* Toronto: Anansi.
———. 1977. "Canadian Monsters: Some Aspects of the Supernatural in Canadian Fiction." In *The Canadian Imagination: Dimensions of a Literary Culture.* Ed. David Staines. Cambridge, MA: Harvard UP. 97–122.
———. 1995. *Strange Things: The Malevolent North in Canadian Literature.* Oxford: Clarendon.
———. 2002. *Negotiating with the Dead: A Writer on Writing.* Cambridge: Cambridge UP.
Aubert de Gaspé, Philippe (*père*). 1863. *Les Anciens Canadiens.* Quebec: Desbarats and Derbishire.
Aubert de Gaspé, Philippe (*fils*). 1837. *L'Influence d'un livre.* Quebec: William Cowan.
Bergland, Renée L. 2000. *The National Uncanny: Indian Ghosts and American Subjects.* Hanover: UP of New England.
Bhabha, Homi. 1994. *The Location of Culture.* London: Routledge.
Birney, Earle. 1952, reprinted 1966. "Bushed." In *Selected Poems 1940–1966.* Toronto: McClelland and Stewart. 117.
———. 1966, reprinted 1977. "Can.Lit." In *Ghost in the Wheels: The Selected Poems of Earle Birney.* Toronto: McClelland. 49.
Boyden, Joseph. 2005. *Three Day Road.* New York: Viking.
Brydon, Diana, ed. 1995. *Testing the Limits: Postcolonial Theories and Canadian Literature.* Special issue of *Essays on Canadian Writing* 56.

———. 2003. "Canada and Postcolonialism: Questions, Inventories, and Futures." In *Is Canada Postcolonial?: Unsettling Canadian Literature*. Ed. Laura Moss. Waterloo: Wilfrid Laurier UP. 49–77.

Castricano, Jodey. 2006. "Learning to Talk with Ghosts: Canadian Gothic and the Poetics of Haunting in Eden Robinson's *Monkey Beach*." *University of Toronto Quarterly* 75(2): 801–13.

Coleman, Daniel. 2006. *White Civility: The Literary Project of English Canada*. Toronto: University of Toronto Press.

Crummey, Michael. 2001. *River Thieves*. Toronto: Doubleday.

Davies, Robertson. 1981. *The Well-Tempered Critic: One Man's View of Theatre and Letters in Canada*. Ed. Judith Skelton Grant. Toronto: McClelland and Stewart.

———. 1982. *High Spirits: A Collection of Ghost Stories*. Harmondsworth: Penguin.

———. 1989. "Robertson Davies in Conversation with Michael Hulse." In *Conversations with Robertson Davies*. Ed. J. Madison Davis. Jackson: UP of Mississippi. 252–69.

De Guise, Charles. 1863. *Le Cap au diable: Légende canadienne*. Saint-Anne de la Pocatière, QC: Firmin H. Proulx.

Derrida, Jacques. 1994. *Specters of Marx: The State of the Debt, the Work of Mourning, and the New International*. Trans. Peggy Kamuf. New York: Routledge.

Edwards, Justin. 2005. *Gothic Canada: Reading the Spectre of a National Literature*. Edmonton: University of Alberta Press.

Fanon, Frantz. 1952, reprinted 1967. *Black Skin, White Masks*. Trans. Charles Lam Markmann. New York: Grove.

———. 1961, reprinted 1966. *The Wretched of the Earth*. Trans. Constance Farrington. New York: Grove.

Freud, Sigmund. 1919, reprinted 1956. "The Uncanny." In *Collected Papers: Papers on Metapsychology, Papers on Applied Psycho-Analysis*, volume 4. Trans. Joan Riviére. London: Hogarth. 368–407.

Frye, Northrop. 1965. "Conclusion." In *Literary History of Canada: Canadian Literature in English*. Ed. Carl F. Klinck. Toronto: University of Toronto Press. 821–49.

———. 1971. *The Bush Garden: Essays on the Canadian Imagination*. Toronto: Anansi.

Gabriel, Barbara, ed. 2006. *Tainting History: Essays in Life-Writing*. Munro Beattie Lecture Series. Manotick, ON: Penumbra Press.

Gelder, Ken, and Jane M. Jacobs. 1998. *Uncanny Australia: Sacredness and Identity in a Postcolonial Nation*. Melbourne: Melbourne UP.

Goldie, Terry. 1989. *Fear and Temptation: The Image of the Indigene in Canadian, Australian and New Zealand Literatures*. Montreal and Kingston: McGill-Queen's UP.

Goldman, Marlene, and Joanne Saul, eds. 2006. *Haunting in Canadian Literature.* Special issue of *University of Toronto Quarterly* 75(2).

Gordon, Avery F. 1997. *Ghostly Matters: Haunting and the Sociological Imagination.* Minneapolis: University of Minnesota Press.

Griffiths, Linda, and Maria Campbell. 1989. *The Book of Jessica: A Theatrical Transformation.* Toronto: Coach House.

Gunew, Sneja. 2004. *Haunted Nations: The Colonial Dimensions of Multiculturalisms.* London: Routledge.

Hart, Julia Catherine. 1824. *St. Ursula's Convent, or The Nun of Canada.* Kingston: Thomson.

Heighton, Steven. 1994. "Graveyard in the North Country." In *The Ecstasy of Skeptics.* Concord, ON: Anansi. 47–48.

Highway, Tomson. 1998. *Kiss of the Fur Queen.* Toronto: Doubleday.

Hopkinson, Nalo. 1998. *Brown Girl in the Ring.* New York: Warner.

Huggan, Graham. 1998. "Ghost Stories, Bone Flutes, Cannibal Countermemory." In *Cannibalism and the Colonial World.* Ed. F. Barker, P. Hulme, and M. Iversen. Cambridge: Cambridge UP. 126–41.

Hurley, Michael. 1992. *The Borders of Nightmare: The Fiction of John Richardson.* Toronto: University of Toronto Press.

Kertzer, Jonathan. 1998. *Worrying the Nation: Imagining a National Literature in English Canada.* Toronto: University of Toronto Press.

Kilgour, Maggie. 1995. *The Rise of the Gothic Novel.* London: Routledge.

King, Thomas. 1993. *Green Grass, Running Water.* Boston: Houghton Mifflin.

———. 1993. "A Seat in the Garden." In *One Good Story, That One.* Toronto: HarperCollins. 83–94.

Kirby, William. 1877. *The Golden Dog.* Montreal: Lovell.

Kogawa, Joy. 1981, reprinted 1985. *Obasan.* Toronto: Penguin.

Kulyk Keefer, Janice. 1996. *The Green Library.* Toronto: HarperCollins.

Lai, Larissa. 1995. *When Fox Is a Thousand.* Vancouver: Press Gang.

Lam, Vincent. 2005. *Bloodletting & Miraculous Cures.* Toronto: Doubleday.

Lawson, Alan. 1995. "Postcolonial Theory and the 'Settler' Subject." *Essays on Canadian Writing* 56: 20–36.

———. 2000. "Proximities: From Asymptote to Zeugma." In *Postcolonizing the Commonwealth: Studies in Literature and Culture.* Ed. Rowland Smith. Waterloo: Wilfrid Laurier UP. 19–37.

Lee, SKY. 1990. *Disappearing Moon Cafe.* Vancouver: Douglas & McIntyre.

Luckhurst, Roger. 2002. "The Contemporary London Gothic and the Limits of the 'Spectral Turn.'" *Textual Practice* 16(3): 527–46.

MacDonald, Ann-Marie. 1996. *Fall on Your Knees.* Toronto: Knopf.

Mackey, Eva. 2002. *The House of Difference: Cultural Politics and National Identity in Canada.* Toronto: University of Toronto Press.

Miki, Roy. 1998. *Broken Entries: Race, Subjectivity, Writing*. Toronto: Mercury Press.

Moodie, Susanna. 1852, reprinted 1991. *Roughing It in the Bush*. Toronto: New Canadian Library.

Moss, Laura, ed. 2003. *Is Canada Postcolonial?: Unsettling Canadian Literature*. Waterloo: Wilfrid Laurier UP.

Northey, Margot. 1976. *The Haunted Wilderness: The Gothic and Grotesque in Canadian Fiction*. Toronto: University of Toronto Press.

Paravisini-Gebert, Lizabeth. 2002. "Colonial and Postcolonial Gothic: The Caribbean." In *The Cambridge Guide to Gothic Fiction*. Ed. Jerrold E. Hogle. Cambridge: Cambridge UP. 229–57.

Punter, David. 1999. "Introduction: Of Apparitions." In *Spectral Readings: Towards a Gothic Geography*. Ed. Glennis Byron and David Punter. London: Macmillan. 1–10.

Richardson, John. 1832. *Wacousta; or, The Prophecy: A Tale of the Canadas*. London: T. Cadell.

Robinson, Eden. 2000. *Monkey Beach*. Toronto: Knopf.

Said, Edward. 1978. *Orientalism*. New York: Pantheon.

Service, Robert. 1907. *The Spell of the Yukon and Other Verses*. New York: Barse and Hopkins.

Shanly, Charles Dawson. 1859. "The Walker of the Snow." *Atlantic Monthly* May: 631.

Slemon, Stephen.1990. "Unsettling the Empire: Resistance Theory for the Second World." *World Literature Written in English* 30(2): 30–41.

Steffler, John. 1992. *The Afterlife of George Cartwright*. Toronto: McClelland and Stewart.

Sugars, Cynthia. 2003. "Haunted by (a Lack of) Postcolonial Ghosts: Settler Nationalism in Jane Urquhart's *Away*." *Essays on Canadian Writing* 79: 1–32.

———. 2004a. "Introduction: Unhomely States." In *Unhomely States*. Ed. Cynthia Sugars. Peterborough: Broadview. xiii–xxv.

———, ed. 2004b. *Unhomely States: Theorizing English-Canadian Postcolonialism*. Peterborough: Broadview.

———. 2006a. "The Impossible Afterlife of George Cartwright: Settler Melancholy and Postcolonial Desire." Special "Haunting" issue of *University of Toronto Quarterly* 75(2): 693–717.

———. 2006b. "'Saying Boo to Colonialism': Surfacing, Tom Thomson, and the National Ghost." In *The Open Eye: Reappraisals of Margaret Atwood*. Ed. John Moss. Ottawa: University of Ottawa Press. 137–58.

Tiffin, Helen. 1996. "Plato's Cave: Educational and Cultural Practices." In *New National and Post-Colonial Literatures: An Introduction*. Ed. Bruce King. Oxford: Clarendon. 143–63.

Traill, Catherine Parr. 1836, reprinted 1989. *The Backwoods of Canada*. Toronto: McClelland and Stewart.

Turcotte, Gerry. 1998a. "Australian Gothic." In *Handbook to Gothic Literature*. Ed. Marie Mulvey Roberts. London: Macmillan. 10–19.

———. 1998b. "English-Canadian Gothic." In *Handbook to Gothic Literature*. Ed. Marie Mulvey Roberts. London: Macmillan. 49–53.

———. 2001. "Collaborating with Ghosts: Dis/possession in *The Book of Jessica* and *The Mudrooroo/Müller Project*." In *Siting the Other: Re-Visions of Marginality in Australian and English-Canadian Drama*. Ed. Marc Maufort and Franca Bellarsi. Amsterdam: Rodopi. 175–92.

———. 2004. "Postcolonial Pedagogy and the Uncanny Space of Possibility." In *Home-Work: Postcolonialism, Pedagogy and Canadian Literature*. Ed. Cynthia Sugars. Ottawa: University of Ottawa Press. 151–65.

———. 2009a. *Peripheral Fear: Transformations of the Gothic in Canadian and Australian Fiction*. Bruxelles: Peter Lang.

———. 2009b. "First Nations Phantoms and Aboriginal Spectres: The Function of Ghosts in Settler-Invader Cultures." In *Postcolonial Ghosts*. Ed. Mélanie Joseph-Vilain and Judith Misrahi-Barak, *Les Carnets du Cerpac* no. 8. Montpellier: Presses universitaires de la Méditerranée [forthcoming].

van Toorn, Penny. 1992–93. "The Terrors of *Terra Nullius:* Gothicising and De-Gothicising Aboriginality." *World Literature Written in English* 32(2) and 33(1): 87–97.

Watson, Sheila. 1959. *The Double Hook*. Toronto: McClelland and Stewart.

CHAPTER ONE

Catholic Gothic: Atavism, Orientalism, and Generic Change in Charles De Guise's *Le Cap au diable*

Andrea Cabajsky

Introduction: Atavism and the "Time" of the Gothic

Literary historians from Edmond Lareau to Robert Viau have credited Charles De Guise with introducing the theme of the Expulsion of the Acadians into French-Canadian literature in *Le Cap au diable: Légende canadienne* (Lareau 1874, 327; Viau 1997, 55).[1] De Guise's novella is framed as an oral "tale" narrated by an unidentified storyteller to his unnamed grandson. It is the tragicomic story of an Acadian woman known only as "Mme. Saint-Aubin," whose madness is precipitated by her belief that she has been widowed and rendered childless after being forced to flee Acadia in a series of violent encounters with the British in the late 1750s. At the close of *Le Cap au diable*, the Saint-Aubins have been reunited with one another, but the subplot involving the "Devil's Cape" persists beyond the novella's conclusion, for the local landscape continues to "haunt" the inhabitants — a mnemonic of lived history and a symbol of Catholic memory.

In this essay, I argue that the fractured plot of *Le Cap au diable*, along with the various concepts with which the trope of Catholicism is emburdened, should be seen as emblematic of the epistemological challenges that faced De Guise when he transformed metropolitan British Gothic into an argument for the viability of Catholic modernity.[2] The first section of this essay examines the historical roots of the Catholic trope in eighteenth-century British gothic fiction and cultural discourse. It argues that *Le Cap au diable* reworks conventional Burkean aesthetics of terror and the sublime in its attempt to transform the history of Acadian dispossession into a recuperative national French-Canadian narrative. The second section pries apart the combination of narrative styles and literary conventions that inform *Le Cap au diable* at the same time as they disrupt the flow of its narrative. I argue that the narrative unevenness of *Le Cap au diable* represents an important formal register of larger epistemological dilemmas that confront an emergent national literature. My conclusion takes a step back from the plot of De Guise's novella in order to ask what makes *Le Cap au diable* a "gothic" text? I propose that the roots of such a deceptively simple question lie both in nineteenth-century debates about literary forms as well as in more recent discussions about the value of early Canadian literature to postcolonial discourse.

Colonial Gothic: Catholicism and Terror as "Weapons of the Weak"

[T]he rise of the Gothic novel, and the development of the aesthetics of terror in Edmund Burke's landmark *Enquiry into the Origin of the Sublime and Beautiful* (1757), all coincide with the Seven Years War in America and India, and the unprecedented expansion of the British Empire.
    —Luke Gibbons, *Gaelic Gothic*

Set in a recognizably Catholic landscape, *Le Cap au diable* begins by establishing a visual contrast between "sharp cliffs" and "alpine valleys," between "haphazard" mountains, rock faces, and overhangs and the charming villages that "repose in peace" under the "protection of the old churches that dominate" the landscape (De Guise 1863, 3). This is a typically Burkean scene — the juxtaposition of the sublime and the picturesque encouraging onlookers (and the readers whose place they take) to "contemplate" the contrast between the variously "wild" and "beautiful" landscapes (3). The narrative style of the opening paragraphs represents an obvious adaptation of Ann Radcliffe's trademark style of contrasts whereby scenic transformations reflect the larger thematic oscillations between morality and dread with which the narrative is suspended ([1794] 1998).[3] De Guise's description of the St. Lawrence River valley, dotted by villages that are "protected" by church steeples and bounded by magnificent precipices, openly resembles the Italian landscape of Radcliffe's *The Mysteries of Udolpho* ([1794] 1998), which contains similarly quaint villages, nestled in valleys and dominated by Catholic architecture and symbols: "On the edge of tremendous precipices, and within the hollow of the cliffs, below which the clouds often floated, were seen villages, spires, and convent towers; while … perpendicular rocks of marble, or … mossy crags, rose above each other, till they terminated in the snow-topt mountain, whence the torrent fell, that thundered along the valley" (164). While Radcliffe's modular passage describes a similar landscape to De Guise's derivative opening scene, the two passages diverge from one another in their tones. The Catholic landscape of *Le Cap au diable* provides a soothing contrast to the terrible scenes that will follow, while the opposite dynamic is largely at work in Radcliffe's novel.

Le Cap au diable demonstrates an application of the model of Radcliffean Gothic, which famously provides everyday explanations for apparently supernatural events. Briefly put, the novella recounts the story of the Saint-Aubin family, whose arcadian existence is shattered by the sudden arrival of the British. The narrative opposes the violence and destructiveness of the British characters to the peacefulness of the Acadians and suggests, at the same time, a fundamental incompatibility between British and Acadian national characters. As a result of the Expulsion, the three members of the Saint-Aubin family are separated from one another for roughly a decade: Monsieur Saint-Aubin is deported, first to the New England colonies and then to England itself, while Madame (Mme.) Saint-Aubin is separated from her four-year-old daughter, Hermine, as they subsequently attempt to flee Acadia. The story of the expulsion of the Saint-Aubins is interconnected with a second narrative thread that adapts conventions from eighteenth-century Gothic and novels of sensibility to tell the story of Mme. Saint-Aubin's descent into madness. Unaware that her husband has been deported, Mme. Saint-Aubin waits days, and then weeks, her initial impatience at her husband's protracted absence turning quickly to debilitating anxiety. Her neighbour, Jean Renousse, has escaped the hands of the British and, though injured and bleeding openly from a wound on his head, thinks of little else than his desire to bring Mme. Saint-Aubin news of her husband. Mme. Saint-Aubin receives a near-fatal shock when she hears footsteps approaching her front door and, believing that her husband has finally returned, finds instead a bleeding, monstrous figure at her doorstep. Mme. Saint-Aubin faints,

3

nearly dies, and, although her motor skills return, is never the same again. Things become worse when she and her daughter board a ship full of Irish immigrants destined for Quebec. Mme. Saint-Aubin nearly loses her life through a combination of maltreatment by the British and a sudden hurricane that arises on the St. Lawrence River and takes the lives of all of the ship's passengers. Believing her daughter to be dead, Mme. Saint-Aubin goes mad.

While *Le Cap au diable* ultimately provides "everyday" explanations for the hauntings and catastrophes that repeatedly torment the characters, these "everyday" explanations are far from reassuring. Mme. Saint-Aubin has gone mad due to her catastrophic encounters with the British. The world of the "real" thus represents a world in which the Acadians have been deported and in which New France has fallen to the British. The horrific events that De Guise's novella describes do not belong to the realm of the supernatural but, rather, to the realm of historical, lived experience. The symbol at the heart of this experience is Mme. Saint-Aubin herself, who doubles as the terrifying "apparition" that registers, physically and psychologically, the traumatic effects of lived history. The narrator introduces Mme. Saint-Aubin to readers, whom he addresses using the second-person pronoun, by fusing their perspective with that of the actual observers, so that the readers become "witnesses" to the strange "apparition" on the cliff:

> At times, I tell you, you would have seen a woman with a haggard eye, unkempt hair, naked arms, clothing in scraps, tighten her hands at the bottom of the chasm and mutter a prayer, a touching supplication; at others, [you would have seen her] uttering threats, imprecations, as if she were trying to reclaim a victim, someone who used to belong to her. Only the boldest sailor could have seen this apparition and heard its voice without immediately turning back to the shore, muttering a prayer as he went. Yet others... have claimed to have seen the apparition crawling on the edge of the beach, in tears of despair, beseeching the tide to return to it what it had lost.... There is no doubt that if this fantastic being were really a woman, then the poor thing had to have been in the clutches of immense sorrow. (De Guise 1863, 5)[4]

A Canadian example of what David Punter has called the "domestic Gothic" genre,[5] *Le Cap au diable* deals with suppressed histories by having them erupt onto the domestic landscape (2002, 106–07). For example, the suddenness with which the British soldiers appear, as though out of nowhere, imbues them with a monstrous quality that the narrative underpins with its repeated descriptions of their "rapacious" appetites and almost mechanical obsession with destruction (see especially De Guise 1863, 19–21). By conflating historical events with characteristically gothic preoccupations with ruptured historical descent, usurped patrimony, and what Ian Duncan has described as "a cultural heritage grown balefully strange," *Le Cap au diable* establishes a precedent-setting equation between a lost origin shared by the Acadians and the French Canadians and an alien force (the British) that invades their home ground (1992, 23). Mme. Saint-Aubin becomes a figure loaded with semiotic energies, which transform a history of lost origins into a gothic tale of ruin, of physical and ideological bondage, and, ultimately, of cultural alienation. While the Saint-Aubins will eventually be reunited with one another, the "Devil's Cape," readers learn, will continue to "haunt" the local inhabitants, as though the landscape itself has been irremediably altered by the events that have taken place.

The transformation of the French-Canadian landscape into a site of historical trauma performs a variety of important functions. It establishes the "Devil's Cape" as a kind of repository of the past and Mme. Saint-Aubin as the figure representing a desire for revisionary historiography in her role as a witness to this lived history. Through the interplay between hearsay, spectatorship, and testimony that characterizes the extended passage quoted earlier, the narrative sustains the legalistic tenor of Mme. Saint-Aubin's role as a witness. As Victor Sage suggests, the narrative form of gothic fiction "is demonstrably 'legalistic' — it calls attention to itself as testimony.... Witnessing [thus, has an] 'objective,' almost scientific significance, as well as an overtly religious sense" (1988, xix). It is thus important that, at the close of the novella, after the Saint-Aubins have moved back to Acadia, the "Devil's Cape" continues to "haunt" the local inhabitants, a mnemonic of recent events. There is an inescapable irony to the notion that the "Devil's Cape" comes to represent a repository of Catholic memory and, as its name suggests, a "devilish" setting — a realm outside of God. One of the key questions that underpins my examination of *Le Cap au diable* is the following: how would a Catholic writer subvert metropolitan Gothic? Would he simply invert the pattern standardized by metropolitan writers — that is, would he simply locate his novella in a Protestant setting? It is interesting to see that De Guise has chosen not to do this, but, rather, to set key scenes of *Le Cap au diable* in what is at once a verifiably French-Canadian setting and a realm beyond God.

At the close of *Le Cap au diable,* the Saint-Aubins return to an Acadia that has been miraculously cleared of British invaders. The plot of *Le Cap au diable* seems thus to be motivated by an overarching desire to revive a superceded past — in this case, a kind of pre-British, pre-contact, Acadian "pre-history." This desire results in a fundamental paradox that, according to Michel Lord, represents a characteristic feature of French-Canadian gothic fiction (1994). While eighteenth-century British gothic novels respond in various ways to the seismic ruptures of recent history (namely the French and English Revolutions), French-Canadian Gothic, suggests Lord, seems content to deny history or even to ignore that it happened. Historical reality, be it the fact that the Acadians were deported or the fact that New France did fall, is rejected in favour of a fictional "dream-state" whereby a lost past is imaginatively restored. For Lord, this persistent atavism is responsible for French-Canadian Gothic's conservative tenor. A potentially radical literary genre ends up echoing the ideology of Quebec's dominant clerical elite, who frowned on revolutionary sentiment and argued that moral rectitude was superior to political muscle. Lord's comments on French-Canadian Gothic's ideological conservatism echo those of Maggie Kilgour, who describes the British gothic novel as ultimately untransgressive: that which "appears to be a transgressive rebellion against norms... ends up reinstating them, [while] an eruption of unlicensed desire... is fully controlled by governing systems of limitation" (1995, 8). For Lord, French-Canadian Gothic typically represents the restoration of the "time-before" history as divinely sanctioned, thereby aligning itself with nationalist theology and ultimately supporting the status quo.

Is it sufficient to describe French-Canadian Gothic as a fantasy for a vanquished culture to imaginatively obtain the moral upper hand? Is the example of generic adaptation not more complicated in this case? Judie Newman has articulated the dilemma facing colonial and postcolonial writers who embark on a "self-conscious project to revise the ideological assumptions created by Eurocentric domination of their culture": "Such [revisions] can, of course, give the impression that non-metropolitan culture can only rework, has no creativity of its own, and is dependent for its materials on the 'centre'" (1996, 172). While Lord does not discuss *Le Cap au diable,* I consider myself to be responding to his concerns about

French-Canadian Gothic's atavistic reflex and complicity with the clerical elite, although I draw different conclusions about their significance to *Le Cap au diable*. It is noteworthy that by the novella's close Mme. Saint-Aubin has not only returned to Acadia but she has also apparently had a permanent effect on the laws of nature. The "Devil's Cape" continues to be a "theatre of infernal apparitions" (De Guise 1863, 4). Mme. Saint-Aubin's singular presence has incited a horde of other spirits, including those of the Irish Catholics who sought refuge in Canada and died there, to haunt the cliffs with their "cries for vengeance" against British wrongdoing (4). While the narrator suggests cryptically that the sources of these supernatural apparitions will never be known — for "victims and murderers" are now "before God" (4) — it is clear that *Le Cap au diable* represents an attempt to explain them while openly condemning Britain's treatment of its Catholic constituents. By the novel's close, the narrative has effectively "split" into two: one narrative thread follows Mme. Saint-Aubin to Acadia, while the other remains tied to the "Devil's Cape." Each narrative thread, moreover, carries with it a separate message: the first of peaceable retreat; the second of revenge. Both narrative threads converge uncomfortably in the trope of Catholicism and the message of retribution and revenge with which it is emburdened throughout *Le Cap au diable*.

Literary historians have variously described the emergence of gothic literature's anti-Catholic theme in eighteenth-century Britain as an aesthetic reaction to at least two monumental developments: the consolidation of Protestant theology and the expansion of Britain's internal and overseas colonies. In the first instance, the French and the English Revolutions figured as foundational events, and Edmund Burke's *Reflections on the Revolution in France* can be seen as a foundational text ([1790] 1999). One of the most influential (and notorious) contemporary reviewers of gothic fiction, the Marquis de Sade, proposed that the trauma of the French Revolution was the source of the Gothic's thematic preoccupation with prelatic and aristocratic tyranny. Sade saw the novels of Ann Radcliffe and Matthew "Monk" Lewis as paradigmatic texts in this context (see Sade [1800] 1990, especially 49). As a partial corrective to Sade, Maurice Lévy traced the gothic novel's rise to prominence in the eighteenth century to England's "Glorious Revolution" in the seventeenth century (1968). For Lévy, as for Sage, the Gothic's foundational anti-prelatic theme is intricately tied to the formation of the English political state and thus to the Protestant Settlement of 1688 (see Lévy 1968, 46; Sage 1988, xi–xviii).

Luke Gibbons, however, has observed that gothic discourse was not always straightforwardly aligned with the interests of Britain's Protestant majority, even when it arose in reaction to the cataclysmic events of the French and English Revolutions (2004). Gibbons reminds readers that the expression of terror in Radcliffean Gothic represented a larger fear for the integrity and viability of monarchical power and aristocratic privilege, which had been the targets of revolutionaries in France. Burke's achievement, Gibbons explains, lies in his suggestion that "it was the remnants of the old order—including the Catholic Church—who were the *victims* of terror" (14).[6] Burke's representation of the Revolution as a tragedy, in part for Catholic victims, thus resonated in the British context, where Irish Catholics had historically been the victims of metropolitan policy makers. If, in France, the Jacobins and the republican modernity that they represented had become "the new monsters of the Gothic imagination," then in Ireland this "monster" became "the oppressive Protestant Ascendancy that arrogated all power to itself, depriving the mass of the Irish population of their most basic liberties" (14). By connecting the French Revolution's Catholic victims to Britain's minority Catholic constituents, Burke demonstrated how the Gothic, "as a literary and cultural form[,] could be turned, through acts of semiotic and narrative appropriation, against itself, thereby becoming a weapon of the weak" (15).[7]

Gibbons's comments on the subversiveness of the Catholic trope make it clear that the rise of gothic literature and cultural discourse in Britain coincided not only with the aftermath of the French and English Revolutions but also with the development of cultural relations between Britain's Protestant majority and Catholic minority. As Gibbons also observes in the epigraph to this section, the rise of the gothic novel was inextricably linked to the territorial expansion of the British Empire in North America and elsewhere. As I aim to demonstrate, the fall of New France and the Expulsion of the Acadians were foundational political events that were just as integral to the development of gothic literary and cultural discourse as the French and the English Revolutions and Britain's "internal colonial" policies towards its Irish Catholic constituents.[8] It is beyond the scope of this essay to trace the intricate logic that interconnected politics with religion and shaped the discourse and attitudes of the English metropolis towards Acadian colonists in the eighteenth century. It is, however, instructive to note the interconnected attitudes towards religion, social order, and imperial expansion that informed the contemporary vocabulary with which the Acadians were described in metropolitan newspapers in the years surrounding the Expulsion. In 1760, for example, the anonymous author of "An Impartial and Succinct History of the Origin and Progress of the Present War" identified the Acadians' proximity to French-speaking Catholics in nearby Canada and Nova Scotia as a primary threat to the security of Britain's North American possessions: "As [the Acadians] were all bigotted papists, it was therefore deemed impossible to expect any fidelity from them, whilst they remained so near their countrymen in Canada and Cape Breton" (1760, 291). A few years earlier, an anonymous article published in the *London Magazine* bearing the deceptively straightforward title, "A Description of Nova Scotia" outlined some potential consequences for the Acadians should they continue "to disturb or prejudice the peace and welfare of the colony": "I see no reason why they should not be put under the restraint of such laws, as may reduce them into proper obedience, [to] the condition of *hewers of wood* and *drawers of water* [as] the natural subjects of the *mother country*" (1749, 184 [emphasis in original]).

As historians of the Expulsion have regularly observed, the Acadians were intensely scrutinized by English and Anglo-American commentators who questioned their loyalty to the British Crown based on their Catholicism and semi-feudal society. Not surprisingly, the theme of Acadian loyalty became central to revisionary French-Canadian literature on the Expulsion, beginning with *Le Cap au diable,* which addressed the paradox that the Acadians could simultaneously represent a foundational and diasporic culture by transforming the tropes of loyalty and Catholicism into arguments for the Acadians' status as a kind of Biblical "chosen people." It is difficult to overlook the "gothic" tension between transgression and punishment that characterizes the anonymous newspaper articles and weaves its way into the pre-emptive political action that their authors advocate. This tension between transgression and punishment suggests the multifaceted nature of the Gothic as a literary form, an expression of cultural unease, and a rationale for legislative and political action for those who attempted to use it in their favour.

The fact that French-Canadian literature on the Expulsion reworked the same themes of loyalty, revisited the same historical scenes of expulsion, and represented the Acadians' fate in similar terms of divine ordination for roughly a century has been the subject of complaint by recent literary historians (see Viau 1997; Runte 1997). I have, however, connected the theme of Acadian loyalty to metropolitan "gothic" unease about the Acadians in order to emphasize the literary historical significance of *Le Cap au diable*'s inaugural use of the Catholic trope in the service of an oppositional historiography. The process of generic transfer carries with it, in this instance as in so many others, important epistemological consequences. The questions on my mind as I read *Le Cap au diable* are: What purpose does the trope of Catholicism serve? Does *Le Cap au diable* perform a kind of Burkean subversion and transform Gothic's anti-prelatic theme into a "weapon of the weak?" (Burke [1757] 1998). Or does it merely pander, as Viau suggests, to the religious elite (see especially 1997, 56)? Instead of seeing the Saint-Aubins' move back to Acadia as an atavistic denial of history, I see "time" and history working towards markedly different ends. For example, the "time" of the narrative is fractured at the novella's close, for it is effectively divided between an Acadian idyll, in which time is suspended, and real historical time, which is, significantly, written in the gothic mode in which recent history resides in the landscape in a kind of perpetual present. This type of temporal fracture is significant, not in terms of a narrative failure but, rather, as a symptom of the challenges facing French Canada's emergent writers who attempted, on the one hand, to satisfy readers' tastes for popular gothic and historical fiction while they worked, on the other, to build a national literature. As *Le Cap au diable*'s fractured themes and temporality would suggest, in De Guise's day literary nation-builders had not yet worked out how to incorporate a history of dispossession and trauma into the national narrative.

Orientalism and the Gothic: Generic Changes, Choices, and Strategies

[N]o working model of... the dynamics of formal and stylistic change is conceivable which does not imply a whole philosophy of history.
—Fredric Jameson, *The Political Unconscious*

When he describes the ways in which genres change over time, Fredric Jameson proposes that generic change is not a kind of "genetic process" from which a text emerges, as though it were a product of "this or that prior moment of form or style" (1981, 57). Instead of conceiving of generic change as an organic process in which a genre materializes at a given moment in literary history, Jameson argues that "formal," "logical," and "semantic conditions" make a text possible (57). The analysis of how genres change therefore involves literary historians in a kind of textual and cultural archaeology that, as Jameson concludes, carries with it "the hypothetical *reconstruction* of the materials — content, narrative paradigms, stylistic and linguistic practices — which had to have been given in advance in order for that particular text to be produced in its unique historical specificity" (57–58). Like other "social formations," such as literary periods or epochs, literary genres are thus "perpetual cultural revolutions" in which different social experiences, and the formal conventions to which they are attached, compete for "ascendancy" (97).

I am particularly interested in the competitive dynamic that Jameson ascribes to literary genres and their constituent features, for it provides me with an important revisionary perspective from which to consider *Le Cap au diable*. While literary historians have readily acknowledged *Le Cap au diable*'s thematic importance, they have traditionally been unforgiving of its hodge-podge of formal features. De Guise has enthusiastically selected features from gothic fiction, novels of sensibility, history proper, and literary realism, although he has poorly integrated them into his narrative so that each set of features seems to compete with others for narrative supremacy. This selection results in some unexpectedly comical scenes in the midst of tragedy (such as the hurricane that suddenly arises on the St. Lawrence and briefly turns *Le Cap au diable* into an adventure tale at sea), but literary historians have not been laughing. For example, in his response to *Le Cap au diable*, Edmond Lareau, Quebec's first literary historian, adopts both an indulgent and admonitory tone to describe De Guise as a promising writer but points out that the "form" of his novella is "worth more than its frame" (1874, 327).[9] Much more recently, Viau has complained that, "in this text, improbabilities accumulate" (1997, 54).[10]

When I am faced with the question of what to do with *Le Cap au diable*'s hodge-podge of narrative styles, I admit that I am inclined to be more forgiving of them. In fact, I find *Le Cap au diable*'s stylistic unevenness intriguing. This is partly due to my approach to literary genres as structurally heterogeneous and ideologically capacious — differently put, literary genres are "always already" aesthetic and ideological assortments of things. The fact that a work of colonial gothic fiction does not structurally come together poses important questions about what the author was trying to achieve when he selected certain generic features and not others for adaptation and about why he selected some features to represent dominant or socially acceptable views and still others to perform the infinitely more challenging task of addressing obscure, ambiguous, or incomprehensible aspects of French Canada's lived history. In this respect, I see myself as responding to, and extending, the views of Kilgour, for whom Gothic's greatest interest and importance lie where other critics have attributed its "failure" — in its "piecemeal … corporate identity" (1995, 5). It is important to keep in mind that the publication of *Le Cap au diable* roughly coincided with that of French Canada's first historical novel, Philippe Aubert de Gaspé's *Les Anciens Canadiens* ([1863] 1994). De Guise's novella represents, therefore, one of French Canada's first works of fiction, an early attempt to adapt the Gothic to French Canada and an early attempt at literary nation building during a decade that literary historians would come to call the "School of the 1860s" to account for the unprecedented wave of literary activity and efforts to "Canadianize" European genres. The choice to select some generic features for adaptation and not others in this time of dynamic literary production is thus highly self-conscious.

Le Cap au diable adapts features from historical fiction, history proper, literary realism, and gothic romance in order to represent the Expulsion of the Acadians in the eighteenth century as a national tragedy and foundational event for French Canada's collective identity in the nineteenth. Typical of historical fiction written in the vein of Sir Walter Scott, the main characters are cultural "types" who are unwittingly caught up in the political events that will come retroactively to define their age. They are uniformly history's victims and not its agents. The narrative assumes the measured style of history proper in passages devoted to statistics, dates, and numbers (such as numbers of men deported from Acadia or numbers of ships necessary to have them carried away). The narrative shifts abruptly into a realist mode of description when it portrays the "antebellum" Acadian landscape, characterized by the Acadians' industriousness and their unique technological advancements in agriculture. (The Acadians invented a complex system of dykes in order to reclaim the land from the sea for much of their farmland fell below sea level.) The novella's hero, Jean Renousse, is Mme. Saint-Aubin's "saviour," as well as an "Artful Dodger" figure — a mischievous orphan with a propensity for thievery who, by contrast to his prototype, has the exemplary Acadian community, and the Saint-Aubins in particular, to help set him on the right path in life (De Guise 1863, 16).

The didactic purpose that underpins *Le Cap au diable*'s hodge-podge of narrative styles becomes apparent in passages that rely on extensive quotations from the French historian Edme Rameau de Saint-Père who, as a result of such landmark works as *La France aux colonies*, became known as the first historian of Acadia (1859). The narrator quotes from Rameau when the emotional charge of a particular scene prevents him from sufficiently describing it. Rameau's history, then, effectively provides the details of the Expulsion as the Acadians might have experienced it. While this recurrent appeal to the historian may be the result of stylistic choices that De Guise made—and Lareau suggests that this is the case (1874, 327)—it is important because it affects how the story is told, which parts of it remain untold, and which scenes demand to be told differently. In effect, the details of history as lived experience, and the events themselves that surround the "expatriation" of the Acadians, prove to be unnarratable by fiction (De Guise 1863, 17). It is this way, I believe, for two reasons. First, it corresponds to De Guise's didactic patriotism, whereby the blame for the Expulsion is placed squarely on the shoulders of the British. And, second, the appeal to a respected French historian thus lends the weight of authority to the lesson that readers are meant to learn. This type of revisionary dynamic corresponds to a pattern that recurs in colonial and postcolonial fiction and that Newman has described as "revision as redemonisation": "The clock turns back to horror stories of 'barbarism' rather than forward to confront the legacies of imperialism in the present" (1996, 172).[11] A central feature of *Le Cap au diable*'s revisionism, this "redemonization" plays a crucial role in enabling De Guise to "write" his way into, and beyond, metropolitan history in his effort to construct an oppositional historiography. The appearance of Rameau's revisionary voice nearly always coincides with a shift in setting as the narrative moves further back in time to "antebellum" Acadia—to the "time before" the Expulsion when "Nova Scotia" was called "Acadie" (De Guise 1863, 5). The historical voice thus functions as an ideological marker alerting readers to a thematic difference between a "time before" history happened and a "time after." It also suggests that each pocket of "time" requires different narrative modes to give it expression. In this case, the "real" events that took place in the past are relayed through the voice of the historian, while the "unreal" aspects of the present are written in the gothic mode.

My inclination to be forgiving of *Le Cap au diable*'s narrative unevenness lies in my perception of De Guise's novella as being characteristically gothic, which is in contrast, say, to Viau, who sees it instead as a kind of failed historical novel. The notion that one can effectively "choose" a text's genre leads me to my second reason for beginning this section with Jameson. In his study of British Romanticism's gothic roots, Michael Gamer responds to Jameson's definition of genres as "social contract[s]" that occur between any "writer and a specific reading public" (2000, 1; quoted in Jameson 1981, 160). Gamer agrees that processes of "generic classification," whereby a given text is deemed to belong to a particular genre by virtue of the characteristic features that it displays, depends upon "readers, publishers, and critics who ultimately determine a text's identity and value." Gamer worries, however, that when genres are defined as "contracts" they are presented as instances of "friendly socialization or businesslike negotiation, where various parties combine to determine textual meaning, and where a significant majority of participants must agree on the nature of a text's 'participation' before any act of 'belonging,' however temporary, can occur" (1).[12] Gamer is interested in the Gothic as a paradigmatic instance of contractual negotiations "break[ing] off" or "ending in deadlock": "Where writers and readers agree fundamentally on a text's cultural status — implicit in Jameson's idea of 'contract' — negotiations may run smoothly and even invisibly. Where writers and readers disagree — or where readers disagree among themselves — we enter into a different situation, one in which writers find themselves placed in generic spaces that they never intended, and where texts do not get to choose their own genres" (2).

According to Gamer, one of the characteristic features of the Gothic's early literary history is precisely this lack of consensus on the part of readers, commentators, and reviewers about what gothic fiction was trying to achieve. Such a lack of consensus characterizes not only the reception history of French-Canadian Gothic but also the reception of *Le Cap au diable,* where even the same literary critic, Viau, has arrived at two fundamentally different conclusions about it. In his most recent examination of *Le Cap au diable,* Viau rightly points out that De Guise justifies Acadian history and diaspora using the recuperative discourse of Christian theology (1997). Viau concludes that this discourse results in an ideologically transparent plot: "The author tries to convince readers to blame the English for so much unmerited suffering. Moral torments multiply" (56). In an article-length study of *Le Cap au diable* published three years earlier, however, Viau sheds a markedly different light on the ideological significance and complexity of Catholicism as a revisionary discourse (1993). Viau counters the view that the providential, or "messianic," nationalism of early French-Canadian fiction on the Expulsion represents a "facile" or even "evasive" historicism (105). Instead, he suggests that messianic nationalism should be seen as a "convalescent nation's response to a time of crisis." Messianism, Viau concludes, "supplies [the minority culture with] an instrument of combat against the invading culture." More importantly, it "projects to the world that culture's determined optimism about the foundation of [its] society which is radically other, which is opposed to the monolithic order of the British. Messianic nationalism is thus a means of collective survival, necessary in the beginning... to enable [a minority culture] to participate in power, let alone to reclaim that power" (105).[13]

Viau's divergent responses to *Le Cap au diable* are particularly relevant to this essay for they represent recent examples of the dynamic that Gamer describes as critical "disagreement" about a text's cultural status (2000, 2). This disagreement is, I believe, symptomatic of a larger, crucial question that faces literary critics of early French-Canadian fiction who must, at some point, grapple with the meaning of messianic nationalism: is it always conservative and reactionary? Does it merely reinforce the status quo? Can it be seen in a more positive light as a kind of reverse "orientalism"? I am adopting my terms not only from Edward Said but also from Ian Duncan, who, in his important study of the Romantic and Victorian British novel, describes Gothic's foundational anti-prelatic theme as a "spiritual orientalism": "The Gothic setting [of eighteenth-century British novels] is most often Catholic — French, Spanish, or Italian — marking Catholicism as a spiritual orientalism in the British Protestant imagination" (1992, 24). In Duncan's formula, the Catholic trope that defines eighteenth-century British gothic novels functions as a discursive strategy that, to adapt Said's terms, puts the Protestant majority "in a whole series of possible relationships" with the foreign, Catholic "other" without "ever losing [for Protestants] the relative upper hand" (1994, 7). Given gothic fiction's characteristic preoccupation with broken historical descent, contaminated genealogies, and usurped patrimony, and given the obvious connections between Gothic's characteristic themes and the patterns of dislocation that structure French-Canadian and Acadian histories, I am left with the following question. Was it possible for early French-Canadian writers to negotiate their history of displacement and dispossession in anything *but* the gothic mode?

Conclusion: Gothic as a "Pretext" for Working through Ideas

What makes *Le Cap au diable* "gothic"? This question is not rhetorical, for literary critics have been surprisingly reticent to describe *Le Cap au diable* as a "gothic" text. One obvious reason for this hesitation is that *Le Cap au diable* is considered to be a minor literary text and is rarely treated at length. It is not, for example, mentioned in Lord's book-length study of early Quebec gothic fiction, in part because it was published outside of his primary temporal bracket of 1837–60 (1994). This bracket reflects Lord's understanding that, for a work of fiction to be considered "gothic," its narrative must contain a mood of terror that the writer sustains (or at least attempts to sustain) throughout. It also reflects his conclusion that no strictly "gothic" work of fiction was published in French Canada after 1860, when other genres (namely historical novels) became prominent. While I share with Lord my interest in exploring French-Canadian Gothic's relationship to history and dominant social ideology, I disagree with him over some basic ideas, such as my definition of "gothic." Like Margot Northey, I believe that it is important to approach early Canadian gothic as a mode that pervaded "varieties of fiction" (1976, 8), for, as Sage argues, the "narrower [our] conception of genre, the more one [risks] moving away from the possibility of explaining it" (1988, xiii). I thus define French-Canadian Gothic as containing various modes of writing, from novelistic prose and historical narration to dramatic tableaux and oral narrative frames.

When I take a step back from current debates about what constitutes a gothic text, I am reminded of the fact that this debate is not new. Neither is the connection that literary commentators make today between questions of aesthetics, literary tastes, and the politics of generic transfer. In late-nineteenth-century French Canada, "the fantastic" ("le genre fantaisiste") represented a formal component of French-Canadian oral tales and legends as well as of historical novels and novellas whose storylines incorporated elements of the supernatural. Debates about "the fantastic" were inextricably bound up in local insecurities about metropolitan literary genres, particularly novels, being "carriers" of foreign tastes, assumptions, and political ideologies. The importation and adaptation of much metropolitan fiction was strongly discouraged by conservative nationalists, for whom the vibrancy of the French-Canadian national character depended on French Canada's impermeability to foreign influences as well as on the assumption that the local literature, in form and content, could be sufficiently inspired by the local landscape and way of life. In my examination of the trope of Catholicism in *Le Cap au diable,* I have attempted to demonstrate that the adaptation of the Gothic from the metropolitan to the French-Canadian contexts could simultaneously represent an act of complicity with dominant conservative ideology as well as an important starting point from which to construct an oppositional, revisionist cultural voice.[14] By means of wrapping up this point, I would like to emphasize the fact that contemporary debates about "the fantastic" also revolved around the matter of its usefulness as a vehicle for effecting moral and social change. An influential voice in this debate was that of French Canada's first "national poet," Octave Crémazie, who defended the moral and social utility of "the fantastic" (1984, 63). Defining "the fantastic" not as a literary genre at all, at least not in the narrow sense, Crémazie conceived of it instead as a form beyond the "everyday rules of poetics" and, as such, as a valuable "pretext for working through [one's] ideas" (63).[15] While his discussions of literary genre should not be seen as being separate from his belief in the moral and social superiority of poetry over fiction (a belief he shared with Quebec's dominant clerical elite), Crémazie's defence of the "genre fantaisiste" and its paradigmatic text, Goethe's *Faust* (1999), as a vehicle for moral debate and thus of moral and social improvement remains important in this context (63).

In the preface to *Is Canada Postcolonial?* Laura Moss asks if it is possible "for the discussion of postcoloniality to go beyond contemporary writing to include writing from earlier times?" (2003, v). The importance of this question is underscored by a number of contributors to the volume who variously demonstrate the complementary interests of postcolonial scholars with early Canadian novelists who have explored the uneasy relationship between history, revision, and Canada's emergent national consciousness (see, for example, Devereux 2003; Ivison 2003; Perkins 2003). In this essay, I have examined a little-known text, *Le Cap au diable,* whose decidedly non-canonical status raises important questions about aesthetics, ideology, and literary knowledge. For if, on one level, literature can reflect a nation back to its readers, then fiction that is rarely studied (even a novella as popular as *Le Cap au diable* was in its day) should prompt literary historians to pursue the connections between changing literary tastes and changing conceptions of the national character.[16] If postcolonial studies makes possible the recovery of little-known texts to the purview of modern readers, then such recovery carries with it unique opportunities to enrich our understanding of today's literary climate with a broader understanding of earlier climates whose key representatives, though they may have employed terms different from our own, were similarly preoccupied by the dialectics of "self" and "other," and "centre" and "periphery," which had been shaping the cultural and political life of their nation.

Notes

1 Two American texts on the expulsion precede *Le Cap au diable:* Catherine Williams's *The Neutral French* (1841) and Henry Wadsworth Longfellow's infamous long poem *Evangeline* ([1846] 2003).

2 Recent scholars who have variously questioned the accuracy of the term "genre" to describe the Gothic include Michael Gamer (2000), James Watt (1999), Maggie Kilgour (1995), and Robert Miles (1993).

3 My examination of the descriptive, thematic, and moral dynamics at work in Ann Radcliffe is indebted to Ian Duncan's influential and meticulously researched investigation of the "culture of Gothic" in eighteenth-century Britain (1992, esp. 20–50), as well as to feminist explorations of the "female gothic" (see, for example, Moers 1976; Wolff 1983; DeLamotte 1990).

4 *Le Cap au diable* was first published serially from 1862–63 in the conservative agricultural weekly *La Gazette des Campagnes*. It was published in book form by Firmin H. Proulx in 1863. All citations in this essay are from the latter publication.

5 David Punter distinguishes between "domestic Gothic" and "foreign Gothic" or Scottish and Irish as opposed to metropolitan gothic novels whose different settings were symptomatic of their divergent approaches to dealing with suppressed histories. In the former, historical traumas and losses are typically enacted on the domestic terrain while in the latter they are displaced onto a "fictionalized 'third location'" (2002, 106–07).

6 For his discussion of how Edmund Burke's *Reflections on the Revolution in France* ([1790] 1999) "imparted to the word *Gothic* a new political charge," see Robert Miles (2002, 42–43).

7 See also James Whitlark (1997) for a relevant discussion of the "pro-Catholic nostalgia" that runs throughout gothic novels by Matthew "Monk" Lewis ([1796] 2008) and Ann Radcliffe ([1794] 1998), thereby creating a highly-charged tension in metropolitan treatments of the anti-Catholic theme. A telling representation of Catholicism as a source of inspiration can be found in Radcliffe's *The Mysteries of Udolpho*: "As she listened, the midnight hymn of the monks rose softly from a chapel, that stood on one of the lower cliffs, an holy strain, that seemed to ascend through the silence of night to heaven, and her thoughts ascended with it" (47).

8 I have adapted the term "internal colonialism" from the title of Michael Hechter's influential study of Britain's national minorities, *Internal Colonialism: The Celtic Fringe in British National Development* (1975).

9 "Son style est meilleur que l'invention du plan; la forme vaut mieux que la charpente." All translations in this essay are my own.

10 "Dans cette oeuvre, l'auteur accumule les invraisemblances."

11 Judie Newman (1996) makes these comments in her discussion of the problems that confront readers of Jean Rhys's *Wide Sargasso Sea* (2000) and V.S. Naipaul's *Guerrillas* (1975).

12 The internal quotations in this citation are from Michael Gamer's (2000) references to Jacques Derrida's "The Law of Genre" (1980).

13 The original quotation reads as follows: "Le messianisme fournit un instrument de combat contre l'occupant et projette sur le monde un optimisme déliberé: celui de participer à la fondation d'une société radicalement autre, qui s'oppose à l'ordre établi anglais... trop monolithique... Le messianisme se présente donc comme un moyen de survie collective, nécessaire au début, qui dissimule une visée politique: la participation au pouvoir, sinon la reprise du pouvoir."

14 Marie Vautier has made a similar point about the thematization of Catholicisim in the postcolonial Canadian context (2003, especially 275-79).

15 The original quotation reads as follows: "La fantaisie n'est pas un genre dans le sens ordinaire du mot. [C]'est un prétexte pour remuer des idées, sans avoir les bras liés par les règles ordinaires de la poétique."

16 *Le Cap au diable* was published four times in one decade—twice in book form and twice serially. In 1865, for example, it was published in the influential and very respectable literary journal *La Revue canadienne*.

Works Cited

"A Description of Nova Scotia." 1749. *London Magazine* or *Gentleman's Monthly Intelligencer* April: 184.

"An Impartial and Succinct History of the Origin and Progress of the Present War." 1760. *London Magazine* or *Gentleman's Monthly Intelligencer* June: 291.

Aubert de Gaspé, Philippe. 1863, reprinted 1994. *Les Anciens Canadiens*. Montreal: Bibliothèque québécoise.

Burke, Edmund. 1757, reprinted 1998. *A Philosophical Enquiry into the Origin of Our Ideas of the Sublime and Beautiful*. Ed. Adam Phillips. Oxford: Oxford UP.

———. 1790, reprinted 1999. *Reflections on the Revolution in France*. Ed. L.G. Mitchell. Oxford: Oxford UP.

Crémazie, Octave. 1984. "Lettre à l'abbé Casgrain sur la littérature." In *Essais québécois, 1837–1983: Anthologie littéraire*. Ed. Laurent Mailhot. Quebec: Éditions Hurtubise HMH. 57–67.

DeLamotte, Eugenia C. 1990. *Perils of the Night: A Feminist Study of Nineteenth-Century Gothic*. New York: Oxford UP.

Derrida, Jacques. 1980. "The Law of Genre." *Glyph: Textual Studies* 7: 202–29.

Devereux, Cecily. 2003. "Are We There Yet? Reading the 'Post-Colonial' and *The Imperialist* in Canada." In *Is Canada Postcolonial? Unsettling Canadian Literature*. Ed. Laura Moss. Waterloo, ON: Wilfrid Laurier UP. 177–89.

Duncan, Ian. 1992. *Modern Romance and Transformations of the Novel: The Gothic, Scott, Dickens*. Cambridge: Cambridge UP.

Gamer, Michael. 2000. *Romanticism and the Gothic: Genre, Reception, and Canon Formation*. Cambridge: Cambridge UP.

De Guise, Charles. 1863. *Le Cap au diable: Légende canadienne*. Saint-Anne de la Pocatière, QC: Firmin H. Proulx.

Gibbons, Luke. 2004. *Gaelic Gothic: Race, Colonization, and Irish Culture*. Dublin: Arlen House.

Goethe, Johann Wilhelm von. 1999. *Faust*. Ed. David Luke. Oxford: Oxford UP.

Hechter, Michael. 1975. *Internal Colonialism: The Celtic Fringe in British National Development, 1536–1966*. Berkeley: University of California Press.

Ivison, Douglas. 2003. "'I Too Am a Canadian': John Richardson's *The Canadian Brothers* as Postcolonial Narrative." In *Is Canada Postcolonial? Unsettling Canadian Literature*. Ed. Laura Moss. Waterloo, ON: Wilfrid Laurier UP. 162–76.

Jameson, Fredric. 1981. *The Political Unconscious: Narrative as a Socially Symbolic Act*. Ithaca, NY: Cornell UP.

Kilgour, Maggie. 1995. *The Rise of the Gothic Novel*. London: Routledge.

Lareau, Edmond. 1874. *Histoire de la littérature canadienne*. Montreal: J. Lovell.

Léger, Antoine J. 1940. *Elle et lui: Tragique idylle du peuple acadien*. Moncton: L'Évangéline.

Lévy, Maurice. 1968. *Le Roman gothique anglais, 1764–1824*. Toulouse: Association des publications de la Faculté des lettres et sciences humaines.

Lewis, Matthew. 1796, reprinted 2008. *The Monk*. Ed. Emma McEvoy. Oxford: Oxford UP.

Longfellow, Henry Wadsworth. 1846, reprinted 2003. *Evangeline: A Tale of Acadie*. Halifax, NS: Nimbus Publishers.

Lord, Michel. 1994. *En quête du roman gothique québécois, 1837–1860: tradition littéraire et imaginaire romanesque*. Quebec: Nuit blanche éditeur.

Miles, Robert. 1993. *Gothic Writing, 1750–1820: A Genealogy*. London: Routledge.

———. 2002. "The 1790s: The Effulgence of Gothic." In *The Cambridge Companion to Gothic Fiction*. Ed. Jerrold E. Hogle. Cambridge: Cambridge UP. 41–62.

Moers, Ellen. 1976. *Literary Women: The Great Writers*. New York: Doubleday.

Moss, Laura. 2003. "Preface." In *Is Canada Postcolonial? Unsettling Canadian Literature*. Ed. Laura Moss. Waterloo, ON: Wilfrid Laurier UP. v–viii.

Naipaul, V.S. 1975. *Guerrillas*. London: Deutsch.

Newman, Judie. 1996. "Postcolonial Gothic: Ruth Prawer Jhabvala and the Sobhraj Case." In *Modern Gothic: A Reader*. Ed. Victor Sage and Allan Lloyd Smith. Manchester: Manchester UP. 171–87.

Northey, Margot. 1976. *The Haunted Wilderness: The Gothic and Grotesque in Canadian Fiction*. Toronto: University of Toronto Press.

Perkins, Pam. 2003. "Imagining Eighteenth-Century Quebec: British Literature and Colonial Rhetoric." In *Is Canada Postcolonial? Unsettling Canadian Literature*. Ed. Laura Moss. Waterloo, ON: Wilfrid Laurier UP. 151–61.

Punter, David. 2002. "Scottish and Irish Gothic." In *The Cambridge Companion to Gothic Fiction*. Ed. Jerrold E. Hogle. Cambridge: Cambridge UP. 105–24.

Radcliffe, Ann Ward. 1794, reprinted 1998. *The Mysteries of Udolpho*. Ed. Bonamy Dobrée. New York: Oxford UP.

Rameau de Saint-Père, Edme. 1859. *La France aux colonies: études sur le développement de la race française hors de l'Europe*. Paris: A. Jouby.

Rhys, Jean. 2000. *Wide Sargasso Sea*. London: Penguin.

Runte, Hans R. 1997. *Writing Acadia: The Emergence of Acadian Literature, 1970–1990*. Amsterdam: Rodopi.

Sade, Marquis de. 1800, reprinted 1990. "Ideas on the Novel." In *The Gothick Novel: A Casebook*. Ed. Victor Sage. Basingstoke: Macmillan. 48–49.

Sage, Victor. 1988. *Horror Fiction in the Protestant Tradition*. New York: St. Martin's Press.

Said, Edward. 1994. *Orientalism*. New York: Vintage.

Scott, Walter. 1814, reprinted 1985. *Waverley: Or, 'Tis Sixty Years Since*. Ed. Andrew Hook. London: Penguin.

Vautier, Marie. 2003. "Religion, Postcolonial Side-by-Sideness, and *la transculture*." In *Is Canada Postcolonial? Unsettling Canadian Literature*. Ed. Laura Moss. Waterloo, ON: Wilfrid Laurier UP. 268–79.

Viau, Robert. 1993. "Le Messianisme des premiers romans de la déportation acadienne." *LittéRéalité* 5(2): 95–107.

———. 1997. *Les grands dérangements: la déportation des Acadiens en littératures acadienne, québécoise et française*. Beauport, QC: MNH.

Watt, James. 1999. *Contesting the Gothic: Fiction, Genre and Cultural Conflict, 1764–1832*. Cambridge: Cambridge UP.

Whitlark, James. 1997. "Heresy Hunting: *The Monk* and the French Revolution." *Romanticism on the Net*, <http://www.erudit.org/revue/ron/1997/v/n8/005773ar.html>.

Williams, Catherine R. 1841. *The Neutral French: Or, The Exiles of Nova Scotia*. Providence, RI: self-published.

Wolff, Cynthia Griffin. 1983. "The Radcliffean Gothic Model: A Form for Feminine Sexuality." In *The Female Gothic*. Ed. Juliann E. Fleenor. Montréal: Eden. 207–23.

CHAPTER TWO

Viking Graves Revisited: Pre-Colonial Primitivism in Farley Mowat's Northern Gothic

Brian Johnson

[T]he exhumation of old bones and their assembly into some sort of order is an honourable and useful task.... I believe that those well-guarded tombs, which hide our greatness from us, contain—not an array of pallid ghosts— but a concourse of living men possessed of such a superb and vital presence that their entombment becomes a reproach to all of us.

—Farley Mowat, *Coppermine Journey*

The archaeological manifesto with which Farley Mowat prefaces his heavily abridged and modernized edition of Samuel Hearne's *A Journey from Prince of Wales's Fort to the Northern Ocean* (1795) illustrates a conjunction between the nationalist discourse of exploration and a gothic vocabulary of tombs, graves, and ghosts in Mowat's considerable body of northern writing that even his most thoughtful critics have been slow to recognize. Indeed, when the literary features of this *oeuvre* are considered at all, it is usually within the rubric of the pastoral. T.D. MacLulich's early and important appraisal of Mowat's ethnographic and ecological writing, for instance, emphasizes Mowat's use of pastoral structures and motifs in *People of the Deer* (1952) and *Never Cry Wolf* (1963) in order to locate him within "the last phase in the development of the Canadian literature of exploration"—a phase marked aesthetically by a "deliberately literary presentation of its subject" and thematically by the explorer's concern with overcoming his earlier role as "a fearful intruder or a conquering invader, or even a skillfully temporary resident" in order to "spiritually become a part of the new land" (1977, 233 and 237). Echoing Alec Lucas's nearly contemporaneous assessment of Mowat as a national-ist and social satirist prone to idealizing "natural men" and "the simple life" (1976, 3 and 5), MacLulich suggests that Mowat's work instantiates a form of "cold pastoral" that eschews "escapism or naive primitivism" but, nonetheless, creates "a northern version of the Edenic pastoral retreat, with primitive Eskimos or idealized wolves serving as inhabitants of his wilderness Arcadia" where a spiritual merger with the land becomes pos-sible (1977, 237–38). John Moss's more recent and more scathing assess-ment of Mowat in his own northern book, *Enduring Dreams,* repeats and amplifies the terms of MacLulich's analysis to emphasize the "inadver-tently imperialistic" nature of Mowat's northern romanticism and to condemn his presumption "to speak for the land itself and for its people" (1994, 31, 33, and 75).[1] Dismissing *People of the Deer* as "a reassuringly derivative text," Moss blasts his Arctic rival as a neo-imperialist "Rider Haggard hero" who purports to "hurtle back through time to the prehis-toric past and across a perilous and empty space where he will discover and champion a lost tribe of benighted primitives" (1994, 68).

Such evaluations usefully foreground the complementarity of primi-tivist and imperialist discourses within the meta-narratives of indigeniza-tion and romantic nationalism that Mowat's work obsessively revisits. Yet they do not explain the significant strand of gothicism that runs through even the most "pastoral" of Mowat's northern visions. *People of the Deer* contains an extended evocation of the northern barrens as a mass grave-yard haunted by the Indigenous victims of colonial contact in a chapter entitled "Stone Men and Dead Men." It also contains a significant chapter on Indigenous "Ghosts, Devils, and Spirits" whose account of the female demon Paija becomes the basis for a frightening tale in *The Snow Walker* (1975a), Mowat's only collection of adult fiction and a veritable cache of Arctic horrors. In stories dealing with blinding, doppelgangers, ghosts, madness, cannibalism, and murder, Mowat evokes the gothic northlands not only of Robert Service (1907a) and Jack London (1907) but also of their Old World precursors, Mary Shelley (1831) and (in a more circuitous way) Samuel Taylor Coleridge ([1798] 1951). More generally, the ruins, graves, and cairns left by Arctic explorers as well as the *inukok* (or "stone men") of the Ihalmiut are a leitmotif in Mowat's northern writing that is not only visible in his ethnography, history, and geography but also constitutes the imaginative core of his young adult fiction, including *Lost in the Barrens* (1956) (originally titled "Phantom in the Wilderness" [King 2002, 114]) and its sequel, *The Curse of the Viking Grave* (1966).

My concern in this essay is to explore the function of this gothic thread in Mowat's northern writing by situating Mowat's work within a specifically New World tradition of northern Gothic and showing how Mowat both extends and complicates this tradition. More particularly, I want to examine how Mowat's reinvention of northern Gothic as *heimlich* ("homely") rather than *unheimlich* ("uncanny") allows him to manage the tensions that emerge in the primitivist/imperialist discourse of indigenization during moments when Aboriginal demands for political redress become audible, openly contradicting the settler-invader meta-narrative of romantic nationalism that constructs the Native as silent or vanishing. Focusing on the intersection between gothicism and ethnicity in Mowat's enormously popular and commercially successful northern fiction and northern history, I will consider how Mowat's writing simultaneously registers and evades Indigenous challenges to settler-invader narratives of national belonging by constructing a primitivist myth of white indigeneity centred on pre-Columbian "arrivants" in northern Canada. Mowat's desire to exhume a primordial Viking presence from the Canadian North, I argue, is not a simple repetition of late-imperial racialism but, rather, an historically specific strategy for out-manoeuvring and ultimately displacing Aboriginal claims to authority over a region that occupies a central place in settler-invader constructions of Canada as a "northern" nation.

Spectral Primitivism: From Indigenization to Homely Gothic

> The white Canadian looks at the Indian. The Indian is Other and therefore alien. But the Indian is indigenous and therefore cannot be alien. So the Canadian must be alien. But how can the Canadian be alien within Canada?
> — Terry Goldie, *Fear and Temptation*

> [H]*eimlich* is a word the meaning of which develops in the direction of ambivalence, until it finally coincides with its opposite, *unheimlich*.
> — Sigmund Freud, "The 'Uncanny'"

As Terry Goldie defines it in his now classic study, *Fear and Temptation*, "indigenization" is the process whereby arrivants in settler-invader colonies such as Canada attempt to overcome the "separation of belonging" that results from their late arrival in a space already inhabited by Native peoples (1989, 12). Confronted by an indigeneity that is desired but out of reach, the settler-invader produces compensatory narratives of indigenization founded on the production of stereotypes that associate the indigene with nature and the land. The resulting narratives are typically structured by complementary rhetorics of "penetration" and "appropriation" or, as Goldie also calls them, rhetorics of fear and rhetorics of desire (15). In narratives of penetration, indigenization proceeds by demonizing the Native as the embodiment of a threatening, primitive nature that must be subdued or destroyed. Conversely, narratives of appropriation reify the indigene as a spiritual embodiment of the land, representing Native culture as pure, authentic, and desirable, and Native peoples themselves as vanishing or dead. In this latter form — which, Goldie suggests, has largely replaced the earlier discourse of penetration — indigenization proceeds through initiation and absorption. The settler "goes native" in order to "become of the land" at the very moment that the Native himself conveniently disappears (16).

As useful as it remains, this influential account of settler-invader literature owes a great deal to Edward Said's theorization of colonial discourse in *Orientalism* (1994) — a debt that is particularly evident in Goldie's emphasis on the semiotic consistency of the stereotype over time and in his defence of a synchronic mode of analysis. Like Said, Goldie tends to imply that colonial stereotypes emanate from the centre to the margin, enabling and reinforcing "a history of invasion and repression" that "awarded semiotic control to the invaders" (1989, 5). "Since then," Goldie maintains, "the image of 'them' has been 'ours.'" However, as Homi Bhabha argues in his critique of Said, colonial discourse is not as monological as it appears (1994, 66). In fact, the paradoxical structure of the stereotype itself — "a form of knowledge and identification that vacillates between what is always 'in place,' already known, and something that must be anxiously repeated" — points to the precariousness of the "knowledge" it supposedly displays. The stereotype's incessant reiteration, in other words, is a case of protesting too much, for it exposes the dominant discourse's constant vulnerability to challenges from those it claims to represent. As Ania Loomba points out, for example, the tendency of "representations of the 'other' [to] vary according to the exigencies of colonial rule" affirms the power of colonized peoples to force the semiotic field of the stereotype into new configurations (1998, 133). In the context of settler-invader nations such as Canada, where colonial relations remain entrenched and where Indigenous voices have not died away but continue to gather authority and make tangible political gains, the strain placed on indigenizing meta-narratives that derive their authority precisely from the disappearance of the indigene is considerable.

As Daniel Francis wryly observes, "the image of the Vanishing Indian did begin to die out" in the decades following the First World War precisely because "[a]s a literal fact it could no longer be substantiated":

> Not only were their numbers increasing, but Native people were asserting themselves more and more strongly.... Far from being a vanishing people, Native Canadians seemed to be increasingly alive and kicking, determined to speak for themselves, and to be heard. It was hard to characterize them as passive, doomed people when they were in the headlines and in the courts. Despite a century of being told about their own disappearance, Indians were here to stay. (1992, 57–58)

As a result of this discursive victory, he suggests, the dying race stereotype was forced to "change content" in order to retain its managerial power, transforming itself into the elegiac cultural fetishism of the 1960s, which lamented not the literal death of a people but, rather, the symbolic destruction of a way of life "threatened by the forces of consumer culture" (57–58).

Significantly, such challenges to the meta-narrative of indigenization emerge not only within Canadian culture at large by mid-century but also within the body of Mowat's own writing of this period as well. In fact, a great deal of Mowat's northern writing of the 1950s and 1960s is not only directly bound up in, but also partially precipitates, this "crisis" and symptomatically displays a number of contradictory impulses. On the one hand, Mowat's works of Arctic history and popular ethnography tend to conform to conventional structures of indigenization in both of its varieties. His celebration of the imperial adventurers who "grappled with and came to terms with the great polar adversary" in works such as *Coppermine Journey* (1958) and his *The Top of the World* trilogy—consisting of *Ordeal by Ice* (1960), *The Polar Passion* (1967), and *Tundra* (1973)—indicate the persistence of the nineteenth-century narrative of penetration and domination (Mowat 1973, 13). Moreover, his account of initiation into a northern Inuit society and his representation of the Ihalmiut as a vanishing tribe in *People of the Deer* and its sequel, *The*

Desperate People (1959), rehearse an elegiac structure of loss that helps to rationalize the narrative of penetration implicit in his work on northern exploration. Yet, as Margaret Atwood points out in her introduction to Mowat's most recent Arctic memoir, Mowat has been (perhaps despite himself) an important stimulus to the interrogation of national meta-narratives since the 1950s. *People of the Deer,* in particular, she suggests, was "an X in the sand" whose publication

> marked a crucial turning point in general Canadian awareness. Before it, the only "Eskimos" southern Canadians might recognize were on ice cream bars. Who knew or cared anything about that part of the north? After it, not only was consciousness expanded, conscience was — however sporadically — engaged. *People of the Deer* was to support for increased autonomy among northern peoples as Rachel Carson's *Silent Spring* was to the environmental movement: a wake-up call, the spark that struck the tinder that ignited the fire from which many subsequent generations of writers and activists have lit their torches, often ignorant of where that spark came from in the first place. (Atwood 2002, ix)[2]

There is clearly a recuperative effort at play in Atwood's appreciation of Mowat as "Ancestral Totem" that bears on Atwood's own fascination with the North as a site of national consciousness as well as her concerns with northern, and indeed global, ecology (x).[3] Moreover, it would be a mistake to take Mowat's northern crusades strictly at face value. Mowat's representations of the North as a neglected resource throughout the 1960s and 1970s remain intensely nationalist, even flagrantly imperialist, calling for greater northern settlement to protect Canada's resources from American predation. Nonetheless, the "plea for the right of the Eskimos to decide their own destiny" through "self-government," which Mowat eventually articulates, does mark a significant shift — not only in mainstream representations of what was once rather cavalierly and romantically called the "plight" of northern Native and Inuit peoples but also within Mowat's own discourse on this subject as well (Lucas 1976, 13 and 17).

As Alec Lucas has noted, Mowat's response to the disruption of Indigenous northern economies and cultures in the original editions of *People of the Deer* (1952) and *The Desperate People* (1959) is marked by horror and despair, leading him to promote assimilation as a solution of last resort (1976, 13–17). In the revised versions of these books published in the mid-1970s, however, Mowat recoils from his earlier support for assimilation, arguing instead for Native self-determination. The striking final chapter of the 1975 edition of *The Desperate People,* in which Mowat dramatizes the response of a university-educated "Eskimo" to the original edition of his book, is emblematic of the complexities and contradictions inherent in this shift:

> "I read that book you wrote — *The Desperate People.* When you stuck to the story of what happened you wrote close to the truth about us. But when you got talking about what we needed and wanted you talked bullshit! You and pretty near every other white man I ever heard. I'll tell you what we want!
>
> We want you whites to leave us make our own decisions. *We'll* decide how much of your phoney world we have to have to stay alive...
>
> There's no big difference between you people and any other colonial sons-of-bitches. You don't give a frigging hell that it's *our* country — always *was* our country...
>
> Just give us back the chance to live in our own country the way *we* figure out we want to live. A place to live in... that's what we want! Our *own* place to live in." (1975, 213)

Echoing Atwood, Sherrill Grace argues that despite its taint of "appropriati[on]," this kind of "ventriloquizing" marks a genuine shift in "the discursive formation of North" — one that "represent[s], for the first time, an Indigenous North existing in history and moving into the present" and "open[s] a space for a speaking and listening that had been denied, repressed, or simply ignored hitherto" (2001, 176–77). Mowat's concluding gloss of his scathing interlocutor — whom he lauds as "the true, the authentic voice of the Desperate People of the Canadian north" — certainly supports this reading insofar as it redefines Inuit "authenticity" in terms of agency and an attitude of judicious cultural syncretism (1975, 213). This move does appear to undermine the romantic assumption of Mowat's earlier ethnographic elegy that, to retain his identity, the indigene must remain sealed within a static primordial world, untouched by history or Western culture as well as the either/or prescription of his assimilationist solution. Yet, the language of "authenticity" is double-edged here because the degree to which Mowat's text sanctions syncretic solutions that are hinted at by his reviewer's vaguely specified intention of "decid[ing] how much of your phoney world we have to have to stay alive" is by no means clear. Indeed, Mowat's ventriloquism of Indigenous demands for autonomy and self-determination might almost be read as a surreptitious reinvention of the very pastoral space of "authenticity" that his earlier position on assimilation had accepted as irrecoverable, even if Mowat himself would presumably be barred from re-entering this hypo-thetical space of potential indigenization by the terms of his own narra-tive's self-reproach.

The impasse that begins to emerge within Mowat's discourse of indig-enization anticipates the contradictions of a more recent and self-con-scious settler-invader postcolonialism that is likewise torn between the desire to indigenize and the uneasy awareness of the illegitimacy of a national romance. As Cynthia Sugars has argued, this contradiction between an acknowledgement of colonial injustice and an attempt to recuperate the indigenizing meta-narrative is a recurrent pattern in con-temporary Canadian literature—one whose ambivalence is increasingly expressed through the multi-layered trope of "a settlement of the land-scape with ghosts" in order to "(ghost)writ[e] the nation into being" (2003, 7). Sugars suggests that the ubiquitous phantom of contemporary Canadian literature is singularly well-suited to exposing the repression of Indigenous ghosts that founds the nationalist meta-narrative because, "[b]y definition, a ghost is an unsettled neurotic, which also makes it an inherently problematic metaphor of cultural/national authenticity" (9). Yet she also warns that the ideological mystifications this "(ghost)writ-ing" performs may ultimately overshadow its subversive power. "The par-adox here," she notes, "is that the unsettling and uncanny experience of being haunted is what produces a feeling of familiarity and home" (7).

Thus, whereas Sigmund Freud's psychoanalytic definition of the uncanny as "that class of the frightening which leads back to what is known of old and long familiar" because its object is "something repressed which *recurs*" famously plays on the sliding linguistic usage of the German word *heim-lich* to make its case, pointing out that its meaning "develops in the direc-tion of ambivalence, until it finally coincides with its opposite, *unheimlich*" ([1919] 1990, 340, 363, and 347), recent settler gothicism typically reverses this trajectory by "discovering" that the supposedly repressed content of its uncanny fears is nothing other than a reassuring image of itself.[4] Such a reversal founds a specifically "homely" form of gothic discourse that not only rejects Susanna Moodie's claim that "[t]he country is too new for ghosts" (1852, 267) but also reconfigures a thematic tradition that founds the imagined national community on a more conventional set of gothic tropes that are centred on the galvanizing experience of fear — a mythic confrontation with a gothic bush garden, a haunted wilderness, a Wacousta syndrome, or a survivalist set of wilderness tips.[5] Adapting Goldie's account of how the discourse of indigenization typically oscillates between poles of "fear" and "temptation" to Freud's account of the *(un)heimlich* as an uncannily shifting signifier, it becomes possible to see the discourse of New World (northern) Gothic as inherently double and generically split, inhabiting not simply the potentially unsettling terrain of terror but also the "homely" space of desire.

Mowat is not only — to borrow Atwood's term — the "Ancestral Totem" of homely Gothic in Canada but also one of its most virtuosic, critical, and sustained practitioners. It is not a coincidence that, until quite recently, this self-described "saga man" was arguably Canada's most popular national myth maker, rivalled only by Pierre Berton and, more recently, Atwood herself. Given his stature within this discourse, it is not surprising to find that Mowat's indigenizing strategies are themselves mythic in both scope and content. Whereas the production of settler ghosts is seen by some authors as a sufficient solution in itself, Mowat attempts to move beyond a mere disavowal of Indigenous presence and imagine a white primitive whose antiquity telescopes the now troubling moment of imperial penetration back into an increasingly dehistoricized, pre-colonial, and mythic past. If Goldie is correct, that "all indigene images contain at least a residue of a pre-white past" (1989, 148), then Mowat's northern project is meant to awaken a primitive Viking ghost whose spectral presence in the North will displace the indigene's claim to historical priority by imaginatively — if not literally — outmanoeuvring it. Since this project is an extension of Mowat's profound and as yet unexplored fascination with northern Gothic, I will briefly explore the roots of this discourse and sketch the terms of its adaptation to New World contexts before moving on to consider Mowat's particular interventions and innovations.

Killing the Albatross: A Genealogy of New World Northern Gothic

I am going to unexplored regions, to "the land of mist and snow"; but I shall kill no albatross, therefore, do not be alarmed for my safety, or if I should come back to you as worn and woful as the "Ancient Mariner"? You will smile at my allusion; but I will disclose a secret. I have often attributed my attachment

to, my passionate enthusiasm for, the dangerous mysteries of the ocean, to
that production of the most imaginative of modern poets.
— Mary Shelley, *Frankenstein*

As she stared back uncomprehendingly, a spasm of anger shook him. What a
fool he'd been to take her aboard at all … now she was a bloody albatross
around his neck.
— Farley Mowat, "Walk Well, My Brother"

Mary Shelley's wry meta-fictional nod to Samuel Taylor Coleridge in the
epistolary frame narrative of *Frankenstein* marks a crucial juncture in the
genealogy of Old World Gothic, permanently entangling Coleridge's tale
of a nightmare journey to the South Pole within the imaginative geography of specifically northern gothic tradition. The allusion could hardly be
more apt. As John Livingston Lowes points out, Coleridge's extensive
reading of northern exploration narratives meant that even though "[t]he
Mariner's ice-fields swim in Antarctic seas … the ice itself is good Arctic
ice, seen, heard, and felt in the 'infernall bitter cold' of Barents's Sea, and
in the 'stinking fogge' of Hudson's Bay, and off the 'snowy Clifts' of Greenland and Spitzbergen" (1927, 139). For this reason, Mary Shelley's tongue-
in-cheek reinvention of the ancient mariner as Native northern explorer
Robert Walton is less an instance of cartographic alchemy than a direct
acknowledgement that "South is North, where the albatross is shot" (139)
and an explicit reappropriation of Coleridge's poem for the psychic geography of an Arctic sublime in which ice-choked landscapes provide the
backdrop for daemonic encounters between the Romantic self and its
monstrous doubles.

As the examples of Coleridge and Shelley suggest, polar regions have
played an important role in the geography of the gothic imagination
from a very early point in the development of the genre, and, as Atwood
has shown (1995), Canadian works such as the ballads and poems of
Robert W. Service, which populate their uncanny northern landscapes
with a profusion of madmen, doppelgangers, and Coleridgean *femmes
fatales,* affirm a significant degree of continuity between Old and New
World versions of northern Gothic. The eerily personified "Northern
Lights [that] have seen queer sights" in "The Cremation of Sam McGee"
(Service 1907b, 64 and 70) recall the dancing nocturnal "death-fires" that
animate the frigid water "like a witch's oils, / Burnt green, and blue and

white" of the mariner's nightmare journey (Coleridge [1798] 1951, 53), just as the alluring but voracious female embodiment of the *genius loci* who presides over Service's "The Law of the Yukon" (1907c, 9) recalls the vampiric splendour of Coleridge's dice-playing "Life-in-Death" ([1798] 1951, 55). The prominent motif of the double and the centrality of madness (often culminating in suicide or murder) as an organizing theme of Service's northern verse similarly suggest the degree to which Service simply redeploys the psychic paradigm of Old World northern Gothic in New World northern settings. The incendiary climax of "The Cremation of Sam McGee," for instance, in which Sam's disturbingly animate corpse apparently addresses the cremator-speaker from "the heart of the furnace roar" (Service 1907b, 69), beseeching him to close the door of his fiery northern coffin lest he admit a draft, is a darkly comic repetition of the climactic scene of *Frankenstein* where a horrified Walton hears the monster's suicidal plan to reach the North Pole by ice raft, "ascend [his] funeral pile triumphantly, and exult in the agony of the torturing flames" (Shelley 1831, 223). More subtly, the poem's isolated Arctic setting, daemonic motifs, and apparently supernatural ending raise the tantalizing possibilities of diseased interiority and psychological projection that haunt all gothic tales of this sort. It is not without cause that Margaret Atwood sees Service as "reflecting an already-existing body of lore and cliché…when he wrote poem after poem describing both the uncanny allure of the North and the awful things it could do to you" (1995, 17).

Yet, the transposition of an uncanny, psychologically inflected literature of northern Gothic from Europe to Canada is less straightforward than the case of Service initially suggests. Whatever its psychological interest (which remains considerable), northern Gothic acquires an overtly nationalist dimension in Canadian literature and culture, largely because not one but both of its discursive elements — the North *and* Gothic — have historically been invoked as critical foci for the imagining of a national community in Canada, often in directly overlapping ways. In fact, as Grace suggests, these complementary nationalist discourses converge in Service's northern Gothic, where his Nordic racialism idealizes the Viking as the ultimate conqueror and a "monstrous female Yukon waits to be ravaged by R.G. Haliburton's 'Men of the North'" (2001, 91). Renée Hulan is more circumspect, arguing that "[i]n Service's poetry, the north is primarily a place where rugged individuals thrive rather than a symbol standing for the new nation" (2002, 118). Nonetheless, she too locates Service's gothic

verse within a late nineteenth-century tradition of male adventure writing premised on "the racial superiority of northern white races" and cele-
brating the Viking "as an ideal of northern masculinity" (118).

Service's work thus provides an invaluable starting point for exploring
how Old World northern Gothic is transformed by the romantic nationalist preoccupations of the Canadian context — but only a starting point.
For as Hulan points out, "in the twentieth century, certain aspects of the
adventure have changed" — most notably the representation of Native
people who "are no longer adversaries and extensions of the [hostile]
wilderness" — even if "[w]hat is perhaps most striking about the adventure genre, despite the changeability of its content, is its relative formal
integrity to the present day" (119–20). If Shelley's appropriation of Coleridge
marks the consolidation of an Old World tradition of "unhomely" northern
Gothic and Service's rewriting of both represents a transitional moment
in the colonial reterritorialization of romantic terrors, Farley Mowat's
allusion to Coleridge — in a story that has a dying Eskimo woman play
albatross to the white protagonist's ancient mariner — marks the extraordi-
nary distance that northern Gothic has travelled in its journey from Old
to New World contexts to become a crucial site for the expression and
management of a "homely" national identity.

Focalized through the perspective of a young Canadian pilot who sur-
vives the Second World War only to crash land in the Arctic while trans-
porting a tuberculosis-stricken passenger to a Yellowknife hospital that is
"already stuffed with dying Indians," Mowat's "Walk Well, My Brother"
(1975b, 134) rewrites Coleridge's "unhomely" northern Gothic as a nationalist fable of indigenization. Reiterating the pattern of imperialist boys'
adventure narratives that Hulan finds to be at the core of Mowat's fiction,
the tale evokes a journey north that becomes a journey into national
belonging where "the impossible necessity of becoming indigenous"
(Goldie 1989, 13) is mediated by the protagonist's relationship with an
Indigenous female character — the dying Eskimo woman, Konala, whom
the protagonist initially identifies as "a bloody albatross around his neck"
(Mowat 1975b, 133). This striking allusion to the ancient mariner's guilt
is the story's strongest evocation of colonization as the primordial crime
and uncanny secret of settler-invader society — a criminal secret whose
literal and cultural effects are figured metonymically by the woman's
tuberculosis. Yet the text raises this spectre of self-accusation only to
refute it. The guilt of colonization is conveniently absolved by the "alba-

tross" herself, as Konala not only rescues the protagonist at the expense of her own life but also teaches him "that what had seemed to him a lifeless desert was in fact a land generous in its support of those who knew its nature" (141). Her final act of fashioning a pair of caribou-skin boots, which she bequeaths to the protagonist with the blessing "Walk well in them ... my brother," defines the text's ideological horizon by papering over the threat of an uncanny national story (147).

Within this context, the story's scattered Coleridgean allusions provide a loose sequence of gothic landmarks by which to chart the protagonist's initiation into national northern mysteries that he increasingly experiences as "homely." Beginning with the reference to the albatross, the story proceeds to invoke and rework crucial elements of the ancient mariner's journey, often with ironic effect.[6] The narrator's early description of Konala as a version of Coleridge's vampiric and leprous "life-in-death" — "her cheeks ... flushed a sullen red by fever and a trickle of blood ... dried at the corner of her mouth.... [h]er dark eyes ... fixed upon his with grave intensity" (134) — is typical of the narrative's complex relationship to Old World northern Gothic. This allusion to Coleridge's *femme fatale* condenses the entire indigenizing narrative into a single suggestive figure, simultaneously reflecting the protagonist's disavowal of colonial violence, his ambivalent attraction to a woman who is "young and not bad looking — for a Husky" (134), and his initial alienation from the northern "wasteland" with which Konala is obsessively identified (138). Ultimately, the allusion is an ironic reversal of "life-in-death" that effects a transition from *unheimlich* to *heimlich*. Konala is anything but vampiric. In fact, it is her northern expertise at finding "a miracle of life" and "a veritable flood of life" — the "undulating mass of antlered animals ... pouring out of the north" — that saves them and becomes part of her legacy to the protagonist who is "[r]evitalized by the living ambience of the great herd" (144–45). Mowat's transformation of Coleridge's icily vampiric leper into a beneficent and forgiving northern mother unsurprisingly reverses the significance of the ancient mariner's lonely northern odyssey, culminating in the protagonist's understanding that "[n]o longer was he an alien in an inimical land. He was a man now in his own right, able to make his way in an elder world" (146).

What is most remarkable about this classic fable of indigenization is neither its playful rescripting of Old World northern Gothic to suit a nationalist agenda nor its archetypal design but, rather, its relative unselfconsciousness when compared to the rest of Mowat's northern work. For unlike this unapologetic fantasy of appropriation, the indigenizing narratives that Mowat has tirelessly been producing and refining since the 1950s are haunted by the bad conscience that Mowat himself was instrumental in promoting. This bad conscience, embodied in *The Desperate People*'s nameless Eskimo accuser and his demands for political agency and autonomy, placed enormous pressure on Mowat's romantic nationalism, leading him to re-imagine and restructure the indigenizing meta-narrative in much of his later work. Mowat's young adult adventure novels — *Lost in the Barrens* (1956) and *The Curse of the Viking Grave* (1966) — are particularly useful for exposing this process of revision and recuperation. The fantastic evasions that characterize their plots as well as their overt didacticism broadcast the type of symbolic management that Mowat attempts as well as the precise nature of the blockages he encounters.

The Phantom in the Wilderness: *Lost in the Barrens* and *The Curse of the Viking Grave*

Mowat's turn to northern adventure fiction is itself revealing, for as a number of critics have recently shown, this sub-genre of imperial discourse is synonymous with the articulation of a romanticized Canadian nationhood that marginalizes Native presence. As Hulan has argued, such novels naturalize imperial ideology by grafting the *bildungsroman* narrative of a boy's journey to manhood onto a parallel narrative of romantic nationalism whose fulfilment depends on the boy's journey north towards successful indigenization (2002, 98–109; see also Grace 2001, 184–85). In many ways, Mowat's novels conform to this pattern. In *Lost in the Barrens,* the protagonist, Jamie, begins in Toronto and travels north, proceeding by degree through a series of encounters that mark his increasing initiation into personal and national becoming. Jamie's voyage into the primitive is coded racially and culturally, as his movement — from his uncle's cabin at Macnair Lake to the camp of the Crees and then to that of the Chippewayans, through the barrens and, finally, to the camp of the Eskimos — enacts an implicit regression through evolutionary time. Within this narrative, the "stone-age" Eskimo represents the *ne plus ultra* of Canadian primitivism and thus serves as the guardian of a precious national essence. As one might expect, the protagonist's movement towards this essence is marked by the usual paraphernalia of indigenization, including Indigenous friends (a Cree boy named Awasin and a boy named Peetyuk who is of mixed Inuit-English ancestry), episodes of bonding with animals, enduring the elements, and learning "respect for the land." However, mere initiation and experience are not enough, as the protagonist's discovery of a lamp in an Eskimo graveyard makes clear, for narratives of indigenization characteristically seek to legitimize the substitution of the settler for the Native by a passage through the grave that will make the transition clean:

> The fire burned down, and from the table shone the gleam of a light that had been reborn after a hundred years of darkness. Once an Eskimo woman must have treasured the little soapstone lamp, and over its moss wick, cooked food for her family. Now it lived again. And the arrow points that had belonged to some long forgotten hunter of the dim and dusty past were also ready for new life.
>
> The dead out on that lonely windswept ridge were friendly spirits. They had made gifts to the living of another race across a century of time. (Mowat 1956, 174)

Such a scene is immediately recognizable as a soft variant of the extinction discourse that marks settler-invader literature's perennial representation of "the indigene as corpse" in order to facilitate "a superior means of indigenization" (Goldie 1989, 158). As Goldie pithily explains, extinction discourse is a privileged form of indigenization because it "leaves no 'native' contradiction" but, instead, follows the logic of perfect substitution: "We had natives. We killed them off. Now we are natives" (157). What makes Mowat's novels unusual, however, is that emblematic moments of indigenization such as this one do not perform their usual magic. Throughout both books, the efficacy of such gestures is constantly threatened by the emergence of Native dissent and assertions of Native authority over the North at the very moment that the hero's indigenization seems imminent. Thus, Jamie's appropriation of the Eskimo lamp and the symbolic implications of this act are challenged by Awasin's belief that "[r]obbing from the dead is evil" (Mowat 1956, 172) — an objection whose focus on taboos concerning the disturbance of remains is in itself revealing, especially since Awasin's objection re-gothicizes a site that Jamie's desire would render prematurely "homely." In *The Curse of the Viking Grave*, Indigenous challenges of this nature also take the form of a growing solidarity between the Indian and Eskimo characters that threatens to exclude the white protagonist from the brotherhood of the North altogether. When the boys try to imagine a solution to the rescuing of the Ihalmiut, whose sickliness and near-starvation motivate the action of the plot, Jamie believes that he can shame the Canadian government into providing assistance. Yet Awasin is not convinced:

> "How will you do that? You are only one person.... Who will listen to your voice. I know how Peetyuk feels, Jamie, but you can never know. You are my best friend, and a friend of the Indians and the Eskimos, but you can never know what we feel. We will get little help from the white men."
>
> For the first time since he had come to the North, Jamie was aware of the chasm yawning between him and the people of that land. The sensation frightened him. (Mowat 1966, 136–37)

Contrapuntal moments such as these that allude obliquely to a history of colonial violence and ongoing struggles for self-determination recur in both texts, but they are ultimately dismissed, for Mowat is writing national allegories that rationalize imperial violence as a necessary stage in the dialectical progression towards a higher unity—a unity that is imagined as a highly structured synthesis of the novel's three "races": the European, the Indian, and the Eskimo. *Lost in the Barrens* concludes with a managerial gesture towards pluralism in its inclusion of the Indian and Eskimo boys into the novel's resolution, but the implicit hierarchies of this national vision are confirmed by the opening tableau of *The Curse of the Viking Grave*, in which the three boys are gathered in the cabin on Macnair Lake, which has been transformed into a neo-colonial schoolroom superintended by the craggy benevolence of Jamie's uncle Angus. Significantly, Uncle Angus is exciting the imaginations of his nephew and his Indigenous charges with a book about early Norse voyages to North America.

As a result of the political and cultural stalemate between settler and indigene that compromises Jamie's indigenization, Mowat must avail himself of other means by which to secure the settler's claim to the land and to legitimize his position in the hierarchy represented by Uncle Angus's rustic schoolroom. As the scene of colonial education suggests, this transition from fraternal disagreement to paternalistic national harmony is mediated by the figure of the Viking, which is introduced early in the first book by a cache of weapons and artifacts that Jamie discovers at a northern site known as the great stone house. From the beginning, it is clear that this site is marked for Jamie alone, as the Native and Inuit characters regard the stone house as an evil place and what he finds during his exploration of the dank gothic structure — a northern haunted house where a giant hare leaps out "like a gray ghost" — implicitly sanctions his trespass (Mowat 1956, 78). His realization that he has stumbled upon a Viking gravesite resembles those scenes of colonial adventure about which Patrick Brantlinger has written, in which one white man meets another in the heart of an African jungle (1988). This unexpected moment of recognition in the Canadian North confers upon Jamie the deed of entitlement that it is the novel's business to secure. Jamie's removal of the sword from the stone house, with its heavy Arthurian echoes of national destiny, signals the beginning of a just new polity. In this context, one can only agree with Hulan's assessment that the Viking motif in Mowat's adventure novels draws on a larger tradition of northern fiction that imagines contemporary adventures as being the revival of northern European sagas on the basis of both climate and race (2002, 120).

However, Jamie's association with a northern heroic tradition cannot itself remove the barriers to his full indigenization, because although the presence of the Viking grave grants Jamie a northern lineage, it is still an imperial lineage and thus leaves him vulnerable to the indigene's charge that he is merely an outsider. The narrative of imperial destiny in these books must therefore be supplemented by a manoeuvre that will remove the Viking from historical time and embed him in the mythic time of the northern primitive. Such a manoeuvre is suggestively schematized in the cover illustration to *The Curse of the Viking Grave*, which depicts an Eskimo character holding a sword and a skull crowned by a horned Viking helmet high in the air above his head — an image that makes the indigene acknowledge the proof of Jamie's legitimacy while simultaneously undermining his own symbolic priority in the Canadian North. For the cover's juxtaposition of the living Eskimo with the Viking skull reverses their temporal sequence and effects a symbolic transference of indigeneity from the former to the latter. The fact that this scene is an extrapolation by the cover artist and does not represent an event in the narrative itself is a telling comment on the efficacy and power of the novel's operations.

Such an invention of white indigeneity proceeds in the text itself through a process of levelling and analogy that repeatedly suggests the equivalence of Viking and Eskimo. For instance, Jamie's extraction of artifacts from the Viking grave in the second book repeats his extraction of artifacts from the Eskimo grave in the first book. Their equivalence is further suggested by Jamie's construction of a "little stone igloo" that refashions the indigeneity of the Eskimo in terms of the great stone house (Mowat 1956, 113). This symbolic economy transforms the Viking from the hero of imperial narratives of penetration into a white primitive towards whom later gestures of appropriation can be directed, effectively outmanoeuvring the Native prerogative of an exclusive indigeneity.

The function of the Viking grave as a mediator between "races" divided by colonial violence and the text's facile vision of a unified nation is evident in the enormous ambivalence that is attached to the grave itself. On the one hand, it is the scene of reconciliation between the fragmented group of friends, who resolve their cultural differences by leaving offerings to the dead as recompense for removing the Viking artifacts. The gifts of Awasin's tobacco, Peetyuk's deer meat, Jamie's pocket knife, and Angeline's tea transform the Viking grave into the primitive origin of Uncle Angus's cabin, which likewise serves as a national microcosm, containing "a pot-bellied Quebec heater, woodcarvings done by the Indians, and the well-worn rows of Angus's [English] books" (Mowat 1956, 7). On the other hand, the grave renews the crisis of Indigenous voice that has plagued the narrative since the beginning, leading to a return of the repressed problem of colonial history and ongoing contestations of its legacy. This is because the "curse" mentioned in the novel's title comes not from the dead Viking but, rather, from an Eskimo shaman who cannot accept the plundering of the Viking grave, even though it has ostensibly been performed for his benefit.[7] By forcing the reader to choose between the shaman's cultural values and the survival of his own people, Mowat's text requires the old man's perspective to be marginalized, and Jamie himself can dismiss him as "the old devil" (1966, 162). Symptomatically, the fulfilment of the gothic-sounding curse exacts only a symbolic pound of flesh from Jamie's group. In a chapter entitled "The Curse of the Flies," the friends are attacked by a plague of mosquitoes and black-flies that "crawled into every crevice in their clothing and when they found flesh they bit, leaving a little drop of blood and a rising welt that itched furiously" (197). This "itch" is bad conscience, a comic reduction of the "curse" of the novel's title that threatens to withdraw the blessing Konala bestowed in "Walk Well, My Brother." It is the hangover of an irreducible historical violence and an ongoing history of injustice and resistance that Mowat's vision of Canada as a fully indigenized northern nation attempts in some ways to acknowledge but seeks ultimately to subvert.

Hekwaw's Crossbow: From *Westviking* to *The Farfarers*

> I am an amateur anthropologist who has lived with and written books about the men who really owned the north—the Eskimos. As for the Norse, their proud and violent ghosts have haunted me since I was old enough to lift a book, or turn a page.
>
> —Farley Mowat, *Westviking*

If Mowat's northern writing is principally concerned with staging (and stage-managing) a contest between "the men who really owned the north" and the "proud and violent ghosts" with whom Mowat seeks to supplant them, then Mowat's favoured spectres appear fatally outmatched. For despite the ingenuity of Mowat's symbolic management in his *Boy's Own*-style Viking fantasies, the idealization of the Viking as a white "indigene" in these texts is marked by a structurally insurmountable problem. For all of his pre-Columbian pedigree and his comparable primitive vigour, the Viking remains a belated visitor to the New World when seen from the perspective of "pure prehistoricity" that Goldie identifies as a typical feature of the "reified indigene" and thus cannot be fully divorced from his imperialist associations (1989, 148). Indeed, Mowat himself has explored this analogy in an early story that evokes and then pointedly critiques the very conventions of "homely" northern Gothic that his writing usually privileges.

In a similar way to "Walk Well, My Brother," "The Iron Men" revisits and revises the gothic terrain of Coleridge's "Ancient Mariner"—this time to imagine the presence of northern European races in the Canadian North. The "iron men" or *Innuhowik* of the title are Vikings, and the story is primarily the recounting of an early moment in the history of Norse-Inuit contact in pre-colonial North America by an Inuk narrator named Hekwaw. Self-consciously drawing both its narrative structure and central motif from Coleridge's ballad, the story frames Hekwaw's oral recitation with the words of an unnamed "Kablunait" (white) narrator who plays wedding guest to Hekwaw's ancient mariner.[8] As the story opens, the unnamed narrator is watching Hekwaw fashion a crossbow "made out of antler bone, black spruce and caribou sinew," which seems to have

41

"no place on those northern plains" (Mowat 1975c, 51–52). Hekwaw's story goes on to recount how his people acquired the knowledge to construct this surprising article of Coleridgean weaponry from a Viking "shaman" named Koonar, leader of a party of wayward Norse explorers who stumbled onto their land many centuries before (61).

In many ways, the story Hekwaw tells appears simply to embroider upon the indigenizing paradigm epitomized by Konala's blessing in "Walk Well, My Brother." The yellow-bearded Koonar is integrated into the Inuit tribe, marries the shaman's daughter, and fathers a line of sons — all significantly named Hekwaw — who pass down the secret tale of Koonar's death to the present bearer of that name. In this way, the frame-narrator's ancient Norse proxy is absorbed into the bloodline of the Inuit in "another age," symbolically undermining any claim that Hekwaw might have to a discourse of purity that would grant him special ownership of the tale to which the frame-narrator seeks access (51). Koonar's immemorial hybridization of the Inuit "race" thus tacitly marks his tale as belonging not simply to Hekwaw but, rather, to the frame-narrator as well — in effect making the story of his own death a meta-fictional Viking grave that is then symbolically exhumed and repatriated by Hekwaw's telling. The tale itself, moreover, which concerns a Viking funeral on *Innuit Ku,* the River of Men, is a *tour de force* of northern Gothic's domestication of the uncanny. The mysterious "tongue of fire [that] thrust upward as if to join the flickering green flames of the spirit lights" sighted by people at the Inuit camp, turns out to be Koonar's floating funeral pyre, which the shaman, Kiliktuk, has made for "the stranger who had become his son":

> Kiliktuk drove away as he had been ordered to do [by the dying Koonar], and when he looked back, flames were already lifting above the boat. So the last of the Innuhowik went from our lands to that place of warriors where, he had told us, his people go at the end of their time. (65)

The merger of the flames from Koonar's ship with "the flickering green flames" over the camp and the story's deliberate blurring of culturally distinct metaphysical spaces — Valhalla and the northern "spirit" lights — inflate the indigenizing strategies of *Lost in the Barrens* and *The Curse of the Viking Grave* to mythic proportions.

Significantly, however, these ideological manoeuvres are subordinated to — and literally framed by — the story's didactic anti-colonial *mea culpa*. As Hekwaw's refashioning of the mariner's archaic crossbow with Indigenous materials suggests, the story proposes simultaneously to revise its Old World gothic sources and to critique their appropriation by New World discourses of romantic nationalism through a ventriloquized Indigenous voice whose features are by now familiar. The hybrid Inuit-Norse crossbow is, of course, a recreation of the ancient mariner's archaic weapon. Yet rather than shooting an albatross (which, in "Walk Well, My Brother" had been a sign of innocent indigeneity), Hekwaw turns the crossbow around and takes aim at a version of the very mariner or "grey-beard Loon" (Coleridge [1798] 1951, 11) whose narrative authority he intends to usurp:

> Laying an unfeathered wooden bolt in the groove, [Hekwaw] drew back the sinew string with both hands and lodged it in a crossways slit. On the shadowed river a red-throated loon dipped and swam. There was a sudden, resonant vibration on the still air. The bolt whirred savagely over the river and the loon flashed its wings in a dying flurry. (Mowat 1975c, 52)

Having thus both parodied and dispatched the symbolic author of Old World northern Gothic, Hekwaw silences even his sympathetic interlocutor, not pausing for his questions but, rather, launching immediately into "a tale which had been called back to life across many centuries by the vibrant song of the crossbow" (52).

This seizing of narrative authority by the Indigenous speaker is perhaps only gestural, but it does indicate the story's profoundly ambivalent, if not hostile, relationship to the story's Norse material, which eventually becomes the basis for its critique of imperial violence, symbolized by Kablunait "gifts" such as the gun and the "fire" of disease that "burned in their bodies, rotting the flesh so they stank like old corpses" (66). Indeed, Hekwaw explicitly identifies the Norse explorers with agents of European imperialism, whose arrival is pointedly referred to as the "return" of "the strangers" (66). Ultimately, although the inner tale evokes a Viking fantasy of indigenization, Hekwaw's conclusion implicitly critiques this fantasy by igniting a fourth fire within the dramatic scene of the frame narrative into which he deposits the crossbow, saying: "Take back your gift, Koonar. Take it back to the lands of the Innuhowik and the Kablunait...."

its work here is done" (67). These words conclude the story, symbolically ridding the community of the deadly prototype for all subsequent white "gifts" while, once again, silencing the white frame-narrator and analogously expelling Koonar's indigenized spirit from his metaphysical home amid the northern lights by renaming his gift as a curse.

As the sliding significance of the identification between Kablunait and Viking in "The Iron Men" suggests, the search for Viking graves is a precarious strategy for indigenization that inevitably risks exposing the homely Gothic as a second-order gothic form, designed to keep the genuinely uncanny — that is to say, repressed — violence of colonial invasion at bay. The generically inscribed romanticism of imperial boys' adventure fiction allowed Mowat to largely avoid the danger of such an uncomfortable exposure in *Lost in the Barrens* and *The Curse of the Viking Grave*. In his writing for adult audiences, and particularly in his popular histories of pre-Columbian voyages to North America, however, Mowat is unable to sustain the fantasy of a purely benign, non-imperial Viking ghost. For example, in *Westviking* (1965), a magisterial attempt to establish conclusively Viking presence in North America prior to Columbus is foundational to Mowat's indigenizing project, and it marshals evidence from the Sagas as well as assembling the available archaeological "evidence" from the Kensington Stone, the Vinland Map, and the Viking settlement at L'Anse aux Meadows to make its case.[9] However, as Lucas observes, "Mowat never seems sure about his Norsemen, for they are epic characters, courageous in war and at sea, and, at the same time, bloody marauders and pillagers" (1976, 32). As a result of this impasse, Mowat is unable to make the Viking voyages serve as a heroic foundation for a transcendent narrative of national integration and indigenization and, instead, is reduced to claiming the Vikings in terms of the old imperial paradigm of indigenization by penetration:

> The sanguinary nature which had enabled the Vikings to overrun so much of Europe was their prime undoing in the western continent. Instead of giving them suzerainty over Newfoundland and Labrador, the ready hand with sword and battle-axe cut them off from the prospects of occupying the magnificent new world they had discovered. Nevertheless their westward voyaging was not a sterile and bootless episode in history, as some historians would have us believe.
>
> It was not a dead-end venture leading nowhere and to nothing. Although the Norse failed to settle the New World, they pioneered and established sea

routes to the west which were followed by later waves of European venturers in the fifteenth century. (Mowat 1965, 372)

This problematic "ambivalen[ce]" precipitates Mowat's most ambitious and revealing attempt to rewrite the meta-narrative of homely northern Gothic in *The Farfarers: Before the Norse* (1998) — a work of imaginary or speculative history that seeks, as its subtitle indicates, to thrust the ever-troubling moment of the European "discovery" of North America further back in time, "[b]efore the Norse" (Lucas 1976, 32).

Like *Westviking* and its many fictional counterparts in Mowat's work, *The Farfarers* is stimulated by Mowat's abiding fascination with northern archaeological sites that could potentially suggest an antique European presence in the Arctic. In this book, however, he attempts to steer safe passage between the Scylla of prior Indigenous presence and the Charybdis of proto-imperialist Viking ghosts by "discovering" a new group of "insubstantial wraiths" to haunt the ruins and stone beacons of the high Arctic, which Mowat interprets as traces of pre-Norse voyages to northern North America (Mowat 1998, xiii). The Albans, as Mowat calls these people who are chased across the Atlantic in a series of stages by the rapacious, slave-holding Vikings, are in fact a sort of benign, phantom projection of the Vikings themselves. Not only are they idealized as "natural people in a natural world," they are importantly identified as "the indigenes who inhabited Europe, Asia Minor, and probably also North Africa, until they were displaced from their lowland territories by largely Indo-European invasions," eventually becoming the pre-Celtic inhabitants of the British Isles (47–48). In this way, the "Albans" come to embody the key virtue of innocent autochthony as a paradoxically mobile and transplantable trait. Their eventual migration to the high Arctic, where Mowat claims they dwelt in harmony with a late Dorset people called the Tunit, allows Mowat to imagine an alternative, non-violent history of "British"-Inuit contact, which he fictionalizes from the point of view of a "prehistoric" Tunit speaker in ways that recall and decisively rewrite Hekwaw's damning association of Innuhowik (Norse) with Kablunait "strangers" in "The Iron Men":

They had no wish to remain on our land — only to stay long enough to gather walrus tusks and other things they valued, most of which had little worth to us. We did not begrudge them what they wanted. They were peaceable folk....

The Far Ones came every year thereafter—sometimes as many as a dozen boatloads. We shared the country and our lives with them. It is certain that some of us carry their blood in our veins. I must be one such, for dreams come to me of places I have never been. It may be that I am seeing the Far Ones' homelands.

They came amongst us for the space of three lifetimes; then one summer they failed to return. That was long ago. Now lichens cover the fallen stones of their great houses and the fireplaces where they boiled good oil until it was no longer fit to eat.

Aieee.... they have been gone a long while ... but we still keep watch to the southeast. Some day the Far Ones may come again. (150–51)

In fact, the "Far Ones" have not really left at all—at least not in the sense that is most important to Mowat's indigenizing epic of national belonging. For they remain within the bounds of what will become Canada, settling in Newfoundland and entering the hybrid national microcosm of St. George's Bay where "the indigenes consisted of nomadic Micmac Indians from Nova Scotia; some Acadian French; and dark-skinned, dark-eyed, dark-haired 'natives' called Jakatars," the latter of which Mowat identifies as the travelling "indigenous" Albans (319).

As Mowat's northern discourse sails further and further into the realm of nationalist fantasy to imagine increasingly remote and transcendent genealogies of white indigeneity for Canada, it is worth recalling the lessons of his earlier forays into New World northern Gothic, which dwelt not upon the search for phantom settler-invaders but, rather, on the potentially unsettling power of restless Native ghosts. I have argued in this essay that Mowat's quest for Viking graves instantiates a reactionary discourse of homely northern Gothic that continues to haunt contemporary cultural production. Yet this argument should not be taken to imply that a reversal of this paradigm—the search for Native or Inuit graves—necessarily implies a process that would unsettle the indigenizing meta-narrative or render it permanently unhomely. As Mowat's example illustrates, this meta-narrative is extraordinarily supple, adaptive, and sly, and invocations of a subversive postcolonial uncanny can themselves become the material of indigenizing appropriations. Mowat's rhetorically powerful, but politically ambiguous, account of the barrens as an uncanny space that is meant to haunt the complacent national imagination in *People of the Deer* is a case in point, as its evocation of the dead is ambiguously poised between consoling elegy and disturbing provocation. As we continue to theorize the unsettling potential of gothic discourse for a critical Canadian postcolonialism, we should remain vigilant that we do not end up reifying the very representations we seek to deconstruct.

Notes

1 Despite its promising title, John Moss's "From *Frankenstein* to Farley Mowat, Words Turn the Arctic Landscape into Unreality" (1991) does not address the gothic contexts of northern representation.

2 Despite her attribution of the 1952 edition, Margaret Atwood's argument bears on the revised 1975 edition of *People of the Deer*, though it may also reflect the earlier edition's role in establishing Mowat's reputation and on the public debates it provoked (2002). Mowat articulates the need for Native autonomy most forcibly in *The Desperate People*, a sequel to *People of the Deer*, which represents a significant revision of Mowat's earlier position on assimilation, a revision that I discuss later in this essay. On the reception of *People of the Deer*, see James King (2002, 119–23).

3 For Atwood's analysis of northern myths, see *Strange Things: The Malevolent North in Canadian Literature*. The incompleteness of Atwood's critique of northern nationalism is evident in her concluding exhortation to this series of lectures: "Canadians have long taken the North for granted, and we've invested a large percentage of our feelings about identity and belonging in it. But the bad news is coming in: the North is not endless. It is not vast and strong, and capable of devouring and digesting all the human dirt thrown its way.... The edifice of northern imagery we've been discussing in these lectures was erected on a reality; if that reality ceases to exist, the imagery, too, will cease to have any resonance or meaning, except as a sort of indecipherable hieroglyphic" (1995, 115–16). This line of argument, which recuperates the North for the nation in the name of ecological protectionism, in many ways recalls the double edge of Mowat's own ecological discourse in *Canada North Now* (1976).

4 For a more detailed discussion of the relation between Freud's uncanny and settler nationalism, see Brian Johnson (1999).

5 For a useful overview of this gothic nationalist tradition, see Sherrill Grace (2001, 32–33) and Jonathan Kertzer (1998, 120–28).

6 When the protagonist of Mowat's story re-awakens to second life after being rescued from the Barrens by Konala, he recalls "the unbearable sense of loneliness... [that] finally sent him, in a heart-bursting spasm of desperation, toward a stony ridge that seemed to undulate serpent-like on the otherwise shapeless face of a world that had lost all form and substance" (1975b, 140). This quotation recalls a similar turning point in Coleridge's poem, where the mariner experiences a redemptive epiphany that frees him of the albatross when he watches water-snakes as "[t]hey coiled and swam" and blesses them "unaware" ([1798] 1951, 272–91). Konala herself assumes multiple Coleridgean masks in the story, transforming the natural and supernatural threats of Old World northern Gothic into the material of New World accommodation. Most notably, her spontaneous song, "a high and

plaintive chant without much melody which seemed as much part of the land as the fluttering of curlews," which "join[s] her voice to the voice of the land and to the spirits of the land" recalls both the many birdsongs of the "Rime" and its presiding polar spirit. Both narratives, of course, conclude with tentative homecomings (Mowat 1975b, 142).

7 Jamie and his friends intend to sell the relics to a museum to raise money to feed the starving Ihalmiut.

8 Despite his ostensible role as Native listener, the scolding, didactic narrator who describes the setting as "the world that we, in our ignorance, chose to call the Barrenlands" already displays the tone and preoccupations of the story's author. He is plainly a mask for Mowat himself.

9 For a critical discussion of this evidence, see Jeffrey Redmond (1979).

Works Cited

Atwood, Margaret. 1995. *Strange Things: The Malevolent North in Canadian Literature.* Oxford: Clarendon Press.

———. 2002. "Introduction." In *High Latitudes: A Northern Journey.* Ed. Farley Mowat. Toronto: Key Porter Books. ix–xi.

Bhabha, Homi. 1994. *The Location of Culture.* New York: Routledge.

Brantlinger, Patrick. 1988. *Rule of Darkness: British Literature and Imperialism, 1830–1914.* Ithaca: Cornell UP.

Coleridge, Samuel Taylor. 1798, reprinted 1951. "The Rime of the Ancient Mariner." In *Samuel Taylor Coleridge: Selected Poetry and Prose.* Ed. Elisabeth Schneider. New York: Holt, Rinehart and Winston. 49–69.

Francis, Daniel. 1992. *The Imaginary Indian: The Image of the Indian in Canadian Culture.* Vancouver: Arsenal Pulp.

Freud, Sigmund. 1919, reprinted 1990. "The 'Uncanny.'" In *The Penguin Freud Library: Art and Literature,* volume 14. Ed. Albert Dickson. Trans. James Strachey. Harmondsworth: Penguin. 335–76.

Goldie, Terry. 1989. *Fear and Temptation: The Image of the Indigene in Canadian, Australian, and New Zealand Literatures.* Montreal and Kingston: McGill-Queen's UP.

Grace, Sherrill. 2001. *Canada and the Idea of North.* Montreal and Kingston: McGill-Queen's UP.

Hearne, Samuel. 1795, reprinted 1958. *A Journey from Prince of Wales's Fort in Hudson's Bay to the Northern Ocean, 1769, 1770, 1771, 1772.* Toronto: Macmillan.

Hulan, Renée. 2002. *Northern Experience and the Myths of Canadian Culture.* Montreal and Kingston: McGill-Queen's UP.

Johnson, Brian. 1999. "Unsettled Landscapes: Uncanny Discourses of Love in Ostenso's *Wild Geese.*" *Wascana Review* 34(2): 23–41.

Kertzer, Jonathan. 1998. *Worrying the Nation: Imagining a National Literature in English Canada*. Toronto: University of Toronto Press.

King, James. 2002. *Farley: The Life of Farley Mowat*. Toronto: Harper Flamingo.

London, Jack. 1907. *Love of Life and Other Stories*. New York: Macmillan.

Loomba, Ania. 1998. *Colonialism/Postcolonialism*. New York: Routledge.

Lowes, John Livingston. 1927. *The Road to Xanadu: A Study in the Ways of the Imagination*. Princeton: Princeton UP.

Lucas, Alec. 1976. *Farley Mowat*. Toronto: McClelland and Stewart.

MacLulich, T. D. 1977. "The Alien Role: Farley Mowat's Northern Pastorals." *Studies in Canadian Literature* 2(2): 226–38.

Moodie, Susanna. 1852. *Roughing It in the Bush; or, Life in Canada*. Toronto: McClelland and Stewart.

Moss, John. 1991. "From *Frankenstein* to Farley Mowat, Words Turn the Arctic Landscape into Unreality." *Arctic Circle* (March-April): 32–40.

———. 1994. *Enduring Dreams: An Exploration of Arctic Landscape*. Concord: Anansi.

Mowat, Farley. 1952, revised 1975. *People of the Deer*. New York: Pyramid.

———. 1956. *Lost in the Barrens*. Toronto: McClelland and Stewart.

———. 1958. *Coppermine Journey*. Toronto: McClelland and Stewart.

———. 1959, revised 1975. *The Desperate People*. Toronto: Seal.

———. 1960. *Ordeal by Ice: The Search for the Northwest Passage*. Toronto: McClelland and Stewart.

———. 1963. *Never Cry Wolf*. Toronto: Seal.

———. 1965. *Westviking: The Ancient Norse in Greenland and North America*. Toronto: McClelland and Stewart.

———. 1966. *The Curse of the Viking Grave*. Toronto: McClelland and Stewart.

———. 1967. *The Polar Passion: The Quest for the North Pole*. Toronto: McClelland and Stewart.

———. 1973. *Tundra: Selections from the Great Accounts of Arctic Land Voyages*. Toronto: McClelland and Stewart.

———. 1975a. *The Snow Walker*. Toronto: Seal.

———. 1975b. "Walk Well, My Brother." In *The Snow Walker*. Toronto: Seal. 132–48.

———. 1975c. "The Iron Men." In *The Snow Walker*. Toronto: Seal. 51–67.

———. 1976. *Canada North Now*. Toronto: McClelland and Stewart.

———. 1998. *The Farfarers: Before the Norse*. Toronto: Key Porter Books.

Redmond, Jeffrey R. 1979. *"Viking" Hoaxes in North America*. New York: Carlton Press.

Said, Edward. 1994. *Orientalism*. New York: Vintage.

Service, Robert W. 1907a, reprinted 1957. *Songs of a Sourdough*. Toronto: Ryerson.

————. 1907b. "The Cremation of Sam McGee." In *Songs of a Sourdough*. Toronto: Ryerson. 64–70.

————. 1907c. "The Law of the Yukon." In *Songs of a Sourdough*. Toronto: Ryerson. 9–16.

Shelley, Mary. 1831. *Frankenstein or The Modern Prometheus*. Oxford: Oxford UP.

Sugars, Cynthia. 2003. "Haunted by (a Lack of) Postcolonial Ghosts: Settler Nationalism in Jane Urquhart's *Away*." *Essays on Canadian Writing* 79: 1–32.

CHAPTER THREE

Coyote's Children and the Canadian Gothic: Sheila Watson's *The Double Hook* and Gail Anderson-Dargatz's *The Cure for Death by Lightning*

Marlene Goldman

Sheila Watson's novel *The Double Hook* begins with a biblically inflected introduction to its characters who live "under Coyote's eye":

> In the folds of the hills
> under Coyote's eye
>> lived
> the old lady, mother of William
> of James and of Greta. (1959, 19)

The introduction is immediately followed by a description of James's murder of his part-Native mother, the old lady.[1] The remainder of the text details the other characters' repeated, uncanny encounters with her ghost, which is always associated with Coyote. Similarly, in Gail Anderson-Dargatz's *The Cure for Death by Lightning* (1997), the narrator, Beth Weeks, a fifteen-year-old white girl also under Coyote's eye, is menaced by this ghostly force who ultimately possesses the body of a man aptly named Coyote Jack.[2] Canadian texts that feature haunting[3] and possession are valuable sites to study the role played by the Gothic and the treatment of desires that society deems unnameable, unacceptable, and unspoken. Intriguingly, in Watson's *The Double Hook* and Anderson-Dargatz's *The*

Cure for Death by Lightning, spectral effects associated with gothic conventions are linked both to unbridled male and female desires and to Indigenous mythology, specifically the figure of Coyote. This study aims to contribute to the current debates about what constitutes a Canadian gothic novel[4] and what differentiates it from other national manifestations of the Gothic by analyzing the treatment of the uncanny gendered and racialized nature of desire in Watson's and Anderson-Dargatz's novels. Both texts are set in the interior of British Columbia and explore relations between the Natives and non-Natives in the area—a two-hundred-year-old struggle within the province of British Columbia that continues to this day. Viewed in this light, it is not surprising that the ghostly spirit of Coyote haunts the settler-invader's land. Indeed, with the exception of a very few coastal bands, the Native peoples of British Columbia "never made any agreement for the sale of their aboriginal rights, nor had they fought and been conquered by the whites." Thus, unlike most of the Indigenous peoples elsewhere in Canada, "they are non-treaty Natives, and land laws were imposed on them without any recompense" (Balf 1978, 13).[5] Owing to their implicit engagement with the tensions surrounding the ongoing Aboriginal land claims in British Columbia, Watson's and Anderson-Dargatz's novels constitute important examples of the Canadian Gothic.

As Arnold Davidson asserts, citing Margot Northey (1976), "Canadians have long been haunted by *their* wilderness" (1981, 243 [emphasis added]). The use of the possessive "their" is both troubling and relevant to this discussion because it highlights the vexed question at the heart of the Canadian Gothic concerning rightful ownership of the land. As Davidson observes, one form of haunting in the Canadian Gothic involves "the new immigrant, the settler who would remain firmly grounded in the values he brings with him," finding the *"unsettled* forest or prairie appalling" (243–44 [emphasis added]). Indeed, the settlers' haunting fear that they are being hunted by "an indefinite thing with no name," according to Davidson, "is almost always invoked or created by those who find their sense of reality, which is the source of their security, at odds with the different reality of the empty land that they see all around them" (244). Recognizing that this type of haunting is based on the misguided perception of an "empty land," Davidson argues further that a second, more complex form of haunting involves the recognition that "a wild, empty land...is empty only according to the prevailing civilised standards of what constitutes a full one" (244). In keeping with these insights, I would suggest that the spectre of Coyote that haunts both Watson's and Anderson-Dargatz's novels serves as a figure for the settler-invader society's anxious and barely repressed awareness of the Native people's prior claim to the land. Ultimately, in both novels, Coyote remains more of a ghostly absence than an actual presence, serving both as the trace of Native people's unjust treatment by the settler-invaders and as a screen for the latter's projection of a variety of threats to the image of a patriarchal, Christian, Canadian nation-state.

Watson and Anderson-Dargatz lived in neighbouring regions of British Columbia (the Cariboo District and the Thompson Okanagan, respectively), both of which featured an uneasy juxtaposition of Native reserves, small towns, farms, and ranch land—regions that later served as the inspiration for the settings of their gothic novels.[6] These regions highlight the fact that colonial space "is by its very nature a bifurcated, ambivalent space, where the familiar and unfamiliar mingle in an uneasy truce" (Paravisini-Gebert 2002, 233). Far from anti-realist fantasies, Watson's and Anderson-Dargatz's texts register the uncanny status of Canada and of British Columbia, in particular, by representing conflicts between those aligned with the patriarchal, Christian, settler community and those aligned with the unsettling trickster-god Coyote. A transformer-god who provided sustenance for his people, Coyote embodies, for the settler-invader society, the uncanny, Aboriginal claim to the land.[7]

The term "uncanny" is appropriate for a study of Watson's and Anderson-Dargatz's para-colonial[8] gothic texts because within the word "uncanny" two seemingly antithetical terms circulate: *heimlich,* which Freud glosses as "home," a familiar or accessible place; and *unheimlich,* which is unfamiliar, strange, inaccessible, unhomely (Gelder and Jacobs 1999, 181). As Ken Gelder and Jane Jacobs explain, an uncanny experience may occur "when one's home—one's place—is rendered somehow and in some sense unfamiliar; one has the experience, in other words, of being in place and 'out of place' *simultaneously.* This happens precisely at the moment when one is made aware that one has unfinished business with the past, at the moment when the past returns as an 'elemental'...force to haunt the present day" (181). As they assert, "[a]n Aboriginal claim to land is quite literally a claim concerning unfinished business, a claim which enables what should have been laid to rest to overflow into the otherwise 'homely' realm of modernity" (181). In essence, the "uncanny" can remind us that within settler nations, "a condition of unsettled-ness folds into this often taken-for-granted mode of occupation" (182).

Watson based *The Double Hook* on her two-year experience teaching during the Depression in the Cariboo District of British Columbia, which she describes as "a country of opposites": "heat and cold; flat rolling plateau and sheared-off hills; streams, rivers, potholes and alkali waste; large ranches and small holdings; native Indians and expatriated Europeans and great stretches where no one lives at all" (Watson, quoted in Morriss 2002, 55). In her unpublished commentary on the novel, Watson describes the district as "devious" and "hostile," filled with "the isolation of which spatial separation is a symbol, the isolation of mind from mind" (55). As Shirley Neuman explains, "[w]riting about a region and a time in which English, American, Spanish, Japanese and Chinese settlers, among others, lived alongside an aboriginal population, Sheila Watson asks what common knowledge could possess them, make them into a civilised community" (1988, 1). Indeed, Watson admits that she wrote the novel because she was deeply troubled by the fragmented and isolated community that she encountered: "The theme of the book is simply this: If men...have neither an image of church or state or even tribal unity, if they are cut off from a rooted pattern of behaviour...they respond to life with violence or apathy" (quoted in Morriss 2002, 55).

To resolve the apparent isolation, "unsettled-ness," and lack of civility, the novel portrays the once-isolated inhabitants forming what Morriss refers to as "a true community" (56). Yet the community that constellates, in true gothic fashion, remains predicated on the expression of direct threats to its cohesion, namely the unsettled and unsettling desires of nomadic Native peoples and women who refuse patriarchal and Christian models of domestication. In using the term "expression," I am drawing on Rosemary Jackson's insights about fantastic literature, which, as she says, can operate in two ways (according to the different meanings of "express"): "It can *tell of,* manifest or show desire (expression in the sense of portrayal, representation, manifestation, linguistic utterance, mention, description), or it can *expel* desire, when this desire is a disturbing element which threatens cultural order and continuity (expression in the sense of pressing out, squeezing, expulsion, getting rid of something by force)" (1981, 3–4). Indeed, "in many cases fantastic literature fulfils both functions at once" (4).

In keeping with Jackson's insights, the formation of the new community in Watson's novel is quite literally predicated on expulsion and sacrifice. Two threatening, part-Native women die violently: the non-maternal, selfish old lady is murdered by her son James — an overt example of "getting rid of something by force": "Pushed by James's will. By James's hand. By James's words: This is my day. You'll not fish today" (Watson 1959, 19). In addition, the old lady's daughter, Greta, whose transgressive sexuality is incestuously directed towards James,[9] commits suicide:

And Coyote cried in the hills:
I've taken her where she stood
my left hand is on her head
my right hand embraces her. (85)

Although Coyote claims both Greta and her mother, the old lady's apparition, always in association with Coyote, haunts the community throughout the novel.[10] Scorning notions of property and propriety and restlessly and shamelessly fishing on everyone else's land, her ghost acts as the trace of an Aboriginal claim that, to borrow Gelder and Jacobs's words, overflows "into the otherwise 'homely' realm of modernity" (1999, 181).

Ann Radcliffe, famous for gothic novels such as *The Mysteries of Udolpho,* wrote that gothic protagonists live in a world that seems "more like the visions of a distempered imagination, than the circumstances of truth" ([1794] 1990, 329). Her view of the gothic world is echoed in *The Double Hook:* "The whole world's got distemper he [James] wanted to shout… The ground's rotten with it" (Watson 1959, 43). In the case of Watson's novel, the distemper and rot are tied to unresolved Native land claims. Moreover, because the old lady embodies these repressed claims that disturb the mainstream cultural order, the other characters condemn the old lady both for her non-maternal, nomadic lifestyle and for her defiant insistence on looking for something that has been hidden or lost. Early on, the old lady's daughter-in-law Ara sees the old lady's ghost fishing along the creek and remarks bitterly: "Passing her own son's house and never offering a fry" (20). Later, Greta complains:

I've seen her standing looking for something even the birds couldn't see. Something hid from every living thing. I've seen her defying. I've seen her take her hat off in the sun at noon, baring her head and asking for the sun to strike her. Holding the lamp and looking where there's nothing to be found. Nothing but dust. No person's got a right to keep looking. To keep looking and blackening lamp globes for others to clean. (31)

However, Angel, the only "pure-blooded Indian" woman in the novel (see Morriss 2002, 61), reminds Greta that "[o]ne person's got as much right as another. ... There's things people want to see. There's things too ... there's things get lost" (Watson 1959, 31). Indeed, what "gets lost" or, perhaps, more accurately, sacrificed in *The Double Hook,* are the desires that threaten the sex-gender system and resist the Christian, assimilationist project of the Canadian nation-state.

Viewed in the larger context of the Gothic, the old lady represents the familiar figure of the occulted female (see Bowering 1988, 62–68; Atwood 1985, 41).[11] At the forbidden centre of the Gothic "is the spectral presence of the dead-undead mother, archaic and all-encompassing, a ghost signifying the problematics of femininity which the heroine must confront" (Kahane 1985, 336). Yet in Watson's Canadian Gothic, the old lady's identity simultaneously represents both the "dead or displaced mother" (335) and the spectre of Native "survivance (survival plus resistance)" (Powell 2002, 400). Indeed, by fishing upstream to the source, the old lady may be

seen as finally attempting to resolve after her death one of the ambiguities of her life. Searching for Coyote, she could at last ground her being in its Indian source, a source that well may be itself in the process of disappearing or at least becoming something else as indicated by Coyote's propensity (protecting disguise?) to pass himself off as the Christian God. (Davidson 1988, 36)

Although Davidson suggests that Coyote is passing himself off as the Christian God, a more vexed and vexing reading of the novel locates the imposition of the Christian religion on Native peoples within a broader colonial framework. As Native educators assert, "the erosion of Shuswap authority over their own lands and people started with the Hudson Bay Company's imposing British justice on Shuswap people. This was the most insidious and fundamental political change that occurred from 1800 to 1858" (Wolf 1996, 26). However, this change was followed by the equally insidious and fundamental imposition of Christianity in 1842 (Balf 1978, 6). Replicating the ongoing pattern of colonial imposition,

Watson's narrative transforms Coyote, a Native-American trickster figure, into an Old Testament version of God.[12] In essence, the transformation of a Native spirit into the Holy Spirit reflects both a nationalist and a modernist agenda to "clean house."

In his introduction to *A Companion to the Gothic,* David Punter asks: "Where might we locate the 'Gothic moment' in modernism?" (2000, ix). He goes on to wonder whether we might "prefer to see in modernism precisely that movement of the mind that seeks to exorcise the ghost, to clean out the house . . . and assert the possibility of a life that is not haunted as it situates itself resolutely in a present and strains toward the future." *The Double Hook,* one of Canadian literature's most celebrated modernist texts, seemingly confirms Punter's observations owing to its apocalyptic conclusion in which the old lady's son James envisions building a new house on the charred ruins of his mother's home:

> In his mind now he could see only the seared and smouldering earth, the bare hot cinder of a still unpeopled world. He felt as he stood with his eyes closed on the destruction of what his heart had wished destroyed that by some generous gesture he had been turned once more into the first pasture of things.
>
> I will build the new house further down the creek, he thought. All on one floor. (Watson 1959, 131)[13]

Despite both the text's powerful and apocalyptic attempts to clean house by transforming living Native peoples into ghosts, *The Double Hook* can still be read in ways that do not so easily banish its uncanny spirits. For instance, although Coyote frequently speaks with a biblical cast, does he necessarily become God — as the majority of critics have argued — or does he function instead, in accordance with gothic conventions, as God's uncanny double (see Davidson 1988, 35)? Moreover, even if mainstream critics equate Coyote with God in order to make Coyote God, as Davidson asserts, "why could not the same equation have the opposite resolution and make God Coyote?" (35). In fact, readings that emphasize the subversive power of Coyote are reinforced by Watson's own revisions to the conclusion, which underscore Coyote's continued spectral presence.[14] In earlier drafts, Coyote's blessing of James's newborn son appeared before the conclusion, but the published version ends with Coyote's voice crying out from "a cleft in the rock" to herald the birth:

I have set his feet on soft ground;
I have set his feet on the sloping shoulders
of the world. (Watson 1959, 134)

As Morriss argues, "Watson's simple adjustment gives Coyote, the pre-
ternatural focus of discord and abdicated humanity, the last word" (2002,
63). Calling out from the vaginal cleft, the womb/tomb to which Greta
and the old lady have been banished, the spectre of Coyote ensures that in
Watson's Canadian Gothic the claims of both the displaced mother and
the Shuswap Nation continue to haunt the text.[15] At bottom, Watson has
fashioned a divided text. On the one hand, *The Double Hook* promotes
colonial and apocalyptic values associated with the fantasy of a new Eden,
yet, at the same time, the novel remains haunted, as Watson herself was
haunted, by the victims of this fantasy and the outstanding claims of the
Natives of British Columbia.[16]

The Cure for Death by Lightning, like *The Double Hook,* emphasizes
gendered and racialized contests over spiritual and geographic territory
and continues to raise unsettling questions about the settler-invaders' status in Canada. Set in BC's China Valley, *The Cure for Death by Lightning*
initially highlights global disputes over territory by virtue of its temporal
setting during the Second World War, when imperial powers were
engaged in struggles over the borders of nation-states. These overarching
conflicts have an impact on the protagonist's family. Early on, we are told
that the narrator's father suffered a head injury during the Great War
that left him "irritable and demanding" (Anderson-Dargatz 1997, 10).
Like James in *The Double Hook,* Beth's father suffers from "distemper."
Later the narrator states: "The blood of a war a thousand miles away
rained down on us," linking the distempered, macrocosmic struggles over
territory to the microcosmic level where Beth's father, John, and his
neighbour, the Swede, battle to establish the border between their farms
(63). At this same microcosmic level, the narrator's father forcibly
attempts to contain the threat of the Native population who live on and
near the reserve by ordering them off his property. When the Shuswap
elder, Bertha Moses, criticizes Beth's father for exploiting Native youth—
"You hire our boys because they don't know how to ask for what they're
worth...You treat them as if they were slaves"—he shouts: "Get out of
my house!" (14). Faced with a disturbing element that threatens mainstream cultural order and continuity, he responds in the same way as

James in *The Double Hook* and forcibly attempts to banish the threat from his house.

Within Anderson-Dargatz's novel, as in *The Double Hook,* contests over territory are also envisioned as a battle between Native and Christian spiritual traditions. Again, both novels accurately encode the traumatic experience of the Shuswap Native peoples with Christian missionaries from 1842 onward. When Beth visits the reservation, she notices that the latter was "overwhelmed by the church" (112).[17] Yet, as Bertha Moses explains, "[t]hose Christ people rule this village here, but Coyote owns the bush. He always has" (117). In keeping with gothic conventions, Coyote's possession of the bush is initially aligned with the familiar binary opposition between helpless young women and male victimisers whose erotic and incestuous tendencies raise the spectre of complete social disintegration (Botting 1996, 5). Indeed, in the novel, the overt, familiar threat springs from unrestrained sexual, patriarchal forces: "[M]en on the rampage" (Ferguson Ellis 2000, 263).[18] When the mysterious, threatening force chases Beth through the grass, she says: "[I]t could be anything: a man like the ones my mother's friend Mrs Bell warned of, who would catch a girl in the bush and do unspeakable things to her" (Anderson-Dargatz 1997, 4). And although Beth is ultimately raped by her father, a much more covert, Aboriginal, and sexually transgressive desire encrypted within the familiar melodramatic gothic context gradually emerges as the most subversive challenge to the dominant patriarchal order—a threat so terrifying that it must ultimately be banished from the text.

Early on, Beth is befriended by Nora, Bertha Moses' granddaughter, a Native girl who sports "boys' jeans and a western shirt that stretched a little at the buttons across her breasts" (9). The attraction between the two women is immediate. When their eyes meet in a crowd for the first time, we are told: "The room grew womanly" (10). Interestingly, as their relationship develops, a curious shift occurs in the menacing spectral force: Coyote is increasingly aligned with Nora:

> I saw a motion in the grass coming towards me, a splitting of the grass as if an animal or a man were running through it, but there was nothing there … The swishing of grass filled up my ears and came at me faster than anything possible. Then a hand was on my shoulder. I swung around and Nora was there, her hand on my shoulder. (129)

Scene after scene aligns Nora with Coyote, rendering her phantomlike perhaps because, as Terry Castle asserts, "to love another woman is to lose one's solidity in the world, to evanesce, and fade into the spectral" (1993, 32 and 34):

> One woman or the other must be a ghost, or on the way to becoming one. Passion is excited, only to be obscured, disembodied, decarnalized. The vision is inevitably waved off. Panic seems to underwrite these obsessional spectralizing gestures: a panic over love, female pleasure, and the possibility of women breaking free — together — from their male sexual overseers. Homophobia... the order of the day, entertains itself wryly or gothically with phantoms, then exorcizes them. (see Anderson-Dargatz 1997, 96, 152, 163, 189, and 259)

By repeatedly inviting Beth to run away with her, Nora embodies the possibility of "women breaking free-together" (see, for instance, 213, 272, and 280–82). Yet, in accordance with Jackson's observation about fantastic narrative's characteristic shift "from expression as the manifestation to expression as expulsion," the narrative invokes the subversive power of lesbian desire only to exorcise it to maintain the patriarchal order (1981, 3–4). When Beth's father discovers his daughter consorting with Nora, he confronts the latter and shouts: "Get off my property. Get away from here. Lousy Indian! Get off my property" (Anderson-Dargatz 1997, 98).[19] Toward the conclusion, however, Beth also playfully confronts Nora: "Maybe it's you that's following me... You're some spy, like them Germans. Or them Japs. Maybe you're a Jap spy" (189). Her comments subtly reinforce the connections between internal and external territorial threats, equating the unsettling challenge posed by her Native, lesbian lover to global threats to the Canadian nation-state.

Like Watson's Native revenant, the old lady who wanders between two worlds, Nora poses a threat both to the patriarchal order and to the Canadian nation-state. This dual threat is conveyed by her unusual eyes and is registered when Beth first sees Nora: "Each of her eyes was a different color, one blue and one green. She was a half-breed, then" (15). Later, Beth muses that Nora "was Indian enough to be an outcast in town and white enough be an outcast on the reserve" (97). In addition to marking her unsettled and unsettling status as part Native and part white, Nora's differently coloured eyes also mark her as a lesbian, what Native North Americans refer to as "two-spirit people": "This close I could see that her eyes of two different colors, one green, one blue, were startling, the eyes of two women in one face" (71). Her eyes function in this case as an emblem of what Castle terms "the embodiment of female-female Eros" (1993, 41). Due to the threat posed by her liminal status—a Native/non-Native and a girl/woman who, by virtue of her dress and sexual preference, acts like a man—Nora and those who associate with her are taunted and attacked by members of the Native and white community alike.

In her study of the Gothic, Claire Kahane traces the fears and desires associated with the figure of the lesbian who tempts the female protagonist with the possibility of "remaining bound within a mother-daughter relationship—erotically bound, that is, to a woman, a transgression of heterosexual convention" (1985, 342). In *The Cure for Death by Lightning,* the relationship between Nora and Beth is explicitly likened to a mother-daughter bond. For instance, when Nora runs her hands through Beth's hair, we are told: "It felt good and calming, like my mother brushing my hair before bed" (Anderson-Dargatz 1997, 109). Later, when Nora sneaks into Beth's room and slips into her bed to calm Beth after a nightmare, Beth remarks: "Nora rocked me and sang quietly... When Nora finished the song, she combed my hair with her fingers, as my mother used to when I was a small child. I became aware of my mother, listening at the door. After a moment she moved away" (264). Nora's maternal gestures, and her juxtaposition with Beth's actual mother in this quote, reinforce Nora's role as a surrogate mother, a replacement for the mother who failed in her role because she allowed her husband to sexually abuse her daughter.[20]

In keeping with gothic conventions, the dystopian, patriarchal family dynamic leaves Beth feeling like a prisoner in her home. As she tells her mother, "it's so dark in here, I feel like I'm suffocating" (125). By contrast, the utopian possibilities associated with Beth's and Nora's relationship are symbolized by their discovery of a secret house in the wilderness. Shortly after they meet, Nora leads Beth to a house buried in the earth that once belonged to Bertha Moses: "This is Granny's old house," Nora explains, "A winter house" (111). Although it belongs now to Granny, as Nora explains, before that it was her "great-granny's house," indicating that it has been in the family for generations (112). With its "opening into darkness at the centre of... [a] mound of dirt and weeds" (111), the structure recalls women's genitalia. Later, Bertha makes the connection between the winter house and the maternal body explicit, telling the girls that her mother "used to say the winter houses were safe like a mother's hug" (115). In actual fact, what the girls discover is the remains of a kekuli or pit house, the circular, underground winter homes of the Shuswap that were built along riverbanks.[21] These houses have become crucial to Aboriginal land claims in British Columbia since remnants of kekuli have provided archaeological evidence that the Shuswap people lived in, and laid claim to, the interior of British Columbia for 4,000 years (Jack, Matthew, and Matthew 1993, 6). If, as critics recognize, the primary locus of the Gothic is "the castle [which] gradually gave way to the old house"—a topos that refers both to a building and to a family line—then the girls' discovery of the ancient, underground Native home simultaneously affirms the prior claim of the Native peoples of British Columbia and the potential for escaping and radically revising the structure of the mainstream, patriarchal family (Botting 1996, 2–3). This potential is made explicit when Nora explains to Beth that the winter home is passed down through the maternal line and thus now belongs to her. Beth replies: "My dad wouldn't give nothing to me... The farm goes to Dan when he's done with it, even though Dan wants nothing to do with it" (Anderson-Dargatz 1997, 112).

In *The Cure for Death by Lightning,* as in *The Double Hook,* however, rejecting paternal, civilized authority ultimately proves too threatening. In fact, Davidson argues that the decision to uphold supposedly civilized principles and propriety is characteristic of Canadian gothic fiction:

> Huck can recognize where his real interests lie, abjure the dubious benefits of civilization, and light out for the territories. But his Canadian counterpart acts in quite a different fashion. Already inhabiting the territories, Niels Lindstedt, in Frederick Philip Grove's *Settlers of the Marsh* (1925), will still retain, and abide by, all the principles he picked up at his mother's knee. (1981, 245)

Similarly, although Beth ultimately confronts her father and demands that he keep his hands off her, the novel's conclusion reinforces what Kahane calls "the real Gothic horror" in which the heroine "is compelled to resume a quiescent, socially acceptable role" (1985, 342). Rather than continue to grapple with the pathology of a patriarchal, Christian social system, *The Cure for Death by Lightning* re-installs the familiar, conservative, and masochistic gothic conclusion in which "the master of the house is discovered as the evil source of her [the protagonist's] tribulations and is vanquished by the poor-but-honest (and inevitably later revealed as noble) young man, who marries the woman" (Massé 1992, 10). Ironically, in a novel whose title foregrounds the need to effect a "cure," Anderson-Dargatz's heroine, like so many gothic heroines before her, is supposedly "cured by the *medicina libidinis* offered in the conservative and comic resolution" (11). Generally speaking, in the Canadian Gothic, the cure is figured as the death of female and indigenous agency and subjectivity.

Not only does the narrative submit to the imperatives of heterosexual sexuality — "the reality principle before which the problematic pleasures of the female body yield" — it also pathologizes Nora and other powerful Native women (11). As noted earlier, Nora possesses differently coloured eyes. But Beth notices that several other women in Bertha Moses's household are similarly marked. When readers first encounter Bertha, Beth remarks that she "had no husband and no son. Her house was a house of women" (Anderson-Dargatz 1997, 9). She goes on to observe that one of "the daughters' daughters was pregnant, another had webbed fingers" (9). In effect, the syntax of Beth's casual observation align independent women, the female body, and reproduction with freakishness. Later, Beth remarks that Nora's mother has "a man's voice" (116) and "an extra finger on her right hand" (116). In her study of the female Gothic, Ellen Moers confirms that the modern female Gothic is populated by "freaks" — "creatures poised on a sharp, thin line between opposites: of sex, of race, of age" (1976, 108). Nora — a child/adult, white/Native, with her girl's body concealed in a man's clothes, and her attraction to Beth — sits on this knife's edge. Whereas Moers argues that the appearance of freaks indicates the presence of a "haunted and self-hating self," the situation is more complicated in Anderson-Dargatz's Canadian Gothic where the threat posed by independent, phallic women is projected specifically onto *Native* women (109). In this case, the haunting and hating spring from a double source: mainstream culture's misogyny and its racism and suppression of Native rights.

In fact, both misogyny and racism are foregrounded when Beth asks Nora about these bodily signs of difference that run in her family: "A lot of your aunts and cousins have webbed fingers and things...Like your mum and her extra finger. That's weird, all that stuff happening in one family" (Anderson-Dargatz 1997, 189). Yet, as Nora tells her, "Granny says they're Coyote's daughters. If Coyote's inside some man when he's with a woman, you know, then the child that woman has by him is like that. Webbed fingers, or extra fingers, or weird birthmarks, or each eye a different color" (189). Nora goes on to explain that, according to her mother, her father "was some white man...who caught her in the bush. She told my uncles and they went and beat the white man up. Then the Mounties came and put my uncles in jail" (189–90). Rather than maintain the familiar, disquieting, and supposedly essentialist gothic link between the female body and freakishness, Nora's response, which describes the rape of a Native woman by a white man and the Mounties' perverse response, suggests, instead, that the weird "stuff happening" in Bertha's family is the bodily trace left on the Shuswap by the rapacious, unjust settler-invaders (189). As argued earlier, in both Watson's and Anderson-Dargatz's novels, Coyote figures as the trace of the repressed aspects of colonialism—its violence and its impact. This notion is emphasized when Bertha Moses tells Beth: "Did you know your ancestors, you white people, came from Coyote? You are his children. That's why you act like that. Always greedy. Got to have everything for yourselves" (170). In forging a direct link between white people and Coyote, Bertha simultaneously restores primacy to Coyote and invites Beth, a child of the settler-invaders, to consider negative effects of colonialism that are glaringly evident in both the non-Native and Native communities.

Despite the narrative's selective attempts to reveal the repressed violence and traumatic impact of the settler-invaders on the Native peoples of British Columbia—a revelation that challenges the supposedly essentialist link between freakishness and the racialized female body[22]—*The Cure for Death by Lightning* ultimately reinforces this link and, in so doing, performs the traditional spectralizing and "'whiting out' of lesbian [and Native] possibility" (Castle 1993, 28). In this case, the term "whiting out" is especially apt because Nora, the figure subjected to abjection, is a Native woman who is displaced by a lighter-skinned man. Beth eventually spurns her lesbian lover from the reserve, paving the way for the heteronormative pairing of the protagonist and Billy, the Native youth who assists Beth in vanquishing the demonic spirit of Coyote on Christmas Eve. In light of the tension between Native and non-Native spiritual traditions in the novel, this date is particularly significant.[23] At bottom, the narrative's logic of abjection calls for both the sacrifice of Coyote Jack and of Nora. As Beth explains, on Christmas night "Coyote Jack hung himself" (Anderson-Dargatz 1997, 275).[24] And, after repeatedly pleading with Beth to leave with her in late winter, Nora gathers her belongings into a bundle and disappears down Blood Road. In this Canadian, postcolonial gothic fantasy, the troubling indigenous spirits willingly commit suicide or vanish into thin air.[25] As Malea Powell observes, "the Indian (whatever that may be) must disappear so that 'America' can live" (2002, 402). This narrative trope, in turn, recalls the actual work performed by the Christian missionaries: "Indian reformers throughout the nineteenth century most certainly believed that the salvation of the tribes meant the sacrifice of the 'savage' to Christianity and civilization" (403).

Nevertheless, both the sacrificers and the sacrificed in Anderson-Dargatz's *The Cure for Death by Lightning,* as in Watson's *The Double Hook,* leave a disturbing trace. In *The Cure for Death by Lightning,* the trace is palpable. As noted, the rape of Native women by the settler-invaders leaves a physical mark on the bodies of their victims. In addition, those who have been injured are compelled to repeat the injury.[26] Nora repeatedly cuts her arm: "Spots of blood dropped from her arm to the snow, creating a trail behind her" (Anderson-Dargatz 1997, 283). At one point, she cuts herself while Beth watches in horror:

> "Pretty, isn't it?" she said.
> "Stop that!" I cried. "There's nothing pretty about it."
> "It's so red." She sucked the blood from the cut on her arm. "So salty. You'd think you were drinking the ocean."
> "Stop," I said. "You're making me sick."
> Nora looked up at me. She'd been crying. Her lips were smeared with the blood from her arm. She licked them clean. (270)

References to blood throughout the novel underscore the theme of female and Native abjection and the violence that must be erased or "licked clean." In the passage cited, however, blood overtly marks Nora simultaneously as masochistically female and Native (a Blood or Red Indian). Moreover, her gesture of sucking the blood from her arm is also linked to vampirism, rendering Nora racially, sexually, and monstrously Other.[27]

In contrast to characters such as Nora and Coyote Jack, scapegoats who serve as figures of abjection, Nora's cousin Billy, who settles on the farm and protects Beth from her father and from Coyote, embodies the conservative message conveyed both by the Gothic and by the nation-state. In essence, as the youthful saviour who ultimately vanquishes and replaces the evil father and tends to both Beth and the farm (the father's property), Billy replicates the Gothic's consoling image of heteronormativity and redeemed masculinity. However, he also serves as propaganda for the nation-state's equally conservative program of Native assimilation. Readers are alerted to the latter when Beth remarks that unlike Nora and Billy's cousin Dennis, who is "Indian all over," Billy is different: he "cleaned his nails and shaved daily. He wasn't as Indian as Dennis was. He had fairer skin" (21). Whereas Nora starts off as a girl of flesh and blood and ends up as a phantom, Billy begins as a monstrous figure of abjection, aligned with Coyote, and ends up as a real (white) man. Early on, readers learn that Billy's nickname is Filthy Billy because "he does not own his voice" and shouts and mutters obscenities (22). As Billy tells Beth, "that thing you (shit) got following you—that follows me. (Fuck) You don't have to name it Coyote. (Shit) You call it demon or ghost, but it's the same thing. Coyote (shit) won't kill me. I'm his house" (257). By the end of the novel, however, boundaries between self and other are reinforced, and Coyote is evicted. "Listen," says Billy, "I'm not swearing! He's gone!" (277).

As noted earlier, the Old World castle and, later, the old house are primary topoi of gothic fiction—as the title of Edgar Allan Poe's gothic story "The Fall of the House of Usher" ([1839]2003) suggests. Moreover, as Davidson argues, in the Canadian Gothic, "the Old World castle and the empty New World land are analogous. Both require inhabitants" (1981, 243). I would argue, however, that in the Canadian Gothic both the Old World castle and the New World land are also sites of ongoing struggles over possession. Thus, owing to both the primacy of the generic trope and the specific historical tensions concerning land claims in Canada, Watson's and Anderson-Dargatz's novels are preoccupied with houses (in terms of the physical structure, namely the property, and in terms of lineages, namely race). In *The Cure for Death by Lightning,* Beth's father brutally governs his house until he is taken away to the local asylum. By contrast, Bertha Moses oversees a matriarchal, nurturing home on the reserve. Beth and Nora finally rebuild Bertha's "winter house" deep in the earth, a structure that, like the concluding image of Coyote's cleft in the rock in *The Double Hook,* recalls both the womb and the tomb, thereby underscoring the fears and desires instigated by Native and matriarchal forces (Watson 1959, 134). In light of the primacy of the gothic trope of the house, the fact that Billy ceases to serve as Coyote's house in *The Cure for Death by Lightning,* much like the burning of the old lady's house in *The Double Hook,* signals the supposed triumph of the Christian, nuclear family over the tribal and nomadic spirit of Coyote. Although, to an extent, *The Cure for Death by Lightning* resists mainstream culture by portraying a mixed race, lesbian relationship, ultimately, Anderson-Dargatz's novel, like Watson's, remains complicit with the masculinist imaginary that informs the patriarchal, Christian nation-state by attempting to exorcise the perceived essential, uncanny otherness of lesbian desire and Native resistance.

In *The Double Hook*, the birth of James's son, like Christ's birth, supposedly effects the redemption of the isolated community. Similarly, in *The Cure for Death by Lightning*, allusions to Christ's sacrifice and resurrection abound. As Bertha Moses states, Billy's father sacrifices himself to save humanity (Anderson-Dargatz 1997, 172–73). In addition, Beth insists that after Coyote leaves, Billy is reborn: "It was as if he'd been remade, as if that old Billy had been sloughed off and he'd grown a new skin. ... Nobody, not even Dennis, called him Filthy anymore" (285). Despite the supposed triumph of the Christian, patriarchal family — a triumph predicated on the Christ-like sacrifice of the Native — *The Cure for Death by Lightning* ends, like *The Double Hook*, with the spectre of Native resistance. Beth stands in the middle of Blood Road watching Nora "leave all over again. She was walking way from me, down the stretch of road. A trail of blood chased her ... Then she was gone and Billy was standing behind me, holding my shoulders" (292). By concluding with Beth (a white girl) "in the middle of Blood Road," watching Nora (a mixed-race girl) move away or, more accurately, be chased by a trail of blood, the text juxtaposes stasis with movement, the settled with the unsettled. On one level, like *The Double Hook*, *The Cure for Death by Lightning* seemingly ends with an affirmation of civilized community. Beth reaches over and clasps Billy's hand. At the same time, Beth's father takes his wife's hand "in his fist and ... [holds] on to it for dear life" (292). Yet just as Coyote has the last word in *The Double Hook*, the repetition of the static, heterosexual, farming couples and their desperate clutching of hands signals in *The Cure for Death by Lightning* a panicked and futile attempt to ward off the spectral threat with its familiar trail of blood — evidence of both a crime and a wound that cannot be erased.

Notes

1   I refer to the old lady as part Native because the first and second drafts of the novel provide background information about the characters' race. As Margaret Morriss explains, "Old Man Potter was an Englishman ... Kip and Angel are 'pure-blooded'

Indians," and, while "no one knows where the Old Lady came from," she must be at least part-Native because her children "William and James (and presumably Greta) are 'a mixed lot'" (2002, 61).

2 The novel features a scene of horrific transformation: "Suddenly he got up. He twisted, batted the air, and screamed, and the scream became a howl. His body flitted back and forth between man and coyote, then the coyote dropped on all fours and cowered away from me ... A movement made me look up, and there was Jack standing at the edge of the path, covering his puckered genitals with one hand" (Anderson-Dargatz 1997, 272).

3 In using the word "haunting," I am referring to the *Oxford English Dictionary* definition: "Of imaginary or spiritual beings, ghosts, etc: To visit frequently and habitually with manifestations of their influence and presence, usually of a molesting kind. *to be haunted*: to be subject to the visits and molestation of disembodied spirits."

4 For more information about the Canadian Gothic, see Margot Northey (1976), Arnold Davidson (1981), Gerry Turcotte (1998), Justin D. Edwards (2005), and Marlene Goldman and Joanne Saul (2006).

5 The recent decision by the Supreme Court of Canada in *Delgamuukw v. British Columbia*, [1997] 3 S.C.R. 1010, confirmed that Aboriginal title had not been extinguished in any land that was not covered by treaty—virtually the entire province. For information about the *Delgamuukw* decision, see Stan Persky, *Delgamuukw: The Supreme Court of Canada Decision on Aboriginal Title* (1998). Although it does not deal directly with the current Shuswap Nation's land claims, the *Delgamuukw* decision nevertheless sets a precedent.

6 The area that Watson writes about is now represented by the Cariboo Tribal Council, which comprises four member communities located around the Williams Lake area: Williams Lake Band (T'exelc), Canoe Creek Band (Xgat'tem/ Stwecem'c), Canim Lake Band (Tsq'escen), and the Soda Cree Band (Xats'ull/Cmetem') (for more information, see <http://www.cariboolinks.com>).

In a personal e-mail, Anderson-Dargatz explains that she grew up "in Glen Eden near Salmon Arm, on the Shuswap Lake" and that the novel is based in "China Valley nearby" where her parents grew up. She goes on to explain that she "grew up right next to the reserve near town." This area falls within the traditional territory of the Ktunaxa Nation and is represented by the Ktunaxa/Kinabaset Treaty Council (see <http://www.bctreaty.net/nations>).

7 Coyote is known for introducing salmon, for creating the fishing places, and for making the world safe for the Shuswap Nation (see Jack, Matthew, and Matthew 1993, 11–12).

8 I use the term "para-colonial" to highlight the fact that, as Malea Powell observes, "the occupying force has not been, nor will it ever be, withdrawn" (2002, 399). Gerald Vizenor's term "para-colonial" thus appropriately denotes "a colonialism beyond colonialism, multiple, contradictory and with all the attendant complications of internal, neo- and post-colonialism" (quoted in Powell 2002, 399).

9 In earlier drafts, the sexually transgressive incest theme was much more explicit. Morriss speculates that it was toned down because it was "too sensational" (2002, 69).

10 John Grube observes that Mrs Potter is "always associated with the chilling sound of the coyote" (quoted in Jones 1985, 43). Moreover, John Lennox argues that Mrs. Potter "expresses the spirit of Coyote, for it is more her presence than her person which is perceived and felt in the community" (1985, 49). Morriss also observes

that in earlier drafts Greta, like her mother, was a palpable presence even after her death: "Ara fears that 'she would see Greta fleshed and sinewed, standing in the ruin she had made'" and later that "Ara also sees Greta's death as somehow facilitating the birth of Lenchen's baby: 'If it's not too late, she said to the boy, Greta's death will turn down the covers for Lenchen and she will bear her child in the hollow Greta made.' During her labour Lenchen cries out: 'It's Greta's baby I tell you. Ask her. She'll tell you,' though immediately after she revokes her odd statement: 'It's a lie, the girl cried. A lie. It's my own. My very own'" (2002, 68).

11 Note, both Angela Bowering and Margaret Atwood are referring to the supposed shift from matriarchal earth goddesses to patriarchal sky gods. Discussions of this shift and the concomitant devaluation of women were prevalent in feminist discussions in anthropology and religious studies during the 1970s and 1980s.

12 Due to the numerous biblical references in the text and its reliance on biblical cadences, critics frequently read the novel as "a Christian parable of life lost in life but all resolved in salvation after death" (Davidson 1988, 34). Margot Northey asserts that "the message of *The Double Hook* is religious. It is a story about redemption written from a Christian vantage point" (1976, 55). In keeping with Watson's intended association between Coyote and God, he is often understood as God or at least to have "his prototype in the Jehovah-figure of the Old Testament" (Mitchell 1985, 111). For an overview of critics who have aligned Coyote with the Judeo-Christian God, see Arnold Davidson (1988, 34).

13 George Woodcock hailed *The Double Hook* as "one of the most important books [since the fifties] for itself and in terms of [its] influence" (1977, 93–94). His summary of the plot likewise emphasizes the gothic nature of the novel: "In which the rural tale of a decaying society is mingled with the native mythology of the *vanished Indians* to create a strange and superb fantasy of moral strife and spiritual terror" (94 [emphasis added]). Woodcock's description not only confirms the work's status as a gothic text, but it also contributes to the gothic effort to express the disturbing element, in effect, to "clean house," by describing the Native peoples as "vanished."

14 Watson changed the ending owing to reservations expressed by a highly influential reader and editor of the manuscript, Frederick M. Salter, who, at the time, was chairman of the Department of English at the University of Alberta. As Watson's biographer explains, "Salter's main concern was with the ending. It did not satisfy him because it seemed too calculatingly right" (Flahiff 2005, 82). As Salter explains,

> I suppose it could be justified as a happy ending, the baby being a promise of the future. Some readers would take it so. And, after all, you have got rid of some poisonous intrusions into your little Eden, and no dread consequences are to be expected from the death[s] of Greta and the old lady. Even Kip has forgiven James, and seems content with things as they are. (quoted in Flahiff 2005, 82)

Salter's comment that Watson has created a "little Eden" is significant in light of the colonial, apocalyptic fantasy of creating a New Jerusalem. Moreover, his account of the expulsion of "some poisonous intrusions," namely the part-Native Greta and her mother, confirm that, in this apocalyptic fantasy, Native North Americans who resist colonial ideology are aligned with satanic forces. With respect to the proposed revision, Salter went on to comment: "I feel the need of a hint or suggestion

of some kind that you have been dealing with things eternal and not transitory."
And as Flahiff observes, "Sheila herself was to achieve something of the effect he
desired by reordering the last lines of this draft" (83).

15 At present, the Dog Creek people are part of the Canoe Creek band, which, in turn,
has united with other bands to form the Cariboo Tribal Council. The council is
currently working with the BC Treaty Commission to resolve outstanding land
claims. At present, negotiations between the government and the Cariboo Tribal
Council are at the fourth stage—that is to say, they have reached an agreement-in-
principle (<http://www.BCTreaty.net>).

16 As Watson herself admitted, "I went to teach in the Cariboo where I sank roots
which I've never really been able to disentangle" (quoted in Flahiff 2005, 39). She
was particularly disgusted by the government's treatment of the Shuswap tribe.
Commenting on the residential school attended by the Native children from Dog
Creek, Watson stated: "The Indian mission school at Williams Lake seemed like a
penal colony out of which children were released, finally into a starving and deci-
mated community in which language and culture—religious and social—had been
destroyed—but not obliterated—not completely" (39). In 1924, Watson wrote to
Emily Carr and asked her what contacts she had made among the Shuswap. Watson
concluded her letter by saying: "Too little is known and too much is being lost of
the spirit which is native to British Columbia." Watson remained haunted by
Canada's treatment of the Shuswap, and, in turn, she left her readers to negotiate
the legacy of this haunting. Perhaps owing to her profound encounter with the
Natives in Dog Creek, her husband, Wilfred, referred to her in his letters throughout her life as "swp," a shortened form for Shuswap (166).

17 The term "overwhelmed" is especially apt given the fact that the missionaries classi-
fied Shuswap Native practices and the language as pagan anachronisms and did
their best to eradicate both (Balf 1978, 8).

18 Kate Ferguson Ellis suggests that contemporary gothic might be titled "men on the
rampage" (2000, 263). In her essay "The Gothic Heroine and Her Critics," she highlights important connections between gender, capitalism, and production, noting
that "an unintended consequence of equality feminism has been that women,
released from their essentialising ties to reproduction, are now theoretically 'free' to
leave the home for the ruthless 'world' of production, with its myths of ever-
increasing economic power—are free, that is to say, to go on the rampage" (265).
This may be one reason that Beth, in contrast to Nora, decides to stay on the farm
rather than flee to Vancouver and work in the factories.

19 In using the word "property" within a patriarchal context, he is referring both to
his farm and his daughter.

20 For an analysis of the cyclical gothic violence against women and children, see "The
History of Abuse" in David Punter and Glennis Byron (2004, 288–92) and Michelle
Massé (1992). Beth's mother presumably fails in her role as mother and protector
of her child because, as the narrator observes, the mother was most likely abused by
her father as a young girl (Anderson-Dargatz 1997, 207).

21 The pit was dug sixty to ninety centimetres below ground level. Then a cone-
shaped framework of poles was erected over the site and covered with grass, cedar
bark and earth (Wolf 1996, 8).

22 According to Sigmund Freud, the female body is profoundly uncanny because it is the former home of mankind: "It often happens that neurotic men declare that they feel there is something uncanny about the female genital organs. This *unheimlich* place, however, is the entrance to the former *Heim* [home] of all human beings, to the place where each one of us lived once upon a time and in the beginning" ([1919] 1955, 221).

23 Christian references abound within the novel. Toward the conclusion, Billy and Beth frolic chastely in the snow making "angels," while Nora, excluded from the game, "disappeared down one of the bush trails" (Anderson-Dargatz 1997, 251).

24 Coyote Jack's body constitutes the ultimate, horrific image of abjection. Even in the dead of winter, his corpse is found writhing with maggots. His father, the Swede, explains: "He must've been there for a week or more. But rotting, can you believe it? Frozen solid and rotting. Full of maggots this time of year. I never seen the likes. I can't believe it. I can't believe it" (Anderson-Dargatz 1997, 278). For a detailed discussion of abjection, see Julia Kristeva (1982).

25 According to Bertha, her son, Billy's father, "took care of Coyote. He was Coyote's house, see?... Once, when Coyote was resting inside him, my son took his own life—so Coyote would have to return to the spirit world with him—so we could walk in peace for a while... My son gave us that as a gift" (Anderson-Dargatz 1997, 172–73). Later, Beth follows a trail of blood in the snow that disappears in a clearing. As Billy tells her, "you (shit) saw blood all right... That was (shit) my father's blood, the trail Johansson (shit) followed when he found him dead. This here spot... This is where my father (fuck) fought Coyote and took him back to the spirit world. (Shit) This is where my father died to (shit) save us" (257). Owing to their sacrifice to preserve humanity, both Billy's father and his son, who for a time serves as Coyote's house but is later reborn, are identified with Christ.

26 For a detailed discussion of the repetition-compulsion phenomenon associated with trauma, see Michelle Massé (1992, 14).

27 As Gina Wisker observes, in "conventional fictions, women vampires connote unlicensed sexuality and excess, and as such, in conventional times, their invocation of both desire and terror leads to a stake in the heart—death as exorcism of all they represent" (2000, 167). Historically, female vampires have represented the threat of the "independent feminist" (171). And, as critics remark, there is often a link posited between the lesbian and the vampire. According to Bonnie Zimmerman, "the lesbian, by selecting same-sex lovers, embarks on a 'journey back to the mother,' equating her with the lesbian vampire who causes a flow of blood equivalent to that in birth" (quoted in Wisker 2000, 176).

Works Cited

Anderson-Dargatz, Gail. 1997. *The Cure for Death by Lightning*. Toronto: Random House.

Atwood, Margaret. 1985. "Excerpt from *Survival*." In *Sheila Watson and* The Double Hook. Ed. George Bowering. Ottawa: Golden Dog. 41–42.

Balf, Mary. 1978. *The Dispossessed: Interior Indians in the 1800s.* Kamloops, BC: Kamloops Museum.

Botting, Fred. 1996. *Gothic.* New York: Routledge.

Bowering, Angela. 1988. *Figures Cut in Sacred Ground: Illuminati in* The Double Hook. Edmonton: NeWest.

Castle, Terry. 1993. *The Apparitional Lesbian.* New York: Columbia UP.

Davidson, Arnold. 1981. "Canadian Gothic and Anne Hébert's *Kamouraska.*" *Modern Fiction Studies* 27(2): 243–54.

———. 1988. "The Double Hook's Double Hooks." *Canadian Literature* 116 (Spring): 29–41.

Edwards, Justin D. 2005. *Gothic Canada: Reading the Spectre of a National Literature.* Edmonton: University of Alberta Press.

Ferguson Ellis, Kate. 2000. "Can You Forgive Her? The Gothic Heroine and Her Critics." In *A Companion to the Gothic.* Ed. David Punter. London: Blackwell. 257–68.

Flahiff, F.T. 2005. *Always Someone to Kill The Doves: A Life of Sheila Watson.* Vancouver: NeWest.

Freud, Sigmund. 1919, reprinted 1955. "The 'Uncanny.'" In *The Standard Edition of the Complete Psychological Works of Sigmund Freud.* Ed. and Trans. James Strachey, 24 volumes. London: Hogarth. 18: 7–61.

Gelder, Ken, and Jane M. Jacobs. 1999. "The Postcolonial Ghost Story." In *Ghosts: Deconstruction, Psychoanalysis, History.* Ed. Peter Buse and Andrew Stott. New York: Macmillan. 179–99.

Goldman, Marlene, and Joanne Saul. 2006. "Talking With Ghosts: Haunting in Canadian Cultural Production." *University of Toronto Quarterly* 75(2): 645–55.

Jack, Rita, Marie Matthew, and Robert Matthew. 1993. *Shuswap Community Handbook.* Kamloops, BC: Secwepemc Cultural Education Society.

Jackson, Rosemary. 1981. *Fantasy: The Literature of Subversion.* London and New York: Methuen.

Jones, D.G. 1985. "Excerpt from *Butterfly on a Rock.*" In *Sheila Watson and* The Double Hook. Ed. George Bowering. Ottawa: Golden Dog. 43–45.

Kahane, Claire. 1985. "The Gothic Mirror." In *The (M)other Tongue: Essays in Feminist Psychoanalytic Interpretation.* Ed. Shirley Nelson Garner, Claire Kahane, and Madelon Sprengnether. Ithaca: Cornell UP. 334–51.

Kristeva, Julia. 1982. *Powers of Horror: An Essay on Abjection.* Trans. Leon S. Roudiez. New York: Columbia UP.

Lennox, John. 1985. "The Past: Themes and Symbols of Confrontation in *The Double Hook* and *Le Torrent.*" In *Sheila Watson and* The Double Hook. Ed. George Bowering. Ottawa: Golden Dog. 47–54.

Massé, Michelle. 1992. *In the Name of Love: Women, Masochism, and the Gothic.* Ithaca, NY: Cornell UP.

Mitchell, Beverly. 1985. "Association and Allusion in *The Double Hook.*" In *Sheila Watson and* The Double Hook. Ed. George Bowering. Ottawa: Golden Dog. 99–113.

Moers, Ellen. 1976. *Literary Women.* Garden City, NY: Doubleday.

Morriss, Margaret. 2002. "'No Short Cuts': The Evolution of *The Double Hook.*" *Canadian Literature* 173: 54–70.

Neuman, Shirley. 1988. "Introduction." In *Figures Cut in Sacred Ground: Illuminati in* The Double Hook. Ed. Angela Bowering. Edmonton: NeWest. 1–4.

Northey, Margot. 1976. *The Haunted Wilderness: The Gothic and Grotesque in Canadian Fiction.* Toronto: University of Toronto Press.

———. 1985. "Symbolic Grotesque: *The Double Hook.*" *Sheila Watson and* The Double Hook. Ed. George Bowering. Ottawa: Golden Dog. 55–61.

Paravisini-Gebert, Lizabeth. 2002. "Colonial and Postcolonial Gothic: The Caribbean." *The Cambridge Companion to Gothic Fiction.* Ed. Jerrold E. Hogle. Cambridge: Cambridge UP. 229–57.

Persky, Stan. 1998. *Delgamuukw: The Supreme Court of Canada Decision on Aboriginal Title.* Vancouver, BC: Greystone.

Poe, Edgar Allan. 1839, reprinted 2003. "The Fall of the House of Usher." In *The Fall of the House of Usher and Other Writings: Poems, Tales, Essays, and Reviews.* London: Penguin.

Powell, Malea. 2002. "Rhetorics of Survivance: How American Indians Use Writing." *College Composition and Communication* 53(3): 396–433.

Punter, David, ed. 2000. *A Companion to the Gothic.* London: Blackwell.

———, and Glennis Byron. 2004. *The Gothic.* Oxford: Blackwell.

Radcliffe, Ann. 1794, reprinted 1990. *The Mysteries of Udolpho.* Oxford: Oxford UP.

Turcotte, Gerry. 1998. "English-Canadian Gothic." In *The Handbook to Gothic Literature.* Ed. Marie Mulvey-Roberts. London: Macmillan. 49–53.

Watson, Sheila. 1959. *The Double Hook.* Toronto: McClelland and Stewart.

Wisker, Gina. 2000. "Love Bites: Contemporary Women's Vampire Fictions." *A Companion to the Gothic.* Ed. David Punter. London: Blackwell. 167–79.

Woodcock, George. 1977. "Possessing the Land: Notes on Canadian Fiction." In *The Canadian Imagination.* Ed. David Staines. Cambridge, MA: Harvard UP. 93–94.

Wolf, Annabel Crop Eared. 1996. *Shuswap History: A Century of Change.* Kamloops, BC: Secwepemc Cultural Education Society.

CHAPTER FOUR

"Horror Written on Their Skin": Joy Kogawa's Gothic Uncanny

Gerry Turcotte

Freud noted that the archaic, narcissistic self, not yet demarcated by the outside world, projects out of itself what it experiences as dangerous or unpleasant in itself, making of it an alien double, uncanny and demoniacal.

— Julia Kristeva, *Strangers to Ourselves*

I live at the west entrance of a haunted house called Canada.

— Rita Wong, "Troubling Domestic Limits"

Introduction: Uncanny Possibilities

This essay takes as its starting point Joy Kogawa's novel *Obasan* ([1981] 1985), which revolves around what Scott McFarlane has called "arguably the most documented instance of ethnic civil rights abuse in Canadian history," namely the internment of the Japanese Canadians during and after the Second World War and their subsequent dispossession and exile (1995b, 401). It also takes as one point of intersection the *Japanese Canadian Redress Agreement*—the decision of the Brian Mulroney government on 22 September 1988 to offer an apology and restitution to the Japanese Canadians for their suffering and unjust treatment.[1] More specifically, this reading is located in the way Sigmund Freud's analysis of "The 'Uncanny'" ([1919] 1956)—and a Gothic modality more widely— can be brought to bear on an understanding of these events.

To begin this analysis, it may be useful to exploit the possibilities of an uncanny register by way of tapping its specific role in narratives of displacement, rupture, and unsettlement. The uncanny, as many critics have now shown, is a central feature of gothic narratives in postcolonial contexts, especially in the way they come to reflect a particular terror of (un)settlement.[2] Ken Gelder and Jane M. Jacobs have mapped this argument usefully in the Australian context in order to show how Freud's well-known essay can be used to read postcolonial Australia's responses to contemporary political developments that have contributed to making that country "unfamiliar to itself" (1995; 1998).

In particular, Gelder and Jacobs focus on *Mabo and Others v. Queensland (No. 2)*, popularly known as the *Mabo* decision, in which the High Court of Australia negated the offensive, and long-held, myth of British colonization that Australia was *terra nullius* — a land owned by no one and therefore legally available for colonization without the need for treaties.[3] Gelder and Jacob argue that the media- and government-generated myth-information that Aborigines would potentially re-claim most of Australia — a perception encouraged by the then Australian prime minister John Howard when he held up a map of Australia covered in red marks representing potential Aboriginal claims on the country — had the effect of making Australia at once familiar and unfamiliar to non-Aboriginal Australians: "Mabo (re)produced a great deal of anxiety; and for those non-Aborigines who even momentarily entertained the possibility, after Mabo, of losing their homes to Aboriginal claims to land, Freud's 'uncanny' might offer an immediate truth" (1995, 150).

Freud's theory of the uncanny provides a useful account of terror-making experiences, suggesting that one of the principal ways in which a feeling of uncanniness is produced is when the familiar is suddenly made unfamiliar. Freud's insight lies in identifying how one becomes the Other — his brief etymological study demonstrates how the *heimlich* becomes *unheimlich,* that is, how the homely becomes unhomely — and in showing how the terms effectively co-exist at the same time. As Gelder and Jacobs insist, "[t]his simultaneity is important to stress since, in Freud's terms, it is not simply the unfamiliar in itself which generates the anxiety of the uncanny; it is specifically the combination of the familiar and the unfamiliar — the way the one seems always to *inhabit* the other" (1995, 150–51).

As has been argued elsewhere, the uncanny is resonant in numerous postcolonial narratives precisely because it enables an emblematic articulation of fears that are, in other circumstances, unmentionable: fears about settlement, dispossession, miscegenation, and contamination. In these narratives, the uncanny is frequently produced as, and by, a crisis of (il)legitimacy—engendering stories that agonize over the right of belonging to an invaded place, or stories that attempt to justify invasion by turning the Native peoples into something monstrous to legitimate genocidal activities. In the nineteenth century, these stories are frequently about bloodlines—unlawful or unjust transportation that severs family ties—or they are settlement narratives in which the newcomer, no matter how the migration is "justified" by the authors in political, moral, or Christian rhetoric, is threatened or surrounded by a resident evil upon arrival in the New World space. Twentieth-century narratives maintain many of these tropes, though frequently the right of place is less overtly questioned, and, instead, identity politics are examined through narratives that explore (or exploit) troubling notions about gender and race.

Monstrous figures stand at the heart of all of these gothic tales, haunting, yet also reflecting, a spectral condition. They generally seem, therefore, at once alien and yet strangely familiar. In some versions, such as *Frankenstein*'s monster, the creature is born of the detritus of humanity and is the child of the individual/culture that rejects him/her—as different, and yet a part of, the very fabric of that which it haunts (Shelley [1831] 1969). In other accounts—for example *Dracula*—the "Other" is framed as a contaminant that will infect the dominant group, so that "us" always finds itself in danger of becoming "them" (Stoker 1897). As Van Helsing puts it in *Dracula*, the vilest threat posed by the vampire "is that we become as him" (Stoker [1897] 1997, 209). And these monstrous analogies are anxiously appended to contemporary fears. Certainly, Canadian and Australian narratives about "Asian" migration are frequently framed through metaphors of invasion. In nineteenth-century rhetoric, the "yellow peril" represents a type of migrating Dracula figure that will overwhelm "us" and that will take over "our" land, "our" women, and "our" selves.

For Gelder and Jacobs, the debates over the *Mabo* case "unsettled" many Australians because they exposed in the law what had hitherto only been understood in an unspoken way that "what is 'ours' is also potentially, or even always already, 'theirs': the one may also be the other" (1995, 151). As they go on to argue,

> because many Aboriginal land claims are either in the process of being dealt with or are yet to be made, a certain kind of un-settlement arises which is

given expression by non-Aborigines and Aborigines alike—at the very moment when modern Australia happens to be talking about "reconciliation." ... In an uncanny Australia, one place is always already another place because the issue of possession is never complete, never entirely settled.... We can think about this process as a way in which "place," as a designation which implies bound-edness, is always at the same time in a condition of unboundedness. (151)

Re-animating History

Joy Kogawa's *Obasan* can be understood in similar terms, both in its own narrative account as well as in its reception. Certainly, Kogawa's book is not gothic in any "familiar" sense of the word, and, of course, it is not an Indigenous text commenting on land rights in the usual understanding of the term. However, it is a text that produces a sense of the uncanny within and without its narrative, by "re-animating" a history of oppression that forces Canadians to confront their own suppressed and unacknowledged violent history. In materialist terms, many Canadians would have had to admit that the very land they owned, the very objects they possessed, were literally stolen from Japanese Canadians. In this sense alone, then, the familiar space of ownership and belonging would have been, for many, made uncanny. Boundaries that were once solid were unbounded by this realization.[4]

As Gilles Deleuze and Félix Guattari have suggested in "What Is a Minor Literature?" in another very real sense, the text, speaking a minority view into a dominant master narrative, produces the effect of deterritorializa-tion ([1975] 1994). And as Roy Miki has argued, "[b]y 'deterritorializa-tion,' [Deleuze and Guattari] point to a disturbed use of language that foregrounds its surface as a conflicted space" (1995, 145). Miki goes on to argue that "[m]inority writers, because of their subordinate position, must work in a language that disrupts the stability of conventional dis-course and communication" (145). He suggests that "[m]inority subject matter, when encoded in forms adjusted to accommodate the expecta-tions of the social majority, can willy-nilly lead to compromise, distor-tion, and misrepresentation. Formal disruptions, such as the generic crossing of fiction, history, autobiography, and documentary in *Obasan*, become strategies of resistance to norms" (145). Rosemary Jackson makes a similar point about uncanny narratives when she notes that

[a] literature of the uncanny, by permitting an articulation of taboo subjects which are otherwise silenced, threatens to transgress social norms. Fantasies are not, however, countercultural merely through this thematic transgression. On the contrary, they frequently serve (as does Gothic fiction) to re-confirm institutional order by supplying a vicarious fulfilment of desire and neutralizing an urge towards transgression. A more subtle and subversive use of the fantastic appears with works which threaten to disrupt or eat away at the "syntax" or *structure* by which order is made. (1981, 72)

Obasan's language is not "opaque" or resistant in the sense defined by Deleuze and Guattari ([1975] 1994). Yet it does produce an effect of opacity in its staccatoed presentation and withholding of the details of its story, and, as Miki suggests, in its blurring of generic conventions (1995). According to Donald Goellnicht, Kogawa's "use of multiple discursive modes, tenses and narrative points-of-view ... disrupts and contests the dominant culture's totalizing, omniscient voice of history" (1989, 294). The effect of this "resistance" yields an uncanny narrative, in which "normal" values are reversed and standard images of normalcy are displaced or entirely emptied of meaning. In many, if not most, fantastic narratives, signification deteriorates and we witness the collapse of language. Fittingly enough, then, *Obasan* is a novel of silences, in which language proves unreliable in so many ways that it produces a general effect of deterritorialization, not only for the characters in the novel but also for the readers who see the language that they take for granted de/scribed in a variety of ways.[5]

Throughout the work, the protagonist struggles to find an identity, attempting to define herself in a language inadequate to the task. In the second chapter, for example, Naomi "spells" what she is for her young students: "'Not "Nah Canny,"' I tell him, printing my name on the blackboard. 'NAKANE. The a's are short as in "among"'" (Kogawa [1981]1985, 6). Later, when Naomi is having dinner with one of her students' fathers, she must answer the inevitable question, "Where do you come from?" In her reply, she explains that she was born in Canada, like the widower himself, and then, once again, "spells" what she is: "'NISEI' I spelled.... 'It means "second generation"'" (7).

Both acts of self-definition are fitting metaphors for postcolonial self-articulation, particularly as they utilize forms and conventions of an older world (pronunciation keys) to define a self not actually accepted in the new environment (her citizenship is questioned by the widower). If Naomi proves unsuccessful in defining herself, it is only because she has not found a language that mediates effectively between her two worlds or one that adequately expresses her situation in her world. Naomi goes so far as to pun on the nature of herself in grammatical terms: "Personality: Tense. Is that past or present tense? It's perpetual tense" (7). To demonstrate the inadequacy of language is to demonstrate the tragedy of the self in transition—in exile.

In *Obasan*, language is severely scrutinized, its indeterminacy foregrounded in many ways. Kogawa underlines language's fragile connection to history, offers examples of the tendentious nature of academic and journalistic language, and stresses the polysemous character of the Japanese and English-Canadian tongues. This thorough progression through all types of information—of both verbal and non-verbal communication—is meant to establish clearly how tenuous the links between actions, words, and meaning are. Kogawa's novel deliberately challenges the labels affixed (by both the government and by the non-Japanese Canadians) to Issei, Nisei, and Sansei, in order to "unname," and so "re-vision," their place in society. Thus, the reader is shown the falseness of the government's "language" and the obscene reality it attempts to misrepresent. Sick Bay, for example, "was not a beach at all. And the place they called the Pool was not a pool of water, but a prison at the exhibition grounds called Hastings Park" (77). If such things can be lied about, the text suggests, then how can equally pernicious accounts about enemy aliens and the need for exile be believed? Such reflections are profoundly deterritorializing.

Miki's comments concerning the generic combinations that occur in *Obasan* form part of that process of deterritorialization. In *Obasan*, the layers of meaning vie for a place on the page, from acute cultural silences—themselves redolent with meaning—to bureaucratic documents that blatantly state the opposite of what they mean. And yet it is also true, as Miki argues in a later essay, that *Obasan* is contained by the fields of knowledge that organize, discuss, interpret, and evaluate the novel (1998). In "Sliding the Scale of Elision," Miki discusses the institutionalizing mechanisms that establish Canadian literature as a field of knowledge, underlining the exclusionary nature of such projects, an "Anglo-European identity politics that imprints itself through a process of differing at the expense of 'its' racialized others" (1998, 130). Numerous critics, even while acknowledging this process, take umbrage behind the fear that too comprehensive an inquiry might dismantle not simply the institution of Canadian literature but also, in Robert Lecker's metaphor, the "peaceable kingdom" itself (1990).[6]

One way to shore up both the stability of the canon — and arguably the "kingdom" — is to gesture towards "challenging texts" without endangering the structure. Indeed, by incorporating such texts — consuming them in other words — it becomes possible to reinscribe "relations of internal dominance" (Miki 1998, 134). Miki's account of *Obasan*'s canonicity articulates this process of consumption. His metaphor signals the voraciousness of the critical, mainstream appetite that, shark-like perhaps, "circled [*Obasan*'s] textual body with interpretive strategies that penetrated its apparent foreignness" (135). Yet does this institutionalized acceptance indicate a change in the dominant structure? Miki's view is that it does not. Far from disarticulating the totalizing Anglo-European frameworks, such incorporation frequently leaves the structure intact. Indeed, the texts, thoroughly digested, can be used to maintain the flexibility and generosity of the policing boundaries without in fact extending them in any way.

In a powerful reading of *Obasan*, Miki demonstrates how the text is compromised because of its recourse to a series of narrative and aesthetic structures that ultimately recuperate the novel into the dominant system — in particular, Naomi's inner journey of self-discovery and the use of Nagasaki as a gesture of resolution. While I accept Miki's point that there is a danger in universalizing Naomi's experience — particularly through a potentially depoliticizing aestheticization of the text so that it speaks a narrative of personal development at the expense of wider issues — it is difficult to read Nagasaki as a similarly aestheticized moment that flattens the horror of Japanese Canadian internment. Rather, the two events are so conclusively interlocked that they must be read as equally horrific — as large-scale events that indict the Anglo-European community that is responsible for such atrocity. If universalizing occurs here, it is precisely — and hence productively — at the expense of the dominant culture.

For Miki, the universalizing of suffering and its interiorization through a range of narrative functions, including the use of Christian symbology to recodify Nagasaki, "performs the personal redemption of history achieved through narrative. As Japanese-Canadian internment is transformed through this lens, race comes under erasure to allow for a depoliticization process in which the power of the victimizer ... is internalized by the victim" (142). Miki goes on to argue that "[t]his misplacement of blame, on the one hand, elides the materiality of history, but on the other, valorizes the humanist allegory of suffering as a 'universal' condition" (142).

Yet, the text also always comments on precisely this process of inversion, in which the victim is made to accept the blame for her/his own suffering. Miki is certainly correct when he argues that the recuperative possibilities that exist in the structures that shape the text's reception, as well as in the available reading strategies that allow for this sleight of hand to take place, explain why the text has figured so centrally — so canonically — "in the institutional hall of CanLit" (142). Despite this fact, there is a danger in yielding the text entirely to this reading at the expense of its phenomenological impact. It is crucial to continue to insist on how the text can be mobilized to resist "methodologies of institutional readings that consistently fail to account for issues of appropriation and misrepresentation" (143); to refuse to allow "the majority white 'we' to inhabit the text" (143); and to resist a construction of the text that would locate the endemic racism it addresses as "past." One way of doing this is to read the text out of frame — or to read the frame itself. How has *Obasan* made the nation — and the traditional literary history of nation — monstrous, as Jonathan Kertzer has argued (1998)?[7]

Re-figuring History

If *Obasan* produces an uncanny effect upon the dominant culture in Canada, it does so in part by cleverly showing that this is precisely the impact that Canadian government policy has had on Japanese Canadians. For these people, the government's response to the outbreak of war — which was to seize property, to imprison people illegally, and to force the repatriation of Canadians back to a country that was not theirs — resulted in making the familiar terrifyingly unfamiliar. Kogawa's text is uncanny in the way that the ordinary gets stripped of its mundaneness. Her account makes frightening reading because it demonstrates the fragility of rights that should have been taken for granted — of belonging, of citizenship, of liberty, and justice. These rights were extinguished overnight and re-written in the name of undisguised racism. Identity was destabilized. The experience seems straight out of a gothic novel — except that it was true.

For a number of commentators, including Jean-Paul Sartre, the world of the fantastic — of the gothic nightmare — is possible only when "someone right-side up" is "transported miraculously into an upside-down world," which "sets off, by contrast, the strange character of the new world" (1968, 57). For Naomi—and, of course, for many Japanese Canadians—this dislocation actually occurred. The safe, "right-side up" nature of the home, which rests on the rightness of law and order, is violently inverted when that law, that home, collapses. As Homi Bhabha puts it,

[t]o be unhomed is not to be homeless, nor can the unhomely be easily accommodated in that familiar division of the social life into private and the public spheres. The unhomely moment creeps up on you as stealthily as your own shadow, and suddenly you find yourself…taking the measure of your dwelling in a state of "incredulous terror." (1997, 445)

It is this process of refiguring the homely that leads critics, such as Rita Wong, to speak of Canada as a "haunted house," one whose entrances are open to some and closed to others (2003–04, 109). Like the homes of the Japanese Canadians, Canada itself as a political and geographical space becomes uncanny to the Japanese-Canadian community, which once lived and moved through a familiar, "owned" landscape. After Pearl Harbour, these individuals were literally deterritorialized and thrust into a gothic landscape, while being forced to live in Canadian ghost towns such as Slocan and later moved into the "alien" landscape of Prairie towns, where Naomi, for one, loses her humanity and becomes a "scarecrow" (Kogawa [1981] 1985, 191).

The landscape of Lethbridge, Alberta, is described in *Obasan* in distinctly gothic terms:

We have come to the moon. We have come to the edge of the world.…Here, the air is a fist.…On the miles of barbed-wire fences, there are round skull-shaped weeds.…Between the shed and the farmer's house are some skeletons of farm machinery.…Every bit of plant growth here looks deliberate and fierce. (191–92)

Everything is unrecognizable to them, prompting Naomi to think, "[t]here are some nightmares from which there is no waking, only deeper and deeper sleep" (194). For all of the propaganda that constructed the Japanese Canadians as monstrous figures—an infection in part identified as the "yellow peril" and turned into a board game that is "made in Canada"[8]—it is the majority culture that is dis/figured as monstrous by

Naomi's narrative.[9] At one stage, Naomi points out that "the worse the news from the Eastern Front, the more ghoulish the public becomes" (88). And despite being forced to live invisibly in various ghost towns, the Japanese Canadians bring life, not death, to them. As Naomi says of Bayfarm in Slocan, "the ghost town is alive and kicking like Ezekiel's resurrected valley of bones" (160).

It would be possible to argue that the very spaces of internment, particularly those located in the British Columbia interior, were themselves paradigms of the duplicitous Canadian government policy of saying one thing and doing another. As Adachi points out, "unlike the arid desert exile of the Japanese-American evacuees, encircled by barbed wire and military police in watchtowers, the detention camps in the interior of British Columbia were another setting altogether. They were set against a splendid physical background" ([1976] 1991, 251). As he goes on to say, however, "[t]he magnificence of the outdoor setting and the echoes of a romantic past were but candy wrapping, hiding a grim reality" (251).

In *Obasan*, the most uncanny space entered into, however, is not the devastating landscape of the prisons and ghost towns but, rather, the memory. It is memory that threatens and allows for the return of the repressed, which is triggered, for Naomi, by her Uncle Isamu's death. As a result of his death, she is forced to reopen old wounds and to return to the past, and the disjunction created by this rupture is gothic in tone and circumstance. Indeed, it seems fitting, given Freud's definition of the *unheimlich* as unhomely, that many of the most unsettling moments in the novel take place within the supposedly safe environment of the home, thereby reminding the reader that this space was permanently violated by the government's racist wartime edicts so that it can never again be a space of security and boundedness ([1919] 1956). The dispossession and violation of the known space is always there. To quote Bhabha again,

> [i]n a feverish stillness, the intimate recesses of the domestic space become sites for history's most intricate invasions. In that displacement, the border between home and world becomes confused; and, uncannily, the private and the public become part of each other, forcing upon us a vision that is as divided as it is disorienting. (1997, 445)

Early in the novel, for example, when Naomi returns to Obasan's house, she is compelled to follow her aging aunt into the attic. Obasan is looking for memories, and her ascent becomes a movement into a profoundly gothic space, undertaken, as one would expect, at midnight. When they get there, Naomi discovers "a whole cloudy scene of carnage.... A grave-yard and feasting-ground combined" (Kogawa [1981] 1985, 25). Here everything is covered in cobwebs and dust — "[a] whiff of mothballs wafts up. The odour of preservation" (25). The preserved corpse — the *revenant* in this case — is the past, which rises up to haunt this narrative and its reluctant witness.

This theme is carried through in *Itsuka* (Kogawa 1993). When Naomi is forced to sell Obasan's house, the act of going through everything that her aged aunt has accumulated through the years is described in specifi-cally gothic terms:

> I'm an undertaker disembowelling and embalming a still breathing body, removing heart, limbs, life blood, all the arteries, memories that keep one connected to the world, transforming this comatose little family into a corpse. We have entered the garbage-dump stage of life and I'm rototilling it all. (69)

After she sells the house, the "new owners of the house bulldoze it. Our shack of memories disappears. I should not have let it happen" (69).

Whereas in traditional Gothic, barriers are physical, with locked doors and dungeons signifying entrapment — here it is memory that imprisons. In *Obasan*, Naomi says: "[W]e're trapped, Obasan and I, by our memo-ries of the dead — all our dead — those who refuse to bury themselves" (Kogawa [1981] 1985, 26). Yet if there is one ghost that haunts this text more than all others it is of course Naomi's mother. The absent mother who haunts the text devours Naomi, who is "consumed by the question" of why she did not return. The language used to address this silent absence is distinctly gothic. Naomi is "[d]evoured alive" by the memory of her (26). Yet no one in the family speaks, and Naomi has no "key to the vault of her thoughts" (26). If the mother is characterized as being mon-strous, however, it is because she is denied a right to speak her/story. As in most ghost stories, this spirit haunts because its pain has not been put to rest. Its story is still untold. So it communicates obliquely: "I waken sud-denly.... Something has touched me but I do not know what it is. Something not human, not animal, that masquerades the way a tree in the night takes on the contours of hair and fingers and arms.... She is here. She is not here" (167).

Again, in *Itsuka,* the metaphor of the mother as ghost is repeated. When Naomi visits Japan, she thinks: "We know so little of their last days, except that they lived within a well of silence, a grave before the grave. A haunted place. Mother hid herself from view. She scuttled through the night" (Kogawa 1993, 83). The act of visiting the hospice where her mother died strips her of identity. It is significant that as she witnesses the "ghost" of her mother—"I hear Mother in the sounds of footsteps, in the swishing of the broom outside"—she is un-named: "When I pick up the pen to sign my name, my hand shakes so much that the N ends up looking like a V. I can't finish my signature. That's Mama's fault" (83).[10]

This spectre is not easy to exorcise because it must first be acknowledged. And for Naomi to do this, she must confront the most terrifying horror at the centre of the narrative—and therefore at the centre of her self/body—the bombing of Nagasaki. As Cecily Devereux has argued in relation to *Obasan,*

> [c]ultural discrimination, like gender discrimination, begins at the body, which always visually identifies otherness in relation to the dominant group. The body is a sign of alterity, and is therefore the first and most important place to be taken over by the oppressor; the body is itself identified as "the enemy," an identification subsequently internalized. (1996, 234)

For any visible minority, skin represents the mark of difference. A particularly powerful aspect of *Obasan* is how it demonstrates the way in which the racism of Canadian culture has made Japanese Canadians foreign *to themselves.* As Stephen says in the text, "[w]e are both the enemy and not the enemy" (Kogawa [1981] 1985, 70). They are Canadian and yet not Canadian. Naomi's mother is there but not there. In this sense, the experience comes across as specifically uncanny.

What the novel also particularly emphasizes is how such valuations are translated into policy and enacted in the brutality of war. The bombing of Nagasaki makes humanity alien to itself. Yet far from universalizing this "self," the moment demonstrates the site-specific—the "racially" specific— nature of warfare: "I am wondering, did Grandma and Mother waken in those years with the unthinkable memories alive in their minds, *the visible evidence of horror written on their skin, in their blood, carved in every mirror they passed,* felt in every step they took" (235 [emphasis added]). As Devereux puts it, "Naomi's mother is effectively erased from discourse, from signification; moreover, as Manina Jones indicates: she is 'de-faced' and 'dis-figured' in the radiation of the bomb" (1996, 241). Humanity becomes unrecognizable to itself because the fiction of its representative homogeneity is shattered. The white "we" cannot inhabit the "skin" of the victim in this scene—it is unthinkable.

For all of the texts of Empire that cast the "Other" in the role of monster, that define migration as a type of disease that will infect the blood, and that posit the outsider as soulless (so much so that they often cast no reflection),[11] the power of Kogawa's narrative is located in the way she demonstrates where true monstrousness lies. It is not the Japanese Canadians who "infect" the West—indeed, they are the West! It is Western technology and policy that disfigures, that contaminates the blood through radiation poisoning, and that carves out the reflection of the Other in the mirror of its own making so that the Other can no longer bear to gaze upon itself. As Julia Kristeva avers in the opening epigraph of this essay, "project[ing] out of itself what it experiences as dangerous or unpleasant in itself, making of it an alien double, uncanny and demoniacal" (1991, 185). Naomi's description of her mother after the explosion is truly horrific:

> One evening when she [Grandma Kato] had given up the search for the day, she sat down beside a naked woman she'd seen earlier who was aimlessly chipping wood to make a pyre on which to cremate a dead baby. The woman was utterly disfigured. Her nose and one cheek were almost gone. Great wounds and pustules covered her entire face and body. She was completely bald. She sat in a cloud of flies and maggots wriggled among her wounds. As Grandma watched her, the woman gave her a vacant gaze, then let out a cry. It was my mother. (Kogawa 1985, 239)

The beast, in *Obasan,* is a gothic creature that, like Dracula, not only consumes but also transforms its prey. The Japanese Canadians are made unrecognizable to themselves by the infection of the government wartime policy.

It would be possible to speak of the history of Japanese-Canadian internment in Canada as a type of *revenant* that haunts the people who were so brutally oppressed by the Canadian government. But it is also a history that will continue to haunt the government and the Canadian people as a whole because such history functions as a narrative that, in the tradition of the uncanny, exposes the illusory nature of totalizing narratives, which underscores the impossibility of wholeness without healing. In revisiting the past, *Obasan* foregrounds Canada's disparate selves despite the nation's repeated attempts to present a myth of unity. Uncanny narratives are ruptured spaces, forever incomplete because of an excess of meaning.[12] The past and the present are forever in competition and, hence, contaminate each other—they inhabit the same space simultaneously—making resolution impossible. History, in this and in all narratives, is un-dead.[13] Like Naomi's dead, the past refuses to bury itself. As Naomi says of her Aunt Obasan, "the past hungers for her. Feasts on her. And when its feasting is complete? She will dance and dangle in the dark, like small insect bones, a fearful calligraphy" (Kogawa [1981]1985, 26). Aptly enough, the body is made to write the fearful story since it is the body that bears the mark of racialization—it becomes the visible signifier, which is either over-invested with, or stripped entirely of, meaning.

Conclusion: Reading against the Grain

This essay began by invoking theories of the uncanny as they can be understood in a range of issues and texts, in particular, that of the Native title legislation in Australia and the way in which it can be brought to bear in coming to terms with the impact of both the novel *Obasan* and the contemporary history of Japanese Canadians. It is certainly a dangerous "land slide"[14] to attempt since it can potentially be charged with "universalizing" the experience of oppression, with obscuring the specificity of experience, and, just as pointedly, with equating the dispossession of Indigenous peoples with the experience of members of a settler community, however disenfranchised they may be.

To some degree, however, this skewing of the traditional models of comparison is enacted to suggest the very way homogenizing and totalizing systems attempt to contain and manage those they oppress, so that there is a certain logic to reading against the grain in this manner. Nationalist narratives typically elide difference, except when they articulate the "reason" for which such homogenization is needed. When the latter issue is addressed, difference is spoken to alert the nation to the monstrous diversity (as opposed to state-sanctioned—that is, "unifying" diversity) that threatens to consume the whole.[15] Scott McFarlane successfully captures the "uncanny" register of such fears when he writes:

> The Canadian State, so dependent on Canadian history for legitimacy, is haunted by the insistent return of armies who challenge its representative authority. And these armies are masked. They doubly challenge the authority of the State so dependent on trust in its vision. The masked armies return like ghosts. (1995a, 20)

Such a cross-cultural reading as has been attempted here, therefore, can play a small role in dis/articulating the wholesome narratives of empire—in fragmenting the putatively cohesive, internally consistent fictions of integrity and design—those performances of nation that figure as non-existent or extinct what is constructed as the unlocatable, unassimilable spectre of the "Other." By dislocating the parameters of the field, the critic can enact an uncanny mis/reading that challenges the binary structures that frequently hierarchize and frame national debates. This enactment also participates in the equally important project of resisting a universalizing blandness by, ironically, opening up the issue—deterritorializing the reading—without evacuating the site-specific dimensions of the story. It is a way of forcing the majority white "we" to be conscious of our role in a wider, ongoing totalitarian project, which should make the "possession" of the text obscene.

To return, then, to the opening proposition, if the *Mabo* decision made the space of Australia suddenly "uncanny" for many of its citizens it is equally true that *Obasan* played a similar role in Canada, reminding Canadians of their fractured identity and exploding the monstrous liberal humanist myth of Canadian democratic unity.[16] Like the *Mabo* decision in Australia, the Mulroney government's redress settlement statement similarly reminded Canadians of this fact. Yet instead of reading this collective, hurtful memory as a necessary step in the process of reconciliation, some commentators chose to re-cast the gesture as a dangerous precedent that would simply further dismember Canada.

Atypically, perhaps, Jeffrey Simpson wrote in the *Globe and Mail* that the "decision to offer financial redress to Japanese Canadians [had set a] precedent…. The Ukrainian Canadian Committee hit Ottawa this week asking for redress…. It followed on the heels of organizations representing Italian Canadians and Chinese Canadians who seek similar kinds of redress for historical injustices" (1990, A16). For Simpson, the gesture of reconciliation is to be feared because it has released the monstrous ethnic appetite once more into the benign, reasonable, and wholesome Canadian space: "Where does this end? Do we compensate Acadians who were expelled? The Irish who were badly treated when they arrived? Those interned during the War Measures Act of 1970?" (A16). Simpson goes on to say:

> History has many, often contradictory, lessons to teach us. It is essential to remember those that cast Canada in a dark light, so that they won't be repeated. But there comes a point at which, in a linguistically and ethnically divided country, the search for restitution for past wrongs not only creates precedents that lead we know not where, but also risks piling up more divisions in a country already quite divided. (A16)[17]

"It is essential to remember those that cast Canada in a dark light, so that they won't be repeated," Simpson says, so long as it does not cost "us" anything. Simpson, like Naomi in much of *Obasan*, prefers to deny the creature lurking in the darkness and wishes to retreat into the shadows of silence. As Himani Bannerji has argued, however, "[i]f one stands on the dark side of the nation in Canada everything looks different" (2000, 104).[18] And, as Naomi learns, to deny the monster does not make it go away. If anything, it proves more invasive and more destructive if it is left unchallenged. Simpson locates part of the problem in the greed of minorities — with their *unreasonable* desire for compensation. If the Canadian government had maintained its silence, "[t]he Ukrainian Canadian Committee might have been satisfied with a statement of apology, some historical plaques and possibly the financing of university chairs in Ukrainian studies" — a few baubles or glass beads perhaps. However, now the floodgates are open, and those who will bear the cost for this ethnic avarice are "today's generation," who will have to "pay for policies and attitudes of generations past," as though we were ever free of our responsibility for/to the past (Simpson 1990, A16).[19]

It is interesting that Simpson, like John Howard, misnames the monster. For Simpson, it is ethnic avarice, just as it is greedy Aborigines for Howard. In one way, this is part of the orientalizing process that makes the "Other" into an insatiable creature that preys on the so-called "real" citizens of Canada and Australia in order to justify past and present actions. The "real" monster, however, is not the people seeking redress but, rather, the acts of violation that impel this call for restitution. Early in the novel, Naomi ruminates on the bad odours emanating from Obasan's fridge and associates them with memories that should be forgotten:

> There are some indescribable items in the dark recesses of the fridge that never see the light of day. But you realize when you open the door that they're there, lurking, too old for mould and past putrefaction.
>
> Some memories, too, might better be forgotten. Didn't Obasan say, "It is better to forget?" What purpose is served by hauling forth the jar of inedible food? If it is not seen, it does not horrify. (Kogawa [1981] 1985, 45)

In the course of the novel, this notion of beneficial forgetting is shown to be false. Naomi is terrified throughout by nightmares—by *not* knowing. The unseen, as any specialist in horror will attest, is always the most frightening and the most crippling. Howard's gesture of holding up the map of Australia, invaded by falsely represented Aboriginal claims of ownership, enacts a dark parody of the British imperial map with its pink landmasses demonstrating power, influence, scope, conquest, and owner-ship. It is fitting that what was once an iconic and positive representation of British power and domination—the world map covered in pink—should be twisted around to represent white disempowerment at the hands of the voracious Aboriginal "spectre."[20]

And yet, in closing, two points need to be remembered. First, that the representation of Aboriginal or ethnic avariciousness is demonstrably false—a fairly typical and long-standing misrepresentation of the facts that recasts the victim as the powerful and evil aggressor—and, second, that it is only in acknowledging the past that any hope of reconciliation becomes possible. However, we need to remember that the act of acknowledgement *is* costly and *is* painful. To think that it could be other-wise seems destructively and monstrously naive.

Notes

A version of this essay was originally published as Gerry Turcotte, "'A Fearful Calligraphy': De/scribing the Uncanny Nation in Joy Kogawa's *Obasan*" (2002).

1 Numerous websites detail the complex history leading up to, and including, the signing of the historic redress settlement where an acknowledgement of the injus-tices, and a small payment of $21,000 per wronged individual, was awarded. See for

example,<http://www.thecanadianencyclopedia.com/index.cfm?PgNm=TCE&Params
=A1SEC914912>.

2 See, for example, a number of studies by Gerry Turcotte (1993a; 1993b; 1995; and
1998).

3 *Mabo and Others v. Queensland (No. 2),* (1992) 175 C.L.R. 1.

4 See Joy Kogawa's comment in Gayle Fujita that the people who now own her parents' home are in possession of "stolen property" (1985, 41, n. 3).

5 For more detailed studies of silence in Kogawa, see King-Kok Cheung (1993),
Arnold Davidson (1993), Gayle Fujita (1985), Kirstie McAlpine (1995), and Gary
Willis (1987). Most critics "reading" *Obasan* comment to varying degrees on the
way language is "destabilized," or on how expectations about linguistic stability are
shattered, in this text (see Miki 1995; Goellnicht 1989; Jones 1990). See also Roy
Miki's extended note in *Broken Entries* for a brief, though important, contextualizing of the numerous critical responses to this text, including the way *Obasan* has
been institutionally appropriated by US academics so that the "site-specific formation of the Japanese Canadian subject...tends to become another version of the
'Asian-American' example" (1998, 155, n. 8). Other important readings include
Erika Gottlieb (1986), Mason Harris (1990), Coral Ann Howells (1987 and 1994),
and Rachelle Kanefsky (1996).

6 See Roy Miki's discussion of this issue (1998, 130–31), and Robert Lecker's argument (1990, 656–71).

7 See Jonathan Kertzer's *Worrying the Nation* (1998, 133), in particular chapter 4.
While I am attracted to certain aspects of this study, I am concerned that Kertzer
homogenizes "difference" in his assessment of the way in which "ethnic, feminist
and Native writers" make "the bourgeois nation" into a monster, "an ideological
aberration to be corrected, rather than a natural habitation." Such a blanketing of
difference reproduces the homogenizing account of the "Other," reductively eliding
the very material specificities that Miki is concerned to foreground.

8 See the quotation in *Obasan:* "The Yellow Peril is a Somerville Game, Made in
Canada" (Kogawa [1981] 1985, 152).

9 A similar reversal occurs in the preface to Ken Adachi's *The Enemy that Never Was,*
when he claims that he had been "the victim since childhood of a particularly virulent strain of racism," which impelled him to "reveal the demon in all its scaly ugli-
ness and perhaps exorcise it" ([1976] 1991, n.p.). Timothy Findley, in his brief
introduction to the 1991 reprinted edition of the book, seizes on this metaphor to
note that, "when he speaks of virulence, Adachi reminds us that racism is a parasit-
ical disease. A sickness. A viral infection that spreads from person to person. It can
even bring death" (1991, n.p.).

10 It is worth comparing this moment of de-scription with the earlier instance when
Naomi attempts to inscribe herself into "white" space — that is, when Naomi is
"spelling" herself for her students. In *Itsuka,* the complete breakdown of even the
act of inscription after her "encounter" with her mother and in the wake of the horror of Nagasaki, restates the connection between the national and the personal, the
public and the private.

11 Again, *Dracula* is a useful example in this instance (Stoker 1897).

12 For a more detailed account of the nature of uncanny narratives as they are
described here, see Rosemary Jackson (1981).

13 See Margaret Sweatman's description of historical writing as a type of necrophilia: "It's ghoulish writing this type of fiction. You get off on these dead people" (2007, 187).

14 I am playing here on W.H. New's configuration and meditation on the term in *Land Sliding* to mobilize, as he does, both actual and yet imaginative crossings of space, place, and imagination (1997).

15 Consider, for example, Australia's nationalist metaphor: "We are one, but we are many." It attempts a similar gesture to the strategies of the Canadian mosaic paradigm. As McFarlane argues, "liberal Canadian nationalism is dependent for legitimation on both historical and contemporary visions of Canada as culturally monolithic. These visions are incommensurate with the alienation experienced by aboriginal people and people of colour" (1995a, 20).

16 For an analysis of the many different writers, film-makers, and poets who have commented on this violent moment in Canadian history, see McFarlane and, in particular, his comment that "no single text concerning the internment has had a greater impact on the Canadian imaginary than Joy Kogawa's *Obasan*" (1995b, 402). He goes on to argue that "*Obasan* played a significant role in the redress movement as evidenced by its being quoted by both Ed Broadbent and Gerry Weiner during the announcement of the settlement with the government" (402). See also Arnold Davidson on this point (1993, 14–15).

17 Compare this with Freud's notion that E. Jentsch's argument is "incomplete" when he maintains that "the uncanny would always be that in which one does not know where one is" ([1919] 1956, 370). The real point is that the uncanny—the *unheimlich*—leads back to the familiar. Or, put another way, the unfamiliar leads back to, is always already imbricated in, the familiar. Jeffrey Simpson's real dread, here, is that he knows very well *where all of this will lead:* to accountability (1990).

18 See Rita Wong, who builds on this observation (2003–04, 110–11).

19 Such re-figurations of minority calls for justice as dangerous, as avaricious, and as blatantly wrong-headed are legion. See Scott McFarlane's discussion of the critical response to the Writing Thru Race conference (1995a). See also columns such as Barbara Amiel's in *Maclean's*, in which she maintains that "it makes no more sense for our government to apologize to our native peoples for past treatment than it would to ask today's Africans to apologize for every missionary who was eaten there in the past" (1998, 11). The extraordinarily offensive and orientalizing nature of the comparison, coupled with the flawed logic, need not be deconstructed at length in this essay. Predictably, however, the nub of the argument, as with Simpson's, is an economic one: "But the best thing we can do is say 'we are sorry.' Period. Compensation cheque will not follow. Sorry" (11). Not surprisingly, in this context, the long-serving Australian prime minister John Howard staunchly refused to offer an apology to the Aboriginal peoples on behalf of the nation, arguing that the present should not be forced to make up for actions of the past. A slightly more complex, though similarly motivated argument for refusing redress is offered in J.L. Granatstein's *Who Killed Canadian History?* (1998), in particular, Chapter 4, "Multicultural Mania." It is significant in this context to note that the first act of newly elected Prime Minister Kevin Rudd in 2008 was to offer the long-awaited apology to the Aboriginal people of Australia. He also opened the first sitting of Parliament with a Welcome to Country, the first time this has happened in Parliament's 107-year history. See <http://www.abc.net.au/news/events/apology/text.htm> for an account of the apology and for a transcript of the address, and

<http://media.news.com.au/multimedia/mediaplayer/skins/black/index.html?id=
769> for a video download of the Welcome. These are but two of numerous such
sites covering this historic event.
20   Again, see Gelder and Jacobs (1995; 1998) and Steve Mickler (1998) for an elaboration of this "inversion."

Works Cited

Adachi, Ken. 1976, reprinted 1991. *The Enemy That Never Was: A History of the
Japanese Canadians.* Toronto: McClelland and Stewart.

Amiel, Barbara. 1998. "Saying Sorry Is Fine, But Only to a Point." *Maclean's,* 25
May: 11.

Apology, <http://www.abc.net.au/news/events/apology/text.htm>.

Bannerji, Himani. 2000. *The Dark Side of the Nation: Essays on Multiculturalism,
Nationalism and Gender.* Toronto: Canadian Scholars' Press.

Bhabha, Homi K. 1997. "The World and the Home." In *Dangerous Liaisons:
Gender, Nation and Postcolonial Perspectives.* Ed. Anne McClintock, Aamir
Mufti, and Ella Shohat. Minneapolis: University of Minnesota Press. 445–55.

Cheung, King-Kok. 1993. *Articulate Silences: Hisaye Yamamoto, Maxine Hong
Kingston, Joy Kogawa.* Ithaca: Cornell UP.

Davidson, Arnold. 1993. *Writing against the Silence: Joy Kogawa's* Obasan.
Toronto: ECW Press.

Deleuze, Gilles, and Félix Guattari. 1975, reprinted 1994. "What Is a Minor Literature?" In *Kafka: Towards a Minor Literature.* Trans. Dana Polan. Minneapolis:
University of Minnesota Press. 16–27.

Devereux, Cecily. 1996. "The Body of Evidence: Re-membering the Past in Joy
Kogawa's *Obasan.*" In *Intersexions: Issues of Race and Gender in Canadian
Women's Writing.* Ed. Coomi S. Vevaina and Barbara Godard. New Delhi:
Creative Books. 231–43.

Freud, Sigmund. 1919, reprinted 1956. "The 'Uncanny.'" In *Collected Papers:
Papers on Metapsychology, Papers on Applied Psycho-Analysis.* Trans. Joan
Rivière. Vol. 4. London: Hogarth. 368–407.

Fujita, Gayle K. 1985. "'To Amend the Sound of Stone': The Sensibility of Silence
in *Obasan.*" *Melus* 12(3): 33–42.

Gelder, Ken, and Jane M. Jacobs. 1995. "Uncanny Australia." *UTS Review* 1(2):
150–69.

———. 1998. *Uncanny Australia: Sacredness and Identity in a Postcolonial Nation.*
Melbourne: Melbourne UP.

Goellnicht, Donald C. 1989. "Minority History as Metafiction: Joy Kogawa's
Obasan." *Tulsa Studies in Women's Literature* 8: 287–306.

Gottlieb, Erika. 1986. "The Riddle of Concentric Worlds in *Obasan.*" *Canadian Literature* 109: 34–53.

Granatstein, J.L. 1998. *Who Killed Canadian History?* Toronto: HarperCollins.

Harris, Mason. 1990. "Broken Generations in *Obasan:* Inner Conflicts and the Destruction of Community." *Canadian Literature* 127: 41–57.

Howells, Ann Coral. 1987. *Private and Fictional Words: Canadian Women Novelists of the 1970s and 1980s.* London: Methuen.

———. 1994. "Storm Glass: The Preservation and Transformation of History in *The Diviners, Obasan,* and *My Lovely Enemy.*" In *Into the Nineties: Post-Colonial Women's Writing.* Ed. A. Rutherford, L. Jensen, and S. Chew. Aarhus: Dangaroo Press. 471–78.

Jackson, Rosemary. 1981. *Fantasy: The Literature of Subversion.* London: Methuen.

Jones. Manina. 1990. "The Avenues of Speech and Silence: Telling Difference in Joy Kogawa's *Obasan.*" In *Theory between the Disciplines: Authority/ Vision/ Politics.* Ed. Martin Kreiswirth and Mark A. Cheetham. Ann Arbor: University of Michigan Press. 213–29.

Kanefsky, Rachelle. 1996. "Debunking a Postmodern Conception of History: A Defence of Humanist Values in the Novels of Joy Kogawa." *Canadian Literature* 148: 11–36.

Kertzer, Jonathan. 1998. *Worrying the Nation: Imagining a National Literature in English Canada.* Toronto: University of Toronto Press.

Kogawa, Joy. 1981, reprinted 1985. *Obasan.* Toronto: Penguin.

———. 1993. *Itsuka.* Toronto: Penguin.

Kristeva, Julia. 1991. *Strangers to Ourselves.* Trans. Leon S. Roudiez. New York: Columbia UP.

Lecker, Robert. 1990. "The Canonization of Canadian Literature: An Inquiry into Value." *Critical Inquiry* 16(3): 656–71.

McAlpine, Kirstie. 1995. "Narratives of Silence: Marlene Nourbese Philip and Joy Kogawa." In *The Guises of Canadian Diversity: New European Perspectives/Les Masques de la diversité canadienne. Nouvelles perspectives européennes.* Ed. Serge Jaumain and Marc Maufort. Amsterdam: Rodopi. 133–42.

McFarlane, Scott. 1995a. "The Haunt of Race: Canada's Multiculturalism Act, the Politics of Incorporation, and Writing Thru Race." *FUSE* 18(3): 18–31.

———. 1995b. "Covering *Obasan* and the Narrative of Internment." In *Privileging Positions: The Sites of Asian American Studies.* Ed. Gary Y. Okihiro, Marilyn Alquizola, Dorothy Fujita Rony, and K. Scott Wong. Washington: Washington UP. 401–11.

Mickler, Steve. 1998. *The Myth of Privilege: Aboriginal Status, Media Visions, Public Ideas.* Fremantle: Fremantle Arts Centre Press.

Miki, Roy. 1995. "Asiancy: Making Space for Asian Canadian Writing." In *Privileging Positions: The Sites of Asian American Studies.* Ed. Gary Y. Okihiro,

Marilyn Alquizola, Dorothy Fujita Rony, and K. Scott Wong. Washington: Washington UP. 135–51.

———. 1998. *Broken Entries: Race, Subjectivity, Writing.* Toronto: Mercury Press.

New, W.H. 1997. *Land Sliding: Imagining Space, Presence, and Power in Canadian Writing.* Toronto: University of Toronto Press.

Sartre, Jean-Paul. 1968. "'Aminadab': or the Fantastic Considered as a Language." In *Literary and Philosophical Essays.* Trans. Annette Michelson. London: Hutchinson. 56–72.

Shelley, Mary. 1831, reprinted 1969. *Frankenstein or The Modern Prometheus.* Oxford: Oxford UP.

Simpson, Jeffrey. 1990. "The Trouble with Trying to Compensate Groups for Historical Wrongs." *Globe and Mail,* 14 June: A16.

Stoker, Bram. 1897. *Dracula.* London: Archibald Constable and Company.

———. 1897, reprinted 1997. *Dracula.* Ed. Nina Auerbach and David J. Skal. New York and London: Norton.

Sweatman, Margaret. 2007. "Ghosts Are Our Allies." In *Speaking in the Past Tense: English-Canadian Novelists and Writing Historical Fiction.* Ed. Herb Wyile. Waterloo: Wilfrid Laurier UP. 165–87.

Turcotte, Gerry. 1993a. "Footnotes to an Australian Gothic Script: The Gothic in Australia." *Antipodes* 7(2): 127–34.

———. 1993b. "How Dark Is My Valley?: Canadian and Australian Gothic." *Scarp* 22: 26–32.

———. 1995. "Sexual Gothic: Marian Engel's *Bear* and Elizabeth Jolley's *The Well.*" *ARIEL: A Review of International English Literature* 26(2): 65–91.

———. 1998. "Australian Gothic." In *The Handbook to Gothic Literature.* Ed. Marie Mulvey-Roberts. London: Macmillan. 10–19.

———. 2002. "'A Fearful Calligraphy': De/scribing the Uncanny Nation in Joy Kogawa's *Obasan.*" In *Reconfigurations: Canadian Literatures and Postcolonial Identities/Littératures canadiennes et identités postcoloniales.* Ed. Marc Maufort and Franca Bellarsi. Bruxelles: Peter Lang. 123–43.

Welcome to Country, <http://media.news.com.au/multimedia/mediaplayer/skins/black/index.html?id=769>.

Willis, Gary. 1987. "Speaking the Silence: Joy Kogawa's *Obasan.*" *Studies in Canadian Literature* 12(2): 239–49.

Wong, Rita. 2003–04. "Troubling Domestic Limits: Reading Border Fictions alongside Larissa Lai's *Salt Fish Girl.*" *BC Studies* 140: 109–24.

CHAPTER FIVE

Familiar Ghosts: Feminist Postcolonial Gothic in Canada

Shelley Kulperger

Since poststructuralism has endowed us with an understanding, following Jacques Derrida, that genre operates within the imperatives of
a law that equates to an "academic apartheid," genre studies has become,
at best, the scholarly equivalent of a tight-rope walking act or, at worst,
the residue of phallocratic thought (1980, 202). For gothic criticism, a
"one size fits all" approach is hopelessly normative and prescriptive
(Richter 1983, 283), while efforts to define gothic narrative structures in
absolute terms, as Judith Halberstam argues, come out of "a humanist
investment in the idea of clarity and identity" (1995, 119). It is into this
minefield that any working definition of the "postcolonial Gothic" must
enter. Any attempt to define a genre such as the "postcolonial Gothic"
needs to be aware of the inadequacy of its capacity to capture a myriad of
literary practices, narratives, and voices. A loosely defined, embryonic,
but increasingly used label, the "postcolonial Gothic" does, however,
require a set of parameters that might allow the term critical currency
and specificity. In risking the kind of academic apartheid that Derrida
suggests is at the heart of classificatory epistemologies, I want to clarify
and identify the narratives, tropes, and strategies that I think qualify texts
as exemplary of the "postcolonial Gothic." In reference to three recent
Canadian novels by women, Ann-Marie MacDonald's *Fall on Your Knees*
(1996), Dionne Brand's *At the Full and Change of the Moon* (1999), and
Eden Robinson's *Monkey Beach* (2000), and in a further (self-conscious)
display of my investment in clarity and identity, I also want to develop a
distinct understanding of *feminist* postcolonial Gothic. I will argue that
feminist postcolonial Gothic surfaces in various intertwined personal,

national, and regional histories through a precise materializing *and* familiarizing of haunting, trauma, monstrosity, and fear.

The development of an understanding of feminist postcolonial Gothic satisfies two aims. First, it provides greater nuance and specificity about what we might mean by terms such as the "postcolonial" and the "Gothic," both of which have been, for the past decade at least, subject to overhaul and debate and which bear even closer scrutiny when brought together. Second, in adding feminist to postcolonialism, it addresses the often suggested salience of the Gothic for both postcolonial nations and for women. The postcolonial nation, like the female body, is routinely and increasingly understood as a gothic space, attracting gothicized discourses.

Anchored in postcolonial feminism, this essay follows a set of interrelated trajectories of race, gender, nation, and history within what are understood as gothic narratives in contemporary Canadian fiction. If the postcolonial Gothic can be defined as a genre that is concerned with the unspeakable traumas and repressed ghosts of colonization, postcolonial feminist Gothic seeks to, above all, materialize and familiarize those motifs of trauma and haunting, grounding them in the brutal realities and ongoing legacies of colonization. It does so by focusing on the hidden stories of women as objects of fear, violence, trauma, and by using traditional gothic conventions to expose the lingering remnants of the past within the present-day postcolonial nation with a particular focus on their impact on women. An important tactic of postcolonial feminism—the merger of the real with the otherworldly, the mundane with the supernatural, the material with the immaterial, the familiar with the unfamiliar, and the domestic with violence—is key to making concrete what otherwise remains private, personal, repressed, or trivialized. Such refractions of the uncanny—the strange made familiar and the familiar made strange—are intricately hinged to the material world.

The trope of haunting as a personal and national memory aid abounds in critical theory. An examination of what might be thought of as the "turn to Gothic" in both literature and theory therefore provides a starting point for clarifying the specificity of postcolonial Gothic.[1] David Punter points to the close "relation between Gothic and contemporary ideas," arguing that "in the 1990s in particular, we have found ourselves at a peculiar confluence between the major motifs of the Gothic and a set of ways of thinking increasingly current in contemporary criticism and theory" (2000, ix). Punter traces this confluence through psychoanalysis to postmodernism:

98

[W]e live in a world peopled by ghosts, phantoms, spectres haunting Europe, or haunting the West; there are, Abraham and Torok affirm, phantoms haunting and distorting the process of psychological transmission down the generations. There are, the theorists of postmodernism assert, perhaps *only* simulacra; entranced by the flickering glow of the new technologies, our bodies vanish from our apprehension, leaving only media constructs, apparitions of desire, hungry *revenants* whose appetite is matched only by their impotence. (1999, 1)

As Punter suggests, it is not just that gothic and contemporary criticism employ similar vocabularies but, rather, that, in keeping with the motifs of the uncanny and the spectral, they imply an impossible, insoluble burden and a certain epistemological crisis:

[W]e also need to say that part of the issue here is clearly that contemporary theory is increasingly itself haunted — haunted especially by a painful understanding of the uncanny nature of knowledge itself, haunted by an awareness of the disjunction between theory and practice, haunted, like Gothic, by the weight of a history, just behind its shoulder, which proves resistant not only to understanding but, more importantly, to change. (2000, ix)

This obsession with the abject, the uncanny, haunting, and ghosts seems appropriate and inevitable. The collapse of modernity's so-called grand narratives has left in its ruins a range of vexed theoretical positions and has made the rhetorical strategies of the Gothic especially pertinent. The "painful understanding" that investigations of colonialism may well involve, including, among many things, the restoration of the discursive frameworks, power relations, authors, and speaking positions of the past, is especially pertinent for postcolonial theory. The adoption of the ghost in postcolonial contexts is then additionally meaningful and deployed to suggest an ethical uncertainty and moral imperative and to signal the imbrication of colonialism/colonialist within postcolonialism/postcolonialist. Roger Luckhurst, on the other hand, sees the ghost as a potent allegory for "amnesiac modernity" in which the insatiable quest for (new) memories and histories is destined to quickly render the object of memory obsolete, passé, and forgotten (2002, 532).[2] In either scenario, the production of history, cultural memory, and knowledge are particularly fraught endeavours.

What seems crucial to the close relationship between theory and the Gothic is a determination to find ways of knowing, articulating, and memorializing the horrors of the past and to account for their haunting trace in the present in a meaningful and ethical way. Punter's exploration of this connection between history and authority involves an engendering of a "painful understanding" for the producer of knowledge and cultural memory, squarely framing the theorist as both haunted and traumatized by the vagaries and impasses inflicted by contemporary times (2000). Andreas Huyssen echoes these sentiments, but, where Punter obliquely inserts trauma into the equation, Huyssen makes it central to understandings of the "spectral turn." He asks:

> What is it that has made trauma a preoccupation in the arts and humanities since the 1990s? And how does the privileging of trauma relate to those other master-signifiers of the 1990s, the abject and the uncanny—all of which have to do with repression, spectres, and a present repetitively haunted by the past? (2003, 16)

This question brings us closer to an appreciation of the issues that circulate within postcolonial Gothic where motifs of haunting, in particular, reflect not just the burden of history but also the burden of transmitting the atrocities and traumas of colonization.

Given the spectral turn's relation to trauma narrative, history, and epistemology, it is no wonder that in postcolonial or settler-invader nations such as Australia and Canada a surfeit of texts thought of as postcolonial Gothic begins to appear. These are nations, after all, that have only just begun to acknowledge such inherently "gothicized" histories as the stolen generation in Australia or residential schooling and slavery in Canada. Ann-Marie MacDonald's *Fall on Your Knees* provides an apt correction to dominant discourses in Canada, warning that "just because it's new doesn't mean it's not haunted" (1996, 18). Technologies of national or regional remembrance have enabled a collective dissociation from "old" or "dead Europe," to use the title of a recent example of postcolonial Gothic in Australia, namely Christos Tsiolkos's *Dead Europe* (2005). Canada's quintessential settler narrator, Susanna Moodie, provided a lasting blueprint by which Canadians have been able to confidently affirm the lack of ghosts or atrocity within the borders of their home ([1852] 1989). "Bad spirits cannot be supposed to linger near a place where crime has never been committed," Moodie writes, adding that "the belief in ghosts so prevalent in old countries must first have had its foundations in the consciousness of guilt" (268).[3] If the old countries are unable to reflect Canadian virtue, America has always been a dependable counterpoint for Canadian imaginings, held up as an "enlightening mirror" (Clarke 2002, 30)[4] to maintain what Glenn Willmott describes as a sense of Canadian *ressentiment,* or moral superiority, over its neighbours to the south (2001, 133).

Neither the "old" countries nor "bad" America, however, are able to deflect Canada's guilty consciousnesses in relation to a number of unresolved and forgotten traumas of colonization. Postcolonial gothic literature serves to remind us that there is ample consciousness of guilt — and justice — to be developed in response to "home-grown" atrocities. Brand, MacDonald, and Robinson clearly reveal that the Canadian historical record is not nearly as spotless as its dominant authors would like it to be. From state- and church-sanctioned violence against the First Nations and against women in the home to the separation of children from "bad" mothers in the maintenance of white supremacy and the formative political economies of slavery, each narrative of haunting carefully surfaces such repressed histories within the narratives of personal trauma. These personal traumas and collective atrocities are then further located within the shared geographies and narratives of the nation. The "stupefying innocence" that Brand sees in Canadian nation-narration is countered in each of the three texts by an awareness of a range of discursive and material violence (1994, 191).

Writers in postcolonial states therefore invoke the conventions of the traditional Gothic — that of the uncanny, the spectre, and the ghost — as mnemonic devices in the recovery of regional and national histories and traumas. Ghosts function, as Roger Luckhurst reads it, as "signals of atrocities, marking sites of an *untold* violence, a traumatic past whose traces remain to attest to the fact of a lack of testimony" or a lack of a "memorializing narrative" (1996, 247). For the writers that I am interested in, the emphasis on siting untold violence and traumatic pasts involves a careful positioning of atrocity within particular bodies, spaces, and histories since the memory needs to become part of the personal, collective, and national conscience. For the purposes of literary criticism, an understanding of haunting as a mnemonic device needs also to account for the specific and prevalent use of the ghostly as mundane, everyday, familiar, domestic, or even, as in Toni Morrison's germinal narrative of haunting and trauma, "beloved" (1987). It would seem that contemporary and postcolonial Gothicists have taken Derrida's decree that "we need to live with ghosts, that we must be engaged in the upkeep and the speaking to ghosts" absolutely seriously and have crafted narratives that combine the mundane with the supernatural in order to convey the ordinariness of the ghostly (1994, 177).

The everyday practice of living with ghosts is no easy task, however, and Dionne Brand's *At the Full and Change of the Moon,* in particular, carefully considers the implications of "living with ghosts" as an ethical (lifestyle?) choice and as a means to access and produce postcolonial cultural memory (1999). As a site of untold atrocity, the ghost's familiarity and ordinariness ensures an understanding of colonization and slavery as commonplace practices that "mark the existence" of nations everywhere. Living with this understanding as a daily, corporeal reality is, however, far different from living with the knowledge of its histories (Derrida 1994, 4). Brand's text shows the precise material embodiment of the theoretical sense of haunting that has permeated critical theory since the 1990s.

Brand's *At the Full and Change of the Moon,* like Toni Morrison's *Beloved,* imbues the spectral with the difficult memories and traces of slave histories. For a nation that, as Maureen Moynagh suggests, can barely "conceive of a female African-Canadian identity" (2002, 120), let alone its place within the nation's history, Brand's tale of a haunted generation of the African diaspora, dispersed across the New World and throughout economic centres in North America and Europe, including Toronto, is pointed in its revision of Canadian history. While the text does not admit of the existence of slavery in Canada exactly, as much recent Canadian literature does, it nonetheless reveals the ongoing flows, benefits, and burdens of this system, effectively closing the distance between the Trinidadian plantation of the past and the globalized (post)colonial capital of the present. Since the text forges, as I see it, an interesting parallel to Morrison's *Beloved,* it also manages to close the distance that permits Canadian national identity to maintain America as the moral degenerate in contradistinction to its "good" self.

The novel's fragmented narrative structure contains loosely connected chapters that trace the descendants of a slave woman and rebel, Marie Ursule, over five generations. Before her execution for the orchestration of a mass-suicide on a plantation, Marie Ursule entrusts her only surviving daughter, Bola, to the fugitive Kamena, who is also Bola's father.

Kamena takes Bola to Culebra Bay and to the rotting ruins of an Ursuline mission and plantation. Left for long stretches on her own as Kamena seeks the notorious Maroon camp of Terre Bouillante, Bola is forced to live with the ghosts of Mère Marguerite de St. Joseph and Soeur de Clémy, two Ursuline nuns who once owned Marie Ursule and, like everyone else who came to the Caribbean, learned "how to multiply ground and ton-loads of sugar and cocoa and whale oil and anything they turned their hand and someone else's labour to" (Brand 1999, 38). Aspiring capitalists, shrewd money handlers, capable plantation owners, and cruel slave own-ers, these ghostly nuns dramatically subvert the traditional gothic figure of the buried innocent nun and expose the mission and the church's hands-on role in administering slavery. On first sight, Bola sees them "crumbling like dust." They appear as

> figures in habits dampened by their strangled pores, pressed by countless suns, black and white turned black, their several hundred years particled in fine little grains. She sees their faces gone over by wood ants' and weevils' gnawing, moss drying for no moisture, the man-o'-war gowns held up like old cupboards for keepsakes, and she screams. (35)

In isolated Culebra Bay, Bola's first encounter with the ghosts induces a terrified scream, but Kamena dismisses the ghosts as nothing (35). "Infected with the nuns' hovering," Bola nonetheless learns to live with them and even thrives with the "spectral Ursulines" even if they are a con-stant nuisance and daily reminder of the traumatic loss of her mother (66). Living with ghosts is, like living with slavery, a brutal hardship, and, for Bola and Marie Ursule before her and her own children afterwards, it is a test of endurance with enduring effects and costs.

Derrida wants us to live with ghosts and favours a politics of testimony—of speaking and listening—that insists justice be done to the debt that the ghost symbolizes (1994, 177).[5] In line with Jean-François Lyotard's dialogic model of justice, *anamnesis,* haunting therefore is a form of witnessing that instantiates "an obligation, a responsibility, or a debt, not only toward thought but toward justice" (1993, 141). Gothic scholars have long seen the ghost as such a figure of testimony, redemption, and dialogue. Terry Castle, for example, argues that to be haunted means "to find oneself obsessed by spectral images of those one loves" (1995, 103). As Castle maintains, such a state of haunting is "to display one's powers of sympathetic imagination:

the cruel and the dull have no such hallucinations. Those who love are by definition open to the spirit of the [O]ther" (103). Brand's use of the ghost as a signal of atrocity and of bad consciousness borne of colonial conquest makes it clear that no love is lost between those "open to the spirit of the Other" and the haunting ghost. The daily reminder of trauma that Bola, and those who are haunted by the ghostly figures of the nuns, must endure is therefore not necessarily a sign of openness or generous dialogue but, rather, the trace of the traumatic histories of colonization. Current understandings of the ghost, and of haunting, therefore, require further clarification to accurately convey the sense of haunting in Brand's postcolonial Gothic. Kamena, like Bola, is neither a romantic individual "open to the spirit of the Other," nor is he willing to engage in the testimonial dialogue required to relieve the haunting debt of the past. He wants only to get away from Culebra Bay and the nuns' spectral presences, and his desire to be done with the past is great enough "for him to consider the debt void, just for some peace" (Brand 1999, 55). Like the others who at the end of slavery "begin to drift" to Culebra Bay, for him the burden of transmitting and reliving the traumas of a painful and recent past needs to be shed and deferred: "There was enough time in the future for recounting but all they really wanted to do was go on, advance into their next years, which had to be sweeter" (64).

Taking the form of man-o'-war birds, these menacing spectres continue to haunt Marie Ursule's descendants, whether they realize it or not, as they begin to drift, over the centuries, away from Culebra Bay and seek opportunities in powerful economic centres across the globe. In an interview with Paulo da Costa, Brand says that her purpose in her creative memoir, A Map to the Door of No Return (2001), was to "contemplate that historical moment" when Blacks were taken to the New World, feeling that that moment "existed still" and "hovered over the lives of the Black Diaspora" (Brand 2004, para. 1). The man-o'-war birds metaphorize this "hovering" moment.[6] By revealing the privilege of not being haunted, beseeched to alleviate guilt or supply testimony and memory, Brand queries the theoretical demand that "we" live with ghosts, while revealing the onerous task that (re)positions Black bodies and voices as suppliers of spectacles of suffering and narratives of trauma in the production of postcolonial cultural memory. In its call for careful attention to a colonial appetite for narratives of others via the "authentic" voice of the "native informant," Trinh T. Minh-ha's foundational text on postcolonial feminism, *Woman, Native, Other,* is apt here (1989). While Geoffrey Hartman points to the production of "two classes which can exist within the same person" — those "who suffer and those who observe that suffering" (1996, 103) — Brand, in the same vein as Trinh, emphasizes two distinct classes, distinctly corporeally marked and positioned within the postcolonial imaginary. For Brand, it is the former class, the colonized body/subject and its pain and suffering, that so heavily bears the burden and has no choice but to learn to live with, and transmit, the haunting of traumatic memory. Being haunted signals the trace of atrocity and the unresolved still-lingering effects of colonial bureaucracy and speaks of a consciousness that leaves its "host" bodies with little peace.

Brand's use of the spectral, therefore, provides some important caveats that need to be considered before rushing headlong into a celebratory heralding of the ghost as a postcolonial model of ethical remembrance. What is striking in Brand's text, as in MacDonald's and Robinson's, is the emphasis on whose spaces, bodies, and lives are inhabited by ghosts. This corporeal and subjective specificity is a distinguishing mark of the postcolonial Gothic. The precise geographical situating of the text is another important aid in making concrete tales of otherwordly haunting. The postcolonial Gothic's residence in local contexts makes it distinct from both the theoretical and epistemological sense of haunting. While the postmodern Gothic might be thought of as a genre without a state, taking place in "anywhere U.S.A." or in the homogenous recesses of suburbia, the postcolonial Gothic is recognizable for its location within the borders of the nation-state and its regional worth (Goodlad 1997, 17). The postcolonial Gothic therefore includes not just national gothics but also regional ones. In Canada, there is the well-known Southern Ontario Gothic and now, with MacDonald and Alistair MacLeod, there is a "Cape Breton Island Gothic," while a blurb on *Monkey Beach*'s cover raves about a "glorious northern Gothic" (Robinson 2000). Richard Cavell argues that the examination of postcolonial space calls for a critical reading practice that restores the recognition that "colonialism has a fundamentally spatial aspect: the seizing of territories, the mapping of sites, the framing of landscapes, the construction of buildings, the displacement of peoples" (1995, 111). This practice enables "a direction for postcolonial theory that deprivileges literature as the sole site of critique." Each of the three texts ensures such recognition. Each features narratives of haunting and trauma that are found within specific time frames, contextualized by actual events, and precisely located within the boundaries of home and nation. Not only is repressed public memory exhumed in each of the three texts, but there is also a direct appeal that takes the reader outside the text and encourages a spatial awareness through details of cartography, landscape, and architecture. This interpellative strategy insists on the text's location within, and in relation to, the outside world. Both MacDonald and Robinson are explicit in their orientation of the nameless reader to geography and space. In *Fall on Your Knees,* MacDonald invites "you" to

> [l]ook down over the street where they lived. Water Street. An avenue of packed dust and scattered stones that leads out past the edge of town to where the wide, keeling graveyard overlooks the ocean. That sighing sound is just the sea.
>
> Here's a picture of their house as it was then. White, wood frame with the covered veranda. It's big compared to the miners' houses. There's a piano in the front room. In the back is the kitchen where Mumma died. (1996, 1)

The telescopic view of the house ends with a shocking throw-away detail — "where Mumma died" — which is so briefly and casually related that it could be glossed over or forgotten. This detail is also significantly out of place, disrupting the superior, transcendent gaze that views the home through a romantic haze. MacDonald brings us in closer and closer, disallowing the blindness to detail (and domesticity) and refusing the distance that the aesthetic gaze from above affords.

Robinson similarly opens *Monkey Beach* with the imperative voice and, offering even more explicit directions, encourages the implied reader to

> [f]ind a map of British Columbia. Point to the middle of the coast. Beneath Alaska, find the Queen Charlotte Islands. Drag your finger across the map, across the Hecate Strait to the coast and you should be able to see a large island hugging the coast. This is Princess Royal Island, and it is famous for its Kermode bears, which are black bears that are usually white. Princess Royal Island is the western edge of traditional Haisla territory. *Ka-tee-doux Gitk'a'ata,* the Tsimshians of Hartley Bay, live at the mouth of the Douglas Channel and surrounding areas just north of the island. During land claim talks, some of the territory is claimed by both the Haisla and Tsimshian nations — this is called an overlap and is a sticky topic of discussion. But once you pass the head of the Douglas Channel, you are firmly in Haisla territory. (2000, 4)

The directions continue until the reader is able to locate the domestic, personal space and the site of trauma:

> If your finger is on Prince Rupert or Terrace you are too far north. If you are pointing to Bella Coola or Ocean Falls, you are too far south. If you are pointing in the right place, you should have your finger on the western shore of Princess Royal Island. To get to Kitamaat, run your finger northeast, right up to the Douglas Channel, a 140-kilometre-long deep-sea channel, to its mouth....Near the head of the Douglas, you'll find Kitamaat Village, with its seven hundred Haisla people tucked in between the mountains and the ocean. At the end of the village is our house. Our kitchen looks out onto the water. Somewhere in the seas between here and Namu—a six-hour boat ride south of Kitamaat—my brother is lost. (5)

As Jennifer Andrews suggests, these directions pointedly provide a different sense of territory and an alternative concept of home that is signalled from the opening of the novel (2001, 11). These detailed directions provide precise bearings for an outsider, and I have followed Robinson's exact directions through the atlas and website to find Kitamaat and to get my bearings. Yet the technologies of mapping are emptied of their traditional knowledge as instruments that contain and seize territory. The Haisla narrator and protagonist, Lisa, defiantly proclaims: "[Y]ou are firmly in Haisla territory." This cartographic exercise serves as a reterritorialization of colonized space.[7]

Both MacDonald and Robinson end their orienting of "real" space with a detail that provides the source of trauma in the narrative. It is here that "Mumma" died; somewhere between "here and Namu" that a "brother is lost." Signalling the postcolonial Gothic's abandonment of an abstract, overview position to one that is on the ground, these directions also progress from the universal to the local, embedding specific domestic traumas in wider national space. Significantly, these personal traumas—connoted both by local space and by the familiarity of "mumma" and "brother"—are inextricably linked to, or result from, colonial and state practices that sustain or promulgate trauma and violence within particular families and communities.

Trauma is therefore geographically situated and contextualized. In the case of *Fall on Your Knees*, a mother's suicide comes as a final self-signatory act after enduring years of domestic violence within a community that not only turns a blind eye to incidences of abuse within the family but also provides the wider discursive and ideological logic in which patriarchal power and domestic violence flourishes unchecked. Not only does the violence enacted against the mother, the Lebanese-Canadian Materia, make sense within a prevailing logic of patriarchal power and control, but it is also reasonable according to the late-nineteenth century racial ideologies and standards within which the novel is set and to which her husband James adheres. James's authority stems from being male, white, and English-speaking, and he subsequently outlaws the speaking of Lebanese between mother and daughters within the home — the mother tongue is therefore silenced and abjected, just as Materia's "darker" skin colour, which was once a sign of her sexual availability and exoticness for James, becomes a worrying blemish that might "stain" his own children and must similarly be denied and repressed. In the case of *Monkey Beach*, a cycle of sexual abuse within the Haisla community, stemming from the sexual abuse of children perpetrated by a priest at the Port Alberni residential school and similarly sustained by church, state, and wider discursive violence against First Nations, sees a young man fatally seek vengeance.

Whether it is a historical or geographical artifact, there is an undeniable (re)assertion of the material within the literary and a return to the "real." Within the postcolonial Gothic, this realism resides, comfortably and naturally, alongside the supernatural and the unreal. This blurring of the real with the surreal is not a marker of postmodern aesthetics but, rather, is very much in keeping with the cultural materialism of the postcolonial Gothic. Joanne Saul provides an important distinction that compels the kind of reading that is required for a revitalization of realism that is undeniably discernible in these texts (2004). Saul argues that a recent trend in Canadian literature reveals a dedicated return to history that is not just a reassessment of the early Canadian search for canon and identity but also, and more crucially, a movement away from the "historiographic metafiction" of the postmodern school of Canadian criticism — a mode that might describe much of Margaret Atwood's *oeuvre* and use of the Gothic. Saul points to "more recent texts" that "want to make much firmer claims about the past" (59). Among the texts that characterize this "less experimental, less self-conscious, less referential" turn to history, Saul names Kerri Sakamoto's *The Electrical Field*, Jane Urquhart's *Away*, and Dionne Brand's *In Another Place, Not Here* (59). The firm historical claims that these authors want to make are strengthened by the *terra firma* upon which their narratives lie. The certainty of "real" historical, material contexts, which are most clearly signified by "real" national spaces and geographies, interspersed with elements of the spiritual and supernatural, operates, then, not so much as an internal self-conscious postmodern formalism but, instead, as Saul notes, as a "(re)turn to history" (59), similarly to that allegedly postmodern "turn to space" (Jameson 1991, 154). The return to history and space in postcolonial Gothic marks a concern for, and recognition of, the work that needs to be done in remembering what happened where (or what is happening here).

Just as there is an assertion of the real, there is also a widening of what is accepted as real to include unknown and mysterious quantities. In postcolonial Gothic, the exhaustion of the ghostly/supernatural as a source of fear, spectacle, awe, mystery, and abnormality significantly reorders the traditional Gothic. The supernatural is right at home in the home — the gothic uncanny blending of the strange and the familiar, the material with the immaterial — and no longer is a source of wonder and fear. Just as Bola learns to fearlessly go about her life with the ghosts of Culebra Bay, MacDonald similarly intones a banality of the supernatural from the outset of *Fall on Your Knees* when she writes: "And certainly it's odd but not at all supernatural to see the surface break, and a real live soaked and shivering girl rise up from the water and stare straight at us" (1996, 3).[8] In Eden Robinson's *Monkey Beach,* a grandmother tells her granddaughter, a Haisla girl who reluctantly accepts the gift of being a shape-shifter: "You don't have to be scared of things you don't understand. They're just ghosts" (2000, 265). Here, Robinson makes the strongest appeal to live with ghosts and, in tying ghosts to the unknown, marks this mundane supernatural as a resistance to the colonizing force of epistemologies. Markman Ellis notes that traditionally "terror and the supernatural is an issue of epistemology: an opening out of imagination that leads to amazement and bewilderment" and, eventually, resolution and mastery (2000, 9). The familiarity and domesticity of the supernatural in each text is not, however, easily resolved, rationalized, or explained, as was the case, particularly, in the Radcliffean female gothic (Radcliffe [1802] 2000). Whereas the traditional Radcliffean "explained supernatural" worked to restore order and faith in the mapping capacity of the rational mind, the postcolonial supernatural announces a politics that resists the need to forbid, control, and contain. If the traditional Gothic has often been read as pushing against the bedrock of Enlightenment thought, postcolonial Gothic leaves the unexplained open and at the thresholds of knowledge in a deliberate and feminist resistance to phallogocentric thought. Such staging of the unknown and the otherwordly operates, then, in a vastly different context from the traditional Gothic's test — and often valorization — of Enlightenment.

It comes as no surprise that these writers characterize women as shape-shifters, speakers with the dead, haunted, clairvoyant, and possessed and that these states are not feared but, rather, normalized and accepted. What is crucial is that such conditions — and conflations of the material and the immaterial — do not require mastery and resolution, triggering the realization that so much academic work and the production of knowledge abides by a colonizing logic. Cavell's reminder that "the forces which a postcolonial reading discerns in literature" are also "active in the academy" points to the nature of academic discourse and its commitment to clarity and order in the face of difference (1995, 111). Simon Critchley looks to the etymology of philosophy to underscore its basic colonial spirit: "[T]o think philosophically is to comprehend — *comprendre, comprehendre, begreifen,* to include, to seize, to grasp — and master the other, thereby reducing its alterity" (1992, 29). The familiar and domestic supernatural in feminist postcolonial texts jams the machinery of colonial modernity and leaves space — indeed nurtures domestic space — for that which cannot be contained by rational phallagocentric discourse. Although it is undeniable that the ghost does in fact signal a certain ethical and moral responsibility for representing trauma, in these texts the emphasis on haunting and ghostliness as a preoccupation with enunciative modalities shifts to a critique of colonizing epistemologies and practices. The question then of "how can I know this" and "how can I speak for/represent this," which has been strongly signalled by the trope of the spectre, becomes "why do I need to know this." The requirement to know and the production of knowledge, in this sense, is unleashed from the mastery, ownership, and colonial pursuit of unknown bodies and bodies of knowledge and removed from the quest of producing useful and rational knowledge.

This aspect of contemporary Gothic — the depletion of the supernatural as a source of mystery and fear — is especially relevant for feminist postcolonial concerns since the mysterious and feared female body itself has so often been the object of relentless colonial rationalism and has so heavily borne the discursive colonial script. The production of the abject and its subsequent release of both fear and desire have been forceful psychic preconditions for the colonization of both the New World and the female body—often seen as one and the same. Terry Goldie long ago revealed the female "indigene" (1989) as a particularly abjected "imaginary body" (Gatens 1995). Her body, like the land itself, is invariably seen as sublime and dangerous, empty and wild and, in either case, requiring the taming and penetrating effects of masculinist imperialism.

In *Monkey Beach*, Robinson emphasizes the collapsing of the indigenous female body and the land as sources of awe and desire in a scene that reverberates with the asymmetrical power relations and transactions of whites and First Nations peoples in Canada since colonization. In it, the protagonist, Lisa, while journeying to find her lost brother, unexpectedly meets a white boy at the eponymous haunted Monkey Beach. The boy muses that "he hadn't realized it would be so empty in the wilderness" and observes "how beautiful it is, how spiritual it is getting back to nature" (Robinson 2000, 216). His remarks reconfirm the schism that allows the white gaze to both erase and exoticize the Other and reactivate the mind-body split that sees both Lisa and nature as distant, exotic objects to "get back to" and to colonize, explore, and exploit. It is as though Lisa was no longer the occupant of her "home" and the "Canadian" landscape was emptied of people and rendered as both a mysterious and abstract space, available for, and awaiting, ownership and occupation.[9]

This familiar colonial and spatial relationship to the great Canadian "wilderness," as students of Canadian culture well know, authorizes white belongings and is matched by an equally dominant articulation of Canadianness in temporal terms—the alleged emptiness of history, identity, and mythology. From Earle Birney's famous poem "Can. Lit," with its oft-cited line "it's only by our lack of ghosts we're haunted" (1964, 37), to Northrop Frye's essay "Haunted by a Lack of Ghosts" (1977), such a "lack" asserts, particularly, white English preoccupations and perceptions. These complementary narratives of nation, one based on the self's relation to geography and the other on the relation to history, are part of a routinely and uncritically adopted sentiment in dominant discourses of Canadian identity. Often turning on its vexed blandness or its dreaded sameness in relation to America and Americans, this is a narrative of nation in which, to use Trinh T. Minh-ha's words, "colonizer and colonized have come to speak the same language," allowing the colonizer to voice loss and prioritize its "victimhood" (1989, 58). These dual constructs—that is, the fear/desire for the Other and the sublime horror of being nothing—have long legitimized the dispossession and appropriation of First Nations' belonging and being in Canada.

A gothicizing of the spaces, bodies, and beliefs of the "Native" is particularly active in this process. Drawing on figures of monstrosity, legends, and myth making in Canada, Robinson highlights the misappropriation of First Nations' cosmologies that emerges from a dynamic that moves from romantic mystification to containment and exploitation. In the third part of her novel, "In Search of the Elusive Sasquatch," Robinson effectively repatriates Haisla objects and beliefs, particularly the "Sasquatchean" monster, which have long circulated and been exploited to fill a perceived void in dominant Canadian culture. Lisa derisively notes the de-contextualization and universalization of this traditional Haisla figure:

> B'gwus is famous because of his wide range of homes. In some places, he's called Bigfoot. In other places, he's Yeti, or the Abominable Snowman, or Sasquatch. To most people he is the equivalent of the Loch Ness monster, something silly to bring the tourists in. His image is even used to sell beer, and he is portrayed as a laid-back kind of guy, lounging on mountaintops in patio chairs, cracking open a frosty one.
>
> B'gwus is the focus of countless papers, debates and conferences. His website is at www.sasquatch.com. Grainy pictures, embarrassed witnesses and the muddy impressions of very large feet keep B'gwus on the front page of tabloids and the covers of books. (2000, 317)

As a commercial product, "Sasquatch" becomes the all-round Canadian guy, a recognizable model of universal white masculinity. In other contexts, he becomes a mystery to solve. It seems significant that Lisa, a shape-shifter, sibyl, and speaker with the dead who is herself visited by a spirit-guide, also actually encounters the B'gwus on Monkey Beach. Unlike her brother who wants to photograph and exploit this creature, Lisa leaves it be. Her "regeneration" and repatriation of the "Native" monster extends to the ethics that she adopts in her final school project, a cultural history of another Haisla figure of monstrosity, T'sonoqua, a woman who eats the flesh of children (Haraway 1992, 295). Where B'gwus becomes a desirable and durable legend of anti-domestic masculinity,

T'sonoqua lingers at the thresholds of dominant Canadian mythologies, reflecting ambivalence for powerful First Nations' female subjectivity and the selective exploitation of First Nations' cultures.[10] Importantly, Lisa looks around her community for other T'sonoqua-like feared and "wild" women like her own grandmother and dispelling the myth of the "savage" and threatening First Nations woman, shows her to be, rather, a subversive model of femininity and a powerful, uncompromising woman of her community. Robinson points to the selective manipulation of particular Haisla cosmologies to support grand narratives of Canadian identity — such as the laid-back (white) guy or the threatening First Nations woman. In doing so, she not only normalizes and deflates the monstrous of its alterity but also reveals its specific meaning, relevance, and place in Haisla communities and knowledges where, brought back into context, the monster figure is demystified and removed from the spectacular realm of awe, fear, and wonder.

Pointing to the stock-standard postcolonial tactic of "writing back," Lisa's school project effectively rewrites archetypes of monstrous female subjectivity. T'sonoqua is first related to the witch in the Grimms' tale *Hansel and Gretel* and then subsequently rendered benign when materialized in relation to contemporary local women. The texts of Robinson, MacDonald, and Brand all contain instances where gothic conventions, from fairytales to the nineteenth-century British canon, are revised. Such revisioning work, however, is consistently reflective of a dedicated materialism: they share a particular focus on the material embodiment of those conventions and, specifically, the *female* embodiment of the monstrous, uncanny, and abject.

Steven Bruhm reads Freud's uncanny as having an acute relationship to the body (1994, xv). It involves, he argues, "a return of repressed anxieties about the body." For Freud, Bruhm notes, "[d]ismembered limbs, a severed hand, a hand cut off at the wrist, feet which dance by themselves… all these have something peculiarly uncanny about them" (244). MacDonald's *Fall on Your Knees* contains a parodic transformation of Freud's uncanny that simultaneously parodies the female gothic canon:

> Back in her room, Mercedes is finishing *Jane Eyre* again. She was thankful when Frances returned her favourite volume apparently unscathed. Now, with that mixture of satisfaction and regret with which one comes to the end

of a beloved book, Mercedes turns the last page only to find Frances's unmis-
takeable scrawl on the flyleaf. It is an epilogue, wherein, Mr Rochester's hand,
severed and lost in the fire, comes back to life and strangles their infant child.
(1996, 224)

Notably, in Frances's ending, a sign of the uncanny in one of Freud's key
terms, the severed hand, comes back to haunt and terrorize the bastion of
family contentment. The new ending given to the text reveals the truth of
MacDonald's fictional Piper family where, at the hand of the father and
in the name of a dutiful Canadian patriarchal imperialism, female bodies
are abused, Bertha-like (that is, racially "impure") women and children
are hidden away from the world, and matriarchy is severed and denied. In
rewriting the ending of that "cult text of feminism," as Gayatri Chakravorty
Spivak has called *Jane Eyre* ([1847] 1992), MacDonald displays a postcolonial tactic that brings to mind Jean Rhys's prologue to *Jane Eyre* in
Wide Sargasso Sea ([1966] 2000), what might be thought of as a cult text of
postcolonialism (Spivak 1991, 798). As the dutiful daughter, Mercedes fever-
ishly and uncritically re-reads and mimics the model of self-sacrificing and
compliant femininity in *Jane Eyre*. She affirms the text's value in turn-of-
the-nineteenth-century Canadian culture. Such an influential "mother
text" of the British female gothic canon is caustically revisited, as MacDonald
makes explicit its themes of violence against women as well as the potential ideological harm the text itself contains (Spivak 1991, 798).

Brand's depiction of Marie Ursule's execution graphically reveals a
gothicized and uncanny figuration of the female body and is similarly
postcolonial in its intertextuality:

> [Marie Ursule] had lost an ear and been shackled to a ten-pound iron for two
> years after the rebellion of 1819 had been betrayed, after the plan to kill de
> Lambert, and all his own, was discovered. While some had been put to death,
> their heads hung on sticks near the bell and their bodies tied to the walls in
> chains, she had been given a ten-pound ring to wear. She had been given
> thirty-nine lashes. She had been given her own ear in her mouth. She had
> been given a heart full of curses and patience. (1999, 5)

The fragmenting of her body and its violent displacement results finally
in a heart and spirit similarly thwarted and deranged. Marie Ursule's
heart of darkness, her heart "full of curses and patience," "so skilled now,

so full of wrath" is "given" to her, a gift of the brutal conditions of the Trinidadian slave plantation (5–6). It can be no mistake that the reference to Marie Ursule's dark heart and the image of heads on sticks so forcefully · evokes a central image within the postcolonial critical canon — as in Joseph Conrad's *Heart of Darkness* ([1902] 1973) — to serve as a potent reminder of where the feared and hated heart of darkness truly resides, despite the conflation of the "dark continent" with, particularly, the monstrous female body.[11]

Freud's dictate that female sexuality and psychology constituted a "dark continent" crystallized the late-nineteenth century impulse to map and produce knowledge of the unknown, within which "Africa" became, for Freud, the surest metaphor to express the mysteries of woman (and vice versa) (Stott 1992, 27). Both the "abjectification" and objectification of bodies grotesquely and uncannily taken apart and reassembled operate as strong signifiers of the Gothic and, in this case, explicitly (re)work colonial discourses and practices that, figuratively and literally, turn the female body into a body in pieces. Brand's materialization of a "heart of darkness" is an instance of the gothic uncanny that, in keeping with postcolonial tactics, locates the proper source of terror that has otherwise been projected onto the monstrous dark continent/female body.

Importantly, too, the explicitly colonized/enslaved female body is not set in a safely removed and overcome past. The narrative of Marie Ursule's trauma continues to haunt as her descendant, a contemporary Canadian woman, Eula, imagines, viscerally, the presence and conditions of Marie Ursule's life in her own:

> I remember what you said about Marie Ursule with her iron ring, limping through forests. I saw her caught in vines and tangles, hurrying back before daylight. I thought that I heard the thudding of her ring on wood and stone until I opened my eyes and it was the rim of my tire on a curb. (Brand 1999, 236)

The string that indelibly tethers the slave woman Marie Ursule to a contemporary woman in Toronto reveals the concern in postcolonial Gothic with inter-generational haunting, which is figured here as a transmission of legacies borne of slavery and the inescapable colonial present. Eula, herself, inhabits the conditions of fugitivity that marked her ancestor, and the somatic link is strengthened when Eula expresses a phenomenology of the self as distinctly *unheimlich*. Psychically split and corporeally disintegrating, walking through the streets of Toronto, she does not belong, is not at home, but is rather just a fragment, "broken up," "swept up," and "falling away" (255). The inherent bond between Marie Ursule and Eula sharpens an understanding of the binds, indeed the haunting traces, between colonial and postcolonial bodies, states, times, and spaces.

If, in the postcolonial Gothic, the ghostly is accepted as mundane, daily, banal, and domestic, then so too are fear and violence. The familiarizing and domesticating of violence and fear — and its proper placement as an internal rather than an external force — reflects the long-abiding feminist critique of the division of public and private spheres and, particularly, the trivialization of domestic violence. It marks an extension — and intensification — of the traditional female Gothic's depiction of haunted and violent domestic space to include, specifically, postcolonial feminist critiques of the displacement and distancing of violence elsewhere.

For the contemporary feminist Gothic, the domestic is often graphically and explicitly a violent space, substantially revising the eighteenth- and nineteenth-century tradition of the female Gothic where, as Kate Ferguson Ellis argues, the conventions of the Gothic were originally mobilized to allow women to express, covertly, the violence and dissatisfaction brewing within, and hidden beneath, the surface of the bourgeois home (1989, 3). The gothic subtext that reveals that the serene and orderly public surface belies a violent and deranged private reality is still intact. Brand pointedly depicts such a dissonance between interior and exterior spaces when a young woman wonders if dutiful wives and mothers like her own mother

> [p]uttered and puttered at domesticity, fixing curtains and chairs and lamps, decorating the abattoir where they were soon slaughtered; primped and laid out doilies and candles to sup up the odours of violence; kept their fingers busy with cooking so they themselves wouldn't cut a throat and perfumed themselves so as not to smell their own fear and rage. Perhaps her mother had done this. Puttered and puttered staving off some violence she sensed in Dovett. Or some violence she sensed in herself. (1999, 212)

When a doilied space is an abattoir and when candles "sup" up the odours of violence, we are surely in the realms of the uncanny and of the familiar made strange and brought into the open. The surfacing of what ought to remain repressed and buried has long been key to understandings of the uncanny and equally integral to the Gothic. This improper display of the private and the subsequent blurring of the lines between public and private has been seized in the feminist Gothic to expose the secrets of the domestic on both micro and macro levels. When brought to bear on the home, the uncanny's discordant clashing of surface and interior, public and private, signals a feminist aesthetic. The collision of distinct discourses, spaces, texts, and knowledges results in the shock of things "ripped out of their original context with a strong seemingly brutal grasp" — something that Walter Benjamin once urged — in order to disclose and grant immediacy to domestic violence (quoted in Buck-Morss 1986, 100).

In the following passage that returns us to a source of trauma in *Fall on Your Knees,* "where Mumma died," MacDonald displays this shocking mixture (1996, 138). It describes, in the most mundane and innocuous terms, what appears to be an everyday practice of domesticity but, in fact, reveals what is, in reality, a violent act, a mother's suicide:

> On the third day she cleans the oven, first turning on the gas to soften up the grit inside, it'll only take a moment. She is so tired. She hasn't slept in three nights, not so much as a tiny zizz, and she has never worked harder. She kneels in front of the oven, peering in, waiting for the gas to do its work, her arms folded on the rack. It'll only take a moment — she rests her head upon her arms. She is so tired. She will start scrubbing in just a moment, just one more moment. (138)

Just as Brand imagines a space covered in doilies as a slaughter house, MacDonald defamiliarizes an ordinary domestic object, the oven, and turns its associations with home-baked meals and maternal nurturance and creativity into the vaporous and deathly odours beckoning a woman to forever rest. The religious allusion "on the third day" morphs into the pressures of a woman's work never done, mixing transcendence and materiality. The fact that "mumma's" name is Materia serves as a reminder of the etymological lineage between mother and matter/materiality in a woman who is not only a down-to-earth domestic woman but also a transcendent-like, dutiful domestic angel. MacDonald uncloaks the hidden abstract meanings — often nostalgic and cozy — of the kitchen within the bourgeois household. It is an instrument of labour, self-sacrifice, and death and a place of women's burial and erasure — both symbolically and literally figured. Such textual incarnations, saturated with the details of domestic materiality, insistently drive the relays between private and public and ultimately bring what is abstract down to the ground and "close to home." By injecting the sacred with the profane, the domestic with violence, the transcendent with the material, MacDonald unmistakably familiarizes domestic violence, thereby removing it from its distant place in the realms of saga, abjectivity, deviance, and the individualized "madman"/villainous gothic tyrant and disclosing its absolute regularity, ordinariness, its frequency, and its entanglement with the wider community, bureaucracy, church, and state.

In MacDonald's text, the familiarizing of violence is met with the corresponding defamiliarizing of domestic objects and spaces. The perversion of everyday domestic objects as women's weapons also works to disclose the everyday conditions of domestic violence. In the Piper household, Materia uses the oven to kill herself but has also used scissors to open up her daughter's stomach during a prolonged and fatal labour and also considers using them to kill her husband. Materia, "awake now, after a 19-year slumber," is "hitting him. Closed fists in his face. If the scissors were handy she wouldn't bother to shut his eyes first" (MacDonald 1996, 145). In the everyday world of female domestic space, scissors destroy in order to create. In the everyday world of domestic violence, such normal domestic objects are a woman's only weapons of self-defence.

In her influential reading of women's writing, Ellen Moers suggests that the "maiden in flight," a mode of "travelling heroinism," is a particularly recurrent motif of the female Gothic (1976, 185). This model hinges on persistent imaginings of imprisoning domestic space and a movement from female bondage to emancipation. Inderpal Grewal, however, argues that "liberatory narratives of the movement from victimage to freedom are especially problematic in the present time because they collaborate with U.S. ideologies of democracy and freedom" (1996, 12). Liberatory narratives, found in the female gothic canon and other spatial narratives of restriction and flight, might equally collaborate with white, liberal, female perspectives. By stripping away the symbolic, allegorical layer of the female Gothic for Brand's female protagonists, bondage and fugitivity are made real. Just as in domestic violence, escape from the home is no longer a metaphorical abstraction of the confines of the private sphere. Consequently, traditional and ubiquitous gothic spatialized female bodies (emancipated/captive, fleeing/static) and particular constructions of space as uninhabitable, labyrinthine, dangerous, entrapping, uncanny, and haunted are, in the feminist postcolonial Gothic, further materialized so as to reveal the specificity of female subjectivity that they uphold. As allegories for female restriction to the private sphere, gothicized spaces and subjectivities traditionally authorize, and have been authored by, in the main, white middle-class women.

Brand, MacDonald, and Robinson are, therefore, circumspect in idealizing the flight from home and in revealing domestic space as gothic since a heightened awareness of both the romantic liberalism of the "maiden in flight" and the absolute privilege (and rarity) of a haven-like home attends their complex textualizations of domestic spaces and identities. This complication of the meanings of home is even more critical given the way that non-white, middle-class homes and families have been pathologized and exclusively subject to state control and surveillance. Recent texts in postcolonial contexts, therefore, articulate the violence of domestic/private space not simply as individual, localized instances (within which a Western liberal heroic and privileged narrative of emancipated and fleeing female subjectivity takes place) but also as very much inseparable from wider state institutions and instances of colonial governance. These texts reveal the enmeshment of public/state and private/domestic violence. Positioning the various institutions of the colonial state as entrapping spaces, violent acts may then occur well beyond the containing spaces of the bourgeois home as clearly they do in *Monkey Beach*. However, even those instances of "domestic" violence are enacted within the borders of the *national* home or take place with the supportive and obliging logic of the state. It is within this understanding of "domestic" violence that First Nations chief justice Mary-Ellen Turpel argues that, "to First Nations people, the expressions 'culture of violence' and 'domestic violence' not only have their customary connotation of violence by men against women but also mean domestic (that is, Canadian state) violence against the First Nations" (1993, 183).

The most complex rendering of violence within the home occurs in *Monkey Beach* where it is hard to disentangle the overlapping and mutually supportive domestic and state, personal and institutional, material and discursive violences that occur within and against the First Nations family. While Lisa's own home is truly a supportive haven, it is not safe from outside conflicts, especially those that mar her extended family and wider community. Lisa's cousin tells her that the conflict in her family is because her grandmother, Ma-ma-oo, sent the two oldest of her four children to the residential school where they were subject to abuse. They were sent, Lisa's cousin tells her, because her grandfather, Ba-ba-oo, "beat Gran. Instead of sending him away, she sent Mick and Mom to residential schools" (Robinson 2000, 59). The protective space of the home is violated not just by the patriarch but also by institutional and colonial regimes and agents whose impact on the First Nations home has been the greatest. But another reason is given for Ma-ma-oo's decision to send the children to residential school when Lisa learns of the coercive bureaucratic state policies that inflicted violence and severed families within First Nations societies in Canada. She learns that

> Ba-ba-oo had lost his arm in the Second World War, at Verrières Ridge. When he came home, he couldn't get a job or get the money he thought he should get from Veterans Affairs because they said Indian Affairs was taking care of him. Indian Affairs said if he wanted the same benefits as a white vet, he should move off reserve and give up his status. If he did that, they'd lose their house and by this time, they had three children and my dad, Albert, was on the way. (81)

This instance of violence drives home a central message within the feminist postcolonial Gothic: it is difficult to maintain distance—be it moral, critical, or spatial—from the various forms of trauma and violence that mark the existence of domestic spaces. Widely understood feminist definitions of domestic violence, then, arise and are informed by histories of colonial governance and the complex relationship of class and race to gender. These understandings clearly mediate feminist deployments of the Gothic in postcolonial states. They work consistently, on the one hand, to locate the sources of state instances of actual violence and, on the other hand, to reveal that what happens in the home is irrevocably sutured to wider cultural apparatuses and discursive frameworks. Feminist postcolonial Gothic not only alerts us to the true sources and victims of violence and fear but also continually pushes us to the realization that what haunts us, what traumatizes us, and what terrifies and terrorizes us can always be located—and it is never far from—home. This reminder would seem to be especially prescient and timely.

Notes

1   Roger Luckhurst, for example, uses the term the "spectral turn" to characterize the resonant and recurrent themes of haunting in literary and critical production (2002, 527).

2   Geoffrey Hartman (1996) and Andreas Huyssen (2003), in different ways, locate the processes that underlie this tension between cultures of memory and cultural amnesia.

3   George Elliott Clarke recognizes the continuum between Susanna Moodie's efface-ment of violence in Canada upon hearing the history of a local lynch mob, framed as a quaint "*charivari*," to the widespread reaction to the death of a Somalian sol-dier at the hands of Canadian special forces. The position, as Clarke puts it, is one of "pretend that we are not implicated," in the provision of a soothing and distanc-ing balm for white Canada (2002, 40).

4   Clarke points out, however, that America as an "enlightening mirror" is not always sustainable (2002, 30).

5   Jacques Derrida calls the spectre a symbol of an irredeemable debt (1994, 177). Jodey Castricano notes that this sense is "best appreciated in the English word *revenant* and in the French *revenance*," which contain "both *revenir* (to return) and *revenue* (the debt)" (2001, 9).

6   In an interview about the novel with Rinaldo Walcott and Leslie Saunders, Dionne Brand explicitly names the nuns as representing that hovering moment (2000, 22).

7   Gilles Deleuze and Felix Guattari's notion of deterritorialization accrues a relation-ship to space in which "territorializing and deterritorializing" consists of a series of moves: "Consolidate the territory by the construction of a second, adjacent terri-tory; deterritorialize the enemy by shattering his territory from within; deterritori-alize oneself by renouncing, by going elsewhere…. Another justice, another move-ment, another space-time" ([1980] 1987, 353). Donelle Dreese's *Ecocriticism* readapts the concept of reterritorialization to frame this question in relation to First Nations people whose movements towards "another justice" involve a need to reterritorialize and reclaim space (2002).

8   This image of the girl rising from the river, I think, is also indebted to *Beloved* (Morrison 1987).

9   Richard Cavell's "Where is Frye? Or, Theorizing Postcolonial Space" (1995) pro-vides an insightful discussion on the abstract production of space in Canada.

10 Julia Emberley reveals this relationship to powerful First Nations women to be more than symbolic, noting "the eventual exclusion of indigenous women from the network of power relations extending throughout Canada in the eighteenth, nine-teenth, and early twentieth centuries became a necessary precondition to the expansion of colonial rule. Whereas colonial and indigenous men received benefits accruing from the historical or economic forces that connected them, indigenous women were placed firmly outside this system of male relations of governance, a system secured through the imposition of a model of the bourgeois family with economic rules and a mode of governance characterized by hierarchical domestic/ civil relations and separate spheres of private and public activity" (2001, 61).

11 For an extension of this dynamic, see Patrick Brantlinger's discussion of the Victorian myth of the "heart of darkness" and its range of representations of Africa as the true site of savage cannibalism and, in a most explicit case of "blaming the

victim," slavery. Moreover, such a myth of the African heart of darkness lives on, in the Canadian context, in a multitude of constructions of "Black" urban criminality (1985).

Works Cited

Andrews, Jennifer. 2001. "Native Canadian Gothic Refigured: Reading Eden Robinson's *Monkey Beach.*" *Essays on Canadian Writing* 73: 1–24.

Birney, Earle. 1964. "Can. Lit." In *Poetry of Mid-Century 1940–1960*. Ed. Milton Wilson. Toronto: McClelland and Stewart. 37.

Brand, Dionne. 1994. *Bread Out of Stone: Recollections on Sex, Recognitions, Race, Dreaming and Politics.* Toronto: Vintage Canada.

———. 1996. *In Another Place, Not Here.* Toronto: Knopf.

———. 1999. *At the Full and Change of the Moon.* Toronto: Vintage Canada.

———. 2000. "The Full and Change of CanLit: An Interview with Dionne Brand." With Rinaldo Walcott and Leslie Sanders. *Canadian Women's Studies* 20(2): 22–26.

———. 2001. *A Map to the Door of No Return: Notes to Belonging.* Toronto: Vintage Canada.

———. 2004. Interview with Paulo da Costa. 15 March [on file with author].

Brantlinger, Patrick. 1985. "Victorians and Africans: The Genealogy of the Myth of the Dark Continent." In *"Race," Writing and Difference*. Ed. Henry Louis Gates, Jr. Chicago: University of Chicago Press. 185–222.

Brontë, Charlotte. 1847, reprinted 1992. *Jane Eyre.* Oxford: Oxford UP.

Bruhm, Steven. 1994. *Gothic Bodies: The Politics of Pain in Romantic Fiction.* Philadelphia: University of Pennsylvania Press.

Buck-Morss, Susan. 1986. "The *Flâneur*, the Sandwichman and the Whore." *New German Critique* 39: 99–140.

Castle, Terry. 1995. *The Female Thermometer: Eighteenth-Century Culture and the Invention of the Uncanny.* New York: Oxford UP.

Castricano, Jodey. 2001. *Cryptomimesis: The Gothic and Jacques Derrida's Ghost Writing.* Montreal and Kingston: McGill-Queen's UP.

Cavell, Richard. 1995. "Where Is Frye? Or, Theorizing Postcolonial Space." *Essays on Canadian Writing* 56: 110–34.

Clarke, George Elliott. 2002. "Raising Raced and Erased Executions in African-Canadian Literature: Or, Unearthing Angélique." *Essays on Canadian Writing* 75: 30–61.

Conrad, Joseph. 1902, reprinted 1973. *Heart of Darkness.* Harmondsworth, UK: Penguin.

Critchley, Simon. 1992. *The Ethics of Deconstruction: Derrida and Lévinas.* Oxford: Blackwell.

Deleuze, Gilles, and Felix Guattari. 1980, reprinted 1987. *A Thousand Plateaus: Capitalism and Schizophrenia.* Trans. Brian Massumi. London: Athlone.

Derrida, Jacques. 1980. "The Law of Genre." *Glyph: Textual Studies* 7: 202–29.

———. 1994. *Specters of Marx: The State of the Debt, the Work of Mourning and the New International.* Trans. Peggy Kamuf. New York: Routledge.

Dreese, Donelle. 2002. *Ecocriticism: Creating Self and Place in American Indigenous Literature.* New York: Peter Lang.

Ellis, Kate Ferguson. 1989. *The Contested Castle: Gothic Novels and the Subversion of Domestic Ideology.* Urban: University of Illinois Press.

Ellis, Markman. 2000. *The History of Gothic Fiction.* Edinburgh UP.

Emberley, Julia V. 2001. "The Bourgeois Family, Aboriginal Women, and Colonial Governance in Canada: A Study in Feminist Historical and Cultural Materialism." *Signs* 27(1): 59–85.

Frye, Northrop. 1977. "Haunted by a Lack of Ghosts: Some Patterns in the Imagery of Canadian Poetry." In *The Canadian Imagination.* Ed. David Staines. Cambridge, MA: Harvard UP. 22–45.

Gatens, Moira. 1995. *Imaginary Bodies: Ethics, Power, and Corporeality.* New York: Routledge.

Goldie, Terry. 1989. *Fear and Temptation: The Image of the Indigene in Canadian, Australian and New Zealand Literatures.* Montreal and Kingston: McGill-Queen's UP.

Goodlad, Laura. 1997. "Postmodern Gothic: The Lost Brides of Frankenstein and the Dark Taste of Fear." *Diegesis: Journal of the Association for Research in Popular Fictions* 1: 17–28.

Grewal, Inderpal. 1996. *Home and Harem: Nation, Gender, Empire, and the Cultures of Travel.* Durham, NC: Duke UP.

Halberstam, Judith. 1995. *Skin Shows: Gothic Horror and the Technology of Monsters.* Durham, NC: Duke UP.

Haraway, Donna J. 1992. "The Promise of Monsters: A Regenerative Politics for Inappropriate/d Others." In *Cultural Studies.* Ed. Lawrence Grossberg, Cary Nelson, and Paula Treichler. New York: Routledge. 295–337.

Hartman, Geoffrey. 1996. *The Longest Shadow: In the Aftermath of the Holocaust.* New York: Palgrave Macmillan.

Huyssen, Andreas. 2003. "Trauma and Memory: A New Imaginary." In *World Memory: Personal Trajectories in Global Time.* Ed. Jill Bennett and Rosanne Kennedy. New York: Palgrave Macmillan. 16–29.

Jameson, Fredric. 1991. *Postmodernism, or the Cultural Logic of Late-Capitalism.* Durham, NC: Duke UP.

Luckhurst, Roger. 1996. "Impossible Mourning in Toni Morrison's *Beloved* and Michele Roberts's *Daughters of the House.*" *CRITIQUE: Studies in Contemporary Fiction* 3(1): 243–60.

———. 2002. "The Contemporary London Gothic and the Limits of the 'Spectral Turn.'" *Textual Practice* 16(3): 527–46.

Lyotard, Jean-François. 1993. *Political Writings*. Trans. Bill Readings and Kevin Paul. Minneapolis: University of Minnesota Press.

MacDonald, Ann-Marie. 1996. *Fall on Your Knees*. Toronto: Vintage Canada.

Moers, Ellen. 1976. *Literary Women*. Garden City, NY: Doubleday.

Moodie, Susanna. 1852, reprinted 1989. *Roughing It in the Bush; or Life in Canada*. Toronto: McClelland and Stewart.

Morrison, Toni. 1987. *Beloved*. New York: Plume.

Moynagh, Maureen. 2002. "'This History's Only Good for Anger': Gender and Cultural Memory in *Beatrice Chancy*." *Signs* 28(1): 97–126.

Punter, David. 1999. "Introduction: Of Apparitions." In *Spectral Readings: Towards a Gothic Geography*. Ed. Glennis Byron and David Punter. London: Macmillan. 1–8.

———. 2000. "Introduction: Ghost of History." In *A Companion to the Gothic*. Ed. David Punter. Oxford: Blackwell. viii–xiv.

Radcliffe, Ann. 1802, reprinted 2000. "On the Supernatural in Poetry." In *Gothic Readings: The First Wave 1764–1840*. Ed. Richard Norton. London: Leicester UP. 311–15.

Richter, David. 1983. "The Gothic Impulse: Recent Studies." *Dickens Studies Annual* 11: 280–311.

Robinson, Eden. 2000. *Monkey Beach*. Toronto: Alfred A. Knopf.

Rhys, Jean. 1966, reprinted 2000. *Wide Sargasso Sea*. London: Penguin.

Sakamoto, Kerri. 1998. *The Electrical Field*. Vintage Canada.

Saul, Joanne. 2004. "'In the Middle of Becoming': Dionne Brand's Historical Vision." *Canadian Women's Studies* 23(2): 59–63.

Spivak, Gayatri Chakravorty. 1991. "Three Women's Texts and a Critique of Imperialism." In *Feminisms: An Anthology of Literary Theory and Criticism*. Ed. Robyn R. Warhol and Diana Price Herndl. New Brunswick: Rutgers UP. 798–814.

Stott, Rebecca. 1992. *The Fabrication of the Late-Victorian Femme Fatale: The Kiss of Death*. London: Macmillan.

Trinh, T. Minh-ha. 1989. *Woman, Native, Other: Writing Postcoloniality and Feminism*. Bloomington: Indiana UP.

Tsiolkos, Christos. 2005. *Dead Europe*. Sydney: Vintage.

Turpel, Mary-Ellen. 1993. "Patriarchy and Paternalism: The Legacy of the Canadian State for First-Nations Women." *Canadian Journal of Women and the Law* 6(1): 174–92.

Urquhart, Jane. *Away*. Toronto: McClelland and Stewart, 1993.

Willmott, Glenn. 2001. "Canadian Ressentiment." *New Literary History* 32: 133–56.

CHAPTER SIX

Canadian Gothic and the Work of Ghosting in Ann-Marie MacDonald's *Fall on Your Knees*

Atef Laouyene

Postcolonial discussions of Canadian identity reflect a relentless search for convenient discursive tropes that may give adequate expression to Canada's uncanny relation to its settler heritage, on the one hand, and to the racially mixed and hyphenated immigrant population that constitutes its contemporary national and cultural fabric, on the other hand. In *Gothic Canada: Reading the Spectre of a National Literature* (2005), for instance, Justin D. Edwards explores the ways in which the discourse of gothicism helps articulate anxieties about the persistent indefinability of Canadian identity—an identity that keeps oscillating between the necessity to remember and take stock of its colonial affiliation (as settler-invader) and the desire to disavow that affiliation and carve a new, post-colonial, multicultural one. Edwards's book offers a bold and insightful examination of the connections between the discourse of gothicism and the history of racial formation with which Canada's national identity is still grappling. "Placed in the context of gothic production," Edwards's study "probes a Canadian fear generated by a lack of a clear national identity and the prevalent fragmentation of subjectivity at the heart of 'Canadianness'" (xiv). The recourse to gothic discourse thus raises a common malaise about the absence of a unifying national meta-narrative—an absence that partly explains the continuing tenuousness of Canadian subjectivity. At the heart of Canadianness, it is often argued, is a sense of being "stuck" between the ethico-political obligation to acknowledge one's involvement in a history of oppression and alienation (with regard to

Aboriginals and to incoming multi-ethnic immigrants) and a concomitant need to move beyond that history and to claim postcolonial independence (with regard to Great Britain and the United States).

The ramifications of this sense of ambivalence and fragmentation raise a number of questions to which this essay seeks tentative answers. How effective is the contemporary discourse of gothicism in disrupting nationalist paradigms and "identitarian" politics when questions of race, sexuality, gender, and national belonging are broached? How does gothic epistemology help articulate this inherent paradox in Canadian settler consciousness — a consciousness torn between the moral and political obligation to recognize, if not to identify with, those whom it has oppressed and repressed? How does gothic discourse allow a reconciliation with the ghost of racial, sexual, and gender oppression, a ghost whose traumatizing return continues to haunt Canada's (multi)cultural memory?

Edwards relates gothic discourse, which he describes as springing from "a language of terror, panic and anxiety," to the anxieties attendant upon debates about Canadian subjectivity, for such debates all too often tend to unearth the ghost of Canada's settler history of dispossession as well as its current cultural fragmentation (xvii). Edwards links the absence of a unifying Canadian meta-narrative to "the haunting trepidation of losing one's true self" (through racial and cultural mixing) — something that he places at the heart of gothic discourse (xvii). Moreover, Edwards concurs with Cynthia Sugars when the latter argues that an imagined sense of unified community is necessary for the continuity and survival of that community. Despite one's disquieting awareness of the imaginativeness of the nation, Sugars insists, one cannot wrest oneself free from its tangible hegemonic power. Notwithstanding this awareness, one continues to believe in a potential sense of national cohesiveness and unity. Sugars describes this psycho-cultural dynamic as "a kind of willing suspension of disbelief that enables the nation's members to 'imagine' that they constitute a cohesive whole, while at the same time realizing that this illusion is always partial and tentative" (2003, 2). The idea of the nation, she goes on to argue, "is not just a socio-political fact but also, as critics such as Benedict Anderson and Homi Bhabha have explored, a way of 'storying' or talking about ourselves" (2). National identity cannot be construed independently of narrative. As much as it determines narrative, narrative also determines it. As Stuart Hall puts it, "identities are the names we give to the different ways we are positioned by, and position ourselves within, the narratives of the past" (2003, 236). National identity is then constituted not simply by the sum of lived experiences within a certain collectivity in a certain era, but by the way it is imagined, narrativized, conceptualized, and, one should add, *spectralized*. In gothic epistemology, the idea of the nation becomes an imaginative (spectral) story, a fairy tale of sorts, whose trans-generational circulation and mutation affect the community in variably intense ways. Both Edwards and Sugars thus conceive of Canada as a spectral nation—a nation that is both real and ethereal. Despite its insubstantial constructedness and its "fairytaleness," as it were, its material/political repercussions are visibly persistent.

The Canadian discourse of the nation is haunted by the spectre of Aboriginal and diasporic others—a haunting that renders problematic the construction of a cohesive national identity. Imagining the nation as a fairytale, however, holds the promise of a transcendent national mythopoeia in which the history of colonial settlement, with all of its violence and disruptions, is tentatively recycled into a creative and potentially unifying grand narrative. In the Canadian settler context, the spectre of colonial violence and dispossession is called upon not simply to be remembered and then laid to rest as a dim and distant memory of historical trauma but, rather, and more importantly, to be sanctified into a powerfully signifying trope within the modern meta-narrative of the nation. Troped within the nation's mythopoeic imaginary, the ghost of settler history thus loosens its haunting and paralyzing grip on the collective conscious and gradually transmogrifies into a new *esprit de corps* invigorating the nation-building project.

The returning spectre is probably one of the most enduring tropes in gothic writing, and many literary critics (David Punter [1980; 2000], Fred Botting [1996], Anne Williams [1995], Julia Briggs [2000], and Michelle A. Massé [2000], to name but a few) have attempted to explain its significance in relation to Sigmund Freud's theory of the uncanny.[1] Freud's famous essay, *Das Unheimliche*, clearly associates the phenomenon of the uncanny with the return of the repressed—the return of that which "ought to have remained secret and hidden but has come to light" ([1919] 1955, 225).[2] In postcolonial hermeneutics particularly, this repressed is often read as an index for the silenced other of history (whether this other be the colonized, women, Blacks, Aboriginals, or fellow citizens), whose return creates a disturbing sense of uncanniness in the oppressor. "Ghosting" offers itself in this respect as a constitutive and useful trope that allows the history of racial, colonial, and gender oppression to make its uncanny apparition *within* and *through* narrative. Taking its cue from such reading, this essay explores the significance of hauntropology[3] in gothic Canadian writing all the while emphasizing its relation to what can be described as the psychic triangulation of remembering, "storying" (telling/narrating), and mourning. More precisely, one could argue that troping the ghost, or "ghostwriting," in contemporary Canadian fiction allows a re-visiting of the traumas of the past in such a way as to facilitate their mourning in the present. Invoking or "presencing" the unhomely Other, to use Homi Bhabha's term (1994, 9), through narrative spectralization puts memory in the service of potentially therapeutic mourning. Ghosting in narrative is the means whereby mnemonic mourning is set in motion.

The presence of the spectre not only blurs the boundaries separating reality from illusion, but it also triggers a process of remembering that eventually leads to the collective re-witnessing and ultimate working through of trauma. Moreover, in order for it to be an effective means of mourning, remembering must take the form of common labour, a shared task in which those affected by the traumatic event (whether they be victims, victimizers, or simply witnesses) collectively reminisce that event. In this way, a collective act of remembering occasions a sort of inter-subjective empathy or an affective osmosis, as it were, by virtue of which the subject(s) may be released from the debilitating hold of trauma.[4] In collective memory, there is a potentially therapeutic transference of the traumatic affect. Taking Ann-Marie MacDonald's *Fall on Your Knees* as my case study, I argue that the book employs gothic tropes in such a way as to negotiate a process of mnemonic narrative mourning. The repetition compulsion dynamic, to which the characters often fall victim, is resolved once the traumatic event in question is commonly remembered, narrated, and passed on from one generation to another. At the same time, while ghostwriting in MacDonald gestures towards the need to story the hitherto "unstoried"—to make room for the absented (often racialized) Other—it simultaneously re-inscribes identity itself (racial and/or national) as inevitably insubstantial and spectral.

Critical studies of *Fall on Your Knees* have invariably emphasized MacDonald's critique of racial, sexual, and gender oppression in Canada's multicultural society. Melanie A. Stevenson, for instance, describes how MacDonald incorporates thematic elements of Shakespeare's *Othello* not only to challenge the racially informed Renaissance master code of

Moorishness (and non-Caucasian otherness, in general) but also to rein-force "the modern idea that racial identity is a fluid social construct" (2001, 34). While Stevenson traces the "Othelloness" paradigm in the novel and its significance in understanding racial and cultural politics in early twentieth-century Canada, Pilar Somacarrera reads "the *Jane Eyre* intertexts" in it, drawing attention to MacDonald's postcolonial (that is, subversive) revisions of traditional, nineteenth-century gothic conven-tions (2004). Both Stevenson and Somacarrera draw analogies between *Fall on Your Knees* and its Renaissance and Victorian proto-texts so as to emphasize, to variable degrees, MacDonald's subscription to multicultur-alism as an alternative to the racial and sexual intolerance that still informs inter-ethnic relationships in Canada. Katarzyna Rukszto, on the other hand, argues that the novel unequivocally exposes "the limits of multiculturalism as a basis for imagining community and nation," for multiculturalism, she notes, hinges upon a reductive classificatory princi-ple that identifies and defines specific cultural groups in terms of their race, origin, language, religion, customs, and so on (2000, 25). Instead, Rukszto proposes the concept of "queer," which signifies, among other things, more "expansive and unpredictable possibilities of identification" (25). *Fall on Your Knees,* Rukszto contends, gestures towards what she describes as the "queerness of difference," a concept designating a resist-ance to the normative racial, sexual, and gender categories of identifica-tion in favour of a transgressive affirmation of more flexible, elusive, and indefinable identity (21, 25).[5]

Without overlooking the analytical insights of these studies, one may nevertheless note that none of them has emphasized the manifest correla-tion between the text's postcolonial gothicism, on the one hand, and the enduring traumas that result from racial, religious, sexual, and gender oppression, on the other. Following a different theoretical line of inquiry and drawing on Freudian/neo-Freudian psychoanalysis and modern trauma theory, I want to suggest that MacDonald's postcolonial narra-tivization of gothicism not only re-focalizes the perception of Canada's haunting/haunted history of racial formation but also, and more impor-tantly, suggests ways of working through the several personal traumas that are dynamically implicated in this history. Focusing on the figure of the returning ghost as a symptom of unresolved trauma, this essay argues that traumatic experiences caused by racial, religious, or sexual abuse need to be re-channelled and meaningfully re-integrated into consciousness through shared narrative labour and common re-witnessing before their invasive, if compulsive, re-enactment is brought to an end.

Gothic Abjection

Fall on Your Knees tells a multi-generational family saga revolving around interracial relationships and indomitable gender politics. Set mainly in early twentieth-century Cape Breton Island, Nova Scotia, and partly in New York City during the jazz era of the early 1920s, the novel opens with an interracial love story between two first-generation immigrants: the Scottish-Irish James Piper, a striving young piano tuner, and the exotic-looking, thirteen-year-old Lebanese Materia Mahmoud. Although dis-owned by her father for eloping with an *enklese* (pejorative Arabic for Englishman), Materia marries James and before long gives birth to three daughters: Kathleen, on whom James lavishes his fatherly but incestuous tenderness as she grows into a promising opera diva; Mercedes, a reli-gious and caring mother figure; and Frances, a mischievous but intelli-gent girl guide who becomes a bar stripper. Upon her sudden return from New York City, where she has been pursuing her singing career all the while flirting with a Black female piano player, Kathleen dies giving birth to Lily, whose true father is revealed later in the novel to be none other than James himself. At this crucial point, and particularly after Kathleen's and Materia's deaths, the narrative sinks into a bleak and phantasmagoric drama where homosexuality, incest, crime, and racism constitute the family secrets with which the Piper sisters have to grapple before they reach self-knowledge and acceptance.

MacDonald's book has the makings of conventional Gothic: ghosts, graveyards, attics, secret chests, Roman Catholic superstition, deserted mines, creepy cats, hidden family secrets, incest, rape, and murder—but the ghost figure is perhaps the most persistently prominent of these. Ambrose, Lily's twin brother who died at childbirth, is a crucial spectral figure, not the least because he brings the entire narrative into focus, especially with regard to the traumas caused by domestic and public repression. However, before delving into the socio-psychical significance of Ambrose's ghost, I would like to examine how he first came into (un)being—that is, how he metamorphosed from short-lived presence, through haunting absence, to uncanny return. The second book opens with a particularly disturbing scene, not only because of the gory, graphic detail in which it is rendered and the mystery in which it is shrouded, but also because it marks the site of a terrifying event that has enduring traumatic effects on its witnesses. On Armistice Day, James Piper, now back from the war, receives an anonymous letter following which he hastily summons Kathleen back from New York. Eight months later, we know she is pregnant and is lying in the attic waiting to give birth. Using "the old kitchen scissors," Materia decides to undertake the surgery herself, killing her own daughter and saving only one of the twins, Lily (MacDonald [1996] 2003, 166). Ambrose dies shortly afterward. Eventually realizing that she has done "the right thing" (to have saved the children) — which is in keeping with the teachings of the Catholic Church — "for the wrong reason" (to have eliminated her own child/rival under the pretext of mercy killing), Materia undergoes a fatal crisis of faith that renders her life a horrifying impossibility (168–69). Three days later, she takes her own life using the gas oven.

Unsettling as it is, the parturition scene is a remarkable dramatization of Julia Kristeva's concept of "abjection" (1982). Not only does it adumbrate the horror typically invoked by gothic writing (musty attics, blood, macabre death, and decaying corpses), but it also enacts what Kristeva identifies, in *Powers of Horror: An Essay on Abjection*, as the self's primordial experience of abjection, an experience that sets in motion an entire process of repeated expulsion and repression. For Kristeva, the abject represents a disquieting otherness that is constantly thrust beyond the cognitive and recognizable realm of the self — although it often emanates from it: "It lies there, quite close, but it cannot be assimilated" by the "I" of the subject. The abject is that which lurks on the outskirts of the known and the acceptable, that which is constantly "ejected beyond the scope of the possible, the tolerable, the thinkable" (1).

More relevant to my argument, however, is the link between the process of abjecting the ostensibly defiled Other and the book's gothic anti-Catholicism. Kristeva argues that in Judeo-Christian scriptures, the abject is persistently associated with a defiling, transgressive, "threatening [often female] otherness" that is "always nameable, always totalizeable" and that must eventually be removed as impure excess (17). According to the church, Materia Mahmoud did the right thing when she sacrificed the mother to save the children, for to have preferred the life of the mother would have brought eternal damnation on her (MacDonald 168). Nevertheless, Materia knows "in her heart of hearts" that she has simply used religious sanction as a pretext to commit self-serving murder—that is, to dispose of her child/rival—something she cannot hide from "His all-seeing eyes" (169). As if to atone for her malefaction, Materia spends the next few days "obsessively" cleaning her household, only to take her own life shortly afterward (169). As a matter of fact, Materia's last-minute decision amounts less to mercy killing a daughter raped by an obsessed father than to deploying one of "[t]he various means of *purifying* the abject—the various catharses—[that] make up the history of religions" (Kristeva 1982, 17 [emphasis in original]). Experienced as loss caused by sin, Kathleen's abjection allows a "redemption or salvation to occur" and promises "a return to unity with the godhead" (LaCapra 1999, 702). It is an act of abjecting, albeit unwittingly, the unholy (m)other in the name of that "institutional Terrible Mother" (that is, the Roman Catholic Church), to which Materia becomes increasingly, if obsessively, devoted (Williams 1995, 117).

In this birth-giving/life-taking scene, MacDonald enacts the horror of potential death that haunts the self at the moment of its birth. While it describes the precariousness of inhabiting, albeit momentarily, that liminal space where the pre-self is *within* and *without* the mother's womb at the same time, the birthing of the twins symbolizes the first act of the self's traumatic separation from the mother and its expulsion/abjection into the outside world. Commenting on a similar birthing scene in Louis-Ferdinand Céline's *Rigadoon* (1974), Kristeva writes:

> The scene of scenes is here not the so-called primal scene but the one of giving birth, incest turned inside out, flayed identity. Giving birth: the height of bloodshed and life, scorching moment of hesitation (between inside and outside, ego and other, life and death), horror and beauty, sexuality and the blunt negation of the sexual. (1982, 155)

And here is how MacDonald renders the process of a twofold abjection whereby Kathleen is cast *out of* the world as defiled, incestuous (m)other, all the while her two infants are cast *into* the world as as-yet-unsplit subjectivity:

> The air splashes and spumes against it, threatening to drown it—*them*—for there are two but they have yet to be cut in half, they are still one creature, really, male and female segments joined at the belly by a common root sys-

tem. It-they is a blood breather and could drown in this fatal spray of oxygen, will drown if they remain silent much longer, will become bright blue fishes in a moment. But the cords are cut, *snip-snap,* and tied just in time, and in an instant the shocking air is gulped and strafed into the lungs. They become babies just in time; slick, bloody, new, wailing, squinting, furious, two. (MacDonald 166–67)

On the one hand, the birthing scene evokes gothic horror through the vivid dramatization of that "immemorial violence with which a body becomes separated from another body" (Kristeva 1982, 10). On the other hand, it echoes what Kristeva describes as the subject's "pre-objectal relationship" — that is, the subject's pre-symbolic consciousness of the world as law and as an alterity that is outside of, and underived from, the self (10). For Kristeva, as Anne Williams argues, gothic horror is "a function of the earliest stirrings of the pre-self's separation from the mother" (1995, 74). In other words, she explains, "[b]efore the speaking subject organizes itself around the split between itself and the other objects, it experiences the 'abject' (the 'cast off') as a sort of 'pre-object.'" While separating the Piper twins from their mother may represent the unavoidable, primal trauma of pre-objectal abjection, separating them from each other stands for the originary split within subjectivity itself as it enters the world of symbolicity. To be able to fit into the order of the signifier — that is, to interrupt its pre-natal silence and birth itself into a speaking/signifying subject — the self must surrender its inchoate ambivalence and amorphousness ("it-they") and become a definite and definable entity, an entity that is "nameable…totalizeable" and, thus, repressible (Kristeva 1982, 17). Lily and Ambrose represent, among other things, the two sides of a split subjectivity. The mark of that split is symbolized by Lily's corporeal but crippled foot and by Ambrose's etherealization into her ghostly double.

"All stories are haunted by the ghosts of the stories they might have been"

The symbolic split in identity at the moment of its origination also coincides with a rupture in the realist flow of the narrative itself. This rupture occurs when MacDonald, with a magic-realist sleight of hand and out of Frances's young but already perturbed mind, *re*-creates Ambrose as a ghost whose haunting presence keeps calling into question the seeming reality of the world that both characters and readers inhabit.[6] More precisely, it is during Materia's funeral, which takes place two days after Kathleen's, that Ambrose is *re*-birthed into a disembodied ghost haunting the margins of the narrative. Up to this point, he has been referred to as "Other Lily," the ethereal half of the real Lily. Now, Frances renames her brother/nephew, whom she has accidentally drowned while secretly baptizing him and Lily in the creek, after St. Ambrose, whose hallowed words are inscribed on the mass card:

> So she [Frances] concentrates on the mass card instead: *ST AMBROSE.* The name detaches itself from the card, leaving its holy prefix behind like a tail, and floats up into her mind, where it wafts about gently until it settles via some mysterious associative route upon the infant boy who died a few nights ago in her arms. Ambrose. Yes. That will be his name. Ambrose. (MacDonald 173)

Interestingly, the subsequent metamorphic *re*-birthing of Ambrose into a ghostly child out of France's infantile mind is also synchronous with the latter's sudden realization that the line between being and seeming is not always easily distinguishable. While the few who have attended the church ceremony are bidding mournful farewell to the departing Materia, Frances, strangely enough, succumbs to a paroxysm of laughter. To her amazement, instead of being "dragged in disgrace from the church" for her irreverent conduct, Frances is offered her "father's sympathetic hand" and Mercedes's "sodden hanky." "*They think I'm crying,*" she thinks:

> Frances learns something in this moment that will allow her to survive and function for the rest of her life. She finds out that one thing can look like another. That the facts of a situation don't necessarily indicate anything about the truth of a situation. In this moment, fact and truth become separated and commence to wander like twins in a fairy-tale, waiting to be reunited by that special someone who possesses the secret of telling them apart…. Some would simply say that Frances learned how to lie. (174 [emphasis in original])

Herein lies a hermeneutic aporia generated by gothic irony. In the church, a stock gothic *locus* for conjuring the otherworldly, MacDonald dramatizes the dissolution of what until now seems to be a clear boundary between the real and the non-real, and she does so by introducing ghostly figures whose intermittent manifestations immediately blur the line between seeming and being and inject an element of uncertainty and uncanniness into the narrative. As Julia Briggs suggests, "[g]host stories have multiple meanings, but one constant element is the challenge they offer to the rational order and the observed laws of nature" (2000, 122). Ambrose's uncanny entrance into the story deprives readers of the luxury of narrative "disambiguation," thus dislocating their smug illusions of truth, reality, and stable identity (Brooke-Rose 1981, 252). Spawned by Frances's mental musings, Ambrose slips into the scene as a disembodied character whose presence throws the readers adrift between reality and illusion, leaving them undecided whether this is going to be an other-worldly fairy tale, a gruesome horror story, or a bleak realist fiction.

From a Freudian perspective, one might go so far as to suggest that "enghosting" provokes a disruption of one's "reality testing" mechanism. Indeed, this is the readerly effect of ghosts populating ostensibly realist fiction. They infuse uncanniness into it—something they can hardly accomplish were one to encounter them in fairy tales (Freud [1919] 1955, 249–50). In realist fiction, one's judgment keeps interfering with the way that one reads and interprets the events by subjecting them to the laws of rationality and logic, whereas in fairy tales, as Freud intimates, one's disbelief is suspended from the start. However, when ghosts make *in medias res* appearances in what originally appears to be a (chrono)logical narrative (the way they do in MacDonald's novel), their effect is nothing less than a disquieting disruption of the reader's habitual modes of intelligibility. As Freud puts it, the author achieves uncanny effects "by promising to give us the sober truth, and then after all overstepping it," thus "betraying us to the superstitiousness which we have ostensibly surmounted" (250).

Ghostly apparitions in *Fall on Your Knees* usually take place at moments when the line between reality and fantasy is blurred. For instance, when Ambrose pays his first unannounced visit to Lily in his tattered baptismal gown, one is not sure whether she is asleep or awake—it is a state "somewhere in between" (MacDonald 279). It is a "shaded area" between "the place called Awake" and "the country of Asleep"; it is called "No Man's Land" (280). Later in the narrative and in the twilight zone between dream and reality, in this "No Man's Land" where the dead and the living may happen to cohabitate, Mr. Mahmoud has a similar uncanny experience, as he feels drawn by the music of a familiar, Oriental love song into the candle-lit front room of his house. There, he sees the ghost of his dead wife, Giselle, in a belly dancer's erotic apparel beckoning him to join her in her luscious dance (423–25). Giselle's ghost appears when the rubies she bequeathed to the family go missing, and Mr. Mahmoud regrets having fired Teresa Taylor, his faithful, lifetime Barbadian servant, for no reason other than his assumption that Black people are innately prone to kleptomania (406). While the spellbinding apparition of Giselle's ghost smacks of necrophilic nostalgia resulting from the discursive admixture of gothic horror and exotic delight at one and the same time, it returns, not to lure Mr. Mahmoud back to the familiar but forgotten pleasures of by-gone marital life but, rather, to remind him that unless he is able to identify the thin line between seeming and being, he will continue to be "a creature of habit" prone to regrettable, racial misjudgments (425).

In postcolonial narrative discourse, the apparition of the ghost is often related to the trope of return of an oppressed Other that haunts the oppressor. Read within the larger context of Canadian settler history, such narrativization of the gothic ghost may be said to mark both the manifestation of the white settler's fear of interracial mixing and the will — on the contemporary author's part at least — to re-imagine more constructive ways of re-scripting Canada's inevitable settler-invader history of displacement, abjection, and absentification. The ghost figure symbolizes not the return of the past, of history, or of a wished-for former identity but, rather, what could have been but was not. "All stories are haunted by the ghosts of the stories they might have been," says Salman Rushdie's narrator in *Shame* (1983, 116). Ambrose is the ghost of an untold story. His spectralization is a metaphor for the stillbirth of what might have otherwise been an enabling narrative. His is the voice of a narrative that yearns to be told but is arrested and silenced precisely at the instant of its conception, and the only way to birth it, to "presence" it, is through a trope of ghosting. Akin to a Derridean trace, Ambrose's narratological and ontological derivation can therefore be read as a reference to that which is there and not there at one and the same time — a presence whose only purpose is to gesture both towards and beyond its absence (Derrida 1994).[7] His frequent manifestations throughout the narrative, particularly to Lily, stand for the presencing of the "absented" narrative of the other.

If the Canadian idea of the nation, like ghost stories, is premised upon a "willing suspension of disbelief," then it is obviously a never-ending one (Sugars 2003, 2). Ghosts and identity (both racial and national) are placed in that liminal space, between reality and fiction, a "shaded area" where one's will to imagine is the *sine qua non* for the construction and potential deconstruction of the idea of the nation. The trope of ghosting in contemporary Canadian writing speaks all too readily not only to Canada's historical indebtedness to the displaced Aboriginals and other immigrant minorities but also to the spectrality of its current constructedness (Edwards 2005, xxix). By pursuing the correlation of incest, race, and subjectivity, I am arguing that Ambrose's ghost represents the haunting return of his father's fears of racial miscegenation. Furthermore, reading the gothic trope of ghosting the other within the larger context of Canada's settler identity, one begins to notice how such an identity is constantly grappling not only with its spectral others but also with its own spectrality. Hybrid and imagined though it is, Canadian national identity still feeds upon the chimera of an originary, mythopoeic idea of the nation, yet what that chimera usually spawns is an uncanny, spectral otherness that keeps re-turning and haunting the nation at large (in the same way that Ambrose keeps forcing himself into the Piper family history as well as into the narrative itself—despite Mercedes's attempts to write him out of the family tree that she is obsessively drawing).

Uncertainty and confusion about racial and national identities are triggered by the interaction of the multi-ethnic groups that populate the novel. I shall limit myself here to James's relationship with the Mahmouds and how this relationship raises issues of race, gender, and national belonging—all of which stymie the facile construction of an ostensibly unified, mono-racial settler identity. As early as the opening pages, one notices how the half-Scottish-half-Irish James is clearly befuddled by the way he is both drawn to, and repulsed by, the Mahmouds. For instance, when Mrs. Mahmoud offers him food, "he was *afraid* she'd feed him something *exotic* and *horrible*" (MacDonald 12 [emphasis added]). Moreover, when he meets Mrs. Mahmoud's daughter, the twelve-going-on-thirteen Materia, young James cannot help but yield to the exotic accent of her "Arabified" English: "She had an accent that she never did outgrow. A softening of consonants, a slightly liquid 'r,' a tendency to clip not with the lips but with the throat itself. What she did for the English language was pure music" (14). However, as soon as James knows that Materia has been betrothed to a Lebanese dentist since she was fourteen, he is quick to condemn the "Old Country" (Lebanon) and its "barbaric," "backward," and "savage" customs (16). Either enchanted by her childish charm or repulsed by the idea of losing her to this unknown suitor/rival (or both), James does whatever it takes to secure Materia for himself.

However, once he has "satisfied his lust for Materia," as Stevenson argues, James's racial prejudices against the Mahmouds come to the fore (2001, 44). And when his favourite daughter Kathleen is born, with her "[s]ilky red-gold hair, green eyes and white white skin," his prejudices become even more pronounced, so much so that he starts doubting the biological adequacy of his own wife, who is after all too young to breast-feed her first daughter, and he even goes as far as to accuse her of having lured him into a regrettable marriage:

> How had he been ensnared by a child? There was something not right about Materia. Normal children didn't run away with men. He knew from his read-ing that clinical simpletons necessarily had an overdeveloped *animal nature*. She had seduced him. That was why he hadn't noticed she was a child. Because she wasn't one. Not a real one. It was *queer*. Sick, even. Perhaps it was a *racial flaw*. He would read up on it. (MacDonald 41 [emphasis added])

Although James does not seem to be completely immersed in turn-of-the-century eugenicist discourse, his book crates, which he never ceases order-ing, include works by both Freud and Darwin — something that explains, at least partly, his tendency to attribute the purported intellectual imbe-cility and moral "deviance" of the non-white Other either to bio-psycho-logical queerness or to racial deficiency. It is worth noting that what seduced James first was Materia's skin colour, her "[s]ummer skin the colour of sand stroked by the tide" (14). Yet after seven years of not-so-felicitous marital life, "one of those things that [is] always before his eyes" is not the extra few pounds that Materia has now gained but, rather, the very darkness of her skin to which he was first drawn and by which he is now repulsed (45). Perplexed by Kathleen's seeming sexual perversity (her lesbian attraction to Rose, the Black piano player) and by his inability to determine its source, James presumes that she has inherited it from her mother:

> James is grateful that all his girls turned out so fair. But there's obviously a morbid tendency in the blood they inherited from Materia that made Kathleen lean towards colour. James has taken delivery of another crate of books. He has dipped into Dr Freud in an effort to discover where to lay the blame for Kathleen's perversity. Freud calls women "the dark continent." James couldn't agree more. He doesn't hate blacks, he just doesn't want them near his bloodline. (448–49)

James's anxieties stem from a disconcerting realization that even the white race, the perfect example of which would be his "peaches and cream" daughter (117), may have within it a "capacity for evil" (DeLamotte 2004, 26). Disavowing his own perverse and irrepressible interracial desire for the dark-skinned, under-aged Materia, James imputes Kathleen's attraction to a Black lover only to matrilineal biological determinants. It must come from a contaminated gene passed down to her by her Arab mother, for James himself, the white Scottish-Irish male, is neither an "*enkelese bastard*," as the Mahmouds like to call him, nor one of those "[f]ilthy black Syrians," as he mistakenly calls them (MacDonald 421 and 422). Moreover, James's conflation of race and gender is nowhere more obvious than it is in the above passage. For not only does he take Freud's phrase "dark continent" literally, associating darkness/blackness and women with threatening inscrutability, but he also subsumes virtually all dark races under the same category, including his in-laws who, interestingly enough, are neither white nor Black. And the deeper James delves into his readings of history, psychology, and biology, the more threatening Materia becomes in his eyes. For, now more than ever, she epitomizes the mysteriously dark and dangerous female, the "dark continent," from which he and his fair daughters should keep away.

James's Lebanese in-laws fulfil a symbolic function that is similar to that of ghosts in the story. Just as the ghost figure blurs the line between reality and fantasy, fact and fiction, so the figure of the white-but-not-quite Arab (in this case, the Mahmouds) disturbs the otherwise clear colour distinction between black and white. The figures of the gothic ghost and the exotic Arab function as disruptive elements in the normative and racialized construction of reality, identity, and otherness. The Mahmouds represent one of the many Canadian ethnicities whose exoticization in the narrative overlaps with their spectralization as excluded and repressed alterities (by such white settlers as James Piper). In terms of racial classification, then, the Mahmouds are neither black nor white — they are somewhere in between, in the space of the "no colour land," as it were. They are white but not quite, representing an immigrant minority whose skin colour allows it to straddle two cultures (black and white) without ever being completely immersed in either:

[T]he Mahmouds aren't really white, are they? They're something else. They are somewhat coloured. What this means in Nova Scotia at this time is that, for the Mahmouds, the colour bar that guards access to most aspects of society tends to be negotiable. It helps that they have money. (145)[8]

Their racial unclassifiability may be tentatively accommodated by what I venture to call the "exothic," a troping of the exotic as an index for cultural difference on the topography of the gothic where that difference may be enunciated. Both the exotic and the Gothic derive their effects from a representational process of "unhoming." The exotic is experienced as such (that is, as exotic) precisely because of its transposition onto an unhomely territory in which it loses its familiar referential grounds. Drawing on J.L. Austin's performative linguistics (1962), Peter Mason equates the geographical displacement of the exotic with the failure of utterances as they occur out of context and thus create an infelicitous dissonance in the intended message (1998, 6). Insofar as it is the effect of a recurrently infelicitous "process of decontextualization and recontextualization," Mason argues, "the exotic is never at home," much in the same way that the gothic ghost is perpetually homeless, doomed to roam the interstitial space between the real and the ethereal, the familiar and the unfamiliar. Troping the exotic on the narrative and psychic geography of the Gothic, therefore, throws into relief the ever-deterritorialized and haunting presence of the nation's multicultural (exotic) Others. The "exothic," therefore, becomes a useful means of conceptualizing the "postcolonial Gothic."

Like the hybrid, uncanny figure of the mulatto, "whose existence acts as proof of miscegenation, the emblem of subversion of racial categories," the Mahmouds and their racial indeterminacy allow MacDonald to deploy exotic tropes in such a way as to draw attention to the uncanny ambivalence of such notions as race, gender, subjectivity, and national identity (Lamothe 2004, 59).[9] The oppression of un-knowable, thus indefinable, diasporic minorities such as the Mahmouds creates what Justin Edwards, by way of Derridean spectrology, describes as "a form of spectral citizenship that haunts the nation" — that is, an uncanny "citizenship wherein the Other inhabits a strangely familiar ground that is simultaneously homely and unhomely" (2005, 48). The spectral liminality of Canadian immigrant populations (such as Arabs, Jews, and Africans) betrays the othering process of displacement and dispossession upon which Canadian settler politics was originally founded. "[T]he act of dispossession," Edwards insists, inevitably "leads to spectralization." And "the liminal sta-

CANADIAN GOTHIC AND THE WORK OF GHOSTING

tus of spectrality—the in-between position held by the dispossessed other—produces a phantasmic figure that slowly contaminates the centre by introducing itself as an unassimilable force" (49–50). The narrative *exothicization* of the Mahmouds, therefore, shakes the illusion of a solid and stable national identity based on clear-cut racial and colour categories and illustrates the fact that subjectivities are by definition insubstantial and spectral.

James's incestuous relationship with his two daughters (Kathleen and Frances), one may argue, is an externalization of his profound anxiety about blood mixing. If Jameel, Mr. Mahmoud's son-in-law with whom James transacts temporarily the speakeasy business, is a fool because he wears the fear of "being seen as coloured" on his sleeve, then James decidedly wears his fear of miscegenation somewhere else (MacDonald 448). So ingrained is the idea of ethnic purity in his mind that inseminating his own daughter, albeit unconsciously, would be the only way to keep the bloodline untainted—to keep it in the family, as it were: "That's when the fear goes out of him" (469). Perpetrating a greater sin (incest), James abjects onto his own daughter his fear of miscegenation, of losing her to this "modern evil [that is] weakening the fabric of our nation," as the "Anonymous Well-Wisher" puts it in *her* letter (291).[10] Miscegenation is that "unclean" abject whose ghost is hovering threateningly above James's world of "the possible, the tolerable, the thinkable" (Kristeva 1982, 1). While Materia abjects Kathleen on the basis of religious unholiness, James does the same thing but on the basis of racial uncleanness. By turning Ambrose into a returning spectre of incestuous rape, MacDonald gestures towards the failure of two myths: maintaining a pure, patriarchal genealogy and constructing a national identity based on a totalizing, exclusionary ideology. MacDonald's narrativization of the ghost undercuts the racial, sexual, and religious oppression that have shaped inter-settler relationships in early twentieth-century Canada, all the while underscoring the lasting traumatic impact that such oppression may have on its victims.

"Memory is another word for story, and nothing is more unreliable"

Cathy Caruth's collection of seminal essays in *Trauma: Explorations in Memory* revolves around the question of how to treat psychic trauma without downplaying the reality and intensity of its impact on those who suffer from it—that is, without encouraging the patient to ignore or to forget the events that led to it (1995, vii). In the preface, Caruth argues that symptoms of post-traumatic stress disorder (PTSD), such as nightmares, flashbacks, and hallucinations, indicate not only a belated and/or distorted response to a traumatizing event but also a necessarily *partial* integration into consciousness of the event at the time of its occurrence. The experience of trauma is so overwhelmingly intense in its immediacy and terror that its assimilation into consciousness by those who go through it takes place only belatedly (6). The PTSD symptom, Caruth explains, marks "the literal return of the event against the will of the one who inhabits it." And it is the very "literality" of the traumatic event and its forceful and "nonsymbolic" return that constitute the pathology of trauma. Caruth postulates that trauma designates above all "a delay or an incompletion in knowing, or even seeing, an overwhelming occurrence that then remains, in its insistent return, absolutely *true* to the event" (5 [emphasis in original]). PTSD thus becomes "not so much a symptom of the unconscious, as it is a symptom of history" (5). It is the symptom of a history that has not been completely possessed by its victims and/or witnesses.

The structure of trauma is marked by "inherent forgetting" and belated return (8). This historical displacement of trauma has crucial implications for psychoanalysis since the modalities of psychotherapy can no longer rely exclusively on presumed childhood fantasies, forbidden drives, or historically fixed scenes (8–9). Since the traumatic event is defined essentially by the impossibility of its immediate cognition and integration as well as by its inevitably delayed return, psychoanalysis becomes constitutively linked to the reality and structure of traumatic survival. For the traumatized subject, "it is not only the moment of the event, but the passing out of it that is traumatic." It is "*surviving itself,* in other words, that *can be a crisis*" (9 [emphasis in original]). Since the *locus* of trauma is no longer simply the event itself but the outliving of it, etiological psychoanalysis therefore becomes less "a statement about others" than a "statement *of* survival" (9 [emphasis in original]). The delayed verbalization of trauma, along with the concurrent transferential mechanism that it sets in motion, thus ordains and shapes the modalities of analytic psychotherapy.

The overwhelming horror of the traumatic experience is such that it creates a schism in knowing that can be filled only through belated verbalization. Holocaust scholar Dori Laub notes that the cognitive inaccessibility of trauma results in what he describes as the "collapse of witnessing"—that is, the failure of the trauma survivor to be a witness to what he or she has survived (1995, 65). Through belated but conscious verbalization, however, the trauma survivor shares his or her experience with another listener, a listener who might or might not be a survivor/witness him- or herself. The telling of the traumatic event is a way of exercising over it, albeit belatedly, the power of conscious witnessing. Giving trauma a narrative frame amounts to "setting the stage for a reliving, a reoccurrence of the traumatic event, in the presence of a witness" (69). In other words, narrating the trauma creates a distance between the event and the ennuciatory position of its survivor, and, by virtue of that distance, the survivor-turned-narrator assumes the temporary role of an external witness to the event. For "*being inside the event*" at the time of its occurrence often makes "unthinkable the very notion that a witness could exist" (66 [emphasis in original]). Such is the power of storying: it subjects trauma to a salutary narrative will. Narrative recovering of the traumatic experiences of the past amounts to (re)admitting them into the realm of consciousness, all the while sharing the pain they involve with another listener-witness. Torn between "the imperative to tell" and the "impossibility of telling," trauma survivors usually cocoon themselves in the haunted house of silence (64): "There is, in each survivor, an imperative need to *tell* and thus to *know* one's story, unimpeded by ghosts from the past against which one has to protect oneself" (63 [emphasis in original]). Yet because of the absence of an ideal audience—that is, of an audience that can be sufficiently "self-effacing" to act fully and authentically as a substitute for the loss experienced by the survivor—the latter often retreats into silence and secrecy (63, 67). The Holocaust survivor's repression of the traumatic event thus leads to the gradual distortion of the event and ultimately to the survivor's perception of him- or herself as being responsible for, rather than "authentic witness to," it (65).

In order to reverse such a collapse of witnessing and bring to an end the anguish of solitary silence to which the survivor confines him- or herself, there must be a will to tell by virtue of which a therapeutic "re-possession of the act of witnessing" is allowed to occur. And "[i]t is the encounter and the coming together between the survivor and the listener," Laub claims, "which makes possible something like a repossession of the act of witnessing" (69). Through such an encounter, retrospective testimony restores the truth of the event and allows the victim of trauma to recover "the internal 'thou,' and thus the possibility of a witness or a listener inside himself" (70).

In *Fall on Your Knees,* James's violent rape can be understood as a clear attempt to force a white, heterosexual imperative on Kathleen, though its violence and overwhelming repercussions are terrifying even to him. The traumatic effect of his act resides less in his failure to remember it than in his failure to halt its persistent *re*occurrence. His adamant disapproval of Kathleen's sexuality, on the one hand, and the unavailability of an adequate social framework that allows him to cope with the traumatic loss he brought upon his family (Kathleen's rape and death and Materia's suicide), on the other hand, bind him to a cycle of repeated abuse directed towards Frances. Since the "shameful" truth about Kathleen's pregnancy and death is not, and cannot be made, public, the "official [that is, public] version" has it that she simply died of influenza while giving birth to a single, fatherless child, thus foreclosing James's chance to mourn and confess and confining him instead to a private prison-house of recurrent abuse and relentless personal guilt (MacDonald 203).

Although he may seem traumatized by the repercussions of his incestuous acts, James is still to be held accountable for them. His redemption, however, begins precisely when he wills to "story" the trauma he has inflicted — that is, when he repossesses the position of a "witness to [him]self" as the principal agent of his family's tragedy (Laub 1995, 61). One day, on the veranda, he tells Frances the story, "*his* story," of what happened in New York, and it took him six long days to exorcize the "steamy ghosts" of his tale — to the expected befuddlement of Mercedes who walks by everyday wondering what both her father and sister are up to (MacDonald 542–43). As he unfolds his own version of the story, "Frances doesn't interject. She doesn't look at him. She knows he will fly away if she does that, so she relaxes and listens to his story" (542). It is here that the "storying" process effects the transference of affect that is essential to the working through of traumatic loss. By consciously and *verbally* re-cathecting his experience in the presence of one of his victims, who also becomes "an empathic listener," James is able to acknowledge the demon of personal guilt and move from the aporia of moribund melancholia to the agency of post-traumatic mourning (Felman and Laub 1992, 68). The act of storying his crime instantiates a metamorphosis from compulsive re-enactment to therapeutic reclamation.

Just as James repeats the original rape by acting it out on Frances, so the latter repeats the original trauma of being a witness to, then a victim of, sexual abuse by displacing its affects onto her yet-all-too-gullible little sister, Lily.[11] In "Beyond the Pleasure Principle," Freud suggests that repetition of unpleasure disguises a primary intention of mastery ([1920] 1991). Unpleasure can be mastered if deliberately repeated, thus leading to a form of sado-masochism. The *fort-da* child repeats the unpleasurable experience of its mother's departure so as to master that experience as a whole and also to revel in the ultimate pleasure of her return. Freud describes this process as "an instinct for mastery that was acting independently of whether the memory was in itself pleasurable or not" (285). Frances's quasi sado-masochistic re-enactment of the primary unpleasure caused first by the horrifying scene of her sister's death and then by the incomprehensibility of her father's incestuous conduct takes the form of numerous gothic horror stories with which she torments Lily.[12] The following passage represents only one sample of those stories:

Lily waits. Listens. Frances tells the story:

"On the day you both [Ambrose and Lily] were born, a stray orange cat came in through the cellar door. It climbed the cellar steps. It climbed the front hall steps. It climbed all the way up to the attic without a sound. It came in here where you both were sleeping and it leapt into your crib. It put its mouth over Ambrose's face and sucked the breath out of him. He turned blue and died. Then the orange cat put its paws on your chest and it was about to do the same thing to you but I came in and saved you. Daddy took the orange cat and drowned it in the creek. Then he buried it in the garden. In the spot where the scarecrow used to be but now there's a stone. I helped."

Lily doesn't move a muscle. (MacDonald 253)

While Lily may be the substitute on whom Frances playfully revenges herself, in the same way that a "child passes *over* from the passivity of the experience to the activity of the game" by passing *on* "the disagreeable experience to one of his playmates" (Freud [1920] 1991, 286 [emphasis added]), Frances's infantile "instinct for mastery" allows her to work through her trauma by remembering shreds of memory of it and re-weaving them into gothic scenarios. If James's verbalization of his experience takes the form of an agonizingly belated confession, Frances's expression of her experiences starts as an inchoate collection of memory fragments and semi-fictive gothic scenarios that ultimately crystallizes into a meaningful narrative precisely following her father's confession. By relating horror stories of drowning infants, predatory cats, buried bodies, half-alive scarecrows, guardian angels—stories relating mainly to the traumatic incident, namely Kathleen's death in childbirth, which Frances had witnessed, and the latter's risky attempt to baptize both Ambrose and Lily in the creek—not only does Frances experience the temporary cathartic (un)pleasure of repeating and *re*-witnessing their affective impact on her sister, but she also hopes to gain mastery over her life and to make sense of the world around her. While Frances's fabricated gothic stories symbolize the unconscious re-enactment on Lily of the trauma caused by Kathleen's grisly death, they also indicate a modality of working through that trauma by trying to accommodate it consciously within a comprehensible narrative frame.

An un-confessed or non-verbalized trauma is potentially subject to repetition and distortion. Verbalizing the trauma, Laub notes, is crucial to the victim's well-functioning in everyday life: "The [Holocaust] survivors did not only need to survive so that they could tell their stories; they also needed to tell their stories in order to survive" (1995, 63). While telling the story of the trauma, Laub continues, helps release the victim from the clutches of its returning ghosts, "'not telling' [it] serves as a perpetuation of its tyranny. The events become more and more distorted in their silent retention and pervasively invade and contaminate the survivor's daily life. The longer the story remains untold, the more distorted it becomes in the survivor's conception of it, so much so that the survivor doubts the reality of the actual events" (64). Gothic *re-emplotment* in *Fall on Your Knees*, I argue, designates an attempt to survive the trauma and to halt its tyrannical re-enactment by tentatively speaking its otherwise unspeakable truth. Two days after Kathleen's death, Frances's "cave mind" (unconscious) interfaces with her "voluntary mind" (conscious) in an attempt to accommodate the inconceivable horror of what it has witnessed:

> By now she has already lost her conscious grip on the events of two nights ago, when the babies were born. She has shivered them away. The cave mind has entered into a creative collaboration with the voluntary mind, and so the two of them will cocoon memory in a spinning wealth of dreams and yarns and fingerpaintings. Fact and truth, fact and truth. (MacDonald 185)

The parturition scene was too frightening to be immediately registered by Frances as conscious memory. Rather, it had to be stowed away in her "cave mind" as a yet unintegrated, unconscious memory:

> The difference between Frances and James is that, although she sees a version of the same horrible picture, Frances is young enough still to be under the greater influence of the cave mind. It will never forget. But it steals the picture from her voluntary mind—grand theft art—and stows it, canvas side to the cave wall. It has decided, "if we are to continue functioning, we can't have this picture lying around." (179)

Resisting incorporation into already "existing meaning schemes," the scene is instantly stored by Frances as an unassimilated "traumatic memory," fragments of which keep resurging as disturbing "recollections and behavioral reenactments" (van der Kolk and van der Hart 1995, 160).[13] In order for those disturbing memory fragments to be assimilated into what Pierre Janet calls "narrative memory," and be part of those "mental constructs [that] people use to make sense out of experience" (quoted in van der Kolk and van der Hart 1995, 160), Frances must re-possess the act of (re)-witnessing the scene either by listening to her father's story or by telling it herself to Lily.

In Janet's constructivist model, while traumatic memory consists of compulsive, solitary, and invariably mechanistic re-enactments of the traumatic scene, narrative memory consists of the conscious retrieval (through verbalization) of that scene and its flexibly meaningful re-integration into the social and historical context of its original occurrence and subsequent remembering (quoted in van der Kolk and van der Hart 1995, 163). It is this attempt to re-contextualize narrativistically that allows the traumatized subject to fill the cognitive hiatus created by the event at the moment of its occurrence and to re-attach that event and its attendant affects to the pre-existing and more cohesive structures of ordinary (narrative) memory.

An untold story is one that is potentially inhabited by distortion (Laub 1995, 64). Unless Frances remembers and tells the story of what happened, her everyday life will remain haunted by gaps and distorted memories. As both victim of, and witness to, unintelligible parental/paternal abuse, Frances spends several years incessantly remembering and constructing presumably meaningful and comprehensible narratives in which the abuse can be assimilated. For instance, while she is eavesdropping on the household of Leo Taylor, the Ginger Man whom she still believes to be Lily's father and with whom she later has her illegitimate Black child, Anthony, her conscious mind delves into her childhood memories, pulling those shivers of "dreams and yarns and fingerpaintings" out of "their silent retention," and strives to reason its way out of the enigma that is her sister's and nephew's demise:

> Kathleen is Lily's mother, Ambrose drowned because we don't know why, Kathleen was not married, she had a tumour in her belly but she didn't really, there was a secret father, it was Ginger—he drove her and they fell in love on the way to school, that's why Daddy says don't play that coloured music from the hope chest—he sent Kathleen to New York Town but Ginger followed in his truck, Daddy took her home again but it was too late, she died of twins. (MacDonald 399)

Although "nothing is more unreliable" than "memory" and "story," as MacDonald's narrator suggests, they become the very means whereby Frances brings her childhood trauma to affective closure: "Frances needs to say a story out loud to divine how much truth runs beneath its surface" (336, 398). Both Frances and James were witnesses to the horror of Kathleen's death. Yet while James seeks solace in alcohol-enhanced oblivion, Frances struggles for an enabling sense of truth by relentlessly recollecting and storying that which still lies beyond her comprehension. In an effort to fathom the truth behind Kathleen's pregnancy and death, she remembers and concocts ever-changing gothic scenarios. Such scenarios may be said to fulfil two functions in the narrative: to suggest that truth and identity are fleeting and untenable constructs and that "storying" is nevertheless the vehicle, if not the origin, of both. In fact, by re-collecting and re-arranging the incidents surrounding and leading up to her sister's death, Frances passes over from the receptivity of a "secondary witness" to the agency of a narrator-artificer (LaCapra 1999, 699). Indeed, she becomes "that special someone who possesses the secret" of distinguishing "the facts of a situation" from "the truth of a situation" (MacDonald 174). Yet it is only upon James's decision to share his own story with her that she is able to reminisce and successfully piece together the shards of childhood memory still lingering in her "cave mind" and to construct what seems, to her at least, a meaningful (that is, an assimilable) story. As soon as "[James's] story is done," Frances's phantasmagoric and gothic scenarios reach, in their turn, formal and relatively meaningful closure (543). What makes Frances's and James's "repossession of the act of witnessing" possible is precisely their "joint responsibility" as addresser and addressee in their conscious re-telling of the trauma. It is their engagement in an empathic "testimonial enterprise" as willing witnesses to and conscious "co-owner[s]" of each other's traumas that exorcizes the ghost of compulsive re-enactment and initiates the process of post-traumatic mourning (Felman and Laub 1992, 70 and 57).

This repossession of the act of witnessing through empathic sharing and unremitting re-emplotment can be read in tandem with the "kind of suspension of disbelief" that allows a re-imagining, through narrative, of a "cohesive" sense of identity (personal and/or national) despite the knowledge that this re-imagining "is always partial and tentative" (Sugars 2003, 2). The story that Frances eventually tells Lily may be "tentative and partial," but it is by no means meaningless:

> "She [Kathleen] went to New York," says Frances. "She was an opera singer. Something happened there. Daddy brought her home. She lay in this room and never said a word. Ambrose drowned in the creek. It was an accident. You didn't drown, you got polio instead. *I was there.*" (MacDonald 549 [emphasis added])

After her father's confession, Frances consciously claims her position as a witness to herself — "I was there" — and takes cognizance of the gruesome scenes of her sister's death and Ambrose's drowning and integrates them into a relatively cohesive and meaningful narrative memory — one that is "relatively cohesive and meaningful" because Lily, to whom the narrative is bequeathed, is still left in the dark about her and Ambrose's true father and about the incest. Yet perhaps this is not of primary importance after all. What is important is that Ambrose, her half-human half-spectral brother, "has become Lily's story. Frances has finally succeeded in giving him to her" (346). The inscription of trauma and its ghostly return within the enclosure of language (that is, narrative) is not so much a guarantee for its preservation and containment as it is a vehicle for its transgenerational migration. In fact, Lily's most valuable inheritance is not the restored scroll on which Mercedes has obsessively inscribed and preserved the names of the family members (with the significant exclusion of the unbaptized Ambrose) but, rather, the variable gothic stories that Frances strove to tell her about Other Lily (Ambrose) — stories she memorizes and is willing to re-construct after her own fashion and pass on to forthcoming generations. Interestingly enough, the book ends with Lily, the infant of incest, unravelling to Anthony, the infant of miscegenation, the tangled story of the Piper family as it is cryptically inscribed on the scroll that he brought to New York where Lily is now sharing an apartment with Rose. MacDonald seems to suggest that the possession *and* transmission of stories, painfully ineffable and fragmentary though they may be, is probably more gratifying and more valuable than any other "family heirloom" (176). For in *re*-telling them and sharing them with others, one occasionally stumbles upon a "trick of light" that reveals, if only for a moment, the fleeting spectrality of one's own being (555). This echoes MacDonald's recent statement about the healing nature of all forms of traumatic confession. In her "Author's Note" for the 2009 National Arts Centre production of her play *Belle Moral*, she writes:

> [A]s long as there are stories, there is hope. If even one person — or indeed, creature — is able to emerge from the rubble of our own making to say, "I remember what happened. Listen, and I'll tell you," that's a happy ending. Bearing witness can be just that: the carrying of a heavy load that eventually must be shared. As long as there is one ancient, flea-bitten, parched and starving mariner able to stagger up to a wedding party and tell his or her tale, there is compassion. (2009, n.p.)

Gothic writing in *Fall on Your Knees* shows how racial and national identities are after-effects of narrative imagination, in the same way that spectres are the effect of blurred distinctions between seeming and being. Brought together, the two highlight processes of "exothic" othering, which underscore the inevitable resurfacing, yet potential transcendence, of colonialist dynamics. Racial and identitarian paradigms are subversively re-inscribed through what David Eng and David Kazanjian describe as the "politics of mourning," whereby the "interpretation [and re-production] of what remains" — that is, the storying of the haunting and traumatizing return of the repressed — occasions liberating and re-defining moments of enunciation (2003, ix). To mourn the traumatic loss and/or abjection of the Other, one must reconcile oneself with its returning ghost and haunting remnants. The return of the ghost thus fulfils two purposes: it triggers the remembering and mourning of those one has lost and/or repressed while gesturing towards the uncanny ambivalence of subjectivity itself through a constant repositioning of the enunciatory "I" of the haunted but ineluctably mourning subject.

Notes

1   See particularly Michelle A. Massé's "Psychoanalysis and the Gothic" (2000).

2   In *Gothic Passages: Racial Ambiguity and the American Gothic*, Justin Edwards ends his analysis of Edgar Allan Poe's *Pym* (1986) with an insightful remark on how both Freud's theory of the uncanny and "gothic epistemology" may help uncover anxieties about racial mixing: "The theory of the uncanny is as much about reading, misreading, writing, and language as it is about the return of the repressed. Indeed, Freud's theory of the uncanny seems to confirm the participation of psychoanalysis in gothic epistemology and narrative structures by laying bare certain hidden forces of terror. In other words, Freud gestures towards an inquiry into the discursive materialization of such hidden forces in narrative (Savoy 10)" (2003, 16).

3   "Hauntropology" is a combination of "haunting" and "tropology," which designates the use of specific gothic tropes and motifs (such as returning ghosts, graveyards, musty dungeons, and creaky attics, and so on) whereby an effect of uncanniness and "being haunted" — "hauntedness" — is created.

4   Commemorative public events are highly significant in Canadian national culture: Remembrance Day, "*Je me souviens*," "Lest we Forget," and so on — all indicate a resistance to collective amnesia and a concomitant desire to construct a Canadian national identity based on the commemoration (that is, the repeated act of public remembering and mourning) of common loss.

5   The *Canadian Review of American Studies* published a special issue on Ann-Marie MacDonald's *Fall on Your Knees*, yet it features only one essay, by Gabriella Parro (2005), that deals with the book's gothicism. Parro's argument reiterates Pilar Somacarrera's thesis (2004) in that it focuses on MacDonald's re-deployment of gothic tropes, particularly that of "hauntedness," so as to critique racial and gender prejudice in early twentieth-century Cape Breton.

6   For a discussion of MacDonald's use of magic realism, see Jennifer Andrews's "Rethinking the Relevance of Magic Realism for English-Canadian Literature: Reading Ann-Marie MacDonald's *Fall on Your Knees*" (1999).

7   Here I draw on Dominick LaCapra's distinction between absence and loss (1999, 700). While the former is understood as a "transhistorical" non-event that "does not imply tenses (past, present, future)," the latter is understood as "historical event" that can "be reactivated, reconfigured, and transformed in the present and the future." The ghost in the novel marks a narrative re-activation, not of an absolute absence but, rather, of specific historical loss resulting from a (witting or unwitting) process of absentification.

8   Ironically enough, and as Stevenson remarks (2001, 43), the Mahmouds' racial/colour difference does not prevent Mr. Piper from doing business with them, nor does it prevent Mr. Mahmoud, early in the novel, from welcoming the piano tuner, the "*enklese* bastard" and the "yellow-haired dog," into his own family (MacDonald

[1996] 2003, 421 and 420). Colour barriers can be ignored if there is profitable business in the equation.

9 In her analysis of Toomer's *Cane* (1923), Daphne Lamothe argues that the Gothic is exceptionally suited for the narrativization of the Mulatto figure mainly because its generic indeterminacy, as well as its interest in themes of death, incest, and transgression of established social and moral norms, approximates the Mulatto's racial ambiguity and resistance to colour categorization (2004, 56). Similarly, in *Fall on Your Knees,* the ontological *unheimlich* of the gothic spectre mirrors the racial ambiguity of the Arab/Lebanese figure. More precisely, both the Arab other and the ghost figure in the novel allow MacDonald to call into question the normative and binaristic construction of reality, identity, and alterity.

10 The author of this letter is later revealed to be none other than Rose's white mother who was herself cast out because of her involvement with a Black man.

11 Here Dominick LaCapra describes the post-traumatic process of mourning among victims as a "necessary acting out" (a repetition compulsion mechanism — tendency to relive past trauma in the present) and that among "secondary witnesses" as a sort of "empathic unsettlement" (1999, 699). Frances is not only a secondary witness to the primary trauma of her sister's death, but she is also a victim of her father's acting out or repeating the trauma of which he is the primary agent. Frances is the victim of a victim's repetition compulsion.

12 I use Frances's sado-masochism here as a reference to a constellation of post-traumatic stress disorder (PTSD) symptoms (such as self-destructiveness, self-humiliation, shame, and emotional numbing), which she displays throughout the novel. For instance, she finds subtle pleasure in tormenting her sister with numerous horror stories about Kathleen's and Ambrose's deaths, in defying her father's commands and in being punished for it, and in exposing herself to humiliation by working as a stripper in a run-down bar owned by Jameel, Mr. Mahmoud's son-in-law. For a more detailed account of clinically diagnosed PTSD symptoms, see the American Psychiatric Association's fourth edition of the *Diagnostic and Statistical Manual of Mental Health Disorders* (1994).

13 Drawing on Pierre Janet's theory of dissociation, van der Kolk and van der Hart note that "under extreme conditions, existing meaning schemes may be entirely unable to accommodate frightening experiences, which causes the memory of these experiences to be stored differently and not be available for retrieval under ordinary conditions: it becomes dissociated from conscious awareness and voluntary control" (1995, 160). "Traumatic memories," they explain, "are the unassimilated scraps of overwhelming experiences, which need to be integrated with the existing mental schemes, and be transformed into narrative language" (176). In the novel, Frances constructs various gothic scenarios for the parturition scene in an effort to transform it into narrative memory and therefore be able to cope with its overwhelming terror.

Works Cited

American Psychiatric Association. 1994. *Diagnostic and Statistical Manual of Mental Health Disorders.* 4th edition. Washington, DC: American Psychiatric Association.

Andrews, Jennifer. 1999. "Rethinking the Relevance of Magic Realism for English Canadian Literature: Reading Ann-Marie MacDonald's *Fall on Your Knees.*" *Studies in Canadian Literature* 24(1): 1–19.

Austin, J. L. 1962. *How to Do Things with Words.* Oxford: Oxford UP.

Bhabha, Homi. 1994. *The Location of Culture.* London: Routledge.

Botting, Fred. 1996. *Gothic.* London: Routledge.

Briggs, Julia. 2000. "The Ghost Story." In *A Companion to the Gothic.* Ed. David Punter. Oxford: Blackwell. 122–31.

Brooke-Rose, Christine. 1981. *A Rhetoric of the Unreal: Studies in Narrative and Structure, Especially of the Fantastic.* Cambridge: Cambridge UP.

Caruth, Cathy, ed. 1995. *Trauma: Explorations in Memory.* Baltimore: Johns Hopkins UP.

Céline, Louis-Ferdinand. 1974. *Rigadoon.* Trans. Ralph Manheim. New York: Dell.

DeLamotte, Eugenia. 2004. "White Terror, Black Dreams: Gothic Constructions of Race in the Nineteenth Century." In *The Gothic Other: Racial and Social Constructions in the Literary Imagination.* Ed. Ruth A. Anolik and Douglas L. Howard. Jefferson, NC: McFarland. 17–31.

Derrida, Jacques. 1994. *Specters of Marx: The State of the Debt, the Work of Mourning and the New International.* Trans. Peggy Kamuf. New York: Routledge.

Edwards, Justin D. 2003. *Gothic Passages: Racial Ambiguity and the American Gothic.* Iowa: University of Iowa Press.

———. 2005. *Gothic Canada: Reading the Spectre of a National Literature.* Alberta: University of Alberta Press.

Eng, L. David, and David Kazanjian, eds. 2003. *Loss: The Politics of Mourning.* Berkeley: University of California Press.

Felman, Shoshana, and Dori Laub. 1992. *Testimony: Crises of Witnessing in Literature, Psychoanalysis, and History.* New York: Routledge.

Freud, Sigmund. 1919, reprinted 1955. "The 'Uncanny.'" In *The Standard Edition of the Complete Psychological Works of Sigmund Freud,* volume 17. Trans. James Strachey. London: Hogarth. 219–52.

———. 1920, reprinted 1991. "Beyond the Pleasure Principle." In *On Metapsychology: The Theory of Psychoanalysis.* Ed. Angel Richards. Trans. James Strachey. London: Penguin. 269–339.

Hall, Stuart. 2003. "Cultural Identity and Diaspora." In *Theorizing Diaspora: A Reader.* Ed. Jana Evans Braziel and Anita Mannur. Malden, MA: Blackwell. 233–46.

Kristeva, Julia. 1982. *Powers of Horror: An Essay on Abjection.* Trans. Leon S. Roudiez. New York: Columbia UP.

LaCapra, Dominick. 1999. "Trauma, Absence, Loss." *Critical Inquiry* 25(4): 696–727.

Lamothe, Daphne. 2004. "*Cane:* Jean Toomer's Gothic Black Modernism." In *The Gothic Other: Racial and Social Constructions in the Literary Imagination.* Ed. Ruth A. Anolik and Douglas L. Howard. Jefferson, NC: McFarland. 54–71.

Laub, Dori. 1995. "Truth and Testimony: The Process and the Struggle." In *Trauma: Explorations in Memory.* Ed. Cathy Caruth. Baltimore: Johns Hopkins UP. 61–75.

MacDonald, Ann-Marie. 1996, reprinted 2003. *Fall on Your Knees.* Toronto: Seal Books.

———. 2009. "Author's Note." In *National Arts Centre English Theatre 08/09: Belle Moral: A Natural History* [theatre program]. Ottawa: National Arts Centre. n.p.

Mason, Peter. 1998. *Infelicities: Representations of the Exotic.* Baltimore: Johns Hopkins UP.

Massé, Michelle. 2000. "Psychoanalysis and the Gothic." In *A Companion to the Gothic.* Ed. David Punter. Oxford: Blackwell. 229–41.

Parro, Gabriella. 2005. "'Who's Your Father, Dear?' Haunted Bloodlines and Miscegenation in Ann-Marie MacDonald's *Fall on Your Knees.*" *Canadian Review of American Studies* 35(2): 177–93.

Poe, Edgar Allan. 1838, reprinted 1986. *The Narrative of Arthur Gordon Pym of Nantucket.* New York: Penguin.

Punter, David. 1980. *The Literature of Terror: A History of Gothic Fiction from 1765 to the Present Day.* London: Longman.

———, ed. 2000. *A Companion to the Gothic.* Oxford: Blackwell.

Rukszto, Katarzyna. 2000. "Out of Bounds: Perverse Longings, Transgressive Desire and the Limits of Multiculturalism: A Reading of *Fall on Your Knees.*" *International Journal of Canadian Studies* 2: 17–34.

Rushdie, Salman.1983. *Shame.* London: Jonathan Cape.

Somacarrera, Pilar. 2004. "A Madwoman in a Cape Breton Attic: *Jane Eyre* in Ann-Marie MacDonald's *Fall on Your Knees.*" *Journal of Commonwealth Literature* 39(1): 55–75.

Stevenson, Melanie A. 2001. "Othello, Darwin, and the Evolution of Race in Ann-Marie MacDonald's Work." *Canadian Literature* 168: 34–56.

Sugars, Cynthia. 2003. "Haunted by (a Lack of) Postcolonial Ghosts: Settler Nationalism in Jane Urquhart's *Away.*" *Essays on Canadian Writing* 79: 1–32.

Toomer, Jean. 1923. *Cane.* New York: Boni and Liveright.

Van der Kolk, Bessel A., and Onno van der Hart. 1995. "The Intrusive Past: The Flexibility of Memory and the Engraving of Trauma." In *Trauma: Explorations in Memory.* Ed. Cathy Caruth. Baltimore: Johns Hopkins UP. 158–82.

Williams, Anne. 1995. *Art of Darkness: A Poetics of Gothic.* Chicago: University of Chicago Press.

CHAPTER SEVEN

A Ukrainian-Canadian Gothic?: Ethnic Angst in Janice Kulyk Keefer's *The Green Library*

Lindy Ledohowski

Ukrainians in Canada find themselves in an interesting position *vis-à-vis* discourses of postcolonialism. Since the first immigrants from Ukraine arrived and settled on the Canadian prairie in 1891[1] and approximately 170,000 more Ukrainians arrived between 1896 and 1914 (with successive waves of immigration at different points throughout the twentieth century),[2] they can be considered at least partially complicit with the colonial project that saw Aboriginal peoples marginalized and displaced from their traditional lands. However, these Ukrainian settlers were also considered ethnic minorities and found themselves limited linguistically, economically, and politically and thus cannot be equated simply with the imperial seat of power. Ukrainian Canadians, therefore, may find themselves in a position similar to other colonized subjects, but their status as not-quite colonial settler nor colonized Aboriginal leaves them in between the binary poles of the colonized and colonizer. They are both and neither.

In her analysis of the politics of home in postcolonial fiction, Rosemary Marangoly George writes that "[t]he search for the location in which the self is 'at home' is one of the primary projects of twentieth-century fiction in English" (1996, 3). In the particular case of Ukrainian-Canadian literature, the "search for the location in which the self is 'at home'" involves Ukrainian-Canadian subjects seeking to define Ukraine as a kind of absent/present "home" to address some of the dynamics of being both/neither colonized and colonizer in a Canadian context. The Ukrainian-Canadian, English-language literary tradition seems invested in a notion of "home" as an oft-sought after reference point around which an ethnic identity can be posited. A Ukrainian-Canadian subjectivity is neither at home as an indigenous presence on the Canadian landscape nor at home as a colonial settler emigrating from the seat of imperial power.

Given the size of this group and its long-standing history in Canada, Ukrainian-Canadian literature can tell us much about Ukraine as the shadowy spectre of "home" that haunts Ukrainian Canadians and informs their conception and construction of themselves as an ethnic minority community within postcolonial Canada. By the time Canadians of Ukrainian descent began writing in English (rather than Ukrainian), "home" could easily be Canada, *tout court*, because questions of citizenship, as an indication of belonging and non-belonging to the Canadian state, had largely been resolved. In 1947, the Canadian *Citizenship Act* was passed.[3] Under this act, those born in Canada became Canadian citizens, not just British subjects. Descendents of Ukrainian immigrants born in Canada before 1947 and those born on or after that date were granted Canadian citizenship along with everyone else. The first Canadian citizenship certificate was given to then prime minister, Mackenzie King, and the second was offered to Wasyl Eleniak, one of the first Ukrainian immigrants who encouraged Ukrainian settlement on the Canadian prairie. Sonia Mycak and Barry Ferguson both note the symbolic significance for Ukrainian Canadians of this act in recognizing Eleniak as a "founding father" of Canada (Mycak 2001, 52; Ferguson 1991, 324). By the time Ukrainian Canadians were writing in English in the post-war period, their official citizenship and status as belonging in Canada had been long established, thus Ukrainian-Canadian writers and characters are Canadian and need not use the hyphenated moniker. However, the persistent presence of "Ukraine" as part of the identity of Ukrainian Canadians indicates this important other "home" outside of the Canadian context. The questions of ethnic identity and belonging that this essay explores, therefore, arise in the literature after real political gains had been made by early Ukrainian immigrants to Canada. By the 1920s, Ukrainians were active in a number of levels of Canadian government (Harasym 1982, 108), and those numbers have increased throughout the latter half of the twentieth century (Harasymiw 1982, 128–36), signalling Ukrainian-Canadian effective involvement in the public life of Canada. To be clear, while the later generations of Ukrainian Canadians are no more homogeneous politically or culturally than any other group, their position, understood as a legitimate ethno-cultural group within Canada, seems to allow for full participation in Canadian life. Therefore, their fixation on constructing a "home" in an imagined Ukraine, outside of Canada, offers insights into a fractured postcolonial Canadian psyche—one that can be applied to other groups beyond Ukrainian Canadians.

My focus, however, remains with Ukrainian-Canadian literature in English. Early Ukrainian-Canadian writers, such as William Paluk, consider Ukraine as the "shadow" that immigrants to Canada find they cannot deny—"it had followed [them] across the ocean" (1943, 11)—and later writers, Vera Lysenko, Janice Kulyk Keefer, and Lisa Grekul employ the language of the ghostly in their separate analyses of Ukrainian Canadianness. Grekul speaks for Ukrainian Canadians when she writes: "We have the chance to write ourselves out of existing shadows and leave new ones, we just need to take it" (2005, 204). While shadows (both Paluk's and Grekul's) are not exactly ghosts, the two are not unrelated: both incorporeally announce the presence of something else. Lysenko makes this connection clear when she writes that "the shadow" of Ukrainian religion "haunted the Ukrainian settlements" in Canada (1947, 63). Further, Avery Gordon, in *Ghostly Matters*, argues that attending to "the ghostly haunt" may indicate what hides "in the shadows" (1997, 15). Ghosts and shadows both evoke secrets lurking in corners, which is where Kulyk Keefer takes us. In "longing for an evolving dialectic to replace the fossilized dichotomy between old world and new, tradition and history, past and future" that Kulyk Keefer sees characterizing Ukrainian Canadianness, she yearns for an "acknowledgement and exploration of dark ghosts—abandoned family, assassinated kobzars, grossly corrupt governments, selves painfully fractured along lines of guilt and relief, memory and amnesia" (2005, 50, 51). These passing comments by scholars of Ukrainian-Canadian literature about the presence of ghosts suggest that the project of defining and locating "home" for Ukrainian Canadians may be a haunted project. "Home" may just be, in Freudian terms, "an *unheimlich* house" or "a *haunted* house" (Freud 1919, 634). In short, the presence of dead Ukrainians in so many of these texts highlights what I see to be a widespread experience of ethnic angst.

If Canadian literature itself is "obsessed with ghosts and haunting," as Marlene Goldman and Joanne Saul put it, and both "transnational haunting" and haunting "bound up with Canada's status as [a] settler-invader society" present the ghostly in national terms (2006, 645, 653, 648), then it should not be surprising to see Ukraine rising as a ghost in literature by Ukrainian Canadians. A country that only came into full independence recently and whose doors were largely closed to outsiders for most of the twentieth century, absent/present Ukraine serves as a vexed trope for ethnic identity formation as authors and characters struggle to define what being Ukrainian Canadian means in terms of finding a "home," not just in spatial terms but also in psychological and physical ones as well. Ukraine appears as a ghostly presence in the literature, haunting the protagonists as they try to account for their own discomfort at being caught in "the in-betweenness of the displaced" (Goldman and Saul 2006, 649), of not being quite Canadian enough, but not being quite Ukrainian enough either, thus potentially turning themselves into spectres as well. For as Cynthia Sugars warns us, "[g]hosts give to the living texture, significance, legacy...culture. Without them, *we* are the ghosts" (2006, 693). If haunting represents sites of theoretical or aesthetic fractures (Goldman and Saul 2006, 647), then the kinds of haunting that emerge in my analysis of Kulyk Keefer's *The Green Library,* as a representative Ukrainian-Canadian text that embodies many similar tropes and themes present in much of the English-language oeuvre of Ukrainian-Canadian writing, can be understood as representing a kind of fracture in the postcolonial subject. Postcolonial theorists have pointed out that one of the over-riding experiences of postcolonial subjects includes a sense of non-belonging, of "various kinds of 'in-betweenness'" (Sugars 2004, xiii). And I contend that in reading the ghosts in *The Green Library* we find an unsettled Ukrainian-Canadian response to this kind of "in-betweenness."

States of "in-betweenness" can be understood as the realm of the ghostly: "[A] reminder that the space of the in-between is palpable; it represents a neither-nor-ness that can break down the symmetry and duality of self/other, inside/outside" (Goldman and Saul 2006, 654). Kulyk Keefer's novel engages the process of locating a Ukrainian-Canadian identity in reference both to postcolonial Canada and to spectral Ukraine. Eva Chown, the protagonist, believes herself to be a Canadian, unhyphenated and uncomplicated, until a mysterious figure leaves her with a photograph of a mother and son. The son looks remarkably like Eva's own, and, thus, she begins to uncover the identity of the child in the photograph. He is her own Ukrainian father, a displaced person (DP) who immigrated to Canada after the Second World War under an assumed name. He has an affair with Eva's mother and fathers Eva. Even though Eva is unaware at the novel's opening of her Ukrainian heritage, her life appears both empty and unfulfilled. She may be uncomplicated in her Canadianness, but the novel wants us to understand that she is also incomplete. She has "[n]o self, no life of her own" and has "grown so empty" (Kulyk Keefer 1996, 16). She is "unreachable" to the man she lives with and has a "hole where her heart should be" (21). These sorts of descriptions highlight Eva's sense of emptiness. The Canadian postcolonial subject, which is what Eva thinks herself to be, is merely an empty shell. We understand that only by engaging in the process of ethnic identity construction can she become complete.

Before Eva begins to delve into the Ukrainian side of her hyphenated, ethnic identity, she first grapples with her minoritized identity within postcolonial Canada. Borrowing Margery Fee's language, Eva engages in a kind of "claim-by-identification" with First Nations (1987, 17). Often the literature of postcolonial setters presents connections between non-Aboriginal and Aboriginal populations as a way of creating a symbolic legitimacy for the immigrant settler who participated in exploitation and colonization, often to assuage a kind of "white-settler guilt" (Sugars 2006, 697). In Canadian literature, this trend takes the form of peopling non-Aboriginal texts with Aboriginal characters and themes to show imagined connections between the two groups to actively construct the settler as somehow indigenous to the colonized space. Fee describes this phenomenon, noting: "Those who do not wish to identify with 'mainstream' anglo-Canadian culture, or who are prevented from doing so, can find a prior and superior Canadian culture with which to identify" (1987, 17). Daniel Francis clarifies this point by explaining that this identification appears in the literature as a kind of transformation from non-Aboriginal to Aboriginal (1992, 123). He writes that "Canadians need to transform themselves into Indians." This pattern of indigenizing in Canadian literature is particularly common among what are often referred to as "non-charter groups,"[4] where one "variant of mainstream nationalism uses the First Peoples' position as marginal, yet aboriginal, to make a similar claim-by-identification for other marginal groups" (Fee 1987, 17). In this group, Ukrainian-Canadian authors seem very similar to other Canadian authors.

Kulyk Keefer's *The Green Library* offers a good example of this kind of "claim-by-identification" that Ukrainian-Canadian literature shares with Canadian (and other postcolonial) literatures. The Aboriginal character, Phonsine Kingfisher, plays a crucial role in Eva's journey of self-discovery, and, as a result, Eva's work to articulate herself as Ukrainian and Canadian also involves appropriating a pseudo Aboriginal status as well. For instance, Phonsine describes Eva's Ukrainian father, saying that he and the other DPs had "faces a little like [hers] — they had these wide, wide cheekbones, and black eyes" (Kulyk Keefer 1996, 48–49). Kulyk Keefer puts this assertion of similitude into the mouth of an Aboriginal character. From her position as "marginal, yet aboriginal," Phonsine adopts Eva's Ukrainian father by aligning his physicality with her own. However, Phonsine not only aligns herself with Eva's unknown Ukrainian father, but she also "births" Eva. She provides Eva with the background information of her mother's illicit affair (and thus the information about her paternity) and of her own role as the birthing midwife. She tells Eva: "I yanked you out and showed you off" (45–46). She functions both as Eva's symbolic midwife, by helping her gain knowledge about her origins, and also as a literal one. The implication that Eva was Phonsine's to be displayed suggests a kind of possession: Phonsine claims Eva. By allying Phonsine with Eva's father and presenting her as a pseudo-mother figure, Kulyk Keefer constructs Eva's inquiry into her ethnic identity as a Ukrainian Canadian as intimately linked with Aboriginal legitimacy. Eva's real mother appears absent, distant, and cold throughout much of the novel, languishing in dementia, and her adoptive father is dead. Her real parental figures are the Ukrainian man she seeks (and eventually finds) and Phonsine. Her ethnic identity, therefore, depends upon a "claim-by-identification" with Canadian First Nations.

Kulyk Keefer also, however, insists that in writing about Ukrainian-Canadian ethnicity she cannot divorce a sense of Ukrainianness in Canada from Ukraine itself (1991, 15–16; 1995, 98; 2005, 20, 24, 35–40), and in talking specifically about *The Green Library,* she says that it is her project to tackle "writing ethnicity, literally" (1995, 84). This Ukrainian ethnicity that she so consciously constructs alongside a postcolonial Canadian identity grows out of familial and national connections. Homes and nations "are built on select inclusions" that "are grounded in a learned (or taught) sense of kinship" (George 1996, 9), and this novel evokes kinship metaphors of blood and belonging that become images of death and dismemberment. On the opening page of the novel we read that "*the dead travel in our blood*" (Kulyk Keefer 1996, 1 [original emphasis]), combining the key metaphors that the book will develop: blood as an image of death and blood as an image of kinship.

The impetus to begin understanding ethnicity as kinship or heredity emerges through Eva's contemplation of photographs. Gordon links photographs with ghosts — they can signal the presence of those who are absent or capture the absence of those who should be present (1997) — and Eva refers to the pictures in her albums as ghosts (Kulyk Keefer 1996, 33). The photograph she mysteriously receives at the book's opening is

> a section of a larger one, gesturing only gradually to what's been cut away. For what first appeared to be bows or roses on the woman's shoulders are really a pair of hands, the hands of a man who's been cut out of the photograph. (20)

After figuring out that the mother and child in the photograph are her own grandmother and father, she dreams of the only family she has known:

> [A] half-grown Eva struggling to free herself from Holly; Garth holding tight to Holly's shoulders, while a pair of scissors cuts him away. Leaving a space for another man to step in, to take his place. A man who never materializes, who remains an absence, a transparent shadow. (25)

Kulyk Keefer deploys the absent "transparent shadow" of Eva's biological Ukrainian father as the first kind of haunting that the book engages with. The painful scissoring done to the photographs of families represents the violence done to Eva's own sense of herself, her own identity, which is made clear when she first feels herself watched by the man she will learn is her father: "[S]he feels his eyes cutting along the edges of her body, cutting her out from everything and everyone she knows" (10). The photograph suggests the haunting absence of her father while also foreshadowing the cutting violence that characterizes Eva's inquiries into her own familial and national past. As she studies the photographs of those she learns are her ancestors, she envisions the link in graphic, bloody terms: "There's a bloodline, not just ink on paper, but a thin, tough line of blood linking her … with these doomed people…. Suddenly, the impossible distance between this young, scowling boy in the photograph and her own son has been bridged, and by nothing more than a line of blood" (99). Again she tries to make the decorporealized "ghosts" of the photographs real through blood imagery. The photographs provide her an avenue not just into a shadowy realm of dead and lost people but also precisely into the pool of blood that is her own family.

Eva thinks of her father as a ghostly Ukraine haunting her. The narrator tells us that "whoever sent [the photograph] has been watching her, shadowing her. This photograph is proof, black and white. As anonymous, as insistent as any shadow" (21). This photograph soon forces Eva to recall her adolescent longings for the only other Ukrainian people she has known. Eva soon merges her attempts to find her father(land) with an attempt to find the Ukrainian son of the woman who cleaned her house when Eva was just a child. Desire—both erotic and filial—blends together in Ukraine as "home." Until Eva visits the site of her own conception, she does not even remember the adolescent Alex Moroz who soon becomes the object of her quest.

After visiting Phonsine, she finds the shore of the lake where her mother and Ukrainian father met. Led by "some kind of magic that's brought her to this place where everything began," she then digs in her attic to find a picture of the young Alex—"the image that's been at the back of Eva's eyes ever since she put her hand into the water of a northern lake" (56, 59). She puts her hand in the water "where everything began" in a clear image of birth and origins, and, instead of finding an originating father, she finds a young lover. Kulyk Keefer evokes both birthing and sexual climax when Eva finds the island where she was conceived:

> Dizziness shakes her, everything inside her leaping, dancing, like light on the water, countless lights, a dance of small explosions. Becoming that smash of light on the water as it beats against her skin. Until her whole body's burning, her hair and her eyelashes, her breasts and the soles of her feet. Until she has to shut her eyes, the dark behind them crowding with a man and woman, naked, nameless, crying out. (56)

As she has her epiphany about the desire between her own parents, imagining it as her own, she dismembers her own body into its parts—hair and eyelashes, breasts and feet. Pieces of bodies and blood function as metaphors for a larger ethnic or national body. At this stage, her own body is fractured, dismembered.

From this point of the novel on, Eva's desire to find her father and learn about Ukraine as a way of understanding her own ethnic identity becomes directed towards Alex as a sexualized, Ukrainian target. In the words of Peter Roman Babiak, "she has all but thrown off the search for her family history and replaced it with intoxicating recollections of the small moments and erotic experiences which constitute her memory of Alex" (2003, 106). As the novel folds back in time to Eva and Alex's youth, we learn of their erotic "watching game" that gives Eva a feeling "as though a thousand matches have been struck inside her, and her whole body crackles with light," an image of power and sensuality, so she "can feel her blood fizzing inside her" (65). Her body alighting and blood boiling once again alerts us to the internal ruptures that her ethnic longing evokes. The two teens stare at each other, never speaking, only watching each other. She comes into a sense of herself as a girl through being an object of a Ukrainian sexual gaze. In a reversal of the kind of feminist critique Simone de Beauvoir offers, which identifies a male tradition of objectifying women and projecting onto them male desires ([1949] 1972), Eva seems to want to be objectified by a male gaze. Importantly, however, the gaze she longs for to define her is not just a male one but also a paternal Ukrainian one. Both Alex and her father occupy the same imaginative space: "[S]he knows her mother's lover was Ukrainian.... Because of Alex, because of the way they've mixed in her head, the man watching her in the park, and that boy with whom she once played the watching game" (Kulyk Keefer 1996, 77). Yet Eva wants more than a shadowy watching game with lost men. In Jacques Derrida's words, one important element in acknowledging the spectral lies in the recognition that "this spectral *someone other looks at us*" (1994, 7 [original emphasis]). Eva wants more than just looking; she wants connecting.

Eva travels to Ukraine to find this connection. More precisely, she travels to find Alex. He stands as a substitute for her absent/present father. When listing all that she brings into Ukraine, Eva includes "risk, memory, desire" (Kulyk Keefer 1996, 132). These three items are about her longing for Alex rather than a dispassionate understanding of the history and politics of her "home-country" or a curiosity about her unknown father. Her journey to find her father and fatherland becomes a quest for sex (by analogy, incestuous sex). If incest, at the symbolic level, represents a fracture in the subject's ability to come into an articulation of the self, and the various images of bodies and blood provide physical fractures, then Eva's journey implies a kind of ethnic fracturing within a postcolonial context.

Despite Kulyk Keefer's statements that this novel focuses on Ukrainian history as being integral to Ukrainian-Canadian ethnicity, the treatment of history in this book is secondary to the treatment of Eva's sexual dramas. When arriving in Kiev, even though "[t]he guide has a great deal more to tell," all "Eva can focus on" is "one thing—getting to the hotel, finding a telephone, and making contact with Dr. Oleksandr Moroz," the Alex of her childhood (127). Everything else becomes incidental to the pursuit of her sexual desires for Alex, particularly the construction of herself as an object of his desire. For instance, when she first meets Alex in Kiev, she says that his words possess "nothing awkward and nothing in the least erotic" (138). In response, Eva merely *thinks* she is grateful for this" (138 [emphasis added]), stressing the fact that, of course, she is not grateful for his unerotic response to her. She says: "[H]e seems somehow absent, distracted" (139), like the ghostly space he has occupied in her imagination since remembering him. Even when with him, he still seems an absent presence.

Only once she metaphorically descends into his shadowy underworld will they seem to relate. Like a modern day Persephone turning the tables and pursuing a Ukrainian Hades, she follows him through the subway into a symbolic death, and only then do they emerge on the other side. "The escalator plunges them underground," and they ride into its depth and must emerge to take an elevator to Alex's apartment: "The elevator is a snug, black coffin. The door shuts and the blackness stays and they are not moving anywhere" (143, 145). Now that Eva transcends the boundary between herself and a shadowy Alex by joining him in "a snug, black coffin," they spend the rest of her time in Kiev in bed, a point that Maxim Tarnawsky makes when he sardonically notes that their relationship occurs "mostly in the loins" (1999, 107). While the novel's narrator tells us that "the lovers push themselves inside each other's skin," this kind of merging made possible through sexual consummation is anything but complete (146). Despite their sexual union, Eva does not successfully amalgamate with the Ukrainian side of herself.

Much has been written about sexual and colonial desire, analyzing the kinds of Orientalist yearnings that an imperial subject feels for his colonized object (see Young 1995; Lane 1995; and Holden and Ruppel 2003), and diasporic longing, analyzing the kinds of expectations a diasporic subject feels for his lost home (Clifford 1994, 311; Stoler 1995, 7, 29; Satzewich 2002, 201–13). In the specific context of *The Green Library,* Babiak identifies the "Cold War Oedipal web" linking Kulyk Keefer's characters, and explains that, while this novel creates Eva as a child born into a new knowledge of herself, birthing and knowledge are contaminated by the taint of incest (2003, 114). Eva feels that she is like "a newborn baby in this place—as clueless, as helpless as a baby wet from the womb...Alex is her eyes and ears, her guide, interpreter, bodyguard" (Kulyk Keefer 1996, 158). Eva's first desires for Alex were desires for knowledge about, and connection to, her father(land), and, once connecting with Alex and moving beyond the photograph and the absence he represents, she views him as a father figure. After spending most of her days in Alex's apartment (even under lock and key, like a child in need of protection during his absences), she asks to be taken to Babi Yar: "She knows she sounds like a child saying this: a spoiled and stubborn child," and once again their romance appears in incestuous terms (183). Not only does Alex deftly stand-in for Eva's father, but Eva also becomes a child. Eventually he takes her to the massacre site of Babi Yar, and as they stand staring into the ravine where thousands were killed during the Second World War, with Alex telling Eva about the gruesome deaths, Eva picks up a leaf flecked with red, which "reminds her of cinnamon candy hearts, the kind she loved as a child. She remembers how she'd take the candy from her mouth and paint her lips with it" (185). Even though she goes on to feel ashamed for having such childish thoughts, she is nonetheless childish. The incestuous link connecting her to Alex as a pseudo-father(land) allows her to retreat into childishness, insulated from the history that Kulyk Keefer thinks is so important to ethnic identity.

Through her character's regression into childishness, Kulyk Keefer presents the fantasy of familial and ethnic connectedness through Eva's Ukrainian family line. Through images of bones and death, Eva begins to see the same line of blood that earlier linked her ancestors to her son. In Kiev, standing by Babi Yar, she "feels she ought to make some gesture, not to [Alex], but to the bones piled under her, and the minute fraction of those bones that belong to her. For they do belong. She feels it tugging at her now: that line between herself and the woman she calls at last, with no awkwardness or forcing, her grandmother" (186). The incestuous connection to Alex strangely turns inwards on itself, allowing Eva access not to her absent/present father but, rather, to her dead grandmother. Lesia Levkovych, her grandmother, was a Ukrainian nationalist poet, shot and thrown into the ravine at Babi Yar, which, Alex tells Eva, "means the Old Women's Ravine" (184).[5] The ghostly and dead Lesia offers Eva a fantasy of Ukrainian belonging. "Ghosts," Sugars writes, "like good ancestors, affirm the continuity between our selves and the past"(2006, 693) and may also signal "a desire for legitimate ancestors" (Goldman and Saul 2006, 651), and Lesia seems to offer Eva both Ukrainian continuity and legitimacy.

In particular, she offers Eva a fantasy of solidarity with persecuted and massacred Ukrainian poet dissidents and Jews at Babi Yar. Babi Yar functioned as a site for the execution of Jews within a larger Nazi program of extermination (Subtelny [1988] 2000, 468; Aronson 1980, 63; Scholes 1973, 534; Gerlach 1998, 797) and has been considered the "largest single massacre by Germans in World War II" (Weinberg 1998, 373). Alex describes it to Eva: "Seventy thousand Jews were murdered here. The poor Jews from Podol, the ones who couldn't leave the city when the government cleared out. Men and women; the very old; small children. And after them, some hundred thousand other 'enemies of the people'" (Kulyk Keefer 1996, 185). Kulyk Keefer co-opts the trauma of the persecution of both Ukrainian intellectuals and Ukrainian Jews to lend legitimacy to Eva's struggles to embrace an ethnicity that Kulyk Keefer is at pains to portray as "problematic or even traumatic for its possessor" (1995, 93). Instead of dramatizing the traumatic nature of Ukrainian immigration to and settlement in Canada that some critics attend to (Motyl 1993, 15; Mycak 2001, 35; Swyripa 1978, 21), Kulyk Keefer emphasizes Ukrainian traumas and, through the figure of Lesia, the murdered grandmother poet, even connects them to the larger trauma of the Holocaust. It seems as though part of Eva's desire for legitimacy as a Ukrainian includes a desire to understand Ukrainianness as a troubled identity, one with claims to public sympathy.

In the end, this link to her grandmother becomes what Eva travels to Ukraine to find. The sliced photograph that instigates her journey presents both Lesia and her son as absent presences in Eva's life, and, after visiting Babi Yar on her last day in Kiev, Eva goes to the Ukrainian art museum and finds a painting that she is convinced is of her grandmother: "It's a portrait of Lesia Levkovych; Eva knows this though the guidebook makes no mention of the name. It's a painting of the woman Eva has seen in a photograph, over whose bones she walked at Babi Yar" (Kulyk Keefer 1996, 209–10). She stares at the painting feeling comforted by the visible presence of her grandmother, and, when she leaves, she thinks: "Absence, presence, like a body and its shadow" (210). This image could not only function as a metaphor for this novel alone, but it could also exemplify the driving concern of much Ukrainian-Canadian literature.

We see Eva's father's significance fading for her once she identifies her grandmother as the real target of her ethnic longing. Continuing the incestuous dynamic established among Eva, Alex, and her father, upon returning from Kiev, Eva finally meets her Ukrainian father, who turns out not only to have been the lover of Eva's mother but also to have been the lover of Oksanna Moroz, Alex's sister — a kind of double for Eva herself. Kulyk Keefer describes Oksanna as having dark hair compared to Eva's blond, and one is given the epithet the "fair-haired girl" and the other the "dark-haired girl," showing their shadowed connection (63). Eva even imagines being part of Oksanna, with the other girl's tongue in her mouth turning into her own, blending the identities of the two girls (85). Meeting as adult women reinforces this shadowed connection from their youth. Eva says to Oksanna: "You've cut your hair," and the only response she gets is: "So have you" (92). Just as Alex can be a substitute, standing in for the absent father, so Oksanna can be another substitute lover, standing in for Eva. When Oksanna makes the revelation of her sexual relationship with Ivan (Eva's father) clear, she says: "He was old enough to be my *father*" (259 [emphasis added]). Yet this relationship between Oksanna/Eva and Ivan has less to do with father-daughter incest and more to do with providing a grandchild with a link to a grandparent — in this case, Eva's son to Eva's father. As a result of Oksanna's link to Ivan, she serves as an intermediary between the grandfather and grandson, allowing them an opportunity to meet by the lake where Eva was conceived. These almost-incestuous couplings close the narrative of Eva's journey of ethnic self-discovery on itself, ending where it began.

For Eva, Lesia becomes the end-point of this incestuous circling. If Eva's only value for her father lies in her being "not a daughter but the woman who has given him his grandson," then she recognizes that his only value lies in the link he offers her to her grandmother (252). As Eva sits by the lake where her conception took place she

> has a sudden sensation of sliding through a chute, a blood-warm, blood-dark chute that is her mother's body, the flesh shiny and fast like the walls of a playground slide. Tipping from uterus down birth canal and through those wide, astonished lips that push her into air and light. Yet the womb which tipped her out is linked to that other womb, the one that harboured the man who is her father. A series of connecting rings: her mother, her grandmother, herself. (261)

Her ethnicity becomes an image of birth and maternity, written not on, but within, women's bodies. The circle of incest turns inwards to the circle of the womb that transforms into a series of "connecting rings" — women

167

become interconnected wombs. Eva's fantasy turns out not to be about uniting with a Ukrainian lover but, rather, about the dynamics of desire that lead her to the fantasy of fusion with her murdered grandmother.

Kulyk Keefer makes clear this fantasy of connectivity not through sex but, instead, through motherhood, when Eva "conjur[es] Lesia Levkovych" to demand answers of her: "My son's pulling away from me; my lover's only a shadow, a shadow cut off from my body. Tell me how to live with this" (229–30). She merges with the identity of her dead grandmother, inscribing herself imaginatively in the roles dictated by the mutilated photograph. But "Lesia's face is turned away" from Eva (230). Through all of Eva's evasion and misdirection, desiring both a father and a lover, and finally finding a grandmother as an originating site of ethnic identity, Lesia remains aloof. She refuses to be anything other than a ghost haunting her granddaughter's imagination.

Kulyk Keefer suggests in this text that a dead and spectral Ukraine—embodied in Lesia—possesses ethnic value. The dead poet offers the lure of connectivity between Ukraine and Canada but ultimately remains beyond the grasp of the woman who longs for her grandmother. Even in this most traditional envisioning of ethnic connection—from one womb through the generations—Lesia never claims Eva, and the one-sidedness of longing highlights a disconnection, a fracture. The chasm that lies between Lesia and Eva, expressed through the disinterestedness of the dead Ukrainian for the living Ukrainian Canadian and the disembodied descriptions of the dead, signals a fracture in ethnic coherence: the Ukrainian Canadian cannot be united with her Ukrainian shadow.

If this is so for Eva in this book, surveying Ukrainian-Canadian literature in general also begins to illuminate dead Ukrainian bodies and ghostly revenants. We begin to see that echoes and shadows of Ukraine haunt this oeuvre, often in the form of Ukrainian bodies—Lesia is not the only corpse. Consider the following examples. The first English language novel by a Canadian of Ukrainian descent, Vera Lysenko's *Yellow Boots* presents a young Ukrainian immigrant girl's story of gaining material success as a pan-ethnic folksinger, but the protagonist's achievements are built on the dead bodies of Tamara, the local Ukrainian-Canadian outcast (whom Mycak [2001, 19–20] argues shares features with Lilli, the protagonist) and Granny Yefrosynia (whom Lilli had hoped could be a "timeless" grandmother figure, like Eva's Lesia, "meant to go on and on" [Lysenko [1954] 1992, 194]). In addition, Myrna Kostash's travel memoir,

The Doomed Bridegroom, offers a chapter focusing on an imagined romantic liaison between the narrator and martyred Ukrainian poet Vasyl Stus. She apostrophizes the dead writer: "Thousands of miles away from your grave I will find you in my books, and I will drag you into my language, my purposes, and my memory" (1998, 35). Like Eva apostrophizing her dead poet grandmother, the narrator of Kostash's memoir (a version of Kostash herself) speaks to the dead Ukrainian, but he does not answer back. A recent novel by a Canadian of Ukrainian descent, Lisa Grekul's *Kalyna's Song* (2003), frames the protagonist's journey from Alberta to Swaziland with the deaths of her Ukrainian piano teacher and mentor, Sister Maria, and her Ukrainian folksinging cousin, Kalyna. The closing scene of the book has the protagonist sitting in the cemetery trying to talk to, and be with, these dead women. Even more recently, Marusya Bociurkiw's *The Children of Mary* (2006) focuses on the narrator Sonya's quest to uncover the details about her father's role in her sister's death. The dead sister literally haunts the text. Similarly, Kulyk Keefer's most recent novel that turns its attention to issues of Ukrainian ethnicity in a Canadian context, *The Ladies' Lending Library,* contains a section entitled "Keepers of Secrets" that is filled with dead girls. This section is haunted by the memory of a sister left behind in Ukraine, but, the novel tells us, she is not just abandoned, but dead: "You can't make people up out of nothing. The dead are dead, and they'll stay dead no matter how much you call them to come back" (2007, 143). Another character is described as being the mother of a "dead baby whose skeleton shape no amount of embroidery and flowers can disguise" (169). Hardships and death in the past sit on display as photographic reminders, absent presences.

Larry Warwaruk's *The Ukrainian Wedding* (1998) provides one of the most graphic examples of these recurring ghosts and bodies. His novel focuses on Lena Melnyk, a young girl living on her family's Manitoba homestead and longing for an escape to the city. At a family wedding, Lena's brother-in-law, Yuri, himself a figure of Ukrainianness as both a Ukrainian scholar and political sympathizer, runs away with Marusia Budka, whom he imagines is a Ukrainian *rusalka* figure. Warwaruk describes Ukrainian *rusalkas* as sirens of classical mythology: "[L]ong-haired maidens [rising] between the waves, water maidens singing, Rusalkas beckoning for sailors to join them in the deep green waters" (3). Seeing Marusia as a *rusalka* haunting the Canadian prairie landscape, Yuri strips Marusia of her humanity and perceives in her the folk creature of his desires.

Ultimately, he murders Marusia, turning her into a body "in an advanced state of decomposition" with "millions and millions of maggots crawling all over it" (280–81). His murder of Marusia, therefore, serves as a warning of the very real dangers inherent in only comprehending Ukraine and Ukrainians as shadowy and spectral presences. If Eva's narrative suggests that Ukraine is dead and cannot be exhumed effectively, Warwaruk's implies that confusing reality with the spectral can lead to gruesome ends.

This list is by no means exhaustive, but it begins to demonstrate that the dead Lesia who emerges as a symbol of the Ukrainian side of Eva's heritage is not an atypical trope within contemporary Ukrainian-Canadian writing. These Ukrainian-Canadian texts, therefore, indicate a kind of unease and discomfort inherent in attempting to construct an ethnic identity in relation both to Canada and Ukraine as potential home sites. Canada appears as not-quite home as characters, such as Eva, attempt to indigenize themselves and associate themselves with Canada's First Nations, and, similarly, Ukraine appears as not-quite home as personifications of Ukraine appear as ghosts and corpses. Thus, while incest, familial secrets, ghosts, and dead bodies do not constitute the sum total of gothic literature, key elements of it that appear in Ukrainian-Canadian English-language literature suggest an affinity between the two — the postcolonial ethnic angst in Ukrainian-Canadian texts emerges through stealthy but inexorable gothic tropes.

Notes

1 The histories of both Wasyl Eleniak and Ivan Pillipiw, as the first two Ukrainian immigrants to Canada in 1891, as well as the efforts of Joseph Oleskiw who advocated settling the Canadian prairie with land-hungry Ukrainian peasants, are well documented (see Kaye 1964; Marunchak 1981, 23–73; Lysenko 1947, 6–33; Kaye and Swyripa 1982, 32, 36–41). Vladimir Kaye and Frances Swyirpa offer this apt, condensed insight: "Pillipiw and Eleniak undoubtedly stimulated the first sustained interest in Canada among the Ukrainian peasantry" and Oleskiw's "writings and speeches gave wide publicity to the free lands in Canada" (1982, 38).

2 Using the conservative and generally accepted figures, after the first and most numerous wave of homesteading Ukrainians (1891–1914), approximately 68,000 Ukrainians immigrated between 1919 and 1939. In the five short years between 1947 and 1952, a further 32,000 arrived. For more information on Ukrainian immigration to Canada, there are a number of excellent studies (see Marunchak 1981; Lupul 1982; Hlynka 1981; Ewanchuk 1981; Balan 1984; Martynowych 1991; Hryniuk and Luciuk 1993).

3 *Citizenship Act*, 1974-75-76, c. 108, s. 1.

4 John Porter first used the term "charter groups" to refer to the two main colonizing forces in Canada, the English and the French. Other ethnic groups (not including First Nations) are often considered "non-charter groups" (1965).

5 Lesia Levkovych is loosely based on Olena Teliha (1906–42), a Russian-born Ukrainian poet who was killed at Babi Yar for her political activism as a member of the Organization of Ukrainian Nationalists (see Subtelny [1988] 2000, 444 and 465). In name and ideology, however, Kulyk Keefer's Lesia also clearly alludes to the earlier poet Lesia Ukrainka (1871–1913), who is one of Ukraine's best-known poets. "Laryssa Kosach-Kvitka, whose pen name was Lesia Ukrainka," writes Subtelny, "was born into one of Ukraine's most cultured families. Her mother was the noted author Olena Pchilka; her uncle was the famous Drahomanov; and she was related to the composer Mykola Lysenko and the playwright Mykhailo Starytsky … Her deep, finely wrought poetry exudes inspiring strength, vigor, and optimism" (304).

Works Cited

Aronson, Ronald. 1980. "Never Again? Zionism and the Holocaust." *Social Text* 3: 60–72.

Babiak, Peter Roman. 2003. "Toronto, Capital of Ukraine: The Ends of Desire and the Beginning of History in Janice Kulyk Keefer's *The Green Library*." *English Studies in Canada* 29(1–2): 97–130.

Balan, Jars. 1984. *Salt and Braided Bread: Ukrainian Life in Canada*. Toronto: Oxford UP.

Beauvoir, Simone de. 1949, reprinted 1972. *The Second Sex*. Trans. H.M. Parshley. New York: Knopf.

Bociurkiw, Marusya. 2006. *The Children of Mary*. Toronto: Inanna Publications.

Clifford, James. 1994. "Diasporas." *Cultural Anthropology* 9(3): 302–38.

Derrida, Jacques. 1994. *Specters of Marx: The State of the Debt, the Work of Mourning and the New International*. Trans. Peggy Kamuf. New York: Routledge.

Ewanchuk, Michael. 1981. *Pioneer Profiles: Ukrainian Settlers in Manitoba*. Winnipeg: Derksen Printers and M. Ewanchuk.

Fee, Margery. 1987. "Romantic Nationalism and the Image of Native People in Contemporary English-Canadian Literature." In *The Native in Literature*. Ed. Thomas King, Cheryl Calver, and Helen Hoy. Toronto: ECW Press. 15–33.

Ferguson, Barry. 1991. "British-Canadian Intellectuals, Ukrainian Immigrants, and Canadian National Identity." In *Canada's Ukrainians: Negotiating an Identity*. Ed. Lubomyr Luciuk and Stella Hryniuk. Toronto: University of Toronto Press. 304–25.

Francis, Daniel. 1992. *The Imaginary Indian*. Vancouver: Arsenal Pulp Press.

Freud, Sigmund. 1919. "The 'Uncanny.'" Trans. James Strachey. *New Literary History* 7(3): 619–45.

George, Rosemary Marangoly. 1996. *The Politics of Home: Postcolonial Relocations and Twentieth-Century Fiction.* Cambridge: Cambridge UP.

Gerlach, Christian. 1998. "The Wannsee Conference, the Fate of German Jews, and Hitler's Decision in Principle to Exterminate All European Jews." *Journal of Modern History* 70(4): 759–812.

Goldman, Marlene, and Joanne Saul. 2006. "Talking with Ghosts: Haunting in Canadian Cultural Production." *University of Toronto Quarterly* 75(2): 645–55.

Gordon, Avery F. 1997. *Ghostly Matters: Haunting and the Sociological Imagination.* Minneapolis: University of Minnesota Press.

Grekul, Lisa. 2003. *Kalyna's Song.* Regina: Coteau Books.

———. 2005. *Leaving Shadows: Literature in English by Canada's Ukrainians.* Edmonton: University of Alberta Press.

Harasym, Rose. 1982. "Ukrainians in Canadian Political Life, 1923–45." In *A Heritage in Transition: Essays in the History of Ukrainians in Canada.* Ed. Manoly Lupul. Toronto: McClelland and Stewart. 108–25.

Harasymiw, Bohdan. 1982. "Political Participation of Ukrainian Canadians since 1945." In *A Heritage in Transition: Essays in the History of Ukrainians in Canada.* Ed. Manoly Lupul. Toronto: McClelland and Stewart. 126–42.

Hlynka, Isydore. 1981. *The Other Canadians: Selected Articles from the Column of "Ivan Harmata" Published in the "Ukrainian Voice."* Winnipeg: Trident Press.

Holden, Philip, and Richard Ruppel, eds. 2003. *Imperial Desire: Dissident Sexualities and Colonial Literature.* Minneapolis: University of Minnesota Press.

Hryniuk, Stella, and Lubomyr Luciuk, eds. 1993. *Multiculturalism and Ukrainian Canadians: Identity, Homeland Ties, and the Community's Future.* Toronto: Multicultural Society of Ontario.

Kaye, Vladimir J. 1964. *Early Ukrainian Settlements in Canada 1895–1900: Dr. Josef Oleskiw's Role in the Settlement of the Canadian Northwest.* Toronto: University of Toronto Press.

Kaye, Vladimir, and Frances Swyripa. 1982. "Settlement and Colonization." In *A Heritage in Transition: Essays in the History of Ukrainians in Canada.* Ed. Manoly Lupul. Toronto: McClelland and Stewart. 32–58.

Kostash, Myrna. 1998. *The Doomed Bridegroom: A Memoir.* Edmonton: NeWest Press.

Kulyk Keefer, Janice. 1991. "From Mosaic to Kaleidoscope: Out of the Multicultural Past Comes a Vision of a Transcultural Future." *Books in Canada* 20(6): 13–16.

———. 1995. "Coming across Bones: Historiographic Ethnofiction." *Essays on Canadian Writing* 57: 84–104.

———. 1996. *The Green Library.* Toronto: HarperCollins.

———. 2005. *Dark Ghost in the Corner: Imagining Ukrainian-Canadian Identity.* Saskatoon: Heritage Press.

———. 2007. *The Ladies' Lending Library.* Toronto: HarperCollins.

Lane, Christopher. 1995. *The Ruling Passion: British Colonial Allegory and the Paradox of Homosexual Desire.* Durham: Duke UP.

Lupul, Manoly. 1982. *A Heritage in Transition: Essays in the History of Ukrainians in Canada.* Toronto: McClelland and Stewart.

Lysenko, Vera. 1947. *Men in Sheepskin Coats: A Study in Assimilation.* Toronto: Ryerson.

———. 1954, reprinted 1992. *Yellow Boots.* Edmonton: CIUS Press and NeWest Press.

Martynowych, Orest. 1991. *Ukrainians in Canada: The Formative Years, 1891–1924.* Edmonton: CIUS Press.

Marunchak, Michael. 1981. *The Ukrainian Canadians: A History.* Winnipeg: Ukrainian Academy of Arts and Sciences.

Motyl, Alexander J. 1993. *Dilemmas of Independence: Ukraine after Totalitarianism.* New York: Council on Foreign Relations Press.

Mycak, Sonia. 2001. *Canuke Literature: Critical Essays on Canadian Ukrainian Writing.* Huntington: Nova Science Publications.

Paluk, William. 1943. *Canadian Cossacks: Essays, Articles, and Stories on Ukrainian-Canadian Life.* Winnipeg: Winnipeg Ukrainian Canadian Review.

Porter, John. 1965. *The Vertical Mosaic: An Analysis of Social Class and Power in Canada.* Toronto: University of Toronto Press.

Satzewich, Vic. 2002. *The Ukrainian Diaspora.* New York: Routledge.

Scholes, Robert. 1973. "The Illiberal Imagination." *New Literary History* 4(3): 521–40.

Stoler, Ann Laura. 1995. *Race and the Education of Desire: Foucault's* History of Sexuality *and the Colonial Order of Things.* Durham: Duke UP.

Subtelny, Orest. 1988, reprinted 2000. *Ukraine: A History,* 3rd edition. Toronto: University of Toronto Press.

Sugars, Cynthia, ed. 2004. *Unhomely States: Theorizing English-Canadian Postcolonialism.* Peterborough: Broadview Press.

———. 2006. "The Impossible Afterlife of George Cartwright: Settler Melancholy and Postcolonial Desire." *University of Toronto Quarterly* 75(2): 693–717.

Swyripa, Frances. 1978. *Ukrainian Canadians: A Survey of their Portrayal in English-language Works.* Edmonton: University of Alberta Press.

Tarnawsky, Maxim. 1999. "What Is Told in *The Green Library:* History, Institutions, Language (Portrayals of the Ethnic Ukrainian Community in Canada and the United States)." *Canadian Ethnic Studies Journal* 31(3): 104–15.

Warwaruk, Larry. 1998. *The Ukrainian Wedding.* Regina: Coteau Books.

Weinberg, Gerhard. 1998. "Unexplored Questions about the German Military during World War II." *Journal of Military History* 62: 371–80.

Young, Robert. 1995. *Colonial Desire: Hybridity in Theory, Culture, and Race.* New York: Routledge.

CHAPTER EIGHT

"Something not unlike enjoyment": Gothicism, Catholicism, and Sexuality in Tomson Highway's *Kiss of the Fur Queen*

Jennifer Henderson

> Uniformly garbed in sky-blue denim shirts and navy denim coveralls, the boys marched out into a long, white passageway that smelled of metal and Javex—everything here smelled of metal and Javex—where lines of Indian girl strangers were marching in the opposite direction. But there was his sister Josephine, hair now cropped at the ears.... He waved surreptitiously at her but, just then, one of the innumerable doors that lined this tunnel swallowed her. Ghost-pale, tight-faced women sheathed completely in black and white stood guarding each door, holding long wooden stakes that, Champion later learned, were for measuring the length of objects.
>
> —Tomson Highway, *Kiss of the Fur Queen*

It is something of a critical commonplace that the transposition of gothic conventions to the literature of North America produces a change in the nature of phobic objects and spaces. A new set of spectral images emerges to haunt the colonial project of establishing order in the wilderness: the castles and convents, the villainous Italian nobles, and the Catholic priests of the European Gothic are replaced by the threats and dangers of the natural world, including, notoriously, the predatory "savages" of its dark, engulfing forests.[1] With this ready-made scheme in mind, it is tempting to decipher a reversal of the colonial Gothic in a late twentieth-century First Nations novel that focuses on the horrors of predatory priests and the mysterious sacrificial rituals of the Roman Catholic church and sets its story of the seduction of innocents in the living tomb of a mid-twentieth century Manitoba residential school. Tomson Highway's *Kiss of the Fur Queen* ([1998] 2005) might thus be read as an account of the terror of colonial institutions. The moonlit chambers, stairs, and corridors of the Birch Lake Residential School invoke the ominous castles and monasteries of the European Gothic, but Highway's reinscription of these details of setting links the horror of the residential school to its program of assimilative correction and training. Descriptions of the school deploy the features of a recognizably gothic *mise en scène* but tie the menace of these gothic features to a regime of prohibition, hygiene, segregation, and regimentation—to the residential school as a space designed to effect the familial, cultural, linguistic, and spiritual dispossession of First Nations people. If, following his residential school "education," Highway's Cree protagonist is characterized by a gothic form of selfhood—"massively blocked off from something to which [he] ought normally to have access" (Sedgwick 1986, 12)—it is precisely due to this series of dispossessions. In this reading, *Kiss of the Fur Queen* would seem to stage a reversal of the colonial Gothic's location of dangerous forces in the irrational "wilderness," deploying elements of the European Gothic to identify the realm of excess and tyranny in the reason of the modern colonial state and its accessory institutions.

However, there are several reasons why such a reading of *Kiss of the Fur Queen* should proceed more cautiously. In the first place, this reading in terms of reversal or inversion is overly schematic in its treatment of the colonial Gothic. One has only to examine the scenes of terror associated with the brutally inflexible reason of the English colonial garrison in John Richardson's *Wacousta* ([1832] 1998) to see that the nineteenth-century Canadian Gothic already exposes the tyranny and excess at the heart of colonial institutions. There are more crucial reasons, though, for proceeding cautiously with a reading of *Kiss of the Fur Queen* in terms of either an inversion or a laying bare of the colonial Gothic. These have to do with the politics of interpreting First Nations texts through a gothic lens and with the complex sexual politics of Highway's novel, which, as I shall argue, hold to a sense of the "queer interdependence of that which harms and that which heals" (Cvetkovich 1995, 373). A recent discussion of the Gothic as it pertains to another contemporary First Nations novel suggests that we should be wary of attempts to apply the Gothic and its critical discourse to the interpretation of texts concerned with the relationship between western European and First Nations world views. Eden Robinson's novel *Monkey Beach* (2000) also treats the effects of European colonialism in terms of the unspeakable and, more specifically, in terms of the conventionally gothic idiom of ghosts and spirits, but, as Jodey Castricano argues, the appearance of these supernatural elements does not license the critic to identify the novel as gothic (2006, 802–03). More specifically, Castricano argues that attempts to apply the "Western European Gothic explanatory model" to Robinson's text obscure important questions about the politics of interpretation that are raised by the novel itself. Castricano reads the novel as asking: "what can the European Gothic possibly tell readers about modern Haisla culture.... In other words... *whose* past is being invoked in relation to the Gothic"? For Castricano, the novel is not so much "gothic" as it is a novel that "deals *in* the Gothic" in order to situate Aboriginal spirituality as a form of knowledge that is necessary to survival and has been repudiated and, indeed, pathologized by the rational materialism of the West (808). In this sense, it is the knowledge practices of European settler-invaders that the novel invokes in relation to the Gothic. The novel is not about the psychological confusion of repressed and traumatized contemporary Haisla characters but, rather, about the effects of the historical process through which their culture's ways of knowing were prohibited and pathologized as primitive occultism.

For Castricano, then, in spite of the conventional association of gothic fiction with the writing of what is in excess of the rational and the socially normative, there is a complicitous relationship between twentieth-century critical discourse on the Gothic and the rationality of the Enlightenment. Insofar as the critical discourse has been overwhelmingly psychoanalytic in its mode of explanation, reading gothic fiction as "the signifier, par excellence, of psychological unease, perceptual disturbance, or atavistic and, therefore, pathological tendencies to be explained — and, perhaps, normalized — in terms of hysteria, neuroses, or 'uncanny' primitivism," it has been reduplicative of the Enlightenment project of demystification (806). The danger of reading texts such as *Monkey Beach* or *Kiss of the Fur Queen* through the lens of the Gothic, then, is that one is likely to carry over these received ideas from the critical discourse. One risks imposing the depth psychology from which gothic criticism has become inseparable and which links the irrational and the magical with the madness or immaturity of "neurotics" and "primitives." When applied to First Nations texts, then, gothic readings risk simply continuing the epistemological work of empire (807).

While Castricano's caveat deserves to be taken seriously because of the provocative questions that it raises about interpretative practices in literary criticism and their sedimentation with historical practices of "psychological colonialism," it is not quite flexible enough, indeed not quite historical enough, to address the complexity of Highway's dealings with the register of the Gothic in *Kiss of the Fur Queen* (808). The novel's irreducibility to questions of responsible interpretation, even when the critic's responsibilities are framed in terms of cultural sensitivity and critical self-reflexivity, says something about the profundity of the challenge stemming from its unapologetic ambivalence about cultural hybridization and its unsettled and unsettling conjoining of sexual colonial violence and queer sexuality. I want to propose that a close examination of the novel's deployment of gothic materials provides a productive pathway through these issues. In order to approach those materials in *Kiss of the Fur Queen,* however, we need first to go back through the "Gothic" from a different angle that takes account of the place of representations of Catholicism in gothic fiction, the fascination with Catholic iconography and ritual as another kind of "primitivism" seen from the perspective of the intensely anti-clerical Protestantism that informs the gothic fiction of England of the late eighteenth and early nineteenth centuries. For if contact with the spirit world among First Nations was framed by colonial epistemology as evidence of the inherent psychopathology of so-called primitive cultures, then "savages" and "papists" are on a par in this gothic fiction (805). The gothic fiction of this period in England promotes a differentiation between the superstitious and underdeveloped Catholic and the civilized Protestant. Associated with the oblique and the symbolic, with mummery and hypocrisy, Catholicism brings into relief the earnest, direct, self-reliant disposition of the Protestant. However, this mundane and widespread anti-Catholicism, bolstered by anti-Jacobin sentiment in late eighteenth-century England, verged on a phobic fascination in gothic fiction. This fascination had to do with the commonplace association of the Catholic countries of the continent with sexual excess — with sodomy and with lurid and exotic forms of transgressive sexual aggression, which were often played out in narratives of predatory priests or nuns and trembling, incarcerated novices (Haggerty 2004–05, para. 8).

As George Haggerty has argued, the Catholic trope functions to map an alien religious context that makes readings of non-normative sexualities conspicuously available. In this sense, Catholicism has functioned in gothic fiction as something of a laboratory for the exploration of same-sex desire (para. 17).[2] This sexual coding goes some way to explaining Highway's curious redeployment of the gothic trope of Catholicism in *Kiss of the Fur Queen*. The narrative seems to refuse the temporality embedded in the gothic trope of Catholicism, which positions Catholicism, like "primitivism," as a state of immaturity to be progressed out of or a mental disorder or perversion to be purged.[3] However, Highway's deployment of the trope is, like so much else in the novel, ambivalent. My reading of the trope's generic function needs to be supplemented by an acknowledgement of *Kiss of the Fur Queen*'s late twentieth-century social and historical context, in which revelations of the sexual and physical abuse of children in church-run educational institutions, most notoriously in denominational residential schools for First Nations children in the middle decades of the century, give a dense resonance to the sexual-religious tropes of gothic fiction.[4] If, as Haggerty suggests, "Catholic gothic fiction and the history of sexuality overlap in countless ways for [the later eighteenth and early nineteenth centuries]" (2004–05, para. 4), they also overlap in our moment in ways that are more difficult to assimilate as a chapter in the recuperative history of non-normative sexualities.

Highway's deployment of the gothic trope of Catholicism works to evoke not only the Christian colonial context of the traumas of residential school but also the terrain of queer sexuality that is encoded in the trope, and this evocation makes gothic fiction a place where desire's links to power and powerlessness are exposed. The novel does not imply that all scandals to propriety are equal, but neither does it allow that they are completely unrelated. The novel's hybridities, as Cynthia Sugars has noted, are difficult and vexed ones rather than naive resolutions of a settler-invader legacy (2002, 73). They are also multiple. For just as twentieth-century Cree and Ojibway cultures are nowhere in the text separable from the historical experiences of missionary education and residential schooling and the incursions of modern capitalism, neither is sexuality in this text ever separable from social practices and representations — not even from fantasies "socially instituted and brutally imposed" (de Lauretis 1995, 64). Thus, just as *Kiss of the Fur Queen* suggests that the Catholic symbolism and Christian narratives into which the two Cree brothers are inducted at residential school provide some of the materials for their later critical and liberating artistic expressions, the novel also takes the risk of associating the brothers' sexuality—including Gabriel Okimasis's unambiguous homosexuality—with their experiences of sexual abuse in the school.

The link between violation and pleasure is of course central to the terrain traditionally explored by gothic fiction, and it is a basic assumption for queer theorists who read against the grain of narrative resolutions that seem to affirm the "heteronormative prerogative" of the dominant social fiction (Haggerty 2005, 386). The conjunction of a good deal of recent critical discourse on the Gothic with queer theory should complicate Castricano's construction of this critical discourse as monolithically and classically psychoanalytic (2006). The key intervention of Eve Kosofsky Sedgwick's *The Coherence of Gothic Conventions,* after all, was to depart from "critical attempts to value the Gothic for its portrayal of 'depth'" and to effect a "shift of focus [that] shows...the strongest energies inhere in the surface" (1986, 12). What has tended to accompany the preference for "'true depths'" in gothic criticism, Sedgwick observes, has been "an extreme critical irritation with the surfaces of Gothic novels, with the superficialities of 'claptrap,' '*décor*,' and 'stage-set'" and a tendency to find sexuality only where it is seen to be evoked thematically as depth (11–12, 141). This observation is relevant to *Kiss of the Fur Queen* because it is in the novel's play with what might be called Catholic surfaces that its queerness is most concentrated. It is also here that the novel's adherence to what might be called an impure aesthetics and politics is most legible as the product of its multiple (and not always commensurable) commitments to First Nations cultural and political integrity, on the one hand, and the queer critique of social-sexual normativity on the other.

Catholic Surfaces

> Below the Fur Queen portrait, Mariesis's rosary lay entwined in Gabriel's fingers. Ann-Adele Ghostrider's old, brown hand removed the beads and replaced them with an eagle feather.... About to throw the rosary in the trash can, she hung it, instead, on a Ken doll sporting cowboy hat and white-tasselled skirt. The medicine woman lit a braid of sweetgrass and washed the patient in its smoke.
>
> —Highway, *Kiss of the Fur Queen*

As I suggested at the outset, it is possible to read *Kiss of the Fur Queen* as a novel that delineates the tyrannical nature of colonial institutions, thereby throwing into sharp relief the repressed subtext of colonial gothic fiction. There is something residual to this reading, however, which has to do with the novel's intense preoccupation with, even eroticization, of Roman Catholic iconography. The novel shares many of the characteristic motifs of European gothic fiction: silences and echoes, doubles, projective mirrorings, metonymies, trancelike states, ambiguous character boundaries, a preoccupation with the unspeakable, with the perverse, and with guilt and shame and their ruinous effects (see Sedgwick 1986, 9–10). Yet most striking is its reinscription of that feature of English gothic fiction that, in writers such as Ann Radcliffe, Horace Walpole, and Matthew Lewis, bears witness to what Ian Duncan has called the "spiritual orientalism in the British Protestant imagination" (quoted in Caballero 2004, 152). The gothic tropes of the strangeness of the Roman Catholic Church, the mysteries of its ceremonies, the threat of its irrational, power-hungry servants, and the danger of being trapped and sacrificed in the labyrinthine structures of its buildings are all integral to Highway's construction of the experience of Jeremiah Okimasis and his younger brother, Ooneemeetoo-Gabriel, in the residential school. The scene of sexual abuse—to which I shall return—is studied in its staging of the classic gothic encounter with the sexual-religious Other. In a moonlit chamber, the victim is immobilized, in a vulnerable dream-state, and the predator, invisible to the victim, approaches in metonymic fragments—"a sliver of light," "the sound of cloth brushing against cloth," until the victim opens his eyes to a frightful sight: "[T]he face of the principal loomed inches from his own" (Highway [1998] 2005, 77). Prior to this moment, Father Lafleur appears to the boys only in the menacing metonymies of a "fleshy voice," "a chunky ruby ring," a "face, now attached to a great black cassock, starched white collar, and silver crucifix" (53, 73, 54). Yet what is more interesting than this generic self-consciousness is the novel's emphasis on the boys' bewildered perception of the apparently sadomasochistic and cannibalistic rituals of the Catholic church and the "grotesque extravagance" of its alien aesthetic, "bristling with images of blood, agony, cruelty" (128, 177).

The defamiliarization of Catholic iconography and ritual from the point of view of two northern Manitoba Cree boys (sons of a caribou hunter, as the text repeatedly reminds us) is partly designed to desacralize the paraphernalia of Christianity by subjecting it to a perspective that either receives it as nonsense or interprets it in humourously slanted ways. Sugars has discussed the boys' restaging of specific Christian stories and rituals—the passion of Christ, the wedding of Canaan, the communion mass, the last supper—as the means by which the two boys are shown to be capable of recasting an imposed culture in more familiar, meaningful terms, disregarding that culture's imposition of guilt and engaging in increasingly "conscious acts of resistance" (2002, 78).[5] While the boys enact this kind of parodic restaging, structurally, the novel itself in its narrative, characters, and motifs is involved in its own displacement of Christian materials, including the annunciation, sacrifice, martyrdom, communion, saviour, chalice, holy spirits, and angels. This displacement often serves to conflate Christian with Cree myths, depriving the former of originality and singularity and, as Sugars points out, producing a blasphemous contamination of Church doctrine that pointedly counters the historical prohibition on the importation of First Nations languages and cultures into residential schools (78). This contamination and loss of originality and singularity works both ways, however. Highway is insistent from the beginning that there is no pure, uncompromised Aboriginal culture available to be recovered (Sugars 2002, 78; Brydon 2001, 24–25),[6] just as, in Richard Lane's view, the novel's representation of sexual abuse (actually, its representation of Jeremiah's representation of the abuse in the play that he writes as an adult) suggests that "there exists no originary or universal aesthetic site that can construct [the sexual abuse], represent it, [or serve] as a norm against which it can be measured" (2002, 194).

Highway names an artistic precursor for his strategy of desacralizing Christian iconography in a homoerotic sixteenth-century Italian baroque painter whose controversial artwork and biography were recuperated for contemporary queer art and politics just a decade before *Kiss of the Fur Queen* was first published in 1998.[7] The reference to the work of Michelangelo Merisi da Caravaggio seems fleeting. In its immediate context in the novel, it specifies the origins of Father Lafleur's taste for boys as the aesthetic of a particular painter in the Catholic tradition: Father Lafleur gazes at the two sleeping brothers, "to him, Caravaggio's cherubs, pink and plump-cheeked, their lips full, ripe cherries" (Highway [1998] 2005, 73). Shortly thereafter, Gabriel is identified with this eroticized object when he is cast as an angel in the school's Christmas pagent: "Gabriel Okimasis...one of God's own cherubin. Hands held together against his chest, the six-year-old knelt on a prayer stool and bent low his perfect head" (80). Needless to say, the desiring lens here is boy loving and specif-ically pedophilic when associated with the sexually abusive priest. The reader's task would be straightforward if the resonance of the reference to Caravaggio were contained there. However, by 1998, the name Caravaggio is inseparable from a queer iconography, associated with historical homo-erotic subcultures, which are in the process of being recuperated as part of a queer cultural politics centred on the archaeology of gay identity (Tweedie 2003, 380–81). In a way that may be discomfiting for some read-ers, Highway seems to want to identify Caravaggio's eroticizing depic-tions of boy angels as part of the aesthetic universe of a pedophilic priest, even as *Kiss of the Fur Queen* aligns itself with broader aspects of the Caravaggian aesthetic.[8] Such images include Caravaggio's humbling of religious materials through a translation of sacred Christian stories into historically "inaccurate," theatrical genre scenes — "neither sacred not profane, but somewhere in between" (Hibbard 1983, 155); his penchant for ambiguously autobiographical paintings in which he inserts portraits of his own face; his refusal of idealism and lyrical beauty in religious painting in favour of a sometimes horrifying realism; his desublimation of symbols into secular, provocatively violent, perverse, sexualized, and often homoerotic scenes, ambivalent in their point of view and almost fetishistic in their insistence on surface or what Mieke Bal has called the "image's skin" (1999, 30).[9]

"Caravaggio," then, has a broader reference in *Kiss of the Fur Queen* insofar as it operates as the sign for the sexualized nature of Catholic iconography and for the queer or "perverse" point of view that recognizes and draws out that iconography's elements of sadomasochism and homoeroticism, giving the lie not only to pretensions of piety but also to the notion of a normalcy of desire. This queer exposure is worked out in a passage in which Jeremiah, newly admitted to residential school, is treated to a classroom lesson about Heaven and Hell illustrated by a chart drawn "in complex detail and swirling, extravagant colours" (Highway [1998] 2005, 58). While the lesson is supposed to inculcate a fear of the devil, Jeremiah is distracted by the "beautiful blond men with feathery wings and flowing white dresses" in Heaven and even more so by the activities enjoyed by the residents of Hell where, he observes, the "dark-skinned people sat": "There appeared to be no end to the imagination with which these brown people took their pleasure; and this, Father Lafleur explained earnestly to his captive audience, was permanent punishment" (60, 61). As if to provide a more immediate confirmation of this coincidence of pleasure and punishment, Jeremiah discerns "a tinge of something not unlike enjoyment" in the priest's tone and hears the word "lust" "burst forth like a succulent, canned plum" from his lips. The ending of the passage, in which Jeremiah mistakenly transcribes "devil" as "evil" in his scribbler, can be read in terms of the child's accidental but incisive demystification of sin, since the absence of the "d" effectively disarms a doctrine that needs the personification of a "devil" in order to intimidate and terrorize. However, it is also crucial to observe that Jeremiah does not just decipher the sadistic relish that is entangled in the priest's religious fervour, but he also shares this enjoyment. Jeremiah's enjoyment is emphasized in the final lines of the passage, which describe his pleasure in the outer shape of "evil": "He thought it rather pretty, especially the way the *V* came to such an elegant point at the bottom, like a tiny, fleeting kiss" (62).

This sensual and corporeal lesson is inscribed much more violently later on, when Jeremiah's brother Gabriel is whipped by the priest as punishment for speaking Cree at school. The whipping scene is embedded in the middle of a chapter that is about the Cree children's schoolyard re-enactment of the passion play, with Gabriel in the role of the suffering Christ dragging his cross up the Via Dolorosa and Jeremiah playing a sadistic, whip-toting Roman centurion, before an imagined bloodthirsty crowd of "ten million" (83). The chapter immerses us immediately in the scene, delaying the provision of contextualizing information that would explain it as a schoolyard performance and the focalizing perspective of "Jesus" as that of Gabriel. This delay supports the investment in realism, which sustains the pleasure of the performers themselves as well as that of the reader. The at first ambiguously focalized narration records the imagined detail of "[b]lood from the victim's lacerated spine splash[ing] the soldier's scarlet tunic, his gold breastplate, his leather leggings, and naked thighs" (83). The initial lack of context and background also makes the sudden appearance in the midst of the performance of Mariesis Okimasis, the boys' mother—drinking red wine from a Javex jug—that much more startling and disturbing.

In the official Stations of the Cross (the sequence of devotional prayers commemorating Christ's final hours), Mary appears to Jesus at the fourth station. The boys' dramatization, however, seems to belong to the unsanctioned theatrical tradition of medieval passion plays that were a "carnivalesque" derivation from the stations.[10] The appearance of a reeling, drunken Mariesis and her account of week-long wedding festivities at Eemanapiteepitat in the place of Mary, in the midst of the boys' perform-ance of Christ's walk to his death, introduces an element of coarse, pro-fane humour that aligns this adaptation of a Christian ritual with a tradi-tion of popular, unsanctioned folk appropriations. But the humour of this irruption of a boisterous scene of Eemanapiteepitat revelry in the midst of the stations of the cross is dampened by the extreme pathos of the mother's condition. Mariesis appears to "Jesus" in such a degraded form — "so drunk she could barely stand," red wine streaking her breasts "like excess milk" — that the effect is to suggest a relation between the sadomasochistic pleasures staged by Gabriel and Jeremiah and the debasement of the mother (84).[11] The suggestion that the boys' inhabit-ing of Christian roles brings about a reorganization of family relation-ships is reinforced at the conclusion of the chapter, when the re-enact-ment of the stations ends abruptly with the children's cruel abandonment of the six-year-old "Cree Son of God" on the cross (86). At the instruction of Jeremiah, the participating children strip Gabriel and leave him wired to a fence as they rush to the dining hall for dinner. Not only has the for-merly exhalted mother been summoned in a marginal and degraded role, but Jeremiah's cruelty and Gabriel's resulting "vow of vengeance" have left the brothers at odds with one another (87).

The text does not permit an unambivalent reading of the re-enact-ment of Christian ritual as destructive, however. The passage is con-structed so that the scene of the re-enactment of Christ's suffering in the schoolyard is interlaced with another scene occurring one week earlier when, we are told, Gabriel "had felt that same sensation, the stinging pain that brought with it a most unsaintly thrill" (84). In this earlier scene Gabriel is whipped by Father Lafleur for having spoken Cree. The details of the scene are ambiguous — the priest may be naked, with "little Gabriel's buttocks splayed across his knees" — but we are told that Gabriel is clinging to a "*vision*" of Father Lafleur as "God the Father" lashing him with his "thunderbolt" (85 [emphasis added]). What is insisted upon is Gabriel's response to the beating, which is to refuse to protest: "He wasn't going to cry. No sir! If anything, he was going to fall down on his knees before this man and tell him that he had come face to face with God, so pleasurable were the blows" (85). Gabriel's intention to express pleasure may be a planned ruse, a means of resisting a punishment that seeks to weaken him. However, at the same time, there is the suggestion that he has learned this complex posture of agential masochism through an identification with Jesus. For if his residential school education prohibits the speaking of Cree, it positively encourages "playing Jesus" as a "supplement" to religious education (84). Gabriel, though, does both at once. The ostensible reason for his whipping is his having sung a bawdy Cree jig when, on another occasion, "he was hanging from the cross and already seven tokens in the red" (84).[12] In the midst of his beating for this offence, he seems to renew his conflation of defiance and submission. *"Kimoosoom chimasoo,"* Gabriel's little Cree voice rang out from the pit of his groin, even as a little English voice beside it pleaded: "Yes, Father, please! Make me bleed! Please, please, make me bleed!" (85). While the involuntary translation of Cree into English here might suggest that the language in which Gabriel has been schooled betrays his body, this does not seem to be the case. The Cree itself is prohibited, but the enjoyment "from the pit of his groin" that the Cree phrase expresses here—an enjoyment of punishment—is decidedly not prohibited. When Gabriel begs the priest to make him bleed, he is in a sense behaving as a correct little pupil who has learned all of the lessons that "playing Jesus" can teach. Just as the distinction between being good and being bad dissolves at this point, so, it seems, does the distinction between Gabriel's spirit of revolt and his enjoyment of a pleasure that is predicated on the very prohibitions that he rebels against.

How to read the meaning of the "special quality of suffering" that Gabriel comes to associate with the body of Jesus, and to stage for himself as an adult gay man, is one of the more perplexing questions raised by *Kiss of the Fur Queen* (Haggerty 2004–05, para. 32).[13] The novel seems to offer abundant evidence in support of a very troubling reading of Gabriel's adult sexuality as an unfortunate, even pathological, effect of childhood "damage." It certainly courts a reading of Gabriel's adult practices in terms of the heteronormative trope of "gay promiscuity."[14] Highway has Gabriel's initiation into anonymous public sex occur in the space of the shopping mall that serves in the novel as the trope for the "monster" of cannibalistic consumer capitalism. He constructs a narrative arc that takes us from the space of the Cree family in Eemanapiteepitat to the lonely and alienated individualism of the city and to Gabriel's death from AIDS, with a parallel narrative of sexual defamiliarization that moves from the exhuberant lovemaking of Abraham and Mariesis Okimasis to their sons' estrangements from reproductive sexuality. When, in a post-residential school encounter between Abraham and Gabriel, Highway's third-person narrator frames the gulf between father and son in the sentimental terms of the former's sexual innocence ("Supposing this kind old hunter could see the hundred other men with whom his last-born had shared... what? Supposing this most Catholic of men could see his baby boy pumping and being pumped"), this interpretation of the novel's presentation of homosexuality as a sad facet of cultural assimilation seems incontrovertible (Highway [1998] 2005, 190).

I want to propose a less reductive reading, however — one that takes its cue from the novel's commitment to epistemological ambivalence. Richard Lane, working with Gerald Vizenor's (1989) theorization of trickster discourse, associates this ambivalence with a mode of trickster signification that works through "comedy, chance, and an aversion to containment" (2002, 193). Via this mode of signification, Lane argues, *Kiss of the Fur Queen* tries to imagine a kind of "restitution" following the "catastrophes" of dispossession and abuse that does not amount to recovery. What seems important is the avoidance of the re-inscription of normativity that the medico-psychological model of "recovery" brings with it. Instead, in Lane's view, Highway's novel attempts to acknowledge the fundamental discontinuity effected by trauma by imagining a form of restitution that does not return to "some unsullied state of being" and does not pretend to heal the divisions "between child and mother, or parents, or community" (194, 195). Lane establishes what is at stake in acknowledging discontinuity in his reading of a key moment in the novel, in which Mariesis's words seem to point to the gulf in understanding between her sons and herself. Mariesis says: "[I]f you ever forgot what those priests taught you at that school, it would kill your father. I tell you, he would just die" (Highway [1998] 2005, 290). "Forgetting," as Lane observes, "is not exactly the problem, which generates a kind of black humour at this point in the story, and being told to remember, while referring to the teachings of Christianity, also becomes a call to remember the abuse as a way of keeping First Nations communities alive" (Lane 2002, 195).

According to the paradox that Lane reads in this passage, "keeping First Nations communities alive" depends upon remembering the abuse and keeping the "teachings" of Christianity as the trigger for that memory. Here I think Lane approaches the real scandal of *Kiss of the Fur Queen,* which is its willingness to draw associations (which are non-totalizing and non-determinative, but associations all the same) between trauma and identity, between sexual abuse and queer sexuality, and between sexual abuse and a queerly assumed First Nations identity. These associations are prohibited in a Left-liberal discussion on progressive grounds and for good reasons. The mere suggestion of a link between traumatic experience and non-normative sexual practices, for instance, seems to produce a pathological taint that colours those practices as compulsive repetition. As I shall argue later in this essay, however, without the kinds of associations that Highway insists on drawing, the subversive, productive possibilities of repetitions that allow differentiation and agency through their creative restaging of traumatic experience are unimaginable.

The risks the novel takes in making these associations are missed when *Kiss of the Fur Queen* is read primarily as the model for an ambivalent or compromised Canadian postcolonialism, although these features of the novel are aptly named in such readings. In response to a Canadian postcolonial criticism that tended towards complacent homogenizations in the 1980s and 1990s, the turn towards Aboriginal writing for a certain re-politicization — for reminders of the different postcolonial constituencies in Canada, marked by their unequal access to institutional resources, for a renewed sense of the "contaminated valency of Canadian postcolonial critique" (Brydon 2001, 24), or for alternatives to assimilationist celebrations of cultural hybridity (Sugars 2002, 73) — was an important intervention. However, the disruption and renewal of Canadian postcolonial criticism that was helpful and necessary at this moment, and that could be so effectively proposed through a mobilization of Highway's novel, also seems to have constituted a missed opportunity to explore the novel's risks. The novel's posing of taboo questions — Does sexual abuse make you gay? Does cultural dispossession and contamination with Christianity make you First Nations? — seems designed to render it unusable as a text that merely re-opens the traumas of national identity. In effect, making *Kiss of the Fur Queen* an emblem of compromised Canadian postcolonialism paradoxically functions to close these traumas, by absorbing them into, or making them meaningful as part of, a reconstruction or retooling of Canadian postcolonialism. In these readings, First Nations cultural production is given a kind of moral agency — that is, it is made to function as the ethical disruption of postcolonial discourse. In order to serve this function, First Nations culture has to be clearly and cleanly "other" to settler culture. However, Highway's insistence on its contamination, its inseparability from colonial history, even production by that history, means that First Nations culture cannot serve this purpose. The colonial history means that there is no such radical otherness to call upon as a corrective. *Kiss of the Fur Queen* thus resists being used to propose a new, improved (that is, more honest) version of Canadian postcolonialism that still retains a fundamentally nationalist purpose. By magnifying the novel's concern with the terrain of sexuality, then, I want to try to show that *Kiss of the Fur Queen* is more scandalous than critics have heretofore acknowledged.

Repetition, Differentiation, and Agency

In Lane's essay, the novel's staging of restitution in a trickster mode that "function[s] symbolically, as with ritual," generating its meaning "within the time of the event itself," is examined through the musical and dance representations composed by the two Okimasis brothers as adults (2002, 196). Yet such restitution must also be seen in the performance that is part of Gabriel's adult sexuality. Well suited to the risky connection between sexual abuse and "perverse" sexuality that Highway seems to draw is Ann Cvetkovich's argument about the centrality of fetish and fantasy to queer culture's response to trauma (1995). Cvetkovich wishes to articulate an alternative to the view within lesbian feminist and mainstream therapeutic discourses that positing any connection between sexual abuse, especially incest, and lesbianism amounts to naming a causal connection — and a causal connection that assumes, furthermore, that there is something wrong with being lesbian or gay (357). This therapeutic view surrenders the possibility of exploring the ways in which the complex relations between these terms "may be productive rather than cause for alarm" (358). Sexual practices with an overtly performative dimension that risk the repetition of scenes of sexual abuse through, for example, relations of dominance and submission, set in motion the power of ritualized repetition to effect differentiations and to transform earlier scenes of violence. Cvetkovich reads Dorothy Allison's semi-autobiographical novel, *Bastard Out of Carolina* (1993), for the connections between pleasure and fantasies of violation that are experienced as shameful because they conjure memories of abuse. She argues that as "the price of sexual agency," Bone, the first-person narrator, must contend with the mixture of pleasure, shame, and anger in the violent fantasies that she cultivates: "The pleasure [Bone's fantasies] produce cannot be separated from the trauma to which they are also connected; to ask for one without the other is to demand that Bone tell her story of violence and leave out her fantasies," that she "offer a truncated narrative that makes her an innocent victim" (Cvetkovich 1995, 369 and 370). Thus, Bone's account does not answer the demand that victims be passive and desexualized in order to be sympathetic. In order to tell the truth about her abuse, she includes her sexual fantasies, and the inclusion of these fantasies demonstrates the way that she comes to claim and possess for her own purposes the power of that which brought her harm (369).

In *Kiss of the Fur Queen*, the scene of Gabriel's first experience of sexual abuse by the priest is both a scene of violation and, as becomes clear when we return to it through Gabriel's adult sexual experiences, an initiation into a particular *mise en scène* of desire. The positions in the scene already prefigure the positions of violence and impassivity that are reassumed in the whipping scene that I have already discussed. Father Lafleur approaches Gabriel while he is sleeping and Gabriel's dream incorporates what we imagine to be the sensations produced by the priest's hand as he commences to masturbate the child:

> A sliver of light flashed once from the dark recesses of the room. It could have been a firefly except that this was mid-December.... The firefly reappeared and disappeared again as it approached the row where the dreaming Gabriel Okimasis was furiously engaged in a do-si-do made particularly complicated because his partner, Carmelita Moose, kept floating up, balloon-like, so that, while his feet were negotiating quick little circles, his arms had to keep Carmelita Moose earthbound. The undisputed fact was that Gabriel Okimasis's little body was moving up and down, up and down, producing, in the crux of his being, a sensation so pleasurable that he wanted Carmelita Moose to float up and up forever so he could keep jumping up, reaching for her and pulling her back down. (Highway [1998] 2005, 77)

Here, the gothic "play of opacity and transparency" in which "each state acquires pathos from its opposite" is designed to absorb the reader too (Sedgwick 1986, 80–81). The narration performs its work of description only partially and through childlike "mistakes." The "firefly," we gather after a delay, is the moonlight catching on the silver crucifix hanging from the neck of the approaching priest. When the focalizing perspective settles within Gabriel's woken consciousness, these ambiguities are resolved, but the pathos of misapprehension, now Gabriel's alone, is only heightened. Gabriel decides that the priest's strange actions must be "the right of holy men," as he observes the priest's face "glowing in the moonlight with the intense whiteness of the saints in the catechism book" (Highway [1998] 2005, 78).

As the priest leans over Gabriel, his crucifix—"the naked Jesus Christ—this sliver of silver light, this fleshly Son of God so achingly beautiful"—moves against Gabriel's mouth. The body of Christ and Gabriel's incipient orality become in this moment bound up in Gabriel's experience of orgasm at the hands of the priest: "[I]n his half-dream state, this man nailed to the cross was a living, breathing man, tasting like Gabriel's most favourite food, warm honey" (78–79). Later on, as a young man, in moments of exquisite sexual pleasure Gabriel tastes warm honey—his body's sensory memory of the abuse, a memory in which is condensed a whole complex of physical and emotional responses as well as contextual religious associations.[15] The invocation of the taste of honey in the adult sexual experiences is always ambiguous. When Gabriel is in an alleyway with a stranger, he sees the "mauve and pink and purple of fireweed and taste[s], on the buds that lin[e] his tongue, the essence of warm honey." The colours of fireweed associate the experience with the flora of his sub-arctic home, whereas the taste of honey pulls the experience in the direction of memories of abuse at residential school (132). When the taste of honey returns again, Gabriel is at an orgy, a penetrated, wounded body, devoured by "serpent-like" tongues (169). Gabriel's lovers in his adult life include a priest and a predatory mentor who is described in terms that suggest his menace through specifically priestly associations. His lover is "[f]lawlessly turned out in black, accessorized with silver." He wears a crucifix around his "whiteman's neck," and follows Gabriel, as Jeremiah observes, "two steps behind him, as in an ecclesiastical rite" (201, 204, 212).

However, while Gabriel's adult sexuality is indeed framed in terms of repetition, this repetition is more creative than compulsive. It is much less about repression than it is about the fetish as a vehicle for sexual activity that attempts to counter victimization and the loss of memory. In this respect, *Kiss of the Fur Queen* seems to support Sedgwick's proposal that, in spite of the depth psychology and the theme of repression that tend to preoccupy gothic criticism, "the most characteristic and daring areas of Gothic convention [are] those that point the reader's attention back to surfaces" (1986, 140–41). In the gothic writing of "contagious, quasi-linguistic" surfaces, metonymy is a privileged trope in the characterization and elaboration of the sexual (142). The fetish functions as a particular type of metonym, with a "strong erotic savour of its own" that prevents it from operating as a pretext or "cloak for something deeper and thus more primal" (144, 143).[16] This sense of the fetish in gothic fiction, as linked to the eroticization of surfaces and material objects, is also what makes the fetish valuable as a potential vehicle for ritualized performances that repeat and transform experiences of sexual abuse in what Cvetkovich names as a queer response to trauma (1995, 360). The emphasis on trans-formative acts that risk repetition in order to produce differentiations in an ongoing process distinguishes this queer response from the "punctual event" of narrative disclosure. The fetish does not lend itself to this regis-ter of disclosure or confession. As a metonym, the fetish is ambivalent, both an access point to, and an effacement of, memory. It also bears an oblique relation to the event of the abuse, carrying its memory as a sub-jective emotional, mental, and physical complex, coloured by contingent associations. The materiality and plasticity of the fetish that make it an access point to this "emotional and physical process" also make the fetish amenable to productive use in new contexts of activity (363). Thus, of the two Okimasis brothers, it is Gabriel who seems to elaborate a desire that takes its own form, even as it deploys the *mise en scène* of his abuse. In an important exchange between the brothers, in which Jeremiah seems to ask a question on behalf of the reader, Highway has Gabriel confront Jeremiah with the cost of his fear of repetition:

> Jeremiah slammed Gabriel against the wall....
>
> "How can you let someone do what that disgusting old priest did to you? How can you seek out ... people like that?"
>
> "And you?" Gabriel grabbed the wrist and flung it to the side with such force that Jeremiah reeled. "You'd rather diddle with a piano than diddle with yourself. You're dead, Jeremiah. At least my body is still alive." (Highway [1998] 2005, 207)

Jeremiah has been provoked to ask Gabriel this question after he sees the shocking sight of his brother with his priestly, "black-garbed" boyfriend. Jeremiah sees this sight iconographically: "there, against the bedroom wall, black on white, Gregory Newman hung nailed to his brother, by the mouth" (198, 204). The effect of this picture, which is to make Jeremiah "wil[l] his body dead," reminds us that the effects of sexual abuse are mediated and unpredictable. In Jeremiah's case, repetition is stark and terrifying. Jeremiah's experience of abuse has become unspeakable and unknowable, and what seems to render it such is the additional trauma of having witnessed his beloved younger brother's abuse. The scene of Gabriel's violation by Father Lafleur does not stop with Gabriel's confusion and pleasure. It continues with a subsequent section that switches focalization to Jeremiah, who is also among the rows of children in the moonlit hall. It is through Jeremiah that we see the scene in terms of a beastly attack with cannibalistic overtones that invert and recode Gabriel's desire to "swallow whole the living flesh" of the crucifix: "When the beast reared its head, it came face to face, not four feet away, with that of Jeremiah Okimasis. The whites of the beast's eyes grew large, blinked once. Jeremiah stared. It *was* him. Again" (79). The adverb suggests that we are already in the time of repetition, but since it is unclear whether the repetition is for Jeremiah or Gabriel, it also produces an ambiguity with regard to the boundary between the brothers. From this point on in the story, this ambiguity becomes Jeremiah's symptom, for the novel plays out some of the clichés of gothic criticism's depth psychology, but — significantly — only in relation to Jeremiah's homophobia and misogyny, which it suggests result from the processes of repression and projected self-loathing, for which the novel offers alternatives in Gabriel's work of queer repetition involving the creative possibilities of fantasy and fetishism.

When Jeremiah leaves his brother to be beaten by homophobic thugs at a pow-wow on Manitoulin Island, what is at stake for Jeremiah is differentiation from a brother who has sometimes seemed to him a threatening, uncanny double: "[H]ow else would he face the truth: that he was embarrassed to be caught in cahoots with a pervert, a man who fucked other men? On an Indian reserve, a Catholic reserve?" (250). The punishment for perversion that Jeremiah knows Gabriel will receive, because he refuses to help him, will replay the punishment that Jeremiah delivered earlier himself, in his performance as the whip-toting Roman centurion who lashed "Jesus" and then saw to his abandonment by the other players. However, the unexamined shame and self-loathing in Jeremiah that is projected outward onto Gabriel is not a sufficient explanation for what happens at the pow-wow. Gabriel's reading of his assailants makes Jeremiah's phobic projection only a specific instance of a wider, historical effect: "[W]here he had anticipated hatred, what he saw, instead, was terror. Of what? The fact that the flesh of the mother had formed their flesh, female blood ran thick inside their veins? Terror that the emotion of a woman, the spirit of a woman, lived inside them?" (251). The novel associates this misogyny—offered here as the root of homophobic violence among the reserve thugs—with colonial Christianity's suppression of First Nations spiritual beliefs and practices and its imposition of a patriarchal religion that required the demonization of the last female shaman of the northern Cree, Chachagathoo (247). Both the name Chachagathoo and the abuse suffered by the boys at the hands of the priests have been rendered unspeakable in Eemanapiteetipat (90–91).

While Jeremiah internalizes this colonial derogation of First Nations spirituality, Gabriel seems to be more receptive to the lessons taught by female characters in the novel (including a torch-singing fox in drag, to whom I shall return) who are associated, through metonymic details, with the trickster figure of the fur queen. It is important to interject at this point that the novel does not allow a reductive dichotomization of the brothers' responses to personal and cultural traumas. Gabriel does not entirely escape the taints of victimhood and consumerist individualism and even demonstrates a certain irresponsibility in relation to the abject figures of raped Aboriginal women whose disturbing presence trails the brothers in the city. Gabriel "brushe[s] past" the scene of a gang rape in an alleyway on his way to a sexual adventure, whereas earlier on Jeremiah attempts to report to the police his witnessing of events leading up to the rape and murder of another Aboriginal woman (132, 107). On the other hand, the novel makes Jeremiah much more resistant than Gabriel to acknowledging the history of spiritual dispossession that is indirectly invoked by these liminal figures of violated Aboriginal women. When Gabriel demonstrates his interest in learning about Aboriginal spirituality and tells Jeremiah that "Indian religion listens to the drum, to the heartbeat of Mother Earth," Jeremiah dismisses him as promoting the pagan practices of "savages" (184). Jeremiah's homophobia and misogyny are represented as the symptoms of a violent, collectively experienced cultural and spiritual dispossession and the imposition of "the sadistic ideology of immaculate motherhood" on a matristic society in which, as Highway writes in his prefatory note, "the male-female-neuter hierarchy is entirely absent" (Bal 1999, 65; Highway [1998] 2005, "Note on the Trickster"). The novel's setting of the homophobic attack on Gabriel on a reserve that is both "Indian" and "Catholic" suggests the extent to which the imposed gender ideology has been absorbed.

The Manitoulin Island reserve that Jeremiah and Gabriel visit is identified as "Wasaychigan Hill," which is the fictional setting of Highway's play *Dry Lips Oughta Move to Kapuskasing* (1989, 249). The allusion to the play at this point in the novel is significant because the play draws some of the same connections between missionary education, misogyny, and violence against women. In the play's climactic scene, Dicky Bird Halked, the damaged, fatherless son of an alcoholic mother, adopted by evangelical Christian Ojibway parents, rapes a pregnant female character, Patsy Pegahmagahbow, with a crucifix. Patsy is one of several female manifestations of the Ojibway trickster figure, Nanabush, throughout the play. As she is being raped, Dicky Bird's real father, the macho leader of the men on the reserve, looks on with his admiring sidekick, Creature, and displaces his discomfort and guilt through a homophobic gesture. Grabbing his friend *"violently by the collar,"* as the stage instructions require, he says: "Get out. Get the fuck out of here. You're nothin' but a fuckin' fruit. Fuck off" (100). Although a connection between misogyny and homophobia is implied, the play's structure and symbolism insist on gender hierarchy and the degradation of female power as the ultimate stains of Christian colonialism on First Nations society, from which other forms of violence emanate. The rape of Patsy serves as a dramatic symbolization of colonial invasion. The effects of Dicky Bird's internalization of Christianity are acted out on a female body that represents the violated and damaged community of Wasaychigan Hill as a whole.

Dry Lips Oughta Move to Kapuskasing is prefaced by the same pedagogical note on the absence of gender distinctions in First Nations languages and the gender liminality of "the central hero figure" in First Nations mythology—"neither exclusively male nor exclusively female, or... both simultaneously"—that is reprinted at the beginning of *Kiss of the Fur Queen* (12). However, the play is much less ambiguous than the novel in its proposal that gender oppression, and rape that is seen as the key "practice" of gender oppression, is an adequate symbol of colonialism. Indeed, something different seems to happen to the status of rape in *Kiss of the Fur Queen* that is an index of the novel's less resolved sense of the relations between colonial racism, gender oppression, and homophobia. This difference also registers a shift in the way that Highway is thinking about the relation between queerness and contemporary First Nations culture.[17] The "Note on the Trickster" at the beginning of the novel implicitly asks the reader to draw a connection between the gender liminality of Cree and Ojibway hero figures and the story that follows. One thread of this story does involve the affirmation of Gabriel's vision of the "Trickster representing God as a woman, a goddess in fur" (Highway [1998] 2005, 298). The fur queen teaches the brothers the trickster's lessons about contradiction and paradox, in her manifold guises as beauty queen, astral tiara, store mannequin, spectral Aboriginal street woman, emaciated dancing "man-woman," and, especially, as the fox in sex-pot drag who counsels Jeremiah in the tough survivalism of the torch-song singer and as the modern female shaman, Ann-Adele Ghostrider, who burns sweetgrass at Gabriel's deathbed and ensures that the rosary in his dying hands is replaced with an eagle feather (168). Instead of throwing out the rosary, however, she drapes it around a cross-dressed Ken doll. Here, it might be said, First Nations struggle and gay struggle come together through the unifying trope of gender diversity. One might argue that Highway invokes a tradition of First Nations two-spiritedness in order to suggest a universalizing conception of gender fluidity that allows gay identity to cohere with First Nations identity. However, *Kiss of the Fur Queen* also opens questions that trouble, rather than confirm, this coincidence of First Nations and gay struggles. Ann-Adele's gesture replaces the rosary in Gabriel's hands with the eagle feather. And the novel's representation of the terrain of sexuality, especially Gabriel's homosexuality, as I have shown, is focused on sexual acts rather than gender identity. The definition of homosexuality in terms of a gender fluidity that can be claimed as part of First Nations culture — even heralded as one of the key values of that culture — is demoted and relativized by a different, competing sense of homosexuality that is about non-normative sexual practices, including those that refuse an absolute opposition between pleasure and violation. The space that the novel opens between gender and sexuality is thus a gap between the issue of the "rape" of Aboriginal socio-cultural systems and the issue of the oppression of queers.[18] The prefatory note's reminder of the absence of gender hierarchy in First Nations mythologies does not suture this gap.

The minoritizing sense of homosexuality in *Kiss of the Fur Queen* prevents the deployment of rape in its function in *Dry Lips Oughta Move to Kapuskasing* as an all-encompassing symbol (Sedgwick 1990, 1).[19] In the novel, rape only accedes to this figurative status part of the time, and uncomfortably. In *Dry Lips Oughta Move to Kapuskasing,* the rape of a woman/trickster figure occurs in the context of a male character's nightmare. In *Kiss of the Fur Queen,* raped and murdered Aboriginal women appear on the streets of Winnipeg as references to a documented history of racist sexual violence. Rape, in this case, is not a figure for colonialism but one specific form that its violence takes, and this form is experienced by the Okimasis brothers as well.[20] The street women whose ghostly presence trails Jeremiah and Gabriel in Winnipeg are unwelcome, uncanny reminders of the young men's own sexual victimization. Yet there is also something about the appearances of these abject, degraded, synthetically clad women — Evelyn Rose McCrae, "the polyester Indian princess," the pregnant "Madonna of the Main" in her *della robbia* blue windbreaker, a "sad plastic rose in her hair" — that recalls the appearance of the degraded Mariesis in the midst of the boys' schoolyard enjoyment of the sadomasochistic pleasures of the stations of the cross (Highway [1998] 2005, 106, 216). Like that appearance of a degraded mother, the appearance of these women is always guilt-inducing — the women become visible in moments of ambition and pleasure for Jeremiah and Gabriel. In this structure of discomfort, I suggest that we read something other than the compulsive tracing of the characters' or the author's shame. I suggest that we read the inadequacy of the trope of rape and the problematic of gender oppression — which the novel does call into play (the suppression of the female shaman Chachagathoo is still offered as the ultimate act of colonialism) — to the text's complex articulation of queer sexuality.[21] If the spectre of the raped woman produces a sullied feeling, it is partly because of the way in which Highway's use of the trope of rape carries with it a model of harm that implies the contamination of an original state not just of integrity but also of purity (the degraded state of the wine-stained Mariesis and the Winnipeg street women robed in plastic carry the weight of this contamination). As I have been arguing, *Kiss of the Fur Queen* sets in motion another understanding of dispossession and, especially, of sexual violation, which refuses to refer back to such a state of purity. The lining up of misogyny, homophobia, and colonial violence that was the work of *Dry Lips Oughta Move to Kapuskasing* therefore breaks down in *Kiss of the Fur Queen,* and the fur queen herself — the novel's master trope of gender ambiguity, cultural hybridity, and gay specificity—can be read as an attempt to resolve this discursive and political disalignment symbolically. The promise of impure integration that she holds out through her capacity to bridge these divergent strands provides the feeling of coherence that the text's wider economy disallows.

Notes

Thanks to Brian Johnson and Pauline Wakeham for numerous discussions of the novel and thoughtful readings of an earlier draft.

1 As Renée Bergland observes, there is an attendant shift in the genre's political implications according to this argument, which was first put forward by Leslie Fiedler (1960) in *Love and Death in the American Novel* (2004, 94–95). Fiedler's psychohistorical approach applies the Freudian (1960) distinction between the forces of superego and id. The European Gothic is revolutionary in its implications because it identifies dangerous irrationality with the repressive authority of ancient aristocratic regimes. By relocating danger in the wilderness, the American Gothic focuses on the threat of the id to the projects of establishing order in the wilderness and in the protagonist's own soul, thereby betraying the conservatism of this version of the Gothic.

2 Haggerty observes that the gothic novel emerges at the very moment "when the battle lines of cultural reorganization are being formed in the later eighteenth century" and suggests that the gothic novel functions to "recor[d] the terror implicit in the increasingly dictatorial reign of those values" (2005, 387).

3 There is an unavoidable irony in the novel's collapsing of Catholicism with the settler-invader project that, at least at the level of national mythology, became an Anglo-Protestant prerogative in nineteenth-century Canada. See Daniel Coleman's *White Civility: The Literary Project of English Canada* (2006) and my *Settler Feminism and Race Making in Canada* (2003). The novel exposes the instrumental contradictions of this project, which could accommodate both anti-Catholic prejudice and the deployment of Catholic institutions in the containment and assimilation of First Nations.

4 First Nations and allied activist organizations' attempts to seek reparations for the genocidal legacy of residential schools are ongoing, as are the state's attempts to respond by seeking to establish closure on the issue. In 2006, the federal government of Canada reached an agreement in principle for a financial settlement with 85,000 First Nations survivors of residential schools. See <http://residen tialschoolsettlement.ca>. The Indian and Northern Affairs minister trumpeted the deal as "a final residential schools settlement agreement" (Fraser 2006, A4). In June 2008, in line with this agreement, the government made a formal apology for its role in residential schooling and established an Indian Residential Schools Truth and Reconciliation Commission (IRSTRC). The differential outcomes of the apology and the IRSTRC for the state and for First Nations are yet to be seen, but concerns about political theatre displacing more substantive political and economic

change have been raised. Highway's anti-confessional, deeply ambivalent representation of post-residential school subjectivity in *Kiss of the Fur Queen* raises additional questions about what it would mean for survivors to speak the truth of their
experience to a commission with public education and reconciliation as its main
mandates. The IRSTRC's potential disciplining of testimony into individualizing
narratives that could be enlisted in a sentimental and self-congratulatory nationalist pedagogy is already anticipated and critiqued by Highway's novel. As I argue, the
novel refuses the teleology of the narrative of violation structured by the opposition of purity or authenticity and contamination. What is at stake is a wider refusal
of the subsumption of Aboriginal peoples' histories, identities, and sexualities
within a paradigm of victimization.

5   The reader of *Kiss of the Fur Queen* is repeatedly reminded of the gulf in sensibili-
ties separating the English and Cree languages — the one a "humourless tongue,"
"hard, filled with sharp, jagged angles," a "dirge" compared to the "descant whirring,
light as foam" of the other (Highway [1998] 2005, 273, 214, and 227). The Okimasis
brothers gradually learn that on "matters sensual, sexual, and therefore fun, a
chasm as unbridgeable as hell separates Cree from English" (190). The implication
is that much is lost or distorted in Highway's second language. This loss may be
comparable to the change in tone that accompanies the change in musical instruments of Jeremiah, a semi-autobiographical character. When he leaves behind his
father's accordion to take up the concert piano in Winnipeg, we are told that the
piano "didn't sound like an accordion; the notes glided, intelligent and orderly, not
giddy and frothy and of a nervous, clownish character" (56). The "clownish," sensu-
ous, and bawdy nature of Cree to which the novel repeatedly alludes suggests that
in spite of the losses in English the novel's transposition of Christian stories into
Cree contexts counters the solemnity of English. Of course the implicit association
of Cree with the flavour of the accordion, a European instrument, also supports the
novel's argument against a cultural authenticity defined in terms of purity and a
pre-colonial past.

6   The novel opens as the boys' father, Abraham Okimasis, becomes "the first Indian"
to win a dog-sled race that is part of an annual Trapper's Festival organized by and
for white settlers in northern Manitoba (Highway [1998] 2005, 6). The boys' parents are devout Catholics, the products of missionary education, who urge their
sons to remember the lessons of the priests at residential school and to continue
attending communion when they move to the city. Of course, the Fur Queen, the
novel's trickster figure, is an emblem of cultural mixture.

7   On this gay recuperation of Caravaggio, see James Tweedie (2003, 379–81).
Caravaggio was in fact conscripted into several contemporary struggles: his baroque
style "became a corrective to formal impasses in abstract and neo-avant-garde art,
and his life a model of rebellion and resistance important to revisionist histories of
the early modern era" (379). On Caravaggio's influence on the baroque revival in
late twentieth-century art and his connection to contemporary baroque thought,
see Mieke Bal (1999). Thanks to my colleague, Brian Johnson, for initially suggesting to me this Caravaggian connection.

8   A number of graduate students in my seminar felt that the novel took politically
inadvisable risks. Even having accepted the suggestion that Highway was perhaps
writing against the constraints of certain progressive pieties associated with normative

sexual and Canadian-nationalist values, they argued that this project was too dangerous in a socio-historical context of homophobia and racism.

9 Of Caravaggio's *Amor Vincit Omnia* (Victorious Cupid), c. 1601–02, Howard Hibbard observes that the artist takes the *other* Michelangelo's cupid, a "pagan, heterosexual symbol that had become a cliché" and turns it into "a boy of the streets and an object of pederastic interest" (1983, 157).

10 Semi-secularized, infused with coarseness, and interspersed with disgraceful and irrelevant farces, these plays were frowned upon by ecclesiastical authorities in the sixteenth century and became a popular tradition sustained by the lower classes.

11 Mariesis/Mary is ostensibly played by one of the other children participating in the schoolyard performance (Highway [1998] 2005, 86). However, the detailed account she gives of the wedding festivities at Eemanapiteepitat and the nature of her appearance as an interruption of the staging of masochistic pleasures ("Not now, Mother, can't you see I'm busy?" said Jesus [84]) suggest that she is as much a fantasy projection of Gabriel's.

12 "Kimoosoom Chimasso" is the name of a jig played by the boys' father on his accordion (Highway [1998] 2005, 17). The jig is translated in the novel's "Glossary of Cree Terms" as follows: "Grandpa gets a hard-on, grandma runs away, diddle-ee, etc. (a non-sensical musical rhyme)" (308).

13 Cynthia Sugars argues that Gabriel ultimately comes to refuse "the cannibalizing discourse of Christianity" but notes that the text does not allow easy dichotomies either: "For it is also the consuming of the body of Christ that triggers Gabriel's erotic fantasies" (2002, 78). Diana Brydon, too, observes the reversibility of the text's trope of cannibalism and reads it as an allegory "for accepting the contaminated valency of Canadian postcolonial critique," inviting others to elaborate the "queer dimensions" of Highway's intertwining of postcolonial, racial, and gay politics (2001, 24).

14 It is important to note that this reading of Gabriel is eventually localized in the repugnant character of Gregory Newman, Gabriel's first boyfriend, who is described in terms that associate him with the predatory priest. Observing a Gabriel who is moving beyond his controlling grasp, Gregory thinks: "Behind the show of innocence and northern piety, what a piece of dirt, a slut, a whore, a slab of meat fucked through every orifice, from Tokyo to Toronto, from Rome to Buenos Aires" (Highway [1998] 2005, 266).

15 And perhaps a historical association too. This motif of orality seems linked to the condition of starvation of the northern Manitoba Cree caribou hunters when missionaries arrived in the nineteenth century. Jeremiah's play, "Chachagathoo, the Shaman," represents this condition of starvation and its implications for the Cree's capacity to resist Christian education when Gabriel, playing the dying hunter Migisoo, ultimately succumbs to a Weetigo creature that leaps into his mouth (Highway [1998] 2005, 294). Throughout the text, as Sugars has observed, the Weetigo (a cannibal monster in Cree myth) is associated with the Catholic priests of the residential school, with the city as site of consumer capitalism, and, in the novel's central trope of ambivalence and reversibility, with the capacity of the boys themselves to internalize these destructive, cannibalizing impulses (2002, 74). The crucifix becomes an oral fetish for Gabriel, but the literal connotations of the symbolic act of consuming the body of Christ in communion also come to repulse him

(Highway [1998] 2005, 125). It is worth noting that Gabriel distracts himself from this feeling of repulsion in the passage in question by gazing longingly at the physique of his teacher, so that his orally focused desire serves, strangely, as a counter to his disgust with communion (125).

16 Eve Sedgwick is reinterpreting the function of the nun's veil in gothic fiction: "The veil that conceals and inhibits sexuality comes by the same gesture to represent it, both as a metonym of the thing covered and as a metaphor for the system of prohibitions by which sexual desire is enhanced and specified" (1986, 143). Of course, fetishism is not other to Freudian psychoanalytic theory, but, as Sedgwick suggests, its psychoanalytic formulation is not part of the Freudian canon that gothic criticism, preoccupied with depths and interiority, draws upon (141).

17 Peter Dickinson also wants to insist that the realm of sexuality in Highway's work needs to be seen as something more specific than "an undifferentiated aspect of the intersection of [the categories of ethnicity and gender]" (1999, 182). However, Dickinson's reading, which is restricted to the plays that Highway wrote before *Kiss of the Fur Queen*, is drawn back towards a model that would only extend these strands by adding sexuality as a third. Thus, "the 'anality' of *Dry Lips*... is sufficient enough to signify an extension of the notion of a 'crisis of authenticity' in Highway's writing to include not only patriarchal constructions of gender and racialist constructions of ethnicity/aboriginality, but also (hetero)normative constructions of masculinity/sexuality" (185). I am suggesting that *Kiss of the Fur Queen* signals a departure from this coalescence in Highway's earlier work.

18 What is behind my thinking here are the so-called "sex wars" within feminism in the 1980s and 1990s where the second wave's way of focusing on rape, sexual violence, sexual aggression, and pornography as the pivotal practices of patriarchy was criticized by queer women and "sex radicals" who argued that this analysis involved a simplistic, indeed, heteronormative understanding of sexuality. Gayle Rubin (1984) and Teresa de Lauretis (1988) took this position, for example. This was the moment when the categories of gender and sexuality, previously collapsed in mainstream feminist analysis, became separated and found their boundaries. To bring this back to Highway's *Dry Lips Oughta Move to Kapuskasing* and *Kiss of the Fur Queen*, I see the texts as standing on either side of this debate, since in *Dry Lips* rape is allowed to function as an all-encompassing trope for "violation," whereas in *Kiss of the Fur Queen*, the meanings of power and aggression in sex acts are much more ambiguous. Therefore, *Dry Lips* can be more easily aligned with a feminist critique of gender oppression than *Kiss of the Fur Queen*. And Highway's invoking in his prefaces the gender fluidity that he sees as being inherent in First Nations culture does not solve the problem for *Kiss of the Fur Queen*—that he is presenting an analysis of sexuality that simply will not jibe with the use of rape as an all-encompassing metaphor for violation.

19 Eve Sedgwick puts forward the distinction between minoritizing and universalizing conceptions of homosexuality in *The Epistemology of the Closet* (1990, 83–90).

20 Even as they stand in for a history of racist sexual assault against Aboriginal women, the names and brutal deaths of "Evelyn Rose McCrae—long-lost daughter of Mistik Lake" and especially of "Madeline Jeanette Lacroix, erstwhile daughter of Mistik Lake" (Highway [1998] 2005, 105–06), seem to evoke the specific cases of Aboriginal women raped and murdered by groups of white men in Canada in the

1960s and 1970s. The character, Madeline, who is found with "a red-handled screwdriver lying gently, like a rose, deep within the folds of her blood-soaked sex" (132), recalls the story of Helen Betty Osborne, who was abducted by four men, stabbed with a screwdriver, and found brutally murdered in The Pas, Manitoba, in 1971. One of her assailants, Dwayne Johnston, was convicted of murder in 1987 (see the website of the Aboriginal Justice Implementation Commission, <http://www.ajic.mb.ca/volumeII/chapter1.html>. His first name is echoed in Highway's novel in the uncertain names of the stranger with whom Gabriel has his first sexual encounter in Winnipeg, after the abuse at residential school. "Gabriel found himself stumbling down a dark passageway, Wayne? Dwayne? — what was his name again? — somewhere in front of him" (131). (Thanks to my colleague Susan Birkwood for alerting me to this important detail.) The repetition of "rose" in the name of the character, Evelyn Rose McCrae, and in the similes that describe the weapons left inside the two female victims (107, 132) may be oblique references to the case of Rose Marie Roper, a member of the Alkali First Nation and a residential school survivor and laundry worker, who was raped, beaten, and left to die by a roadside by three young men near Williams Lake, B.C., in 1967. See Constance Backhouse (2008, 227–62). For ongoing research on missing and murdered Aboriginal women in Canada, see the Sisters in Spirit initiative of the Native Women's Association of Canada, <http://www.nwac-hq.org/ en/sisresearch.html>.

21 Even if rape attains a new materiality in *Kiss of the Fur Queen* through the descriptions of the sexual abuse of the brothers and through the novel's indirect references to the actual murder of Helen Betty Osborne, something of the abstraction and distance of rape as a trope remains in the status of the "madonnas of the North Main" who are never more than liminal figures and still function to point beyond themselves to the brothers' experiences of sexual violence and to the colonial history of spiritual dispossession. Perhaps because the rape of women is called into this tropological service, in *Kiss of the Fur Queen* as in *Dry Lips Oughta Move to Kapuskasing,* the act of rape occurs by means of instruments that substitute for the male anatomy. The cross with which Patsy Pegahmagahbow is raped in *Dry Lips Oughta Move to Kapuskasing* becomes in *Kiss of the Fur Queen* a broken beer bottle and a screwdriver. Interestingly, this pattern of prosthetic rape does not apply to Jeremiah's eventual recollection of his anal rape by Father Lafleur (Highway [1998] 2005, 287). The gap between the representation of female and male rape, and the distancing strategy that tends to make rape a trope in the case of female characters, putting them at a distance from the world of male characters, deserves further attention — especially insofar as it necessarily complicates any attempt to suggest an alignment of Highway's gay politics with feminism (see Dickinson's [1999, 182] discussion of feminist responses to Highway's plays). In *Kiss of the Fur Queen,* although the "out" gay brother seems, according to a clichéd political taxonomy, to be more receptive to women than the repressed, paranoid-homophobic one, political commitments along the axes of sexuality and gender are not shown to be commensurable in any easy way.

Works Cited

Allison, Dorothy. 1993. *Bastard Out of Carolina.* New York: Penguin.

Backhouse, Constance. 2008. *Carnal Crimes: Sexual Assault Law in Canada, 1900–1975.* Toronto: Osgoode Society for Canadian Legal History/Irwin Law.

Bal, Mieke. 1999. *Quoting Caravaggio: Contemporary Art, Preposterous History.* Chicago: University of Chicago Press.

Bergland, Renée L. 2004. "Diseased States, Public Minds: Native American Ghosts in Early National Literature." In *The Gothic Other: Racial and Social Constructions in the Literary Imagination.* Ed. Ruth Bienstock Anolik and Douglas L. Howard. Jefferson, NC: McFarland. 90–103.

Brydon, Diana. 2001. "Compromising Postcolonialisms: Tomson Highway's *Kiss of the Fur Queen* and Contemporary Postcolonial Debates." In *Compr(om)ising Post/colonialism(s): Challenging Narratives and Practices.* Ed. Greg Ratcliffe and Gerry Turcotte. Sydney: Dangaroo Press. 15–29.

Caballero, Soledad. 2004. "Gothic Routes, or the Thrills of Ethnography." In *The Gothic Other: Racial and Social Constructions in the Literary Imagination.* Ed. Ruth Bienstock Anolik and Douglas L. Howard. Jefferson, NC: McFarland. 143–62.

Castricano, Jodey. 2006. "Learning to Talk with Ghosts: Canadian Gothic and the Poetics of Haunting in Eden Robinson's *Monkey Beach.*" *University of Toronto Quarterly* 75(2): 801–13.

Coleman, Daniel. 2006. *White Civility: The Literary Project of English Canada.* Toronto: University of Toronto Press.

Cvetkovich, Ann. 1995. "Sexual Trauma/Queer Memory: Incest, Lesbianism, and Therapeutic Culture." *GLQ: A Journal of Lesbian and Gay Studies* 2: 351–77.

Dickinson, Peter. 1999. *Here Is Queer: Nationalisms, Sexualities and the Literatures of Canada.* Toronto: University of Toronto Press.

De Lauretis, Teresa. 1988. "Sexual Indifference and Lesbian Representation." *Theatre Journal* 40(2): 155–77.

———. 1995. "On the Subject of Fantasy." In *Feminisms in the Cinema.* Ed. Laura Pietropaolo and Ada Testaferri. Bloomington: Indiana UP. 63–85.

Fiedler, Leslie. 1960. *Love and Death in the American Novel.* New York: New Criterion.

Fraser, Graham. 2006. "Ex-Residential School Students Get $1.9 Billion." *Toronto Star,* 26 April: A4.

Freud, Sigmund. 1960. *The Ego and the Id.* New York: W.W. Norton.

Haggerty, George E. 2004–05. "The Horrors of Catholicism: Religion and Sexuality in Gothic Fiction." In *Romanticism on the Net* (November 2004–February 2005), 36–37, <http://www.erudit.org/revue/ron/2004/v/n36–37/011133ar.html>.

———. 2005. "Queer Gothic." *A Companion to the Eighteenth-Century English Novel and Culture.* Ed. Paula R. Backscheider and Catherine Ingrassia. London: Blackwell. 383–98.

Henderson, Jennifer. 2003. *Settler Feminism and Race Making in Canada.* Toronto: University of Toronto Press.

Hibbard, Howard. 1983. *Caravaggio.* New York: Harper and Row.

Highway, Tomson. 1989. *Dry Lips Oughta Move to Kapuskasing.* Saskatoon: Fifth House.

———. 1998, reprinted 2005. *Kiss of the Fur Queen.* Toronto: Anchor-Doubleday.

Lane, Richard J. 2002. "Surviving the Residential School System: Resisting Hegemonic Canadianness in Tomson Highway's *Kiss of the Fur Queen.*" In *Reconfigurations: Canadian Literatures and Postcolonial Identities.* Ed. Marc Maufort and Franca Bellarsi. Brussels: Presses Interuniversitaires Euro-péenes. 191–201.

Richardson, John. 1832, reprinted 1998. *Wacousta.* Ed. John Moss. Ottawa: Tecumseh.

Robinson, Eden. 2000. *Monkey Beach.* Toronto: Alfred A. Knopf.

Rubin, Gayle S. 1984. "Thinking Sex: Notes for a Radical Theory of the Politics of Sexuality." In *Pleasure and Danger: Exploring Female Sexuality.* Ed. Carole S. Vance. Boston: Routledge and Kegan Paul. 267–319.

Sedgwick, Eve Kosofsky. 1986. *The Coherence of Gothic Conventions.* New York: Methuen.

———. 1990. *The Epistemology of the Closet.* Berkeley: University of California Press.

Sugars, Cynthia. 2002. "Weetigos and Weasels: Tomson Highway's *Kiss of the Fur Queen* and Canadian Postcolonialism." *Journal of Commonwealth and Postcolonial Studies* 9(1): 69–91.

Tweedie, James. 2003. "The Suspended Spectacle of History: The Tableau Vivant in Derek Jarman's *Caravaggio.*" *Screen* 44(4): 379–403.

Vizenor, Gerald. 1989. "Trickster Discourse: Comic Holotropes and Language Games." In *Narrative Chance: Postmodern Discourse on Native American Indian Literatures.* Albuquerque: University of New Mexico Press. 187–211.

CHAPTER NINE

Rethinking the Canadian Gothic: Reading Eden Robinson's *Monkey Beach*

Jennifer Andrews

Whatever the reasons, we have largely neglected an important...dimension in Canadian fiction, namely the dark band of gothicism, which stretches from earliest to recent times.
> —Margot Northey, *The Haunted Wilderness*

Magic and monsters don't usually get associated with Canadian literature.
> —Margaret Atwood, "Canadian Monsters"

It's only by our lack of ghosts / we're haunted.
> —Earle Birney, "Can. Lit"

Introduction

In a special issue of *Studies in Canadian Literature* on Aboriginal writers in Canada, the Plains Cree scholar and poet Emma LaRocque calls for a move beyond "reading Native writing stereotypically," which involves not only acknowledging the "humanization of Native peoples" but attending to the complexities of their writing—in political *and* aesthetic terms (2006, 16). Perhaps most revealing is LaRocque's own choice of words when describing the contributions of Native writers and scholars:

By banging on the doors of convention, we are lifting the weight of old and tired traditions. We are the other half of Canada, the half that is shedding light on both the good and the shadowy sides of this land. We are sometimes the Uncomfortable Mirrors. (16)

LaRocque's desire to read Aboriginal literature as "Resistance literature" without exclusively focusing on its politics, and to engage with Native texts in a manner that avoids "the spectre of ghettoization," articulates the primary motivation for the essay that follows—a reading of Eden Robinson's distinctly Aboriginal reformulation of the Canadian Gothic in her novel *Monkey Beach* (LaRocque 2006, 15).

Since 2001, when an earlier version of this article first appeared in print (in *Essays on Canadian Writing*), much important work has been done on the Gothic in English-Canadian literature, including Justin Edwards's *Gothic Canada: Reading the Spectre of a National Literature* (2005) and a 2006 special issue of *University of Toronto Quarterly*, guest-edited by Marlene Goldman and Joanne Saul. Most relevant to this essay is Jodey Castricano's "Learning to Talk with Ghosts: Canadian Gothic and the Poetics of Haunting in Eden Robinson's *Monkey Beach*," one of the contributions to the *University of Toronto Quarterly* special issue, which focuses on how Lisamarie Hill is transformed by learning to talk with those who haunt her because she can reconnect with a "spiritual dimension of Haisla culture in spite of its negation in the wake of European contact" (2006, 802). More broadly, Castricano probes the relevance of applying the term Gothic—and the Eurocentric materialist context that frames it—to a Native-authored text such as *Monkey Beach*. She contends that while "*Monkey Beach* deals *in* the Gothic, it could be said that the novel, paradoxically, stages a resistance *to*…the strangely familiar world of Western Gothic" (808). Castricano's reading of the novel exposes the scholarly challenges of reading Lisamarie's narrative, concluding that *Monkey Beach* ultimately undermines Western tendencies to use the Gothic as a means of normalizing or at least pathologizing what is perceived as primitive or "Other." What Castricano's approach raises for me, at least, is the difficulty of doing scholarly work on Aboriginal texts as a non-Native person, deeply steeped in Western models of reading. As Helen Hoy has so elegantly demonstrated in *How Should I Read These?* there are no easy answers to such a situation (2001). Yet, LaRocque's desire to move beyond the ghettoization of Aboriginal texts also signals the need to bring Native works into larger discussions of Canadian literary criticism and to focus on the intersection of political and aesthetic issues within those texts in a manner that potentially challenges enshrined beliefs about Canadian national identity, the place of Aboriginal literature (or its absence) in the study of Canadian literature, and the relevance of the Gothic to English-Canadian and Indigenous literary traditions.

As Castricano aptly points out, the Gothic is, at first glance, an "easy — and even desirable" (2006, 806) framework within which to read *Monkey Beach* because of its openness "to coming to terms with the unspeakable," at least from a Western perspective (Rand 1994, 21). And the Gothic has played an important role in discussions of English Canada's literary development and the concept of literary nationalism, in part because it offers a space to explore the colonial legacy of Canada's creation. Earle Birney may assert that "[i]t's only by our lack of ghosts / we're haunted," but the reality is much different ([1966] 1982, 116). While Jonathan Kertzer has argued that English Canadians are "haunted by a palpable absence that marks our peculiar identity crisis" (1998, 37–38), it is the legacy of an Aboriginal presence, both past and present, that complicates this nationalistic dis-ease. Thus, perhaps it is more appropriate to understand the following reading of *Monkey Beach* as inflected not only by an interest in how the text accords with, and undermines, a Western gothic framework — and the implications of this strategy for ideas of nation in Canada — but also by my own white Western efforts to understand and engage with a world from which I am ultimately distanced.

The Argument

In a review of Eden Robinson's novel published shortly after its release, Joan Thomas describes *Monkey Beach* as an example of "glorious Northern Gothic," bringing the geographic and literary dimensions of the text together in a single term for which no clear definition is provided (2000, D9). Similarly, Warren Cariou claims that Robinson follows the tradition of Stephen King, using "the trappings of a contemporary Gothic novel" but adding a twist by setting her text in the First Nations Haisla community, located on the British Columbia coastline (2000, 36). Both use the word "gothic" to describe *Monkey Beach*'s narrative, a term that certainly is not new to studies of English-Canadian literature. Margot Northey's *The Haunted Wilderness: The Gothic and Grotesque in Canadian Fiction* (1976) is perhaps the best-known and most substantial study of the significance of the "Gothic" in a distinctly Canadian context.[1] Northey's book offers a "critical analysis" of the "varieties of gothic fiction" in nineteenth- and twentieth-century Canadian literature, surveying a diverse array of English- and French-Canadian texts, ranging from what she calls the "Canadian prototype" of the gothic novel *Wacousta* to *Wild Geese, Surfacing, The Double Hook, Kamouraska,* and *La Guerre, Yes Sir!* (18).[2] Although Northey insists that the Gothic is a relevant term for Canadian literature, few scholars in the 1980s and 90s used this concept in their discussions of Canadian fiction. Moreover, the articles that were published typically explored the same handful of novels that were discussed in *The Haunted Wilderness,* limiting the concept of the Gothic to a narrow selection of works.[3]

Yet the reappearance of this term in reviews of Robinson's book suggests that the Gothic remains a potentially useful term for Canadian literature. If so, what role might it play in discussions of contemporary English-Canadian fiction and, more specifically, Aboriginal-authored fiction? This essay examines the relevance of the gothic novel in a Native and a Canadian context through a close reading of Eden Robinson's *Monkey Beach. Monkey Beach* presents its own version of the gothic novel through the story of Lisamarie Hill, a Haisla woman whose world is "populated by supernatural characters" (Cariou 2000, 36). The novel, which traces Lisamarie's past and present as she waits for word on the fate of her missing brother, Jimmy, who has been lost at sea, focuses on various spiritual connections that link her to both the traditional tribal world and Western popular culture. Robinson's text adheres in many respects to the formal and thematic conventions of the gothic novel, as defined by British, American, and Canadian scholars. Yet her depiction of the Gothic within the Haisla community and through a character whose life blends tribal beliefs and practices with an intimate knowledge of the non-Native world calls for a fundamental rethinking of the significance of the gothic novel for English-Canadian literature generally and Native literature written in Canada in particular.

The word "Gothic" historically has been most commonly associated with a medieval form of European architecture. As a literary term, however, the "gothic novel," which is considered a sub-genre of the novel, can be traced back to Horace Walpole's eighteenth-century novel *The Castle of Otranto: A Gothic Story* (1764), which contains the characteristic attributes of this sub-genre, namely "closed worlds, mediated narratives, ancient houses, dark villains, and perfect heroines" (MacAndrew 1979, ix). In "The Supernatural in Poetry," Ann Radcliffe (1826), the author of several early gothic texts, provides a useful explanation of the significance of terror and horror to the Gothic in literature. She argues that terror expands the soul and awakens the senses, while horror is so powerful that it causes the destruction of the latter and the shrinking of the former. The distinction between the two, in Radcliffe's opinion, is that terror reflects the evil in the environment rather than in humankind itself, and horror posits evil as being inherent in people (MacAndrew 1979, 125). Although Radcliffe treats terror and horror as separate entities, MacAndrew argues that the two effects are increasingly brought together in gothic texts, noting that while horror may disgust the reader and suggest the futility of fighting evil, terror creates sympathy towards otherwise monstrous characters, in whom readers see themselves. By evoking such responses and precipitating an examination of "human nature and the place of evil in the human mind," these narratives were, and still are, intended to educate people and potentially avoid the rise or continuation of such evil in the world within a contained framework (ix). In order to convey the darkness and evil that are central to the sub-genre, gothic novels typically incorporate the depiction of "dream landscapes and figures of the subconscious imagination" (3). Included in the narratives may be "beings — mad monks, vampires, and demons — and settings — forbidden cliffs and glowering buildings, stormy seas and the dizzying abyss" — which function as powerful symbolic representations of a character's mind and emotional turmoil (3).

MacAndrew argues that most of the devices used in early gothic novels remain relevant into the twentieth century, including the use of settings in remote times and places, the presence of a split or tormented hero/villain, the inclusion of fantasy and dreamscapes, the structure of a tale within a tale, the contrast between urban and rural life, and the use of a first person narrator. In particular, the Victorian desire to integrate "'Gothic ideas' with more general ideas about life and society" has led to an increasing awareness of how environment shapes behaviour and a melding of gothic fantasy and realistic fiction. The result in the twentieth century is the creation of "blood-curdling supernatural events in a realistic social setting" (243). Indeed, sources of terror are often part of daily life.

In terms of national affiliation, studies of the gothic novel have focused primarily on British and American authors of the eighteenth and nineteenth centuries. Not surprisingly though, the American Gothic is often treated by scholars as a separate "discursive field" that is both nationally and regionally distinctive (Martin and Savoy 1998, vii).[4] As Robert Martin and Eric Savoy caution in examining the American Gothic, "it may be that broad generalizations about the gothic — overshadowed as they are by the genealogical tracing of British and continental influences — have reached a limit of conceptual or explanatory usefulness, and further particularization is urgently required" (1998, 5). Martin and Savoy's comment suggests that a similar strategy may be useful for discussing Canadian versions of the gothic novel. If the "American gothic," in Martin and Savoy's terms, "does not exist apart from its specific regional manifestations," what, then, constitutes a Canadian gothic novel and what makes it different from other national manifestations of the Gothic (6)? Given Savoy's emphasis on regional distinctions between gothic texts produced by Americans, how, too, might debates over the role of region in Canadian literature shape such a discussion of the gothic novel? In particular, what might Native versions of the Gothic look like, given that Indigenous people in Canada have been historically rendered as ghostly in order to legitimate their colonization and assimilation?

Certainly, the Gothic has played a significant role in the development of Canadian literature. Donna Bennett has argued that "the important images, archetypes, and genres in Canadian literature are tied to concepts of monsters, ghosts, and the Gothic" (1997, 253). Although Bennett's statement is perhaps too broad in its claims, such a relationship is logical in a country where the creation of identity initially involved settling what was presumed to be an empty and potentially savage wilderness. The Gothic allowed early white Canadian writers a means of articulating their own ambivalent relationships to the New World. The profound dislocation experienced by many people who came to Canada before and after Confederation has proven to be a particularly rich subject for those authors who explore how Canadians are haunted by the wilderness — a haunting that takes two forms: the literal fear of the untamed natural world encountered by new immigrants and the accompanying realization that such perceptions of emptiness depend upon often naive presumptions of what constitutes civility and order (see Davidson 1981, 243–45).

This double bind is aptly illustrated by John Richardson's *Wacousta* (1832), a text that portrays the oppressive nature of a "garrison mentality" within the fort and the dangers posed by leaving it (Frye 1965, 830). The central figure in the novel, Wacousta, is perceived as a serious threat to the fort precisely because he, as the internally divided villain, embodies this unresolved tension between savagery and civilization. The result is a monstrous man who has become part Indian and seeks vengeance on the de Haldimar family even though he was born and raised as a British gentleman. As D.H. Lawrence explains in *Studies in Classic American Literature*, the relationship between a writer and the New World is powerful precisely because the land "is full of grinning, unappeased aboriginal demons, too, ghosts, and it persecutes the white man.... Yet one day the demons of America must be placated, the ghosts must be appeased, the spirit of place atoned for" ([1923] 1961, 48). Richardson depicts a similar dilemma in Canada, with the presence of Native tribes, French communities, and Wacousta himself just beyond the walls of the British fort. Thus, the challenges of negotiating the contradictions of the New World and the populations that already occupied the land provide a rich setting for the Canadian Gothic.

Michael Hurley complicates such a reading of *Wacousta* by introducing a regional slant to his understanding of Richardson's text, which he suggests is the literary precursor to the Southern Ontario Gothic texts of writers such as Alice Munro, Margaret Atwood, and Robertson Davies. What Hurley calls the "Native Canadian Gothic" is manifested through the figure of Wacousta himself, a character who is not only "an amalgam of border legend and historical personages as well as of gothic and Romantic hero-villains" but also "bears a curious resemblance to the... figure of the Trickster in North American Indian mythology" (1992, 183). Drawing on Paul Radin's work on the trickster, and his emphasis on the sexuality and disorder that this figure embodies (1956), Hurley contends that Wacousta is an early white version of the trickster, who reappears in various English-Canadian texts ranging from Margaret Atwood's *Surfacing* (1972) to W.O. Mitchell's *Who Has Seen the Wind* (1947), extending the gothic dimensions of the novel in new directions (1992, 183–95).

Hurley reads the trickster in *Wacousta* as an "ambiguous saviour, embracing loss as well as gain, darkness as well as light, energy as well as order" and thus sustaining his contradictory nature to the end of the text (1992, 194). Richardson does reveal the wrongs done to Wacousta—in his earlier manifestation as Sir Reginald Morton—late in the novel as the garrison's destructively confining social structure becomes apparent. Yet this white-authored trickster figure remains marginalized from incorporation into society and relegated to a position of difference that ensures, whether he wants to or not, that he will never be reintegrated into the southern Ontario garrison with its European heritage. How, then, might a reading of *Monkey Beach,* which is set within a Native community and avoids the monstrous "othering" of Aboriginal people, alter recent discussions of what Hurley calls the "Native Canadian Gothic"?

When asked about *Monkey Beach,* Eden Robinson has noted that she destroyed a second draft of the novel because it "was too moody, too gothic. The only ones who liked it were my German publishers" (quoted in Hunter 2000, 68). While the published version of *Monkey Beach* is the third draft of the text, Robinson's novel retains many of the traditional markers of a gothic text, incorporating settings and beings that reflect the emotional turmoil of a gothic protagonist, through a first-person narrative voice. However, she transports the Gothic to a Native context, and, rather than depicting the Haisla characters who populate the novel as potential threats to the safety of a white, Eurocentric community, these individuals form their own world in which monsters exist but are not necessarily a destructive force. What Northey characterizes as Canadian writers' ambivalence regarding the New World and the dislocation experienced by early settlers is replaced in *Monkey Beach* with uncertainty about the world beyond the Haisla community. It is this external world that proves potentially destructive, at least for the protagonist, Lisamarie Hill, who falls into a pattern of drug and alcohol abuse when she runs away to the urban centre of East Vancouver. Furthermore, instead of presenting the Gothic as a means of exploring how non-Native characters are haunted by a Canadian wilderness that they find unfamiliar and threatening, Robinson negotiates a space in which her Aboriginal characters can examine the possibilities inherent in connecting to the natural world, monsters and all. She also reworks the typical settler's realization that the land is "wild, [and] empty" because of prevailing Eurocentric ideals of what it ought to be (Davidson 1981, 244). In *Monkey Beach,* Robinson traces her characters' strong relationships to a wilderness that they recognize as having a burgeoning, though not necessarily just human, population and a powerful tribal history that is far more important than the structural imposition of white, Western standards of civility and the regulations of the nation-state.

Monkey Beach, like many gothic novels, can be read as a response to "cultural disorder" (Northey 1976, 110). Yet Robinson revisions the cultural disorder that Northey's study suggests is the result of Eurocentric perspectives coping with the harsh Canadian landscape. In *Monkey Beach*, Haisla viewpoints dominate, and Robinson's narrative conveys the sense that whatever disorder or confusion the characters are experiencing is a result of negotiating the often jarring juxtapositions between Native and non-Native viewpoints. If the characters in *Monkey Beach* are preoccupied with evil, it is because many of them have had to face the impact of Eurocentricism on their communities and identities. Robinson's novel pays special attention to the role of the residential school system, the transition from a matriarchal to a patriarchal social and political structure, and the long-standing history of governmental attempts to wipe out the Native populations in Canada and the United States through relocation and legal regulation. Moreover, the Native Canadian Gothic described by Michael Hurley, in which Wacousta epitomizes the Native outsider who will never gain access to the southern Ontario garrison (1992), is rewritten by Robinson, who offers a more favourable portrait of Native peoples from *within* their own community. By locating the narrative on the northwest coast of British Columbia, Robinson overturns the southern Ontario focus[5] — which is itself haunted by a historical legacy of Native displacement — and asserts a new narrative centre for her gothic vision — the coastal lands of northern British Columbia, where monsters and the supernatural are embraced and Native populations dominate.[6]

Monkey Beach begins with a Haisla proverb that cautions: "It is possible to retaliate against an enemy, But impossible to retaliate against storms" (Robinson 2000, n.p.). The proverb frames the narrative and overtly acknowledges the power and danger of the natural world, an assertion that is highly appropriate for a gothic novel in which stormy seas are often present. Set in the remote village of Kitamaat, Lisamarie's story begins with yet another gothic convention, a portrait of a seemingly closed world, far from urban centres or the basic geographic knowledge of most readers. To demonstrate the isolation of Kitamaat and to orient readers, in the opening pages of the text Lisamarie provides a substantial description of the village that highlights its inaccessibility even as she pinpoints its location through a game of "hot" and "cold" with the reader's finger. Her orientation of Kitamaat also conveys the centrality of the waterways that link the village and surrounding area to the rest of the world — connections that not only may provide travel routes and sustenance for the locals but also can cause death. Lisamarie's lengthy and detailed account of how to access Kitamaat is contrasted with her

brother's mysterious disappearance into the ocean, an event whose resolution does not come until the end of the novel (4–5). The narrative,
moreover, is mediated by Lisamarie's alternating reflections on her childhood relationships with her family and her present state of anxiety about
Jimmy's potential fate. *Monkey Beach* may lack the overt distinction
between the frame text and the inner narrative that characterizes many
traditional gothic novels. Yet Robinson's story still creates a sense of tension between the immediate reality of the search for Jimmy and Lisamarie's
recounting of her life up to this point. Robinson's narrator weaves connections between the two that reveal Lisamarie's close links to the spirit
world and knowledge of events that she is unable to fully comprehend or
stop from taking place. As the description of Kitamaat suggests, Lisamarie's desire to frame and contain her world in measurable terms is
countered by the tangible experiences of fear and potential loss that are
sustained throughout much of the novel.

Lisamarie, aptly named after Elvis's daughter, a living descendant of a
dead legend, is plagued throughout the novel by a fear of death and a
supernatural ability in many cases to predict the deaths of those most
precious to her. Throughout *Monkey Beach,* she repeatedly dreams about
individuals shortly before their deaths — an experience that she describes
as a "'death sending'" (313). By making Lisamarie the centre of the novel,
Robinson complicates the usual gothic pairing of a dark villain and perfect heroine. She creates a protagonist who reflects on the nature and origins of evil through her relationship to the spirit world. Lisamarie's subconscious continually returns to haunt her, forcing the young woman to
negotiate her supernatural connections and desire to be simply ordinary.
However, the return of the repressed — a crucial aspect of gothic texts —
takes on a larger political significance in Robinson's novel. In *Monkey
Beach,* evil is primarily associated with Eurocentric interventions in the
Haisla community, rather than with individual Native characters, a strategy that creates a more ambiguous and complicated vision of evil than
many gothic novels.

In particular, what is identified as evil lies, for much of Robinson's
novel, beyond the text, a perspective that calls on readers to reflect on
their presumptions of what constitutes an evil or monstrous "Other." For
example, in the concluding section of *Monkey Beach,* titled "In Search of
the Elusive Sasquatch" (a reference to a local monster who has special significance for the Haisla), Lisamarie tries to repair her teenage brother's

relationship with his girlfriend, who is ironically nicknamed Karaoke for her ability to lip-sync songs. Having decided to marry Karaoke and knowing he must raise money to pay for a ring and a ceremony, Jimmy leaves without any explanation to work on the *Queen of the North*, a fishing vessel owned by Uncle Josh. Karaoke, however, presumes he has dumped her. To prove her wrong, Lisamarie searches her brother's room for the promise ring he has purchased to show Karaoke his commitment to her and, in doing so, discovers "an old photograph and a folded-up card," both of which belong to Karaoke (365). The card is a birth announcement, decorated on the front with "a stork" carrying a baby, and the handwriting inside reads: "Dear, dear Joshua. It was yours so I killed it" (365). The accompanying black and white photograph adds another dimension to the already disturbing evidence that Joshua has sexually abused and impregnated Karaoke. The picture depicts Uncle "Josh's head...pasted over a priest's head and Karaoke's...pasted over a little boy's" and contains the caption: "Dear Joshua...I remember every day we spent together. How are you? I miss you terribly. Please write. Your friend in Christ, Archibald" (365).[7] Here, Robinson incorporates traditional British and specifically Canadian gothic elements—what Northey describes as the "overpowering force of human will" and "sexual encounters or conflicts" based on "domination" (1976, 109). The card and photography are all about relationships of domination, as shaped by race, education, the faith invested in the church, and the process of colonization. Yet Karaoke's card to Uncle Josh marks a break in the cycle, expressing a pointed refusal to continue to submit to such abuse, which began with one white, male Christian's sexual abuse of a Haisla child. Robinson's novel thus can be read as exploring not only the legacy of abuse inflicted through residential schools on Native children but also the power of the nation-state, which has permitted, and indeed regulated, this abuse.

While the legacy of Christian conversion may be read as a well-meaning attempt by Canada to civilize and ultimately assimilate Native peoples, Robinson's reading of this process of colonization highlights the systemic spread of evil behaviour among both the oppressors and the oppressed, which has led to Uncle Josh's sexual violation of Karaoke. As Northey notes, in most Canadian gothic texts, "the dominance of one human over another is a prime contribution to the final doom or destructive action of the story" (109). This dominance often results in sexual encounters or conflicts within the narrative that embody the power relations between individuals, communities, and nation-states. *Monkey Beach* is no exception. Colonization has led to the sexual abuse of children, both by the colonizer (Archibald) and eventually by the colonized (Josh), by virtue of power relations that relegate women (and particularly Native women) to a lesser status than men. In this case, the powerlessness of the colonized Native male is countered by abusing the colonized female. The increased interest in the moral ambivalence and psychological dimensions of evil in nineteenth- and twentieth-century gothic texts is depicted in *Monkey Beach* from a somewhat different perspective. Robinson gives gothic conventions a Native twist in order to show how the desire to civilize what white settlers first perceived as an uncivilized "other" race has resulted in evil behaviour by both colonizer and colonized. Thus, the evil posited within the community through Lisamarie's discovery of these documents is redirected back outside the text to non-Native readers, such as myself, who can wrestle with the disturbing legacy of attempts to Christianize and assimilate Native peoples with the help of the nation-state.

Part of Lisamarie's challenge in *Monkey Beach* is to negotiate the relationship between traditional Haisla culture and the pervasive presence of popular culture and to find a balance between the two, especially given the young narrator's connection to spirits and monsters. Lisamarie not only can see and hear the red-haired man, a night-time visitor, but also comes face to face with a sasquatch, feels an invisible "thing" feeding on her body, and hears voices around her (Robinson 2000, 274). She keeps many of these encounters secret but is so plagued with nightmares and sleepwalking that her middle-class parents, in desperation, send her to a school psychiatrist to understand the cause of the dreams. The psychiatrist that Lisamarie sees tries to convince her that the ghosts she sees do not exist but are simply her "attempt to deal with death" (273). In "Learning to Talk with Ghosts," Castricano rightly asks "*whose* repressed returns," arguing that *Monkey Beach* draws attention to the "spiritual consequences of Western culture's materialist drive that has attempted to eradicate 'superstition' or 'mysticism' in the name of psychology" (2006, 808). The psychiatrist's interpretation of the young girl's behaviour offers one answer to Castricano's question by discounting the legitimacy of the spirit world for the Haisla community along with Lisamarie's ability to communicate with it. But by refashioning the gothic conventions in a Haisla context, Robinson suggests that it is the psychiatrist—with her promise to get Lisa "back to normal in no time" — and not her patient, who is struggling to repress that which cannot be colonized (2000, 274).

In contrast, two of the most significant characters in the text, Ma-ma-oo, Lisamarie's grandmother, a Haisla woman who gives her granddaughter a sense of her traditional heritage, and Uncle Mick, a Native activist who has fought the Eurocentric world to retain tribal rights and freedoms, acknowledge and respect Lisamarie's powers. Both help her to find a way to mediate between the frightening dimensions of this other world and her own purpose in life. Ma-ma-oo cooks salmonberry stew, gathers oxasuli roots to ward off ghosts, and pays tribute to the tree spirits with tobacco leaves when she takes plants from the forest. Yet she balances this transmission of traditional practices with her obsessive love of television soap operas, which she watches on an ancient "relic from the black-and-white era, with foil wrapped around its rabbit ears" (Robinson 2000, 76). Ma-ma-oo roots for the various female characters on these shows, yelling at the television in an attempt to guide their ill-fated behaviour. This gesture echoes her frustration with her own past as an abused young wife, who sent her children to residential school to protect them from the beatings inflicted by her now dead husband.

Most critical to Lisamarie, Ma-ma-oo acknowledges and gives advice to her granddaughter about how to deal with the spirit world. Lisamarie's father dismisses Ma-ma-oo's tendency to think that everyone and everything, from the sasquatches rumoured to have been sighted on nearby Monkey Beach to the soap opera characters that she watches on television, "are real" (10). Yet the older woman helps Lisamarie to mediate between what others see and what she has access to. She relays traditional Haisla stories, educating her granddaughter about the existence of ghosts and what she calls shape-shifters: "Animals and humans [who] could switch shapes simply by putting on each other's skins" (210). Ma-ma-oo even recounts how knowledge was initially passed on from the experienced animals to the newly formed humans until "flesh solidified" and such transformations became impossible except for medicine men (210).

In particular, Ma-ma-oo explains the significance of Monkey Beach, a frequent destination for Lisamarie and her family, through the story of the "B'gwus, the wild man of the woods," who is also known as the sasquatch (7). According to Ma-ma-oo, this mysterious hybrid creature is the result of an illicit love affair between a beautiful woman and her husband's brother. The woman, desperate to get rid of her husband, clubs him during a boat ride, when he stops to urinate just off Monkey Beach. She presumes that she has killed him but when the lovers return to Monkey Beach to bury the body they find "large footprints in the sand" (211). After following the trail into the woods, both the woman and her husband's brother are killed by the husband who has been transformed into a sasquatch (211). Ma-ma-oo's translation of this Haisla narrative gives Lisamarie another perspective on the mass media hype surrounding sasquatch sightings, humanizing the b'gwus in a distinctive tribal context that dispels the sense that monsters are "other." Her story follows gothic conventions by creating "sympathy" for otherwise monstrous characters and thus suspends the immediate "moral condemnation" of readers (MacAndrew 1979, 125). Yet Robinson complicates this moment of sympathetic identification by Lisamarie and the novel's readers with Ma-ma-oo's insistence that "to really understand the old stories...you had to speak Haisla" (2000, 211). Her statement not only emphasizes the power of the Haisla language and accompanying cultural traditions, but it also reinforces Eurocentric readers' sense of distance and exclusion from this world of gothic otherness, inverting the typical privileging of white, Western values and the English language. Those who are familiar with the Haisla language and culture and see ghosts have a unique ability to mediate between these two worlds and to understand the limits of each. As Ma-ma-oo tells Lisamarie shortly afterwards: "You don't have to be scared of things you don't understand. They're just ghosts," ghosts who need to be respected and listened to but not feared (265).

Uncle Mick provides a different sort of support, as a man who has witnessed the oppression of Native peoples, from his childhood in a residential school where he was sexually molested to the death of his wife, Cookie, who died in a racially motivated murder disguised as a car fire. Having spent years working as a front-line Native activist, Mick first appears in Lisamarie's life when, as a child, he arrives at her home with a single pink salmonberry flower for her mother — a visit that initially upsets the young girl because Mick's return causes her father to cry. Notably, in anticipation of Mick's arrival, Lisamarie is visited by her own childhood monsters, which she describes as "a variation of the monster under the bed or the thing in the closet, a nightmare that faded with the morning":

> I was afraid to sleep because of the little man's visit the night before. I lay
> awake with a stranglehold on Mr. Booboo and the lights turned on.... Now

that I think back, the pattern of the little man's visits seems unwelcomely obvious, but at the time, his arrivals and departures had no meaning....He liked to sit on the top of my dresser when he came to visit, and he had a shock of red hair which stood up in messy, tangled puffs that he sometimes hid under a black top hat. (26–27)

This monster, which first appeared "the day before the tidal wave" when she was very young, becomes a barometer of events in Lisamarie's life, a means of reading the world on a subconscious level, which Mick also respects and nurtures in his own playful way (20). When Lisamarie later becomes involved in a playground showdown and ends up in an emergency room, Mick nicknames her "monster" (67). He tries to instill in her both what he calls a "warrior" spirit, a willingness to challenge conventional accounts of Native history, and a respect for the natural world and its rhythms (69). Mick takes her fishing and insists that they return a halibut they have caught to the water, explaining: "It's a magical thing.... You aren't supposed to touch them if you don't know how to handle them" (99). Haunted by his own past, and suffering from nightmares because of his experience in residential schools, Mick willingly turns to the spirit world for relief. He acknowledges his belief in sasquatches and even tells Lisamarie during an early morning campout at Monkey Beach that "[s]ometimes... when there's a storm, you can hear voices singing on the lake" (118).

The ability to see and hear beyond the events of daily life is, ironically, both a gift and a curse that her uncle helps her to understand. Lisamarie has another vision just before Mick sets out on his final round of net gathering, part of a small fishing business that he has set up with Lisamarie's father to sustain him while in Kitamaat. Lisamarie is visited yet again by the little man. This time, he dances on her dresser, then slips and falls into the laundry basket, burying himself in sweaters and t-shirts. The vision is so disconcerting that Lisamarie struggles to catch her breath. Shortly after, Mick goes missing on the water. Worried about his whereabouts, Lisamarie and her father search for him, discovering his body, which has been gruesomely consumed by hungry seals. Though his obsessive love of Elvis may not make him an obvious bearer of tribal tradition, Mick is also intimately connected to Haisla culture and belief systems. Through his reading of himself as a warrior who fights for Native rights and Lisamarie as "'my favourite monster in the whole wide world,'" Mick re-reads the negative perceptions of Natives as monstrously "othered" in a positive light, inspiring the young narrator to take pride in her Haisla roots (67).

The death of Mick and of Ma-ma-oo several years later are two gruesome events that leave Lisamarie uncertain about the future and wrestling with feelings of guilt because she feels she ignored the signs of their death that she was given from the spirit world. The young girl runs off to Vancouver, retreating to the urban world, and a life of drugs and alcohol to bury her grief. She is eventually confronted by Tab, her cousin, who appears in the flesh and then returns to visit her in a ghostly form, telling Lisamarie that she needs to take control of her life: "'Don't look at me like that. You and your fucking problems. Get your act together and go home'" (301). Lisamarie's mourning for those who have died, a "'wallowing in misery,'" as Tab puts it, is broken by the young girl's discovery that although she has seen Tab's ghost, her cousin is not dead or about to die (300). With a better understanding of her powers—both negative and positive—Lisamarie returns to Kitamaat to take stock of her life, finish school, and cultivate her connections to her Haisla heritage.

Rather than seeing this communicative ability with the spirit world as destructive, Lisamarie begins to listen again to the ghosts, monsters, and voices, despite her parents' belief that she is merely "hearing things." As Lisamarie explains at the beginning of the novel, when the family first discovers that Jimmy has gone missing, she hears crows speaking to her in Haisla. Yet when she tells her mother about the crows, transformative trickster figures who repeat the word "*La'es*," meaning "Go down to the bottom of the ocean," Lisamarie's mother insists that the talking crows are "[c]learly a sign, Lisa…that you need Prozac" (1, 3). Willing to listen and use this knowledge to help find her brother, Lisamarie turns to the stories of supernatural beings told by her grandmother and gives herself an identity. In particular, Lisamarie describes herself in the concluding section of *Monkey Beach* in distinctly Haisla terms, writing a school paper in English, which incorporates Haisla words, about an elusive female monster that reflects her own marginalized and yet crucial status within the community. In doing so, she may be invoking the gothic concept of the hero/villain but revises it to suit her own needs as a Haisla woman:

> T'sonoquoa is not as famous as B'gwus. She covers herself in a cloak and pretends to be an old woman. She will ask for your help, feigning a helpless shake in her hands as she leans on her cane. If you are moved to go close enough for her

to see you with her poor vision, she will straighten to her true height, and the hands that grip you will be as strong as a man's. She is an ogress, and she won't let go because, to her, human flesh is the ultimate delicacy and young flesh is especially sweet. But discredited scientists and amateur sleuths aren't hunting her. There are no conferences debating her existence. She doesn't have her own beer commercials. She has a few amusing notes in some anthropology books. She is remembered in scattered campfires. But she is, by and large, a dim memory. (337)

She identifies with this neglected monster, a woman who disguises her youth and feeds on flesh, much like the unseen shapes that nibble on Lisamarie's body. T'sonoqua offers an alternative to the commercial fame of the male sasquatch, one that can be resurrected productively to serve the needs of Haisla women in particular. Lisamarie's mother may want to dismiss her daughter's unusual abilities as merely crazy and suppress the existence of such monsters by turning to modern psychiatry. But, as Robinson's novel suggests, her positive recognition of herself in monstrous terms is a crucial breakthrough for the young girl precisely because it links her to her Haisla culture and gives value to her talents in a context that fuses contemporary concerns with long-standing tribal narratives. Moreover, by reclaiming the T'sonoqua, Lisamarie can embrace the strong matriarchal vision of her grandmother and parlay that ancestral heritage into action.

In the concluding section of the novel, aptly titled "The Land of the Dead," Lisamarie learns of Jimmy's demise, aided by her connections to the spirit world. She has already dreamt of his death prior to his disappearance, seeing Jimmy on Monkey Beach where he "faded in and out of view as the fog rolled by" (7). It is not surprising then that Lisamarie returns to Monkey Beach en route to meeting her parents in Bella Bella in search of her brother. Monkey Beach can be described as a distinctly gothic setting, remote from the rest of the world and populated by mysterious creatures, whose existence in Lisamarie's mind reflects her own psychological confusion about who she is and what powers she possesses. While on the shore of Monkey Beach, Lisamarie hears the voice of "the thing" — the invisible monster that has repeatedly visited her over the course of her childhood (370). Rather than simply letting herself be fed upon by the monster, she demands that it show her what has happened to Jimmy. Her wish is granted, and Lisamarie sees a series of images of her brother out on the *Queen of the North* with Uncle Josh, who it turns out has been murdered by Jimmy to revenge his abuse of Karaoke. In a gothic twist of fate, however, Jimmy is not destined to survive either, despite his heroic killing of the villain. Jimmy abandons the sinking *Queen of the North* to swim to shore but does not make it. Lisamarie, having watched this vision and knowing her brother is dead, is torn between giving in to the monster and trying to escape and drowning in the waters just off Monkey Beach, choosing between two versions of the gothic novel's "dizzying abyss" (MacAndrew 1979, 3).

Having witnessed the iniquities of evil at work, Lisamarie prepares to let herself drown but is visited by the ghost of Ma-ma-oo who demands that her granddaughter acknowledge her power and use it wisely not self-destructively: "'You have a dangerous gift.... It's like oxasuli. Unless you know how to use it, it will kill you.... When it's time to go, you go.... Nothing you can say or do will change it. We're where we belong, but you have to go back. Do you hear me?'" (Robinson 2000, 371–72). Instead of allowing Lisamarie to join the world of the dead, Ma-ma-oo's ghost insists that she remain alive despite the pull of the water. In a final series of encounters between the living and the dead, the young girl meets the watery ghost of Jimmy, who pulls her away from the seals and up to the surface. Lisamarie then climbs onto the beach where a group of ghosts, including Mick, have gathered around a bonfire, singing a farewell song about "leaving and meeting again" (374). Listening to the voices, as Mick has instructed her to do in childhood, gives Lisamarie a chance to hear and understand the importance of her survival and her intimate relationship to the dead. Left on the beach, alone, Lisamarie has a final transformative experience while lying in the sand, describing herself as "so light I could just drift away" just as she hears the howl of a nearby b'gwus (374). In this moment, Lisamarie finds peace with the past and present, recognizing the need for her continued survival despite her desire to join the ghosts of family members. She also acknowledges her own powers to hear and see what is beyond the realm of most other people. The setting of Monkey Beach becomes a source of inspiration and mediation for Lisamarie, who may hear the howl of the b'gwus but can also envision her own female monsters and place in the world.

Monkey Beach can be read as including multiple aspects of the gothic tradition, with its setting in the closed world of Kitamaat and nearby beach, a narrator whose movement between past and present creates distance from the story itself, and an emphasis on danger and evil that is manifested through the depiction of supernatural beings, stormy seas, and the constant threat of death. Approaching Robinson's text through the Gothic is especially helpful for drawing readers beyond the Haisla community into an unfamiliar and mysterious world ripe with imaginative possibilities because it is a familiar set of conventions. Yet in *Monkey Beach*, Robinson repeatedly rewrites the strictly conventional gothic plot to serve her own purposes, employing the "unlicensed indulgence of an amoral imagination" to create a narrative that is both "subversive" and decidedly moral in its condemnation of the white settlers' treatment of the Haisla people (Kilgour 1995, 7). The novel, for example, lacks a single perfect heroine or dark villain. Lisamarie is no passive, angelic female, and the only real dark villain of the text is Uncle Josh, who poses an indirect threat to Lisamarie and her family through his abuse of Karaoke, an abuse rooted in Christian assimilation and Josh's own experience as a child victim. Certainly, how evil functions in the human mind is an integral part of Robinson's narrative, precisely because Lisamarie herself must wrestle with an ability to connect to spirit beings that is not always pleasant or successful in saving lives.

What Northey describes as a shift over the past century in the Canadian Gothic from external to internal conflicts over the relationship between the natural and civilized world is also relevant to this reading of *Monkey Beach* (1976, 110). Lisamarie continually negotiates her own sense of ambivalence about her place in the world as a Haisla woman who is trying to couple traditional values with contemporary experiences, finding strength in the past and a way to cope with the challenges of the present. Arguably, the "cultural disorder" of Native tribes in Canada who are trying to find a place within — or beyond — Eurocentric ideas of nation would be a logical site for a gothic narrative. However, what is most fascinating and radical about Robinson's novel is her pointed reversal of the Native as "Other," which has shaped most previous Canadian gothic texts. Moreover, by setting *Monkey Beach* outside of the regions that have typically characterized the Canadian Gothic and portraying the Canadian North not as an unexplored world but, rather, as a vibrant place that has been romanticized for the purposes of marginalization, Robinson raises questions about how and why readers (like myself) see these communities as Gothic and who such labels serve.

Who is being criticized in *Monkey Beach,* a text in which the struggles of the community and the tribe reflect the long-term impact of colonization?

By positing evil on the margins of the novel and exploring the potential empowering aspects of the natural and supernatural worlds, Robinson can be read as suggesting that the Gothic may be a way of distancing— and, paradoxically, bringing forward—what is uncomfortable for non-Native readers to confront: a historical legacy of monstrosities that continue to impact on the Haisla tribe. In doing so, Robinson creates a text of terror that includes elements of horror (adhering to the traditional gothic distinction) but is further complicated by the subject matter of the novel itself. *Monkey Beach* reveals the dangers (and virtues) of the natural environment, epitomized by the seals that consume parts of Mick's body; recognizes the way in which painful experiences often lead to evil acts, as with Uncle Josh's abuse of Karaoke; and acknowledges the existence of evil in characters such as Lisamarie's grandfather, Ba-ba-oo, whose beatings of Ma-ma-oo remain unexplained. Perhaps most obviously, Robinson's text traces the return of the repressed (and the imposition of such Western concepts) from a distinctly Native perspective, insisting upon the complex and lasting impact of non-Native colonization, especially the legacy of residential schooling, and exploring the increasing presence of Western mass culture in tribal communities.

Robinson's use of gothic conventions allows her to further complicate what can be read as a narrative of suffering and the need for reparation. The gothic dimensions of *Monkey Beach* enable Robinson to explore the contradictions of Lisamarie's identity and her relationships with various family members in their intricacies, without imposing a rash or reductive perspective on the evil that is manifested in various forms throughout the novel. At the same time, Robinson's text writes back to a Canadian gothic tradition in which Natives are marginalized, romanticized, or entirely absent from the text, creating a space for Native cultural revitalization that forcefully critiques the traditional association of Aboriginals with what is monstrous. The term "monster," through Lisamarie, becomes empowering, and the haunted wilderness becomes a source of cultural knowledge. If we are to talk about the concept of Native Gothic in a Canadian context, Eden Robinson's *Monkey Beach* provides a rich starting point for rethinking what such a juxtaposition of concepts might mean beyond the fusion of a Native trickster and a gothic hero/villain in a white-authored text such as *Wacousta* (Richardson 1998). Instead, as Robinson's novel suggests, the Native Gothic in Canada explores not only the monstrosities of colonization and incorporates the power of the Native spirit world but also acknowledges the survival of Native populations and their traditions on their own terms.

Notes

I am grateful to Cynthia Sugars, Gerry Turcotte, and the anonymous readers at Wilfrid Laurier UP for their helpful suggestions and to Kevin Flynn and Jack David for permission to reference and use parts of the essay first published in *Essays on Canadian Writing*.

1 Margot Northey includes a discussion of the "grotesque" as a separate term in her introduction but concludes that although they are closely related "I consider the gothic to be the more inclusive category or genre, embracing all works in which terror or horror are major elements" (1976, 8). Given the constraints of this essay and the repeated usage of the term Gothic to describe Robinson's novel, I have chosen to focus exclusively on the concept of the Gothic.
2 See John Richardson (1832); Martha Ostenso (1925); Margaret Atwood (1972); Sheila Watson (1959); Anne Hébert (1970); and Roch Carrier (1968).
3 See Margaret Atwood's essay "Canadian Monsters: Some Aspects of the Supernatural" ([1977] 1982), which includes analyses of the monstrous in several texts not mentioned by Northey, and an article by Lorna Drew (1995) on the gothic links between L.M. Montgomery's *Emily of New Moon* ([1923], 1983) and Ann Radcliffe's *Mysteries of Udolpho* ([1794], 1966) for exceptions.
4 See also, for example, Gross (1989); Mogen, Sanders, and Karpinski (1993); Ringe (1982); Fiedler (1960); and Winter (1992).
5 Notably, the story of *Wacousta* is set in the era of Chief Pontiac's unsuccessful attempt to seize Fort Detroit (1763), a Native-led attack intended to end British military dominance in the area. The fort was built by the French, and like its close counterpart, Fort Machilimackinac, was given over to the British after the capitulation of the French in Quebec in 1760. The two forts were strategically located near waterways as part of a system of trade routes that were originally used by Native peoples but became increasingly complex to use with the arrival of the French and the English.
6 Such an assertion of domination needs to be made cautiously given the number of land claims occurring across Canada right now. However, Kitamaat is the primary residence of the Haisla people, with a population of 700. There are close to 1,500 Haisla members living in various villages throughout their territory.
7 Robinson's "Queen of the North," the concluding section of her short story collection, *Traplines,* tells the story of Karaoke's relationship with Jimmy and her Uncle Josh up to the point of Jimmy's departure on the fishing boat (1996, 185–215). The story, narrated by Karaoke, explicitly describes Josh's molestation of her and the "gift" that she gives him along with the doctored photograph and card: a blood covered maxi-pad, which is evidence of her recent abortion or miscarriage.

Works Cited

Atwood, Margaret. 1977, reprinted 1982. "Canadian Monsters: Some Aspects of the Supernatural in Canadian Fiction." In *Second Words: Selected Critical Prose*. Ed. Margaret Atwood. Toronto: Anansi. 229–53.

Atwood, Margaret. 1972. *Surfacing*. Toronto: McClelland and Stewart.

Bennett, Donna. 1997. "Criticism in English." In *The Oxford Companion to Canadian Literature*. Ed. William Toye and Eugene Benson, 2nd edition. Toronto: Oxford UP. 242–67.

Birney, Earle. 1966, reprinted 1982. "Can. Lit." In *The New Oxford Book of Canadian Verse in English*. Ed. Margaret Atwood. Toronto: Oxford UP. 116.

Cariou, Warren. 2000. "Dreamlike Spiritual Quest in a Vividly Rendered World." Review of *Monkey Beach*, by Eden Robinson. *Canadian Forum* 79(889): 36–37.

Carrier, Roch. 1968, reprinted 1981. *La Guerre, Yes Sir!* Quebec: Stanké.

Castricano, Jodey. 2006. "Learning to Talk with Ghosts: Canadian Gothic and the Poetics of Haunting in Eden Robinson's *Monkey Beach*." *University of Toronto Quarterly* 75(2): 801–13.

Davidson, Arnold E. 1981. "Canadian Gothic and Anne Hebert's *Kamarouska*." *Modern Fiction Studies* 27(2): 243–54.

Drew, Lorna. 1995. "The Emily Connection: Ann Radcliffe, L.M. Montgomery, and 'The Female Gothic.'" *Canadian Children's Literature* 77(21): 19–32.

Edwards, Justin. 2005. *Gothic Canada: Reading the Spectre of a National Literature*. Edmonton: University of Alberta Press.

Fiedler, Leslie. 1960. *Love and Death in the American Novel*. New York: Doubleday.

Frye, Northrop. 1965. "Conclusion." In *Literary History of Canada: Canadian Literature in English*. Ed. Carl F. Klinck et al. Toronto: University of Toronto Press. 821–49.

Goldman, Marlene, and Joanne Saul, eds. 2006. Special issue of *University of Toronto Quarterly* 75(2).

Gross, Louis S. 1989. *Redefining the American Gothic*. Ann Arbor: University of Michigan Press.

Hébert, Anne. 1970. *Kamouraska*. Paris: Éditions du Seuil.

Hoy, Helen. 2001. *How Should I Read These?: Native Women Writers in Canada*. Toronto: University of Toronto Press.

Hunter, Jennifer. 2000. "Growing Up with Elvis and Sasquatch." *Maclean's* 113(12): 68.

Hurley, Michael. 1992. *The Borders of Nightmare: The Fiction of John Richardson*. Toronto: University of Toronto Press.

Kertzer, Jonathan. 1998. *Worrying the Nation: Imagining a National Literature in English Canada*. Toronto: University of Toronto Press.

Kilgour, Maggie. 1995. *The Rise of the Gothic Novel.* London: Routledge.

LaRocque, Emma. 2006. "Opening Address." *Studies in Canadian Literature* 31(1): 11–18.

Lawrence, D.H. 1923, reprinted 1961. *Studies in Classic American Literature.* New York: Viking.

MacAndrew, Elizabeth. 1979. *The Gothic Tradition in Fiction.* New York: Columbia UP.

Martin, Robert K., and Eric Savoy. 1998. *American Gothic: New Interventions in a National Narrative.* Iowa City: University of Iowa Press.

Mogen, David, Scott P. Sanders, and Joanne B. Karpinski, eds. 1993. *Frontier Gothic: Terror and Wonder at the Frontier in American Literature.* Rutherford: Fairleigh Dickinson UP.

Montgomery, L.M. 1923, reprinted 1983. *Emily of New Moon.* Toronto: Bantam Books.

Northey, Margot. 1976. *The Haunted Wilderness: The Gothic and Grotesque in Canadian Fiction.* Toronto: University of Toronto Press.

Ostenso, Martha. 1925, reprinted 1961. *Wild Geese.* Toronto: McClelland and Stewart.

Radcliffe, Ann. 1794, reprinted 1966. *The Mysteries of Udolpho.* London: Oxford UP.

———. 1826. "On the Supernatural in Poetry." *New Monthly Magazine* 16: 145–52.

Radin, Paul. 1956. *The Trickster: A Study in American Indian Mythology.* New York: Philosophical Library.

Rand, Nicholas T. 1994. "Introduction: Renewals of Psychoanalysis." In *The Shell and the Kernel.* Ed. Nicolas Abraham and Maria Torok. Chicago: University of Chicago Press. 1–22.

Richardson, John. 1832, reprinted 1998. *Wacousta.* Ed. John Moss. Ottawa: Tecumseh.

Ringe, Donald A. 1982. *American Gothic: Imagination and Reason in Nineteenth-Century Fiction.* Lexington: UP of Kentucky.

Robinson, Eden. 1996. "Queen of the North." *Traplines.* Toronto: Alfred A. Knopf. 185–215.

———. 2000. *Monkey Beach.* Toronto: Alfred A. Knopf.

Thomas, Joan. 2000. "Glorious Northern Gothic." Review of *Monkey Beach,* by Eden Robinson. *Globe and Mail,* 22 January: D9.

Walpole, Horace. 1764, reprinted 1964. *The Castle of Otranto: A Gothic Story.* Ed. W.S. Lewis. London: Oxford UP.

Watson, Sheila. 1959, reprinted 1966. *The Double Hook.* Toronto: McClelland and Stewart.

Winter, Kari J. 1992. *Subjects of Slavery, Agents of Change: Women and Power in Gothic Novels and Slave Narratives, 1790–1865.* Athens: University of Georgia Press.

CHAPTER TEN

Beothuk Gothic: Michael Crummey's *River Thieves*

Herb Wyile

Historical fiction, suggests Winnipeg writer Margaret Sweatman, is a little like necrophilia: "It's ghoulish writing this type of fiction. You get off on these dead people" (2007, 187). This original characterization of historical fiction points to the potential fruitfulness of approaching the genre through the lens of the Gothic — a genre that has likewise been characterized (at least according to its detractors) by an unhealthy preoccupation with the dead. Like the historical novel, the Gothic has enjoyed increasing critical scrutiny in the twentieth century, including, as David Punter and Glennis Byron observe, from a postcolonial perspective in which the repressed colonial past is seen as returning to haunt the present (2004, 54). The suppressed secrets, hidden bodies, shadowy menaces, and haunted spaces of gothic fiction characterize a paradigm that is readily transportable to the examination of the literature of colonial and postcolonial cultures. Colonial texts frequently use gothic conventions to figure the colonial "Other" as threatening and barbaric. However, because the colonial enterprise is premised on a largely brutal and illegitimate suppression of Aboriginal cultures, this legacy is figured through tropes of ghosts and haunting in many colonial and postcolonial texts. Renée Bergland argues that Indian ghosts are ubiquitous in American literature, for example, because, by virtue of the disappearance or erasure they evoke, they serve as "constant reminders of the fragility of national identity." In this sense, the

> entire dynamic of ghosts and hauntings ... is a dynamic of unsuccessful repression. Ghosts are the things that we try to bury, but that refuse to stay

229

buried. They are our fears and our horrors, disembodied, but made inescapable by their very bodilessness. Ghostly Indians present us with the possibility of vanishing ourselves, being swallowed up into another's discourse, another's imagination. (2000, 5)

Such a formulation has interesting implications for the literature of Newfoundland and Labrador, which for the last two centuries has been preoccupied with the fate of the Beothuk, the only North American Aboriginal group to be entirely extinguished during the colonial period. Furthermore, it might be argued, Newfoundland (courtesy of the vote in favour of Confederation with Canada in 1949) has been "swallowed up into another's discourse" and, especially with the recent moratorium on the cod fishery, has been experiencing "an unprecedented upheaval, a 'sea change' of sorts, which will permanently alter what it means to live [t]here" (Crummey 2004, 32). As Bergland argues, the erasure of the indigene marks an ambivalent founding of the nation, making it both possible and illegitimate from the very beginning:

> The American subject ... is obsessed with an originary sin against Native people that both engenders that subject and irrevocably stains it. Native American ghosts haunt American literature because the American nation is compelled to return again and again to an encounter that makes it both sorry and happy, a defiled grave upon which it must continually rebuild the American subject. (2000, 22)

In a similar fashion, in a literature permeated by loss — "loss of independence, the loss of the cod fishery, the loss of countless lives to the sea, and the loss of opportunity" — the extinction of the Beothuk, as Paul Chafe argues, is "the fundamental loss in Newfoundland's history — the originary moment when *what could have been* was separated from what *is*" (2004, 93).[1] The prevalence of treatments of the extinction of the Beothuk in Newfoundland literature clearly suggests that their story functions as a kind of original sin — their erasure not only facilitating settlement but also destabilizing the settler's sense of belonging.

Michael Crummey's 2001 novel *River Thieves*, which provides a revisionist version of this chapter in Newfoundland's history, makes for an interesting study of the intersection of postcoloniality, historical fiction, and the Gothic. *River Thieves* revisits a central episode in the story of the Beothuk, the capture of one of the last remaining Beothuk, Demasduit (Mary March), in 1819, stressing not so much the experience of the Beothuk as the internal debates and tensions within the settler community at the historical juncture when the eclipse of the Beothuk became palpable. "The formative event here," as Cynthia Sugars puts it, "is not the Beothuk dispersal so much as the European unsettlement that derives from this dispersal" (2005, 162). Although it is a fairly conventional historical novel, *River Thieves* highlights and complicates the demonology characteristic of so many colonial texts, in which "the racial or national 'other' comes to be seen from a Gothic perspective, endowed with diabolical, monstrous or merely melodramatically powerful qualities" (Punter and Byron 2004, 45). More broadly, though, the novel also suggests that historical fiction can be seen as a fundamentally gothic gesture and that animating the dead—particularly with as politically and emotionally charged a story as that of the Beothuk—raises some profound historiographical, political, and ethical considerations.

River Thieves is built around three expeditions into the interior of Newfoundland: the 1811 expedition led by naval lieutenant David Buchan to establish friendly contact with the Beothuk, which culminated in the beheading of two marines; the 1819 excursion to Red Lake by a party of settlers led by John Peyton Junior (known just as Peyton) and John Peyton Senior (known as John Senior), during which Mary March was captured; and the attempt to return her body to her people in the winter of 1820 after her death from tuberculosis.[2] Despite the structural importance of these three expeditions, Crummey stresses in an interview that the fate of the Beothuk, except for moments near the end of the novel, "is very marginal to [the] lives and concerns" of the Europeans (2007, 298). One effect of this narrative strategy is that, to the Europeans, the Aboriginal functions, as Bergland's characterization of the uncanny suggests, as the shadowy and sinister force that is a central feature of gothic texts. "The sense of unsettledness in the word *unheimlich* is important," she argues, referring to Sigmund Freud's notion of the "unhomely," "because it evokes the colonialist paradigm that opposes civilization to the dark and mysterious world of the irrational and savage. Quite literally, the uncanny is the unsettled, the not-yet-colonized, the unsuccessfully colonized, or the decolonized" (Bergland 2000, 11; Freud 1919). For the settlers and colonial authorities who take part, these expeditions are unsettling journeys into the heart of darkness—the Beothuk an elusive and threatening force whose depiction has undeniably gothic overtones.[3]

Crummey's depiction of the Europeans' experience on the three expeditions certainly evokes a central colonial trope: the construction of the indigene in the mind of the settler as a menacing absence and barbarous presence. In many ways, this dual discursive strategy is a fundamentally gothic one, corresponding to the effects of what Jerrold Hogle distinguishes as "terror Gothic" and "horror Gothic" (2000, 3). The former "holds characters and readers mostly in anxious suspense about threats to life, safety, and sanity that are kept largely out of sight or in shadows or suggestions from a hidden past" (3). David Stevens observes that gothic terror is a kind of numinous, sublime, "overwhelming experience that transcends everyday normality" (2000, 50), and the shadowy absence of the Beothuk has a kind of chilling sublimity, suggesting the presence of an ontological divide separating them from the European characters. As the expedition crosses from a forest of "poplar and birch to a dark corridor of black spruce, pine and larch," the change in terrain (the effect of a forest fire some seventy years before) is "abrupt and complete, as if a line had been drawn to separate two worlds" (Crummey 2001b, 115). The men then come upon the deserted caribou fences of the Beothuk, whose lines of birchbark clappers "swung in each breath of wind and raised a racket that was intended to spook the caribou and keep them from leaving the river and escaping into the bush. The noise was irregular but steady, like scattered applause, and it spooked most of the men who were coming up the river for the first time as well" (118). After the disaster of the first expedition, Buchan returns to visit the Peytons at Burnt Island, where they talk of the fleeting sightings of Beothuk "as if they were discussing creatures who had all but disappeared from the earth, ghosts, spirits who drifted occasionally to this side of darkness" (144).

This absence gives to the setting an atmosphere again consonant with the Gothic. As Hogle observes, "a Gothic tale usually takes place (at least some of the time) in an antiquated or seemingly antiquated space" (2000, 2). Although *River Thieves* is not set in a classically gothic space—"a castle, a foreign palace, an abbey, a vast prison, a subterranean crypt, a graveyard" (2)—the vanishing Beothuk leave behind ruins of a sort, as the successive expeditions come across habitations deserted by the Beothuk. While the structures show signs of recent activity, their emptiness has a haunting quality:

There was no lack of evidence of a Beothuk presence — abandoned mama-teeks, recently used firepits, well-marked trails. Twice Buchan and his men approached camps in which fires were burning and birds on wooden skewers were angled over the coals, but the occupants had seen or heard them approach and disappeared into the woods. (Crummey 2001b, 14–15)

The sense of uncertainty created by the absence of the Beothuk is an eerie one, not because the deserted architecture — the ruins of a culture — is ancient but, rather, because, as Sugars suggests, their abandonment is so recent: "The Beothuk, throughout, are conjured primarily as a trace, a series of last sightings" (2005, 164). Indeed, in characteristically gothic fashion, the novel's final scene, during the expedition to return Mary's body to her people, takes place at a deserted tomb (that of Mary's murdered husband), the Beothuk once again having vanished — and this time seemingly for good.

If the Beothuk are mostly a shadowy presence in the novel, the few encounters between them and the Europeans (excluding the captive Mary) are characterized by elements of "horror Gothic," which, according to Hogle, "confronts the principal characters with the gross violence of physical or psychological dissolution, explicitly shattering the assumed norms (including the repressions) of everyday life with wildly shocking, and even revolting, consequences" (2000, 3). The Beothuk are such a feared presence partly because of the past history of violent, gruesome conflict in the area. Their animosity towards John Senior's former business partner Harry Miller, for instance, culminates in chilling, gory violence. First, they burn down his fishing tilt, "shout[ing] into the flames" and singing and "chant[ing] into the night" (Crummey 2001b, 322). Subsequently, they ambush Miller and behead him, leaving his corpse to be picked over by animals, "the bloodied clothes torn and pulled away from the torso. Most of the flesh was eaten away from underneath. Grey lengths of bone showed through, the surfaces pocked with tooth marks. Richmond had said, 'That's hardly worth burying'" (224). To the settlers, these actions provide, as Lizabeth Paravisini-Gebert puts it, the "'mark of savagery' that justifies colonialism, while providing the required element for Gothic terror" (2000, 238).

The execution of the marines during the disastrous first expedition is likewise depicted with unnerving gore. After friendly contact is established with the Beothuk, two marines volunteer to be left behind as security for the Beothuk men who accompany the expedition back to retrieve gifts that have been cached further behind. The three Beothuk men abandon the party in succession, the last fleeing after he stumbles upon the corpses of the two marines:

> The bodies were about a hundred yards apart, stripped naked and lain on their bellies. The heads of both marines had been cut from the torsos and carried off. The flesh at their necks was flayed ragged as if a blunt blade had been used to behead them and loose scarves of blood draped the snow above the mutilation. Their backs were pierced by arrows. The group stood over the scene in a stunned silence until one of the Blue Jackets in the party turned away from the bodies and vomited. (Crummey 2001b, 139)

Such grotesque violence creates an "overwhelming, oceanic sensation" (Stevens 2000, 50), which is evident when the party beats a retreat back to Buchan's ship, unnerved by the slaughter: "Each night one or more of the party started awake from a dream of Butler's perfectly blond head on a stake, of Bouthland's eyes as dead and sightless as the mole on his cheek. Some tried desperately to stay awake then for fear of where their dreams would take them" (Crummey 2001b, 140). While, at first, Buchan is sanguine about their deaths, seeing the expedition as otherwise successful and hoping shortly to rectify what he sees as an unfortunate misunderstanding of intentions, later he is haunted by the idea that they have been the victims of his megalomaniacal desire to champion the cause of the Beothuk.

The depiction of Aboriginal violence as otherworldly in its barbarism is, of course, a staple of North American colonial literature, and a recurring, complementary strategy in postcolonial texts is a turning of the tables, which is a tactical reminder that brutality and barbarism are not the exclusive preserve of the colonial Other. Although for most of the European characters in *River Thieves* the Beothuk function as a source of gothic terror and horror, it is the settlers who are depicted as the principal source of barbaric and grotesque violence. John Senior, for one, sees the Beothuk as incomprehensible and inhuman—"Our lot haven't got but a civil bone in their bodies and there's no amount of charity will teach them any manners" (29). Here John Senior exhibits a characteristically colonial (but also gothic) Manichean logic "in which the land that falls under the rule of empire is perceived as 'empty' because its previous inhabitants...are denied the status of the human" (Punter and Byron

2004, 46). This perspective, in turn, justifies his indiscriminately retributive stance. After the Beothuk burn down Harry Miller's house, John Senior accompanies Miller on a retaliatory raid on a random group of Beothuk. As they approach, John Senior fires into the mamateeks, which contain women and children as well as men. When they enter one of the mamateeks, a wounded old man strikes John Senior with one of his own traps, and John Senior then proceeds to beat the man to death with it: "The battered skull showed through the long shearing wounds and tiny yellow flecks of bone had landed on John Senior's boots. His trousers were sprayed with blood" (Crummey 2001b, 326).[4] Finally, one of the novel's most haunting images is that of a Beothuk girl captured by Dick Richmond (who presumably kills her companions in the process) and ultimately sent to Poole, where she is exhibited, terrified, before unrestrainedly curious crowds disappointed by her lack of exoticism. As Peyton, who witnesses the spectacle, reflects, the "English audience pressing in on her must have seemed like the half-wild and savage creatures they had come hoping to see" (110).

One of the dangers of reversing the terms of the colonial opposition between the savage and the civilized, however, is that it can amount to a retrospective self-congratulation. Richard Budgel questions the validity of sweeping claims about settler brutality and sees them as part of an effort to strike a distance from Newfoundland settler history in order to say: "Look how far we've come from our savage ancestors" (1992, 26). In her comprehensive history of the Beothuk, Ingeborg Marshall argues that relatively few of the English settlers were actively hostile (1996, 106), and Crummey's focus on John Peyton Senior, Harry Miller, and Dick Richmond as prominent instigators of violence accords with this account. Another way in which Crummey avoids this pitfall is by concentrating on the conflicting responses to the Beothuk within the settler community, particularly the opposition to John Senior's tactics by his son and namesake. Indeed, the central spine of the narrative is Peyton's gradual usurpation of his father's authority as they struggle over how to react to the Beothuk's theft of their property. In this struggle, *River Thieves* again harnesses the energies of the Gothic. As Hogle observes, gothic fictions tend to focus on protagonists "caught between the attractions or terrors of a past once controlled by overweening aristocrats or priests…and forces of change that would reject such a past yet still remain held by aspects of it" (2000, 3). Although it would be a stretch to suggest that there was an aristocracy on Newfoundland's eastern shore in the early nineteenth century, John Senior presides over a mini-empire on the River Exploits and, given the frontier conditions of the time and the fact that "most settlers were impoverished members of the working class," can be seen as one of the area's aristocrats (Budgel 1992, 26). Indeed, the title of Crummey's novel seems to be a reworking of the title of *River Lords* (a relatively laudatory biography of the historical Peytons by the wife of one of their descendants), implicitly demoting the barons to robber barons (see Peyton 1987).

As various critics have noted, what has revitalized interest in the Gothic in the twentieth century is that its revolutionary (albeit ambivalent) energies—its preoccupation with the overturning of the established order—have deep and profound psychological resonances. As Hogle contends,

> the features of the Anglo-European-American Gothic have helped to prefigure and shape Freud's notion of Oedipal conflict in the middle-class family. In some way the Gothic is usually about some "son" both wanting to kill and striving to be the "father" and thus feeling fearful and guilty about what he most desires. (2000, 5)

This dynamic is central to *River Thieves,* in which (to put a gothic spin on the relationship) the two John Peytons function as doppelgangers. At the beginning of the novel, Peyton is depicted as being impatient to inherit his aging father's empire, taking heart when his father passes on the care of his trapline to him. From there, the narrative revolves around the son's increasing resistance to his father's authority and around the transition of power from one generation to the next.

Intensifying this archetypal generational struggle are the pair's conflicting attitudes towards the Beothuk. Whereas John Senior is uncompromisingly belligerent in his response to theft or destruction of their property, Peyton is more conciliatory and, somewhat contrarily, supports Buchan's cause of establishing friendly contact. In this struggle, however, Peyton is stirred by more deeply Oedipal sentiments, including a brooding resentment of his father that is motivated by his desire for their housekeeper Cassandra Jure and by the suspicion that she has been his father's lover.[5] Brought from St. John's to tutor the young Peyton as well as to keep house, Cassie (Peyton's senior by six years) is initially a maternal figure, replacing Peyton's mother whom he chooses to leave behind in England in order to accompany his father to Newfoundland. Peyton's hope, though, is that "running his own trapline was a first step towards a station from which he felt he might legitimately declare his intentions" (Crummey 2001b, 54), and John Senior too initially sees Cassie as a potential wife for his son as he grows older. However, an incident in which John Senior surprises Cassie naked while bathing raises the possibility that "he might have her for himself" (191). The possibility that John Senior is indeed "having her" deters his son from openly pursuing her, especially after she resorts to a backwoods abortion, which confirms his suspicions. Peyton is forced by Cassie to keep the abortion secret, leaving him feeling torn between the two: "He felt owned in sections, as if parcels of himself were under Cassie's name, others under John Senior's" (209–10).

This sexual triangle gives the generational struggle a more explicitly Oedipal cast, as Crummey intimately intertwines the Peytons' competition for Cassie with their divergent responses to the Beothuk. Although John Senior is scathingly skeptical of Buchan's colonial authority and his naively Samaritan approach, Peyton devotes himself to aiding Buchan almost to spite his father, who feels himself vindicated when the trust placed in the Beothuk is rewarded by the beheading of the two marines. When Cassie steps in between them to break up a particularly virulent argument set off by John Senior's observation of his son's enthusiasm — "If I didn't know any better ... I'd think you was after a Red bride" — Peyton's reaction highlights the physical tensions of the sexual triangle: "He found it disturbing, Cassie's touch obliquely connecting him and his father that way, and he wondered if he was the only one of the three of them to be bothered by it" (145). The obsession with instinctive drives and the brooding threat of violence that are hallmarks of the Gothic make their presence felt from early on in *River Thieves*.

It is the second expedition, however, that really defines the father-son struggle in a particularly gothic fashion. The ultimate outcome of the expedition is a murder that must be covered up, which is a narrative thread familiar from such classic gothic tales as Edgar Allan Poe's "The Black Cat" and "The Cask of Amontillado" (1843 and 1846), but which in *River Thieves* is part of a broader historiographical, revisionist agenda. If the Beothuk can be seen as the skeleton in Newfoundland's closet, as it were, in *River Thieves* Crummey explores a more specific concealment — the possibility that during the capture of Mary March a murder was committed and subsequently covered up. While this possibility is floated, but not prominent, in the historiography on the Beothuk, in Crummey's novel it becomes central to the narrative intrigue.[6] Contemporary historical fiction often explores the gaps or the contradictions in the historical record, and the tensions between the Peytons in the novel are built around what Crummey sees as a distinct but suppressed possibility in a key moment in Newfoundland history, something suggested by the tensions and inconsistencies in eyewitness accounts of the episode (2007, 310–11).

The second expedition, during which the simmering tensions between father and son come to a boil, develops in response to the theft and vandalizing of the Peytons' fishing boat by the Beothuk. Disappointed by his son's resistance to retaliation on previous occasions — "I didn't realize when I passed off to you … that it was all to go to leeward to keep them cock Indians in gear" — John Senior brooks no opposition to his proposed expedition to the interior to recoup their losses: "Don't lap back at me on this one, laddie boy" (204, 205). In order to stem the potential violence, Peyton, at Cassie's prompting, contacts the colonial authorities and gets their blessing to capture a Beothuk, for which they have posted a substantial reward. However, Peyton's premonition that the expedition would gather "momentum until it was a careening downhill surge he would be helpless to direct or divert" proves to be accurate (217). The Peytons and their men manage to surprise a group of Beothuk on Red Indian Lake, but, after Peyton catches hold of Mary, a man brandishing a birch branch approaches the party and tries to reclaim her. As a struggle ensues between the man and John Senior, Peyton is compelled to order his men to fire after their efforts to beat the man off with their muskets prove futile.[7]

This untoward outcome precipitates a crisis that accelerates the shift in the power relations between son and father. Although Peyton had uneasily attempted to quell the expedition's violent urges, his assertions of authority had met with resistance from his father and most of their men. The killing on Red Indian Lake, however, compels the authorities to launch an inquiry, before which Peyton is called to testify. His claim that the party acted in self-defence is accepted by the jury, which concludes that the "obstinance of the deceased [who turns out to have been Mary's husband] warranted the Peytons acting on the defensive" (258). However, the jury's underlying suspicions are suggested by their caveat that other members of the party be subject to interviews — a somewhat surprising departure from the tendency to presume settler violence against the Beothuk to be justified.[8]

When Buchan takes over the investigation, after almost a decade's absence, he manages to discover from Mary what Peyton has withheld from the inquiry, namely the fact that a second, less defensible killing had taken place—that of a Beothuk man, fatally wounded by John Senior while attempting to flee and subsequently put out of his misery by the Peytons' Irish head man Joseph Reilly.[9] Peyton is forced into suppressing the truth not so much to protect his father, who could potentially have argued extenuating circumstances, as to protect Reilly. As Reilly is a convicted "river thief" who has been exiled to the colonies (the telltale "T" branded on his hand, which is reminiscent of Hawthorne's *The Scarlet Letter* [1850]) and rehabilitated by John Senior, his past and ethnicity virtually guarantee a trip to the gallows. This situation occasions the real shift in power between father and son, as it is Peyton who negotiates with Buchan, effectively dismissing his father: "The old man looked to his son quickly, about to argue with him, but said nothing. In the few months since they'd gone down to the lake John Senior seemed to have lost his place in the world, everything around him had shifted, breaking up like ice rotten with spring heat" (Crummey 2001b, 368). At least in terms of the Peytons, the violence on Red Indian Lake seems to mark the passing of a regime, of a more belligerent, uncompromising colonial attitude.

The Peytons' complicity in this violence, furthermore, complicates and ultimately resolves their competition over Cassie, whose own troubled past further deepens the psychosexual intrigue of the novel and fortifies the gothic overtones of the overthrow of a dissolute old order, one stained by the suggestion of incest. Rescued by John Senior from an abusive father after the death of her mother, Cassie has been keeping his son at bay because she has been harbouring her own secrets. For one thing, the father of the child she aborted, it turns out, was not John Senior but, rather, Buchan, with whom Cassie has had a series of nocturnal liaisons prior to the catastrophic first expedition. This secret, which Peyton discovers after witnessing Cassie divulging the information to Buchan by writing in his notebook, ultimately provides the leverage Peyton needs to blackmail the self-righteous Buchan to prevent him from prosecuting Reilly. The more dramatic revelation, however, is that Cassie was a victim of incest and that the broken leg from which she still has a limp was the result of being pushed down the stairs not by her drunken father (as she had earlier confided) but, rather, by her mother, seemingly in a fit of jealousy. Part of the reason that John Senior was compelled to rescue Cassie was that he had witnessed her father going upstairs to fetch either Cassie or her mother to provide some entertainment for a drunken Harry Miller, and the question of which of the two Cassie's father intended to prostitute has haunted John Senior ever since. Thinking back to the moment of surprising Cassie—"young enough to be the old man's daughter"—in the tub, John Senior exhibits his anxiety of breaching the incest taboo, feeling "ashamed of himself and fearful, as if he'd just woken from his nightmare. *His wife or his daughter?*" (76, 191). However, the question also reflects his indecision over what status Cassie should have in his own household. As Hogle argues, the

> Gothic clearly exists, in part, to raise the possibility that all "abnormalities" we would divorce from ourselves are a part of ourselves, deeply and pervasively (hence frighteningly), even while it provides quasi-antiquated methods to help us place such "deviations" at a definite, though haunting, distance from us. (2000, 12)

John Senior's demonizing of the Beothuk, in other words, can be seen as a displacement of his anxiety over his own repressed "abnormalities."

Cassie's reserve and her ultimate retreat from the Peytons, Crummey observes, is intended to mirror and echo the vanishing Beothuk, and her departure is precipitated by revelations about the Peytons' treatment of the Beothuk (2007, 303). Although Cassie has been vaguely aware of stories about John Senior's brutalities against the Beothuk, her tortured past and John Senior's intervention to rescue her from it have quelled her curiosity. The arrival of Mary, who takes refuge in the Peyton home after her capture, and the revelation about the second killing, however, prompt her to interrogate John Senior about his dealings with the Beothuk and Peyton about the truth of what happened on the lake. John Senior's confession of his wanton violence and his son's concession that they have effectively conspired to cover up a murder prompt Cassie to recognize their complicity in a patriarchal violence that she had hoped to escape. At the end of the novel, after persuading Buchan and Peyton to allow her to accompany the expedition returning Mary's body to her people, Cassie takes leave of the Peytons. Historical fiction often allegorically weaves a romance narrative into the fabric of historical events, and Cassie's departure amounts to an indictment of the Peytons' complicity in both patriarchal and colonial violence.

The outcome of the Oedipal struggle in *River Thieves* suggests what Valdine Clemens sees as a central dynamic of gothic texts, namely "the return of the repressed" (1999, 4). In other words, John Senior and also, by association, his son are undone by the appearance of that which has been contained, not just the brutal history of the treatment of the Beothuk but, more generally, the pathology of patriarchal authority. The latter is suggested by the way in which both Peytons are haunted by the demented decline of their fathers. John Senior guiltily provides palliative care for a considerate father turned abusive and insane, and his rescuing of Cassie is partly to atone for his mother's suffering at the hands of his father (Crummey 2001b, 330). His son, in turn, witnesses John Senior as he is routinely "hag-ridden," haunted by a recurring nightmare in which "he was flailing his arms, hands balled into fists or holding something cold and hard, and he was beating something helpless beneath him, something utterly defenceless" (320).[10] These scenes suggest the cautionary function that gothic tales share with nightmares, "which serve as alarming reminders that things are not as they should be or not what they appear to be" and are "a message from the unconscious, often arising when a given attitude is proving inadequate to a current life situation" (Clemens 1999, 3).

Valdine Clemens's characterization of the role of repression in gothic texts, moreover, speaks to the larger canvas of *River Thieves* and to its revisionist, postcolonial historiography:

This "return of the repressed," or emergence of whatever has been previously rejected by consciousness, is a fundamental dynamism of Gothic narratives. Something—some entity, knowledge, emotion, or feeling—which has been submerged or held at bay because it threatens the established order of things, develops a cumulative energy that demands its release and forces it to the realm of visibility where it must be acknowledged. The approach and the appearance of the repressed create an aura of menace and "uncanniness," both in Freud's sense of *"unheimlich"*—something that becomes apparent although one feels it "ought" to remain hidden—and in the Jungian sense of something possessing an awesome or transpersonal, numinous quality. (1999, 4)

The revelation of the second killing is central to the novel not only because it resolves the struggle between father and son but also because it constitutes an indictment of the suppression of settler violence as the foundation of a colonial culture. *River Thieves* evokes what Punter and

Byron see as "the recurrent sense in Gothic fiction that the past can never be left behind, that it will reappear and exact a necessary price." Indeed, they argue, the "very structure of the term 'postcolonial' itself, its apparent insistence on a time 'after,' on an 'aftermath,' exposes itself precisely to the threat of return" (2004, 55).

The outcome of the romance narrative underscores the postcolonial parallels between Cassie and the Beothuk, especially through the sense of dissonance that her leaving provokes in Peyton—a profound sense of the "unhomely," of having "one's home—one's place … rendered somehow and in some sense unfamiliar … of being in place and 'out of place' *simultaneously*" (Gelder and Jacobs 1999, 181). Earlier in the novel, Peyton finds a moment of reprieve from his tense relations with Cassie and his father in the backcountry, reflecting that his knowledge of it "made him feel he was closest here to belonging, to loving something that might, in some unconscious way, love him in return" (Crummey 2001b, 207). At the end of the novel, though, after a last attempt to float the possibility of a union with Cassie (which is left unanswered), Peyton looks at his surroundings and forlornly observes: "All my life I've loved what didn't belong to me" (408). The remark directly points to the elusive Cassie but is also—in another gesture to the "thieves" of the novel's title—a concession of colonial guilt, a recognition that the Newfoundland to which he has become so attached, for which he has left behind his mother, and for which he has now lost Cassie, does not belong to him. "The Peytons and the other characters," as Chafe puts it, "can never be comfortably at home on this island because they always exist where someone else *was supposed to have existed*" (2004, 97). Although at this point the novel comes dangerously close to the trope, which is recurrent in literary representations of the Beothuk, "of Beothuk extinction as a wound to the European," Crummey's depiction has much in common with the increasing use of gothic tropes and conventions to raise postcolonial questions about settler identity and colonial history (Dalton 1992, 140). As Bergland observes, the presence of ghosts in American literature is intimately connected to "issues of public justice" because the "history of European relations with Native Americans is a history of murders, looted graves, illegal land transfers, and disruptions of sovereignty. Among these, land ownership may be the source of the nation's deepest guilt." In short, "the land is haunted because it is stolen" (2000, 8–9). Peyton's reaction points to the way in which, as Punter and Byron argue, the postcolonial is fundamentally gothic because of its preoccupation with

the haunting ineradicability of paths not taken. The cultures and histories of
colonized nations are shadowed by the fantasized possibility of alternative
histories, the sense of what might have been if the violence of colonization
had not come to eradicate or pervert the traces of "independent development." (2004, 54)

If the framework of the Gothic helps to elucidate Crummey's postcolonial, revisionist revelation of repressed colonial violence, it also helps to
articulate the way in which *River Thieves* foregrounds some of the tensions of the historical novel. The crucial part of the novel in this regard is
Peyton's recollection of being marooned on an island with his father during a storm and taking refuge in what turns out to be a Beothuk burial
site. Initially, John Senior evokes the Beothuk as the gothic Other in order
to unnerve — and implicitly belittle — his son: "Dead Indians are the least
of your worries. It's the quick you got to watch out for" (Crummey 2001b,
112). What transpires as the scene develops, though, is a transfer of gothic
otherness onto the settler. Peyton watches appalled as his father unwraps
one of the corpses from its shroud and cuts away its sacred pouch, presenting it to his son as "a keepsake." "It made him distrust his father in a way he
was never able to articulate clearly," Peyton remembers years later, as he
struggles to sleep during the first expedition down the Exploits River and
turns "onto his side then, drawing his legs up to lie in the exact same position as the dead man he'd uncovered years ago, and waited for sleep"
(114). As Clemens notes, although the genre of the Gothic is coterminous
"with the development of the urban-industrial world," gothic novels also
function as a kind of atavistic reminder of the proximity of "the more dangerous, precarious hunting and gathering life" of the past and of "how the
past continues to shape the psychic realities of the present. They stress the
fragility of civilized constraints on human behaviour and demonstrate
that the world is much older and less anthropocentric than we would like
to think" (1999, 4). This effect is reflected at this point not so much in
Peyton's postural identification with the Beothuk as in his dawning recognition, courtesy of his father's desecration of the grave, of his father's fundamental barbarism. As Budgel observes, "there is, lurking behind many of
the descriptions of early Newfoundland settlers, a premise that our hold
on civilization is tenuous" (1992, 26). Peyton has seen the enemy, and it is us.

The gothic overtones of the scene — a representative of the decadent,
compromised aristocratic order grotesquely desecrating a grave — take on

larger historiographical resonances in a subsequent recollection near the end of *River Thieves*. In one of the novel's key scenes, Peyton, fearful at the prospect of imminent revelation, hesitates before opening Buchan's journal, which he has asked Reilly to pilfer after witnessing Cassie write in the margins:

> He would find himself in there, and his father and Mary, and all the men who made up the party to the lake, but not, he was sure, in the fashion they had conspired to present themselves. The start of their undoing, that little book, now or some time beyond their time. There were things he'd seen and heard in his days he vowed to take to his grave, as if that was a safe place for the truth. But two hundred years from now, he knew, some stranger could raise his bones from the earth and put whatever words they liked in his mouth. It was a broken, helpless feeling. (Crummey 2001b, 347)

In what is in most ways a relatively traditional historical novel, this passage jumps out as a self-conscious disclaimer that is more typical of postmodern historiographical meta-fiction. It seems to be not only a warning to the reader that this text is ultimately fiction — that this is not the past "live and in action," as it were, in textual form — but also a concession of Crummey's consciousness of historical fiction as, in turn, a kind of desecration, a violation of the dead. As Crummey admits, "[t]he 'stranger' that John Peyton points his sadly accusing finger at is me, sitting on the other side of the computer screen. I thought I owed him that much at least" (2001a, 42).

Prior to this point, however, Peyton thinks back to the earlier desecration, providing a more gothic variation on this subsequent moment of historiographical self-consciousness. Peyton opens the journal, the "motion like a mouth talking, the jaws of a skull working open and closed" and remembers his father in the Beothuk grave picking up a man's skull (shades of *Hamlet*) and flapping jawbone and skull "back and forth and [speaking] under this mime in a low-pitched voice. 'Just a dead Indian,' the skull said. 'Nothing to bother your head about'" (Crummey 2001b, 346). Peyton's response captures Crummey's authorial anxiety and his resistance to historical fiction as a kind of necromancy, bringing the dead (that is, the past) back to life: "He could feel the violation in that act, putting words so carelessly and callously in the mouth of the dead" (347).

What this scene suggests, then, particularly through its use of gothic tropes, is the novel's doubled anxiety about the dead. It reflects how the Beothuk continue to be a haunting, unsettling presence in Newfoundland; that the province is, in a way, a "defiled grave"; and that, as a magistrate warns before it happens, "the English nation...may have affixed to its character the indelible reproach of having extirpated a whole race of people" (24). It also reflects an anxiety that to write about the past involves a kind of ghoulish exhumation, that historical figures are not just textual manifestations of the archives, semiotic clusters in historical documents, but, rather, in a more literal sense, bodies being disturbed. As Crummey acknowledges, while writing the novel he was "keenly aware of the fact that many of the names and faces [he] was using belonged to real people, to individuals whose own unknowable selves passed two centuries ago. That [he] was, in some sense, playing God with those lives" (2001a, 40).

Looking at *River Thieves* through the framework of the Gothic ultimately helps to unearth, then, a fundamental tension in Crummey's attitude towards the dead. On the one hand, Peyton's historiographically self-conscious meditations reflect Crummey's wariness of the idea that he is putting words in the mouths of the dead. On the other hand, his revisionist project — his disclosure of the skeleton in the closet — suggests the intent to make history speak, to reveal what has been repressed. As Mary Dalton argues, representations of the Beothuk in Newfoundland literature are rife with contradictions and effectively serve as projections of the writers' anxieties and desires: "The literary works about the Beothuks, full of expressions of empathy and sympathy and awe and guilt, nonetheless exclude and deny them.... We write shadow Indians, who serve us beyond the grave" (1992, 144). Crummey's solution seems to be to write not so much about the Beothuk but, rather, about the settlers' perception of their eclipse, their elusiveness a trope for their ultimate, mute inscrutability. Nonetheless, this approach leaves a tension succinctly identified by Sugars: "The real question...is at what point does this sort of narrative shade into a self-serving nostalgia rather than a genuine act of restitution?" (2005, 171). Certainly, Crummey depicts the settlers (paradoxical as it seems) as being traumatized by the fate of the Beothuk as well as being victimized by a rigid colonial authority personified by the martinet Buchan. This tactic runs the risk of setting up a spurious equivalence between the two in which "Newfoundlanders are tied to the Beothuk by their marginality and their shared understanding of life in a difficult place" and by being likewise "persecuted unfairly" (Budgel 1992, 29). Crummey's novel, though, strikes a balance (albeit uneasy) between the dubious alternatives of a hyperbolic, simplistic indictment of settler violence and a reductive, sentimental, and exculpatory identification of the settler with the Beothuk.

Ultimately, though, the novel *is* about the Beothuk, in the sense that the narrative revolves around the literal skeletons in the closet—the two dead men on the lake. However self-conscious Crummey may be about it, *River Thieves* is a fictional proposition, enacting a desire to challenge certain propensities in the historical record and, in the process, "doing a certain kind of cultural cathartic work, enabling Canadians to speak the crime that has no name" (Sugars 2005, 162). "The dead have their rights, as the living do," the nineteenth-century Irish-Canadian politician Thomas D'Arcy McGee once observed: "Injustice against them is one of the worst forms of injustice" (quoted in Slattery 1968, epigraph). In these terms, Crummey's novel highlights the fundamental Catch-22 that the disappearance of the Beothuk occasions. To leave the dead alone, Crummey's revisitation of the events on Red Indian Lake suggests, is to do an injustice to some of them. To exhume them, however, may well be an injustice to others (among the dead, that is). In this sense, *River Thieves* illustrates how the traditional historical novel—and its revisionist successor—necessarily involves a disturbing of the dead. However, as Punter and Byron suggest, such a gothic gesture may well be a necessary and, indeed, constructive condition of postcolonial cultures:

> The story of the postcolonial, then—here as elsewhere—is in the mouths of ghosts; the effect of empire has been the dematerialization of whole cultures, and the Gothic tropes of the ghost, the phantom, the revenant, gain curious new life from the need to assert continuity where the lessons of conventional history and geography would claim that all continuity has been broken by the imperial trauma. (2004, 58)

To put it in terms of *River Thieves*, just because the Beothuk are gone does not mean they should be left behind. *River Thieves*, in other words, ultimately avoids the consolatory, compensatory, exculpatory tone of much writing on the Beothuk and serves instead as a reminder of how their extinction is implacably part of, rather than erased by, the history of Newfoundland.

Notes

1 Michael Crummey's work is particularly permeated by loss, a preoccupation shaped by the decline of the culture of the inshore fishery and by his growing up in the dying mining town of Buchans in the Newfoundland interior. In "Journey into a Lost Nation," he describes visiting Buchans almost as an uncanny experience: "Going back to visit now evokes the old unsettling feeling of disquiet from my childhood, the fear that my hometown is more imaginary than real. Each time I arrive, something more of the place has disappeared" (2004, 15).

2 Although most of the novel is based on historical events, perhaps the most significant reworking of the historical record is that, in the character of Mary March, Michael Crummey collapses the stories of the two most prominent Beothuk captives, Demasduit (Mary March) and Shanawdithit (Nancy April) (2004).

3 See Paul Chafe's "Lament for a Notion" (2004) and Cynthia Sugars's "Original Sin" (2005), both of which touch on some of the parallels with Joseph Conrad's *Heart of Darkness* (1899).

4 See Ingeborg Marshall (1996, 104) and B.D. Fardy (1988, 8) for historical accounts of this incident.

5 Cassie is the most fictionalized of the principal characters in the novel. See J.P. Howley ([1915] 1974, 175 and 182) and Amy Peyton (1987, 76 and 81) for references to a Mrs. Jure, who served as Peyton Junior's housekeeper when Shanawdithit stayed in the Peyton household in the mid-1820s.

6 It is mentioned by B.D. Fardy in a note (1988, 98), and, in Shanawdithit's version of events, cited by Ingeborg Marshall (1996, 164), there was a second killing.

7 The historical Peyton's culpability on this occasion is the subject of much debate. Ingeborg Marshall criticizes him for not releasing Demasduit "to show his good intentions" (1996, 165) and sees the episode as the unfortunate consequence of the incredibly naive but common assumption that benevolent treatment of captives would reverse the deeply entrenched suspicion and hostility of the Beothuk towards whites. Amy Louise Peyton, in a dubious bit of telepathy, largely exonerates the Peytons by constructing the clash as being initiated by a vengeful Beothuk stirred by the presence of the notorious and hated John Senior: "A very tall Indian suddenly noticed the elder Peyton. He recognized him as their enemy from previous encounters and thinking him to be the 'ringleader,' must have thought that there was now a chance to wreak his revenge" (1987, 42). See Paul Chafe for a compelling Lacanian reading of the Oedipal narrative in the novel, in which Mary and her husband become figures of the mother and father (2004, 109–14).

8 At this point in the novel, Michael Crummey quotes verbatim from the verdict of the historical jury.

9 Reilly is also a more fully fictional character, although Ingeborg Marshall, in discussing how the punishment of offences was extremely biased against the poor, mentions that a "James Reily [sic] had a T branded on his hand for theft" (1996, 106).

10 Chafe reads the hag as a figure of colonial guilt: "The Beothuk will remain the hag lingering just outside Newfoundlanders' perception, nagging their unconscious, disrupting their sleep" (2004, 116).

Works Cited

Bergland, Renée L. 2000. *The National Uncanny: Indian Ghosts and American Subjects*. Hanover: UP of New England.

Budgel, Richard. 1992. "The Beothuks and the Newfoundland Mind." *Newfoundland Studies* 8(1): 15–33.

Chafe, Paul. 2004. "Lament for a Notion: Loss and the Beothuk in Michael Crummey's *River Thieves*." In *Literature of Newfoundland*. Ed. Lawrence Mathews. Special issue of *Essays on Canadian Writing* 82: 93–117.

Clemens, Valdine. 1999. *The Return of the Repressed: Gothic Horror from* The Castle of Otranto *to* Alien. Albany, NY: SUNY Press.

Conrad, Joseph. 1899, reprinted 1995. *Heart of Darkness*. Ed. D.C.R.A. Goonetilleke. Peterborough: Broadview.

Crummey, Michael. 2001a. "Changing History." *Quill and Quire* 67(11): 42, 40.

———. 2001b, reprinted 2002. *River Thieves*. Toronto: Anchor Canada.

———. 2004. "Journey into a Lost Nation." In *Newfoundland: Journey into a Lost Nation*. Ed. Michael Crummey and Greg Locke. Toronto: McClelland and Stewart. 8–39.

———. 2007. "The Living Haunt the Dead." In *Speaking in the Past Tense: English-Canadian Novelists on Writing Historical Fiction*. Ed. Herb Wyile. Waterloo, ON: Wilfrid Laurier UP. 295–319.

Dalton, Mary. 1992. "Shadow Indians: The Beothuk Motif in Newfoundland Literature." *Newfoundland Studies* 8(2): 135–46.

Fardy, B.D. 1988. *Demasduit: Native Newfoundlander*. St. John's: Creative Press.

Freud, Sigmund. 1919, reprinted 1955. "The 'Uncanny.'" In *The Standard Edition of the Complete Psychological Works of Sigmund Freud*, volume XVII. Trans. James Strachey. London: Hogarth. 219–52.

Gelder, Ken, and Jane M. Jacobs. 1999. "The Postcolonial Ghost Story." In *Ghosts: Deconstruction, Psychoanalysis, History*. Ed. Peter Buse and Andrew Stott. London: Macmillan. 179–99.

Hawthorne, Nathaniel. 1850, reprinted 1990. *The Scarlet Letter*. Ed. Brian Harding. Oxford: Oxford UP.

Hogle, Jerrold E. 2000. "Introduction: The Gothic in Western Culture." In *The Cambridge Companion to Gothic Fiction*. Ed. Jerrold E. Hogle. Cambridge: Cambridge UP. 1–20.

Howley, J.P. 1915, reprinted 1974. *The Beothucks or Red Indians*. Toronto: Coles.

Marshall, Ingeborg. 1996. *A History and Ethnography of the Beothuk*. Montreal and Kingston: McGill-Queen's UP.

Paravisini-Gebert, Lizabeth. 2000. "Colonial and Postcolonial Gothic: The Caribbean." In *The Cambridge Companion to Gothic Fiction*. Ed. Jerrold Hogle. Cambridge: Cambridge UP. 229–57.

Peyton, Amy Louise. 1987. *River Lords: Father and Son.* St. John's: Jesperson Press.

Poe, Edgar Allan. 1843, reprinted 1993. "The Black Cat." In *Tales of Mystery and Imagination.* Ware, UK: Wordsworth Editions. 189–96.

———. 1846, reprinted 1993. "The Cask of Amontillado." In *Tales of Mystery and Imagination.* Ware, UK: Wordsworth Editions. 202–07.

Punter, David, and Glennis Byron. 2004. *The Gothic: Blackwell Guides to Literature.* Oxford: Blackwell.

Slattery T.P. 1968. *The Assassination of D'Arcy McGee.* Garden City, NY: Doubleday.

Stevens, David. 2000. *The Gothic Tradition.* Cambridge: Cambridge UP.

Sugars, Cynthia. 2005. "Original Sin, or, The Last of the First Ancestors: Michael Crummey's *River Thieves.*" *English Studies in Canada* 31(4): 147–75.

Sweatman, Margaret. 2007. "Ghosts Are Our Allies." In *Speaking in the Past Tense: English-Canadian Novelists on Writing Historical Fiction.* Ed. Herb Wyile. Waterloo, ON: Wilfrid Laurier UP. 165–87.

CHAPTER ELEVEN

Keeping the Gothic at (Sick) Bay: Reading the Transferences in Vincent Lam's *Bloodletting & Miraculous Cures*

Cynthia Sugars

> They have been taught to beware of counter-transference.... No, not to beware. They are taught to be aware.
>
> — Vincent Lam, *Bloodletting & Miraculous Cures*

> Certain types of patients can arouse feelings which are not yet at our command or use, and hence may significantly interfere with treatment. Before we assume a holier-than-thou attitude, we must ask ourselves whether we have fully plumbed our unconscious in terms of murder, cannibalism, fusion states, envy, and death.
>
> — Robert Marshall, *The Transference-Countertransference Matrix*

> It is interesting that psychoanalysis, which would have us look truth in the eye, also makes use of the most powerful illusion we generate: that we convey ourselves to other people. Sitting silently, "umming" along to sustain the illusion, the analyst supports the patient's belief that he understands everything.
>
> — Christopher Bollas, *Cracking Up*

Vincent Lam's collection of linked short stories, *Bloodletting & Miraculous Cures* (2006), is a book with a deceptively gothic title. Following its nomination for the Giller Prize in 2006, it became an almost overnight sensation because of the uniqueness of its subject matter, which was striking for its notably non-gothic tenor. Indeed, the book is a literary treatment of the profession of modern day emergency medicine without the melodrama typically associated with popular culture depictions of that world. Given its conjuring of the Gothic, it is interesting that the book exhibits a distinct suspicion, yet accompanying fascination, with gothic irrationality, while placing this interest within the hyper-rationalized world of the medical profession. In effect, Lam seeks to "de-gothicize" the common portrayals of modern medicine of their emphasis on horror tales of emergency room gore, medical school pranks, or morbid fantasy, while, at the same time, infusing this world with gothic potential by probing the irrational, bewildering, and mutually vulnerable side of medical practice.[1] This approach is immediately evident in the epigraph to the book from the noted Canadian humanist/physician William Osler: "Medicine is a science of uncertainty and an art of probability." In Lam's stories, the doctor's role resembles that of the intuitive author and critic, who appends a "conclusion" to the story of the patient's disease. As the art of what is likely and the science of what is not, medical diagnosis makes use of a kind of prescience that can seem distinctly uncanny. Yet in Lam's account, this unconscious interpretation is problematized since we are never sure whether what the doctors are perceiving is accurate. To paraphrase Adrienne Rich, the practice of medicine involves courting "what you don't know you know" (1979, 40).

Lam's stories play with this ambiguity, for hovering at the edges of each narrative is a kind of furtive knowledge — something that we are not quite sure of and which we cannot articulate, but which we nevertheless feel that we "know." In effect, *Bloodletting & Miraculous Cures* tantalizes readers with its "almost gothic" subject matter, luring readers with a promise of a gothic plot, taunting them with it, but always pulling back. The stories entice the reader into thinking that they will tip over into the gothic territory of macabre medical experiments and "miraculous" resuscitations, but they never do … quite. Instead, it is in the "stories" that are exchanged between doctor and patient, in the realm of the psychological "transference" between the two, that the Gothic makes its fleeting appearance.[2] In the book, this evocation of the gothic transference becomes a curious act of repression of the gothic genre itself, whereby the fetishization of "narrative" becomes a way of secreting the Gothic to the edges of interlocutory consciousness. Lam's use of the Gothic thus taps into its long history of epistemological ambiguity, particularly as the Gothic has been so frequently read in terms of psychosis. Comparable to Sigmund Freud's delineation of the term *unheimlich* (meaning both *strange* and *familiar*), gothic elements have an unstable ontology in that they can be read as either real or not real (imagined), sometimes both simultaneously ([1919] 1990). By overtly playing on the uncertainty between mental derangement and the real, Lam is able to use the Gothic to access the suggestive realm of uncertainty in interpersonal unconscious communication.

Lam's version of the Gothic is thus very much a "post"-colonial one, in the sense that he is not concerned with the demons and ghosts of the colonial encounter or with the spectres of racism in the Canadian nation-state. It might be more appropriate to speak of his work as post-postcolonial or even in terms of a post-gothic Gothic. Moreover, it is not the Chinese-Canadian experience, per se, that is of interest to Lam in these stories, despite the fact that many of his characters are Chinese Canadian. In a 22 January 2006 review of *Bloodletting & Miraculous Cures* in the *Toronto Star*, Judy Stoffman observes that Lam's writing provides a portrayal of Chinese-Canadian characters that is distinct from those of the "older generation" of writers such as Wayson Choy and Fred Wah. These earlier writers, Stoffman suggests, "paint a harsher reality of displacement, departure, exclusion," while Lam's stories depict a world of "successful, assimilated young Chinese-Canadian professionals." Although one might be able to read the stories for the underlying current of diasporic and other issues as they affect second- and third-generation Canadians, Lam himself confirms Stoffman's perspective: "My generation [of Chinese Canadians] ... are at a unique point in Canadian history because the barriers have fallen."

The focus group in Lam's stories are not Chinese Canadians as such but, rather, another group of individuals who struggle with issues of authenticity, passing, coding, border crossing, role playing, and split subjectivity—namely medical professionals who wrestle with the expectations that are imposed on them by their patients and, more profoundly, by themselves. As Paul Gessell puts it in his review of *Bloodletting & Miraculous Cures* for the *Ottawa Citizen*, doctors are barraged by "the expectations of patients believing in the infallibility of modern medicine" (2006).[3] Indeed, many of Lam's doctors engage in what Fred Wah, in another context, describes as "faking it" (2000), as they prepare a face to meet the faces that they meet. Lam's physicians, writes Kevin Chong in the *National Post*, "must learn not only to practise medicine but how to appear and behave like a doctor" (2006). Internally, the doctors are perturbed by the illusion of their role as miraculous healers. "*Always sit down with the patient*," one doctor says to himself, "*It makes it seem ... that you care*" (Lam 2006, 168). Others are plagued by the absurdity of the central role they assume in strangers' lives. The doctor in "Night Flight," for example, assumes a mask of impenetrable calm as he knowingly lies to a woman about the treatment her husband received before his death: "There is this balance of professing humanity without invading privacy. Should I keep eye contact for another few seconds, or turn away? ... Lies are about belief, about a reality suspended because we want to believe the lie. Both the teller and the recipient must trust each other for everything to hang together" (261, 262). In order for the "lie" to be maintained, both doctor and patient must proclaim a faith in the doctor's infallibility. Recognizing the fiction of medical omniscience, Lam's doctors marvel at the impact that they have on their patients' lives. If indulged in, this cognizance of fictive omnipotence can assume megalomaniacal proportions or, at the very least, an uncanny sense of diagnostic prescience, a kind of medicalized second sight. Doctors become harbingers of death, the catalysts of destiny. In "Afterwards," a doctor who has just treated a fatal heart attack meditates upon his role: he is powerless to alter the determinacy of fate yet also omnipotent in his launching of destiny. He is more than a messenger, for he feels that his speech *enacts* the death: "Mr. Wilhelm himself was gone, but the Mr. Wilhelm who existed with his family was alive until Sri told them of the death.... *What if, just now,* he thought, *I forgot that Mr. Wilhelm died? ... I should just say it, to make it real and end it*" (190–91 [emphasis in original]). There is something indecent about one person being catapulted so profoundly and precipitously inside the existence of another. The doctor, as a kind of gothic master of ceremonies and omniscient storyteller, makes death "real." Yet how is it possible that the doctor-patient barrier can become so easily traversed? Whose stories are we reading: the patient's or the doctor's?

Of central concern in these stories is the zone of interpersonal unconscious communication — the counter-transferential relation between physician and patient. For Lam, it is in the realm of the transference that the Gothic is allowed to emerge, figured as a "potential space" where the irrational finds freeplay alongside the rational, where "the boundaries between fantasy and reality" are blurred (Sprengnether 1993, 96). In this sense, Lam's evocation of the Gothic might be said to conform to one of

the classic descriptions of gothic functioning as a "transgression of boundaries" (Punter 1980, 19; Botting 1996, 6–9). The transferential experience
is, literally, a crossing of boundaries between self and other on the level of
unconscious communication. In this book, as perhaps even for Freud, the
transference *is* the site of the Gothic—the only site of the Gothic that is
possible in a rationalist, medicalized textbook world.

Stalking the Gothic

The courting of the Gothic that takes place in Lam's stories both confirms
and disrupts the analysis of the gothic tradition undertaken by Jodey
Castricano in her essay "Learning to Talk with Ghosts" (2006). Castricano's
critique of the gothic tradition in Western literature rests on its long-
standing alliance with psychoanalysis, which rationalizes gothic occurrences by pathologizing them. Terry Castle claims that such rationalizing
of the Gothic has put it on a solidly psychological footing (quoted in
Castricano 2006, 803). This linking of gothic occurrences with psychic
malaise is the very phenomenon that Lam is playing with in these stories.
According to Castricano, Freud puts gothic "intrusions" in an "occult-free
zone," a form of demystification grounded in scientific materialism (803).
Likewise, Anne Williams notes that Freud "saw himself as a destroyer of
illusions" who asserted "the power of the reality principle" (1995, 243).
For Castricano, the Gothic has come to be the signifier of "psychological
unease" and, by extension, refuses magical, primitive, or supernatural
explanations. Eden Robinson's novel *Monkey Beach,* she argues, "exceeds
a Western European Gothic explanatory model ... by staging the displacement of the twin ghosts of European Gothic and psychoanalysis" (2006,
806; 812). But what do we do with a book such as Lam's, a work that is set
within the "pathologizing" world of the medical profession and appears
to be resisting, yet also courting, an extra-rational explanation? Paradoxically, in Lam's stories the Gothic is held up as precisely the realm of
extra-rational, "empirical" reality, a literalization of gothic effects that has
often been absent in the later gothic critical tradition (see Sedgwick 1999,
11–12). In other words, if one reads Lam's stories for gothic *presence,* the
medical/psychosomatic explanation is undermined. Yet when a medical
practitioner insists on a literal interpretation of psychotic delusion,
whose psychosis is it that we are dealing with: doctor's or patient's? If the
psychopathological explanation is a way of resolving gothic absurdity, in

Lam's stories the literal "gothic" explanation, because it is never wholly allowed in, remains in suspension. Psychotic patients may or may not be telling the truth. Rational doctors may be unstable maniacs beneath a veneer of inscrutable professionalism. Such possibilities makes Lam's approach a kind of playful gothic negation — "Leave the Gothic out of this!" — a post-gothic Gothic, which at once conjures its presence and then submerses it beneath a facade of verifiable and realist referentiality. His book points, ultimately, to an extra-rational desire for gothic verification.

The critique of Freudian psychoanalysis as a rejection of the "supernatural" is valid to the extent that Freud refers puzzling experiences to the realm of the unconscious. Nevertheless, the unconscious, for Freud, figures as a kind of gothic third space, where identities, settings, chronologies, and ontologies overlap and fuse to create a world of bizarre and, often terrifying, internal objects. To dismiss psychoanalysis as an obfuscation of the extra-rational is problematic given what Anne Williams has identified as the gothic nature of Freud's own narratives (1995, 241; Kilgour 1995, 220). Paradoxically, Freud's rationalist inquiry overturned the rationalist basis of the self: "If Freud evokes the Male Gothic plot in insisting on the reality and the implacable force of some power that is counter-intuitive, then accepting that reality has the paradoxical effect of undermining the very authority with which one asserts this principle" (Williams 1995, 246). In effect, the Freudian unconscious represents a subversive discourse that takes seriously the realm of the "inexplicable" and attends to surface manifestations, such as hysterical symptoms, as symbolic messages from an intra-psychic depth that function outside of normal space/time.

Lam, I would argue, is taking advantage of the epistemological instability that is central to the gothic tradition. Indeed, it is expressly *because* his book is set within a world of medical psychopathology that the inherent irresolvability of the Gothic is so attractive. This is especially true of Lam's depiction of the physician/patient transference in his stories. While the Gothic has traditionally been defined in terms of the supernatural, it gradually emerged as a sign "of the need for the sacred and transcendent in a modern enlightened secular world which denies the existence of supernatural forces, or as the rebellion of the imagination against the tyranny of reason" (Kilgour 1995, 3; see also Botting 1996, 1). In other words, it allowed for an expression of the "extra-rational" within highly rationalist contexts (Heilman, quoted in Sedgwick 1999, 1). The Gothic, according to David Punter, may be "representing those areas of the world and of consciousness which are...not available to the normal processes of representation" (1980, 18). More relevant, perhaps, is Maggie Kilgour's discussion of the Gothic as it delineates interpersonal relations. The Gothic, she argues, offers resistance to "a modern bourgeois society, made up of atomistic possessive individuals, who have no essential relation to each other" (1995, 11). In Kilgour's account, the Gothic is double-sided in that it also presents a modern world of detached individuals, showing "the easy slide of the modern Cartesian mind from autonomy and independence into solipsism and obsession, depicting the atomistic individual as fragmented, and alienated from others and ultimately from himself. In the gothic, 'normal' human relationships are defamiliarised and critiqued by being pushed to destructive extremes" (12). Lam's courting of the Gothic in his representations of interpersonal relations conjures its ambivalent yet potentially transformative nature. As Kilgour puts it, "[t]he fragmentation and estrangement of the gothic thus both reflects a modern alienated and estranged world made up of atomistic individuals, and suggests the hope of recovering a lost organic unity" (15).

This is precisely the way the Gothic functions in Lam's collection. In one sense, the medical profession overrides the atomization of individuals in its reliance on interpersonal communication. And, yet, this "dialogue" occurs only on the surface. As Judith Butler puts it, "[s]omething is said, and it appears that an intention is being represented in speech, that correspondence is intact.... But the speech act is a form of address, and it is addressed to one who is not transparently there" (2003, 120). Paradoxically, transference both erects such a barrier (perhaps even epitomizes it) and facilitates communication (of the unconscious). In Lam's stories, the conversations between doctor and patient are frustratingly opaque exchanges that are reaching to become something more and yet cannot due to the inescapable divide between physician and patient. Lam's doctors struggle to reach beyond this gap, while remaining safely on the side of the "professional," yet nonetheless mythologized, miracle worker. Ultimately, the Gothic cannot be fully actualized in Lam's work because of the insistence of this divide. Nevertheless, it is within this divide, via the inevitable triggering of the (sometimes healing, sometimes threatening) transference-countertransference relation, that the Gothic may be glimpsed. In the twenty-first century medical world where psychoanalysis has itself become figured as the domain of quacks and flakes—where psychotherapy has been replaced by cognitive-behavioural or pharmacological therapies of various kinds — the conjuring of the Freudian unconscious marks a subversive departure for Lam. The world of modern medicine is one in which Freud himself has been colonized by the Western rationalist-materialist tradition. If psychoanalysis has typically been construed as a demystification of extra-rational irruptions as unconscious psychic effects, in a secular world it is now perhaps psychoanalysis that remains the last refuge of the irrational.

Yet Lam's stories also bear links with the tradition of Southern Ontario Gothic in their interest in the gothic undercurrent beneath the surface of the quotidian. If the Gothic shares a "general opposition to realist aesthetics" (Punter 1980, 404), in Southern Ontario Gothic it conjures the inherently gothic nature of hyper-realism (that is, the illusion of surfaces). Punter speaks of a body of "paranoiac fiction," which continually places the supernatural in doubt and at the same time "serve[s] the important function of removing the illusory halo of certainty from the so-called 'natural' world" (404). In Lam's stories, the ontological status of the physician's projections and paranoia remains obscure. The physician's code, as one of the doctors in Lam's stories tells himself, is to project an illusion of "equilibrium": "*Always sit down with the patient, I was taught. It makes it seem like you've spent more time and that you care.... If you give this impression* (this is the subtext) *then the patients will do what you say and leave quickly*" (Lam 2006, 168). In other words, the gothic taboo that is evoked in Lam's fiction is precisely the physician's "irrationality" — that is, the physician's projection of unconscious fantasies onto the patient and surrounding circumstances (things that should supposedly be controlled or suppressed).[4]

This process is delineated very clearly in what is one of the best stories of the collection, "Take All of Murphy." The story concerns a group of three medical students who are in the same dissection group at university. Although the transferential relation is complicated in this story because the "patient" is dead, what the story delineates are the different projections of the three doctors/students onto the patient, who, in turn, "speaks" to them through the tattoos that cover parts of his body and that the students are forced to cut into. The first crisis occurs when Sri, one of the members of the group, proposes that they name the cadaver "Murphy" in order to de-abjectify it and re-infuse it with human identity. In response, his emotionally hardened lab partner, Ming, "refused to use any name... [she] made a point of saying 'the cadaver's aorta, the cadaver's kidneys'"

(40). Nevertheless, it is Ming, despite her rationalist pretensions, who is the disrespectful one, making repeated crude jokes about the body—a distinction that the Dean of the faculty archly raises when she says that she would *"rather you be a bit emotional than, shall we say, overly cavalier"* (32–33). The story anticipates readers' gothic expectations of tales of grave robbing and Frankensteinian experiments, not to mention modern medical-school horror stories. The Dean reminds students that *"distasteful incidents regarding cadavers have, in the past, resulted in expulsion"* (33). Later, she reassures the third student of the group, Chen, that the cadavers were once respectable people, not like the corpses of criminals and paupers smuggled by old-time grave robbers. The latter, it is implied, invited gothic projections: *"In my time it was all people from the jails or found dead in fights or ditches. No identification and so forth. What you would call bad people. Yours are different, all volunteers. Elderly, upstanding citizens mostly"* (36). The story thus conjures the Gothic in order to swiftly reject it, yet one cannot help but anticipate a horrific conclusion as the students proceed with their dissection and, within the group, become increasingly fractious. The incongruous detail of the delicate origami lessons that conclude each dissection only adds to this effect. What is the trick, one wonders? When is the jolt going to come?

When the students uncover the tattoos on Murphy's arm, the pictures begin to tell a story, apparently revealing that Murphy was an air-force pilot whose downed planes are recorded in a ring on his upper arm. Ming continually deflates what she sees—"It's good they started the tattoos from the outside'" (42)—while the other two slowly try to piece together the "story" of Murphy, as they peel back one layer of gauze after another. It is Sri's emotional response that is the focus of the story, as he becomes increasingly hostile to Ming and, at the same time, construes Murphy as a kind of Lazarus, projecting onto the cadaver his desperate desire for human significance, dignity, and, it emerges, salvation. "He's here for us,'" he tells his lab partner Chen (53). Sri, throughout, is empathetic with Murphy: "[He] touched the tattooed arm. 'I guess the war ended'" (42). On Murphy's shoulder is a tattooed crucifix underneath which is written in gothic letters: *The Lord Keeps Me—Mark 16* (42). As Ming blithely attempts to cut through the tattoo, Sri becomes obsessed by the message: "It must mean something'" (42). When Ming insists on proceeding with the dissection, Sri resists: "It's bad luck.... You should respect a man's symbols'" (43). Sri becomes increasingly agitated over the course of the year, challenging Ming for her refusal to let her unconscious speak with the dead. As she puts it rather starkly, "'I don't have dreams, because I don't have hang-ups about the stupid corpse'" (50).

It seems clear from the story that the reader is meant to empathize with Sri's inner conflict and not with Ming's detachment. Paul Gessell suggests that "Lam has ... put humanity back into medicine" (2006). This is clear in "Take All of Murphy," which depicts not only the doctor's respect for the dead but also the "patient's" effect on the internal world of the doctor. Sri's response is human — perhaps not rational, as Ming would say — but human. When he finds out that Ming has misplaced part of the cadaver's head, he feels that she has wilfully violated both him and Murphy. Learning that the head is in the bag with the intestines, Sri enters the lab at night to put it in its proper place. In a scene that appears to be building to a gothic climax, Sri and Chen, after a night at the pub, sneak into the anatomy room. And, yet, the conclusion is remarkably gentle. Sri's transference of his own fears of personal invasion, and presumably of death, onto Murphy is epitomized when he and Chen discuss the meaning of Mark, Chapter 16, which tells of Jesus's resurrection from the dead. Chen's summary of the scripture has a reassuring affect on Sri, who concludes the vigil by tenderly wrapping up Murphy (whose head is now intact) for the last time, tucking his ear beneath a fold of the cotton as though performing a final act of respect and burial.

The ambiguity of Murphy's guiding role is compounded by the evocative image of the pages from the dissection manual that have been folded into origami swans and attached floating above each dissection table: "*The swans were hung over the cadavers with twine, and if you forgot something you could look up and see whether it was printed on the wing of a twirling swan*" — helpful messages from the spirit of the dead (Lam 2006, 44). When Murphy's head is lost, Ming tells Sri to "'[j]ust study it from the manual,'" to which he replies that he turned that page into a swan (46). If the swan and the corpse are metonymic equivalents, the message that is potentially revealed on the swan's wing, like a tattoo, is encrypted in Murphy. The message being some kind of "sign" that they are doing the right and good thing. To Sri, Murphy has come back from the dead to speak from the afterlife — rather in the vein of Dante. Nevertheless, it is also clear that Sri has invested too much of himself in his patient and has written a story for him, which may or may not be accurate. Indeed, by continually appealing to his mother's advice when speaking of how they should be treating Murphy, it becomes apparent that Sri has aligned Murphy and his mother as a kind of condensation of a "lost object" that is beyond his reach. By the end of the story, the gothic spectre of the resurrected corpse, as in the Biblical account, is seemingly laid to rest, while the supposed irrationality of Sri's response is left in suspension, for whose response is more "rational": Sri's or Ming's? And what, finally, is the meaning of the reference to Mark, Chapter 16? Sri and Ming, in effect, represent the different responses to the undeniably gothic scene of Jesus's resurrection. Is his ghost real or a figment of the mourners' imaginations? Sri may be right to perceive that there has been something predestined in Murphy's being "here for us" — specifically for the three lab partners who read his tale. However, it may also be a mere flight of fantasy.

The epistemological ambiguity of the gothic transference is a recurring theme in Lam's stories. In many instances, the "irrationality" of the doctor's response is used momentarily to conjure a surreal world, as though the stories were building to a potentially gothic climax that registers as both "real" and "psychotic" and then drop us back into the world of the everyday, yet are nevertheless imbued with the lingering (and uncanny) residue of the gothic plot. In each of these stories, the mental stability of the doctor (or student doctor) remains in question. We are to think that a "rational" explanation is applicable to each circumstance, and yet the inherent irresolvability of the gothic transference has placed this explanation in doubt.

Transference and the Unspeakable

In most instances, Lam's presentation of these not-quite-gothic scenarios hinges on the transferential relations between individuals. Transference, Freud quickly realized, was where the real work of psychoanalysis took place — not only because it was where unconscious elements came to the fore (and where the past became "presenced," like a ghost) but also because of the self's unwilling surrender to its effects. It represents a weird form of ventriloquizing, in which the self becomes "possessed" by the speech of the unconscious. As Butler describes the transference/counter-transference, "aims that the intending speaker does not fully know or control become articulated in the ways speech (whose speech?) is enacted in the course of the interlocutory exchange between analyst and patient" (2003, 120).

Of course, the transference is also the realm of creativity and insight, including that of the interpreting medical professional (as in the epigraph from Osler cited earlier). Christopher Bollas's many discussions of transference are applicable to Lam's work in that Bollas is primarily concerned with narrative exchange and manipulation. The physician responds to the patient by "displacing [his/her] narrative into a counternarrative" (1995, 12), an interaction that causes the physician's inner world to become gothicized. This act of translation is comparable to the way the dream work functions using condensation, displacement, metonymy, and false logic. What results is a kind of gothic geography or gothic experience, as the doctor finds him/herself inhabiting a confused mental landscape in which he/she "carries evolving contradictions and condenses events from differing periods of the analysis, [becoming] *recurrently confused,* wandering in the strange country of even suspension" (13). Bollas thus uses the notion of "counter-transference" to refer to what Sándor Ferenczi describes as "Dialogues of the Unconscious" (quoted in Bollas 1995, 9). As he puts it, the doctor's "thoughts and feelings are derivatives of the patient's unconscious": "I respond by transforming his material into my own, unconsciously resignifying it according to my own unconscious processes" (21, 25). This dynamic echoes Lam's account of his experience as both a literary and medical practitioner: "'The link between doctors and writers is narrative,'" he told John Goddard for the *Toronto Star.* "'What happens is, someone tells me the start of a story, and much of what I'm supposed to do is tell them the ending. The other thing I'm supposed to do is make the ending of the story better.'"[5]

This is precisely what happens in many of the stories. A doctor appends or transfers his/her own "story" onto that of the patient, without always being aware that she/he is doing so. In "Night Flight," the doctor insists on "the relief of confession" (2006, 267), yet, in fact, there is very little overt confession on the part of the physician (indeed, the doctor in this story never does "confess" to the lie he tells his patient, even though he claims that he believes in the primacy of truth). If doctors are meant to contain their patients' anxieties, appending a "happy" conclusion to the patient's story, they also incorporate those anxieties into their own self-constructed gothic scenarios, which, we find out, may or may not have objective validity.

Two of the most interesting stories in this connection, "Winston" and "Eli," concern overt doctor-patient counter-transferences. Although, in each case, it is the patient's name that is foregrounded in the title, each tale is ultimately concerned with the doctor's reaction to the patient's story. "Winston" is perhaps the signature story of *Bloodletting & Miraculous Cures* for its courting of a gothic plotline. At the outset, we are introduced to Winston, a man who believes that he has been poisoned and seduced by his upstairs neighbour when she gave him a strange blue potion at a Halloween party. After days of consideration, Winston, who is suffering from insomnia and hallucinations as a result of the "blue drink," decides to visit the hospital for an antidote. He comes to the doctor with an overtly "gothic" problem: "'The evil in my bloodstream fizzes my brain.... That blue drink—I knew something was funny, not the funny colour, not ha-ha funny, but *funny*. Put down the glass, don't even sip, said my inner voice, but I didn't listen. I was wearing this ghost costume, and ... then she poisoned me'" (119–20).

While Sri initially believes Winston to be delusional, he becomes seduced by Winston's appeal to his rational integrity. Winston, as in the epigraph by Osler, appeals to Sri's commitment to the "science of uncertainty" rather than to the "art of probability." As Sri's practically minded, yet metaphorically inclined, supervisor tells him in relation to the case, "'I admire your open-mindedness.... You've heard that the sound of hoof-beats implies the presence of horses? It is true that we must look carefully for zebras, but for the most part we expect to find horses'" (125). The most "rational" approach is to read for probability (horses not zebras), yet because this approach is inherently anti-empiricist, Sri places his faith in the scientific commitment to empiricism, making it incumbent upon him to investigate the "truth" of Winston's gothic narrative (and, thereby, potentially yielding zebras not horses). In essence, the context is forcing Sri to read (or choose not to read) the surface plot, enacting the scenario that Slavoj Žižek rehearses from Groucho Marx's *Duck Soup:* "'This man looks like an idiot and acts like an idiot—but this should in no way deceive you: he *IS* an idiot!'" (1991, 73). Likewise, Winston says he is being poisoned and acts as though he has been poisoned, so Sri should read him accordingly: he *is* being poisoned.

When Winston places his faith in the doctor—"'Doctor, give me a sign to trust you'"—Sri, taking the patient at his word, unclips his badge and hands it over (120). A clue to Sri's precarious relation with the patient becomes evident almost immediately when Sri fears that the patient "might be taking advantage of him and will at any moment laugh at the humour in a momentary tilt of the balance of power" (120). When Sri subsequently tries to rationalize with Winston by reading his experience metaphorically and insisting that "'some think of illness as a kind of poison'" (121), he performs the Freudian rationalization that Castricano identifies in her reading of the Gothic. Yet, as the hyper-vigilant medical rationalist, Sri cannot let the patient's claims go uninvestigated. After all, he has no concrete proof that Winston is delusional. The patient anticipates Sri's wavering: "'[T]hat's why you, being a doctor and everything, have to treat the poison because this stuff is making me *sound cuckoo*. You've got to fix it before it *does* make me nuts'" (121 [emphasis in original]).

What catches Sri off guard is the patient's lucid insight into the disruption of his thought processes, leading the doctor to search for "zebras" and become the "delusional" one himself. In short, the patient appeals to the doctor as his last hope of receiving a fair hearing of being sane. He implores the doctor to read against the grain of conventional gothic criticism and accept the material reality of his gothic experience *as* real. Interestingly, this is precisely the charge brought against gothic criticism by Sedgwick—that the surface elements become ignored in favour of metaphors of "depth" (1999, 11). Yet the terms are reversed in this story for the doctor is called upon to validate a gothic "depth" (or hidden reality) at the expense of the "surface" reality of mental derangement (the latter of which is usually interpreted as the "depth"). In other words, Lam's doctors want to believe in a verifiably gothic underpinning (poisoning, police brutality, fire, and tattoos) to the "reality" (that is, psychosis) they are presented with.[6]

The effect of this inversion is to make the quest for gothic explanation an expressly rationalist impulse. Sri's exchange with his supervisor reveals his insistence on rational explanation to the extent that he fails to understand his supervisor's metaphorical meaning:

> "Tell me, Dr. Sri, if you woke up one day and saw a purple bird in your room, what would you think?"
> "Excuse me?"
> "A purple bird ..."
> "I would check the windows, the doors, and anywhere else a bird could have flown in."

"But despite that, you would be left with the spectre of a flying, tweeting creature having appeared in your room …"

"I sleep with the windows closed," says Sri. "Even if a bird escaped from a pet shop, or the zoo, it couldn't get in." (Lam 2006, 152–53)

Sri is as far from a gothic mindset as it is possible to be, which, in effect, makes him a prime candidate for gothic contagion, as the history of the Gothic as a response to rationalist bourgeois society suggests. In Lam's stories, the rationalist insistence on "uncovering" buried gothic truths paradoxically turns the doctors into victims of gothic infection — for to believe in gothic *reality* becomes a sign of gothic *delusion*. The quest for an empirical explanation ultimately puts the sanity of the physician into question.

In the case of Sri, it is possible that he yearns for a brush with the Gothic in order to supplement the rationalized world that he inhabits (much as he does in the story "Murphy"). He wants to listen to his unconscious, to deal rationally in a science of uncertainty: "Sri tells himself that this is clearly a psychosis. His gut whispers, *Zebras do exist*. But he is a physician, he tells himself sternly, who should deal not in gut feelings but in facts" (154). Nevertheless, Sri is haunted by what he terms "the presumption of physicians" (155). As his consultations with Winston proceed, he begins to give him the benefit of the doubt. He seriously considers whether there might be "an agent" that could produce the symptoms that Winston complains of, a "'new synthetic substance'" (126) or "'maybe a new rave drug'" (152). Ironically, Sri proceeds in what is simultaneously the most rational and irrational way possible. He takes the patient at his literal word and runs a series of laboratory tests and Internet searches for drugs that might have caused the symptoms that Winston describes.

His supervisor warns him against succumbing to the transference: "'This is the dilemma, to build a rapport, to allow the legitimacy of experience, but never to speak of what is *not* real as if it were'" (126). As it turns out, this is not easy, for rational investigation gives credence to the gothic narrative, hence playing with the inherently tenuous status of the Gothic (as real or imagined). When Winston produces the urine sample for the drug screen, he believes that he is being observed through a door in the bathroom wall. Even though Sri attempts to dispel his paranoia, he has to admit that there is some truth to Winston's perception. He is, after all, constantly being monitored by the hospital cameras: "'I can attest that no one watched you in the bathroom, but' — Sri says carefully, 'Someone is viewing us right now, of course, but that's different. We have a camera system'" (137). Sri's words confirm the truth of Winston's suspicions, and, in his fumbling attempts to rationalize the situation, Sri begins to sound more unbalanced than his patient. Moreover, the reality actually confirms the patient's delusion and, counter to Sri's intention, elicits an "insane" response from him, as though, were the truth to be acknowledged, we would all effectively become insane:

> "We have a camera system ... you know about that, don't you?"
> "What?"
> "Cameras. Not in the bathroom, but all these rooms are, let's not say watched, let's say monitored.... It's a physical camera, with wires, and it's *really there,* but not the way you think someone is *watching you.* You know what I mean?"
> "That's exactly what I feel, that someone is really watching me." (137–38)

The more Sri insists on what is "really there," the more he confirms what is not, thereby neglecting his supervisor's caution "'never to speak of what is *not* real as if it were'" (126).

As Sri attempts to enter his patient's mental world, to rationalize with a madman, he finds himself sounding more and more like him. Stumbling to regain control of the doctor-patient exchange, Sri becomes reckless and tells Winston of his supervisor who is supposed to be observing them at that very moment: "'She's there in the monitoring room but I'm sure that she's not paying attention. In a true sense, no one sees us'" (138). Adhering to his supervisor's admonition "'never to speak of what is *not* real as if it were,'" Sri's heightened rationality speaks the truth in the sense that none of us are truly accessible to one another, hence, "'[i]n a true sense, no one sees us'" (126, 138). This might be particularly true of the doctor, whose role is to be what he is not for the benefit of the patient's cure. However, Sri also speaks what is blatantly untrue, since Winston and he are under supervision at the very moment that Sri utters those words. In a sense, then, Sri has spoken of what is not real as though it were, although, in effect, the transference gives the lie to such an untruth, since in the transference one is both seen and not seen, heard and not heard, depending on whom one believes one's "true" self to be. That meaning does not necessarily emerge from "logical discourse" (Williams 1995, 247) is evident in Sri's exchange with Winston, making it all the more problematic that Sri attempts to apply logic to Winston's narrative. Sri is presented as a naive and impassive reader who is, in effect, figuratively challenged. Yet his dysfunction leads him to resuscitate the verifiably gothic plotline by reading it as "true"—the very interpretative approach that *Bloodletting & Miraculous Cures* undermines in its overall refusal of gothic effects. If in the gothic transference reason is "dethroned" (Williams 1995, 247), the completion of the gothic plot, as conducted by the "reader" Sri, represents an imposition of a rationalist plotline, which, in turn, renders the Gothic all the more palpable.

Winston's delusions become increasingly extreme as, in stages, he convinces himself that he was seduced by the upstairs neighbour when she was dressed as a harem girl, that he overheard her speaking to her husband about her love for him (Winston), and that he and she are going to kill her husband. Although we are witnesses to Winston's gradual descent into madness, the status of these "overheard" conversations remains uncertain (are they imagined or are they real) since they are presented as straightforward text. Moreover, it is also possible that the neighbours are playing mind games with Winston, trying to make him think that he is crazy. As Sri notes in his list of "facts" about the case, "Fact 3: tension and fog can appear between neighbours" (Lam 2006, 155). Like Sri, we are unsure of what the diagnosis will be: gothic or not. Sri, aware that the situation "has slipped out of his grasp," determines "to find out what is real and what is not" and visits Winston's apartment (155). Face to face with Winston's alleged poisoner, Sri begins to feel distinctly uncomfortable. As the details of Winston's gothic story gradually begin to unravel, Sri desperately tries to reassemble the pieces and ground them in gothic reality. The upstairs neighbour, Adrienne, was away during the time of the supposed Halloween party. Sri immediately wonders: "Should he ask how she went to Montreal? Car? Train? Maybe catch her out" (159). He also notices that Adrienne is not surprised when Winston, through a locked door, accuses her of trying to murder him: "Adrienne's expression is completely unchanged ... is it the way that someone who is not surprised is simply not surprised?" (159). Is she engaging in that "special kind of double deception," of which Sri suspects Winston—namely, enacting the truth because it is the truth (Zizek 1991, 73)? Next, he discovers that Adrienne does not have a husband but, instead, lives with a roommate: "Does she have a harem girl costume?" Sri asks himself, "Or maybe is she sort of ... masculine?" When Sri is upstairs in Adrienne's apartment, using the telephone to call for an ambulance, the critical moment takes place when she offers him a cup of tea: "'It's *not* poisoned, you know'" (Lam 2006, 162). Just as he is about to take a sip, he sees flitting out of the corner of his eye a purple bird on the window ledge.

There is something taboo about the doctor's succumbing to the irrationality of the counter-transference. It is at once "unspeakable" yet also premised in the speech act. Winston's irrational thoughts of persecution become echoed in the physician's equally unspeakable counter-transference, in which the gothic content of the patient's thoughts is picked up and given concrete validation. Yet, ironically, what Sri has in fact projected onto his patient is a rational reading of reality. He assumes that Winston is reading correctly, which, in turn, renders the physician's rationality questionable. In other words, the doctor's hyper-rational approach (taking the patient's words at a manifest level) lead him to a gothic plot. However, what if he chooses to believe a mental patient because on some level he wants it to be true? The doctor is projecting his own unconscious gothic fantasies by allowing the patient to maintain his.

The story entitled "Eli" plays out a similar doctor-patient dynamic. A patient is brought to the emergency ward with a head injury, apparently inflicted as a result of police brutality. Fitz, the doctor on call, feels increasingly irritated by the police who expect him to scoot the prisoner to the head of the queue so that they can take him to the police station. Fitz's desire to get at the cops contributes to his belief that Eli has been beaten by them. The two police officers try to warn Fitz — "'Watch yourself with Eli.... He's quick. Watch yourself'" — but almost immediately Fitz suspects that there is something untoward (172). He constructs the officers and their prisoner in terms of his own fantasy family scenarios: "The police are surprisingly kind to the prisoners, as long as they're docile. They treat them like younger siblings, showing them where to sit and filling forms for them. Just like an older brother, the police turn nasty in an instant if the prisoner becomes difficult.... Benevolence and cruelty are separated only by a veneer of whim which, in medicine, we understand" (167–68). Later, he thinks of himself as a parent, sitting on the edge of a child's bed: "*Where is it sore, dear?*" (168). These roles are important, for Fitz will come to behave as both parent and nasty brother in the course of his treatment of Eli. Indeed, a typical form of transferential relation is to replay with the Other early relations with persons (usually family members) from one's past.

Aware of the "veneer of whim," Fitz is also cognizant of himself acting a series of roles, including a doctor, a brother, and a patient. He is only what he allows others to believe him to be. Subsequently, he is offended when the police interpret his role as replaceable. Since he has a sense of himself as "faking it," he assumes that the police are doing the same, although it does not occur to him that Eli might be similarly "performing" the role of the battered victim. When Eli insists that he was "set up," Fitz takes him at his word and accepts the persecutory narrative that Eli relates: "'Fuckin' cops playin' drums with my head say I'm a killer gonna make me pay some shit'" (169). With unaccountable urgency, Fitz begins to "read" Eli's narrative as "true." However, for the benefit of his other interlocutors—the police who wait outside the examining room—he insists on subjecting Eli's seemingly paranoid narrative to a conventional psychological reading (that is, attributing Eli's claims to mental instability) in order to get Eli out of the hands of the police. Fitz "gothicizes" Eli by projecting onto him a fictional paranoid psychosis, leading him with questions that will enable Fitz to undercut the cops who wait outside: "'Are you hearing voices? Are you seeing things... that other people don't see? Is someone out to get you?... Are you receiving radio or telephone messages?'" (171). Imposing onto Eli a series of fictional paranoid delusions, Fitz, in fact, lends credence to Eli's initial paranoid complaint. One delusion is displaced by another, both of which are governed by Fitz's equally deluded assessment of his patient. When Fitz reports to the police, he plays with them by deviously providing a dual diagnosis: "'Eli told me about someone threatening [him].... That would be coercion, police brutality. Can't be true. So, Eli must be paranoid. Psychotic.... Although I guess he's not psychotic if it's all true'" (172–73). Like Sri in "Winston," he orders medical tests as a kind of reality testing. If the tests come out positive, it proves a literal gothic scenario underlying the apparent psychosis (Winston was indeed poisoned, and Eli has an internal brain hemorrhage from the police officer's kick). If they come out negative, the patient is delusional and, hence, conforms to the conventional reading of gothic narratives. In either case, the doctor initiates a gothic plot.

In truth, it is Fitz who feels beleaguered by the police, brutalized by their invasion of his turf: "Police stand and talk and lean on things as if they belong anywhere. For most people, there's a distinction between a place that is theirs and one they are visiting" (166). Subsequently, he feels that the cops are co-opting his diagnosis: "The game is supposed to go like

this. The police give the precis: Look doc, this guy did such-and-such....
Maybe they say what they think the diagnosis will be. The officers usually
imply what they think should happen to the prisoner. They can't say it
outright—'course, you're the doctor, they must say in conclusion, as per
protocol" (167). His paranoia extends to his belief that they are laughing
at him as they watch him treating the patient and, subsequently, to his
belief that one of them consciously allows Eli to attack him.[7] Indeed, the
turning point of the story occurs when Eli lashes out and bites Fitz's
hand, though the doctor is never certain whether or not it was the police
officer whom Eli intended to injure. His overly generous attempt to "rescue" Eli, motivated not by concern for the patient but, rather, by a desire
to get at the police, initiates an irrational degree of anger in Fitz. Instantly,
he becomes the gothic Jekyll-and-Hyde monster, transforming from the
nurturing doctor/mother into the nasty big brother. Behaving more brutally than either of the police officers, he proceeds to staple the wound on
Eli's forehead without having administered enough anaesthetic: "I
squeezed Eli's forehead, not paying attention to the alignment. *Thunk
thunk*, in went the staples. The male officer forced down Eli's knees as he
bucked at the hips. *Thunk thunk*.... 'Shut up, you piece of shit,' I whis-
pered. I leaned the sharp corner of my elbow on his sternum.... *Thunk
thunk*, I put in a few extra just for the sting" (177–78). By the end of the
story, Fitz is panicking, drawing blood from Eli's arm to have it tested for
HIV and thrusting him back into the arms of the police, despite the fact
that Eli is finally claiming that he needs a psychiatrist: "'Hey, I'm seeing....
Dancing elephants and shit.'" "'Never heard you say it,'" Fitz responds (181).

Fitz's sense of betrayal by Eli is apparent in the intensity of his retaliation. However, what is never adequately explained is the revenge he takes
on the police officer who lets slip her grasp while holding Eli. As one of
his last actions before moving on to another patient, Fitz leaves a pair of
scissors within reach of Eli's hand and leaves the room. His infection by
Eli's blood/saliva has now transformed Fitz into a monster, effecting a
kind of vampiric contagion. His thoughts echo those of Winston in the
earlier story when he believes he has poison running through his veins:
"The evil of blood is like a malevolent thought. Once it touches, the very
suspicion of its presence causes it to grow, to distort motive and action,
and to propagate its own dark, spreading reach" (181). At the end, Fitz
gives Eli the means to enact the revenge that Fitz's narrative demands.
According to Fitz's version of the story, this is the logical (and gothic)

conclusion — a form of horrific retributive justice. If the doctor is writing the story, Eli, in an appropriately transferential manner, is to act as his proxy.

These scenarios echo Lam's comments on his work as a doctor-writer. On the one hand, he speaks of the doctor's act of diagnosis as a kind of speech act, bringing the disease into being by pronouncing its presence (very like the doctor pronouncing the patient's death in "Afterwards"). Lam aligns this act with piecing together the elements of a story and appending a logical ending to it. It becomes the doctor's story as well as the patient's. The doctor, conditioned by a counter-transferential relation, enunciates what he/she imagines the patient experiences, which, in some instances, imposes on the patient a gothic narrative (the cops are out to frame you; the upstairs neighbours are trying to poison you), which may be a projection of the doctor's obsessions. The status of the gothic plots remains uncertain. Do the gothic experiences that are described have real world referentiality or are they manifestations of mental illness? Is the "almost gothic" aligned with mental illness or not and on whose part: doctor's or patient's? It is not clear. For Lam, the medical profession itself seems to be associated with this tenuousness. After all, how to get into medical school, the title of two of the stories in the collection, is based on a multiplicity of factors: intelligence, perseverance, hard work and also craftiness, illusion, and duplicity. In his essay "To Do Justice to Freud" (1998), Jacques Derrida assessed Michel Foucault's work on madness and sexuality for its ambivalence towards Freud, "who is... sometimes included among those who liberated us from the strategies of power and knowledge and sometimes put on the side of those who subjected us even further to them" (quoted in Naas 2003, 63). Similarly, Lam's use of both psychoanalysis and the Gothic points to a simultaneous fascination with, and rejection of, gothic effects. Derrida characterizes this back-and-forth movement as a "*fort/da* relation" (quoted in Naas 2003, 63). This is comparable to Lam's stalking of the Gothic in *Bloodletting & Miraculous Cures.* The "fort/da dynamic" provides an illusion of control over a desired external entity by calling it forth and subsequently rejecting it. Lam's stories want to allow the gothic unconscious entrance into the world of medical practitioners, yet they do not want gothic irrationality to run away with the plot — that is, with the respectable rational humanism upon which the practice of medicine is founded.

In one of the final stories of the collection, Fitz has become infected with the SARS virus and is dying in hospital. He is insistent that he no

longer be addressed as a doctor, thereby finally "confessing" his acknowledgement of the pretense of the rational and reliable professional role. "If
a doctor can succumb to disease, what hope is left?" the story seems to
ask, though admittedly each story in the collection has hinted at this possibility. Lam's focus is the vulnerability and humanity of the medical professional, the uncanny underside to the poised persona that we meet in
the medical consulting room. Yet it is also this underside that is the taboo
of rational medical practice, the unspeakable truth of the transference.
This dynamic is evident in the lines from Lam's story "Winston," which
form one of the epigraphs to this essay. In medical school, Sri is taught a
double relation to the transference: he must "beware" of it (avoid it) and
"be aware" of it (confront it). The transference becomes a gothic space of
psychological uncertainty and intuition—a conduit for gothic monsters
that are to be both avoided and courted. It is significant that Sri corrects
himself, changing "beware" to "be aware," almost as an afterthought.
Putting a stop to the transference is to become insular, to remain silent,
even though the transference inevitably highlights the alienated nature of
human communication. The only truly non-transferential state is death.
As Chen puts it in the final story of the book, "[m]ostly, I feel that if only
I do not speak, if only I refrain from uttering a single phrase, then everything will be all right. If I talk, it may allow things to spill from me. It
could set in motion a vertiginous unbalance, a confusion leading to madness, or a hunger that may cause me to eat until I burst and die. If only I
do not speak, I will be fine" (Lam 2006, 337). And, yet, Lam's stories
emphatically do not advocate silence, nor do they conclude with disillu-
sionment about the efficacy of interpersonal communication. Rather,
they are propelled by the furtive, and sometimes oracular, gothic potential within transferential narrative exchange.

Notes

1 Many reviewers commented on a sense of disappointed expectations based on the
book's title. Paul Gessell, for example, stated in the *Ottawa Citizen* that Lam's stories provide "ordinary bloodletting and few miraculous cures" (2006). Similarly, in
the *Montreal Gazette*, Joel Yanofsky notes that "the lurid title notwithstanding,
there's a minimum of gore and heroic measures" in the book (2006).
2 Transference may be defined as "the client's experience of the therapist that is
shaped by his or her own psychological structures and past, and involves displace-

ment onto the therapist, of feelings, attitudes, and behaviors belonging rightfully in earlier significant relationships" (Grant and Crawley 2002, 4). Premised on the belief that communication from unconscious to unconscious is constantly occurring, transference is considered a part of all interpersonal relationships (3; see also Bollas 1995, 10). Indeed, it is part of the process that helps humans make sense of interpersonal experiences. According to Evelyne Schwaber, "it is a powerful concept... [that] highlights our awareness that what we experience in another is a representation of the meaning we give to it, that what we see and feel is a product of what we bring to it" (1985, 3).

3　This echoes Lam's discussion of the Ontario Medicare system in his essay "The Best Medicine," published in *Toronto Life*.

4　This dynamic is what is defined as counter-transference. It typically refers to the physician's response to the "transference" of the patient (Marshall and Marshall 1988, 59), although it is more widely applied to embrace the "whole of the analyst's unconscious reactions to the individual analysand—especially to the analysand's own transference" (Laplanche and Pontalis 1988, 92). Sigmund Freud identifies it as "the patient's influence on [the physician's] unconscious feelings" (quoted in Laplanche and Pontalis 1988, 92). Initially counter-transference was considered an obstacle and a possible sign of "professional incompetence" (Marshall and Marshall 1988, 59). Later, it came to be seen as a useful tool.

5　See also Jason McBride's interview with Lam for *Toronto Life* where Lam provides a similar version of the doctor/writer connection (2006).

6　The gothic reality takes a different form in each story. In "Winston," it is the possibility of poisoning; in "Eli," police brutality; in "Night Flight," a consuming bushfire; in "Take All of Murphy," a tattooed message; in "Before Light," a speeding car. In each of the stories, the gothic undercurrent occurs in the way in which doctors respond to the pressures of the profession. Doctors become increasingly reckless as a result of these pressures, as though psychosis is stalking them. In turn, it becomes unclear whether their awareness of "gothic" surfaces is delusional or not.

7　Fitz is clearly acting out a resistance to authority figures and a fear of victimization. In the transferential situation (between any individuals, not just between doctor and patient), the subject relates to the other in a way that is comparable to how abusive figures in the past related to the subject—that is, you subject the other to the same traumatic and terrorizing emotions that you had to undergo. As J. Laplanche and J.-B. Pontalis point out, it is "psychical reality" that is transferred not "verbatim repetitions" (1988, 460). The plotting of Fitz's development, as delineated in the trajectory of the linked stories of *Bloodletting & Miraculous Cures*, begins in the opening story, "How to Get into Medical School, Part I," when Fitz is betrayed by his girlfriend Ming (who also becomes a doctor). The order of the stories leads the reader to construct this early event as the foundation of Fitz's increasingly aggressive and self-destructive behaviour in later life (among other things, he becomes an alcoholic). There is much that could be said about the development of the characters over the course of the book, but the topic is too broad for me to develop further in this essay.

Works Cited

Bollas, Christopher. 1995. *Cracking Up: The Work of Unconscious Experience.* New York: Hill and Wang.

Botting, Fred. 1996. *Gothic.* London: Routledge.

Butler, Judith. 2003. "Afterword." In *The Scandal of the Speaking Body: Don Juan with J.L. Austin, or Seduction in Two Languages.* Ed. Shoshana Felman. Stanford: Stanford UP. 113–23.

Castricano, Jodey. 2006. "Learning to Talk with Ghosts: Canadian Gothic and the Poetics of Haunting in Eden Robinson's *Monkey Beach.*" *University of Toronto Quarterly* 75(2): 801–13.

Chong, Kevin. 2006. "Critical Moments When Godlike Doctors Crack." *National Post,* 21 January, <http://vincentlam.ca//060121-critical-moments.php>.

Derrida, Jacques. 1998. "'To Do Justice to Freud': The History of Madness in the Age of Psychoanalysis." In *Resistances of Psychoanalysis.* Trans. Peggy Kamuf et al. Stanford: Stanford UP. 70–118.

Freud, Sigmund. 1919, reprinted 1990. "The 'Uncanny.'" In *The Penguin Freud Library: Art and Literature,* volume 14. Ed. Albert Dickson. Trans. James Strachey. Harmondsworth: Penguin. 335–76.

Gessell, Paul. 2006. "Beyond the Miracle Cures of Primetime Television." *Ottawa Citizen,* 4 February, <http://www.vincentlam.ca/060204-beyond-the-miracle.php>.

Goddard, John. 2006. "Doctor-Author Offers His Literary Diagnosis." *Toronto Star,* 9 November, <http://www.vincentlam.ca/061109-doctor-author-offers.php>.

Grant, Jan, and Jim Crawley. 2002. *Transference and Projection: Mirrors to the Self.* Buckingham: Open UP.

Kilgour, Maggie. 1995. *The Rise of the Gothic Novel.* London: Routledge.

Lam, Vincent. 2006. *Bloodletting & Miraculous Cures.* Toronto: Random House-Anchor.

———. 2006. "The Best Medicine." *Toronto Life,* March. <http://www.torontolife.com/features/the-best-medicine>.

Laplanche, J., and J.-B. Pontalis. 1988. *The Language of Psycho-Analysis.* London: Karnac.

Marshall, Robert J., and Simone V. Marshall. 1988. *The Transference-Countertransference Matrix: The Emotional-Cognitive Dialogue in Psychotherapy, Psychoanalysis, and Supervision.* New York: Columbia UP.

McBride, Jason. 2006. "Interview with Vincent Lam." *Toronto Life,* April, <http://www.vincentlam.ca/060401-interview.php>.

Nass, Michael. 2003. *Taking on the Tradition: Jacques Derrida and the Legacies of Deconstruction.* Stanford: Stanford UP.

Punter, David. 1980. *The Literature of Terror: A History of Gothic Fictions from 1765 to the Present.* London: Longman.

Rich, Adrienne. 1979. "When We Dead Awaken: Writing as Re-Vision." In *On Lies, Secrets, and Silence: Selected Prose 1966–1978*. New York: Norton. 33–49.

Robinson, Eden. 2000. *Monkey Beach*. Toronto: Alfred A. Knopf.

Schwaber, Evelyne Albrecht, ed. 1985. *The Transference in Psychotherapy: Clinical Management*. New York: International UP.

Sedgwick, Eve Kosofsky. 1999. *The Coherence of Gothic Conventions*, revised edition. North Stratford, NH: Ayer.

Sprengnether, Madelon. 1993. "Ghost Writing: A Meditation on Literary Criticism as Narrative." In *Transitional Objects and Potential Spaces: Literary Uses of D.W. Winnicott*. Ed. Peter L. Rudnytsky. New York: Columbia UP. 87–98.

Stoffman, Judy. 2006. "ER Doctor a Good Fiction Writer." *Toronto Star*, 22 January, <http://www.vincentlam.ca/060122-er-doctor.php>.

Wah, Fred. 2000. *Faking It: Poetics and Hybridity: Critical Writing 1984–1999: The Writer as Critic VII*. Edmonton: NeWest.

Williams, Anne. 1995. *Art of Darkness: A Poetics of Gothic*. Chicago: University of Chicago Press.

Yanofsky, Joel. 2006. "Stories Examine Doctors' Doubts and Aspirations." *Montreal Gazette*, 21 January, <http://www.vincentlam.ca/060121-stories-examine.php>.

Žižek, Slavoj. 1991. *Looking Awry: An Introduction to Jacques Lacan through Popular Culture*. Cambridge, MA: MIT Press.

Contributors

Jennifer Andrews is a full professor in the Department of English at the University of New Brunswick and co-editor of *Studies in Canadian Literature*. She has co-authored a book on Thomas King entitled *Border Crossings* (University of Toronto Press, 2003). She is currently writing a manuscript on Native North American women's poetry funded by the Social Sciences and Humanities Research Council.

Andrea Cabajsky is an assistant professor of Comparative Canadian literature at the Université de Moncton. She is co-editor of *National Plots: Historical Fiction and Changing Ideas of Canada* (WLUP, forthcoming 2009) and is a founding member of the Early Canadian Literature Society. She holds an FESR/Heritage Canada Standard Research Grant for 2007–09.

Marlene Goldman teaches Canadian literature at the University of Toronto. She is the author of *Paths of Desire* (University of Toronto Press, 1977) and recently completed a book on apocalyptic discourse in Canadian fiction, *Rewriting Apocalypse* (McGill-Queen's University Press, 2005). She is currently researching Canadian fiction that invokes the motif of haunting.

Jennifer Henderson is an associate professor in the Department of English Language and Literature at Carleton University. She has published articles on Canadian fiction and criticism, feminist culture, and discourses of the liberal self and is the author of *Settler Feminism and Race Making in Canada* (University of Toronto Press, 2003). Her two current projects study the government of childhood and the trope of national reconciliation.

Brian Johnson is an assistant professor in the Department of English at Carleton University in Ottawa, where he specializes in Canadian literature and literary theory. Among his recent publications are essays on indigeneity and ecology in the Canadian animal story, northern nationalism in Martha Ostenso's *Wild Geese*, and Jewish masculinities in the novels of Mordecai Richler. He is currently working on a study of race and horror in Canadian representations of the North.

Shelley Kulperger completed a Ph.D. on feminist and postcolonial gothic in Canada in the School of English, Media Studies and Art History at the University of Queensland, Australia. Her research interests include Australian and Canadian gothic, motherhood, and feminist and postcolonial cultural memory. She currently works in multicultural health policy and has published articles on transculturation, urban space, multiculturalism, and feminist cultural memory.

Atef Laouyene is an assistant professor in the Department of English at California State University, Los Angeles. He has published articles on the discourse of exoticism in contemporary postcolonial writing and Arabic culture and literature. His research interests include postcolonial literary studies, Arab diaspora studies, and francophone literatures of the Maghreb. He is currently working on narratives of violence in Anglo-Arab writing.

Lindy Ledohowski completed her Ph.D. in the Department of English at the University of Toronto in 2008 and a SSHRCC postdoctoral fellowship in the Department of English at the University of Ottawa in 2009. She has accepted an assistant professorship in Canadian Literature at St. Jerome's University in the University of Waterloo. Her research focuses on representations of ethnic angst in contemporary Canadian literature. She is currently working on a book analyzing death and haunting in Ukrainian-Canadian English-language literature.

Cynthia Sugars is an associate professor in the Department of English at the University of Ottawa, where she teaches Canadian literature and postcolonial theory. She is the author of numerous essays on Canadian literature and has edited two collections of essays on Canadian postcolonial theory: *Unhomely States: Theorizing English-Canadian Postcolonialism* (Broadview, 2004) and *Home-Work: Postcolonialism, Pedagogy, and Canadian Literature* (University of Ottawa Press, 2004). She has recently co-edited (with Laura Moss) a new two-volume historical anthology of Canadian literature, entitled *Canadian Literature in English: Texts and Contexts* (Pearson, 2009) and is working on a study of Canadian ghosts.

Gerry Turcotte is the dean of arts and sciences at the University of Notre Dame in Sydney, Australia. He is past president of the Association for Canadian Studies in Australia and New Zealand, former secretary of the International Council for Canadian Studies, founding director of the Centre for Canadian–Australian Studies, and was the editor of *Australian-Canadian Studies* for four years. He is the author and editor of fourteen books including the novel *Flying in Silence* (published in Canada by Cormorant Books and in Australia by Brandl and Schlesinger, 2001), which was shortlisted for *The Age* Book of the Year in 2001 and *Border Crossings: Words and Images* (Brandl and Schlesinger, 2004). His new book, *Peripheral Fear: Transformations of the Gothic in Canada and Australia*, will be published by Peter Lang in 2009.

Herb Wyile is a full professor in the Department of English at Acadia University in Wolfville, Nova Scotia. He has published numerous articles on contemporary Canadian literature, co-edited special issues of *Textual Studies in Canada* and *Studies in Canadian Literature*, and is the author of *Speculative Fictions: Contemporary Canadian Novelists and the Writing of History* (McGill-Queen's UP, 2002) and *Speaking in the Past Tense: Canadian Novelists on Writing Historical Fiction* (Wilfrid Laurier UP, 2007). He has recently co-edited with Jeanette Lynes *Surf's Up! The Rising Tide of Atlantic-Canadian Literature*, a special issue of *Studies in Canadian Literature*.

Index

abjection, 131; of Aboriginal/racialized Other, 63–66, 71n24, 130–33, 136, 141, 150, 214–16; and incest, 131–33, 141; Kristeva on, 131–33; mourning of, 150; of women, 63–65, 130–33, 136, 141, 150, 215–16

Aboriginal lands: alleged "emptiness" of, 76, 111–12, 234; in Australia, 76, 77–78, 88, 89, 90–91, 93n19; claims to, 52–54, 55, 56, 62, 66, 68n5, 70n15, 106, 225n6; and geography of trauma/haunting, 106–7, 108, 213–14, 217–18, 221–22, 242; as haunted because stolen, 242; ownership of, 38–39, 52–53, 111–12, 234, 242. *See also* wilderness landscape

Aboriginal literature, 205–6; and British/European Gothic, 175–78, 208–9; and Canadian Gothic, 207–8, 210–12; and as itself gothic, xix–xx, 176–78, 206–7, 208. See also *The Cure for Death by Lightning*; *Kiss of the Fur Queen*; *Monkey Beach*

Aboriginal peoples: abjection of, 63–66, 71n24, 214–16; activism/"warrior" spirit of, 217, 218–20; and challenges to "indigenization" meta-narratives, 25, 26–27, 37–38, 43–44; "disappearance"/extinction of, xix, 25, 26–27, 34–35, 37, 64–65, 69n13, 229–31, 233, 245–46; and "domestic vio-

lence" of state policies, 119–20, 212–13, 214–16, 223, 224; identification with, by white settlers, 159–60, 170, 245–46; land claims of, 52–54, 55, 56, 62, 66, 68n5, 70n15, 106, 225n6; mythological figures of, xx, 112–13, 200n15, 214, 216, 217–18, 221; spirituality of, vs. Christianity, 53, 54, 56, 57–58, 59, 65, 66–67, 69n12, 69–70n14; and white claims to indigeneity, xii, 25, 31, 38–46, 111–12; and whites' process of indigenization, 26, 34–41. *See also* Australia, Aboriginal peoples of; Beothuk, as depicted in *River Thieves*; "indigenization" meta-narrative; Mowat, Farley, *entries on*

Aboriginal peoples, as gothic figures, viii, xi, xvii, xix–xx; and ghosts of troubled past, xviii–xix, xx, 24, 30, 229–33, 245–46; in "indigenization" meta-narratives, 25–31, 36; and misappropriation of mythology, 112–13; in settler-invader context, viii, ix–x, xi, xiv, 25–27; and trickster, xix, 53, 57; and women's supernatural powers, 109, 110–11, 112–13, 206, 214, 216–22. *See also* Coyote; "indigenization" meta-narrative; Mowat, Farley, northern Gothic of

Aboriginal women: abjection of, 63–65, 130–33, 136, 141, 150,

roles as omniscient healers, 253–54, 257; and gothic presence in rational/"pathologizing" world, 255–61, 263–71; and lies told by doctors, 254, 262, 266; and poisoning patient's descent into madness, 262–68, 269; police brutality victim in, 268–71; and Southern Ontario Gothic, 258; and tale told by cadaver, 258–61; title of, 251–52, 272n1; transference (patient–doctor communication) in, 251, 252–53, 256–61, 272–73n2; and *unheimlich*, 253

Bloodletting & Miraculous Cures, individual stories of: "Afterwards," 254, 271; "Eli," 262, 268–71; "Night Flight," 254, 262; "Take All of Murphy," 258–61, 265; "Winston," 251, 262–68, 269, 272

Bociurkiw, Marusya: *The Children of Mary*, 169

Boyden, Joseph: *Three Day Road*, xviii, xx

Brand, Dionne, 101, 113, 118, 119; *In Another Place, Not Here*, 108; *A Map to the Door of No Return*, 104. See also *At the Full and Change of the Moon*

British Columbia: Aboriginal land claims in, 52–54, 55, 56, 62, 66, 68n5, 70n15, 106, 225n6; and geography of trauma/haunting, 106–7, 108, 213–14, 217–18, 221–22; Haisla territory in, as connected to spirit world, 106–7, 212–13; and imposition of British law/Christianity, 56–57; as setting of Japanese-Canadian internment, 84. See also *The Cure for Death by Lightning*; *The Double Hook*; *Monkey Beach*; *Obasan*

British/European Gothic, 208–9; and Aboriginal literature, 175–78, 208–9; anti-Catholicism in, xx, 1–10, 15, 178; castle/old house in, 62, 66, 208; decadent aristocracy in, 235–36, 243; "distemper" in, 55, 58; as "domestic," 4, 18n5; features/tropes of, 130, 151n3, 208–9; and historical fiction, 108–9, 229–31, 235, 237–38, 240, 241, 242–46, 247n2; and imperial expansion, 2, 8–9; as northern Gothic, 24, 31–32, 34–35, 41–43, 47–48n6; revolutionary backdrop to, 6, 7–8; and subversion of "contract" between writer and reader, 14; terror vs. horror in, 209, 224, 225n1, 232–34; as testimony, 5; 1–5, 7–10, 12–15; as "weapon of the weak," 8, 10. See also Canadian Gothic, as transformation/variation of British/European Gothic

Brontë, Charlotte: *Jane Eyre*, 113–14, 129

Burgess, Tony, xviii

Burke, Edmund, 2, 7, 8, 10

Canada: apparent lack of ghosts in, xiii–xiv, 30, 100, 111, 205, 207; as gothic space, xiii–xvi, xxi; as haunted, vii–xxi, 83; national identity of, xvii–xviii, xxi, 125–27; postcolonial status of, x

Canadian Gothic, 207–8, 210–12; and Aboriginal literature, 207–8, 210–12; absence of, ix, xii–xiii; conservatism of, 6–7, 10, 17, 62–63, 65–66; dominance/sexual power imbalances in, 215–16; ghosts/haunting in, vii–xxi; monsters in, vii, viii–ix, x, xi, xii, xiii–xvii, xx; and national identity,

Cohen, Matt, xvii

Coleridge, Samuel Taylor, "The Rime
of the Ancient Mariner": as evoked
by Mowat, 24, 32, 34–36; and
Frankenstein, 31–32, 34

counter-transference, in *Bloodletting
& Miraculous Cures*, 251, 254–55,
261–72; definition of, 273n4; and
doctors' roles as omniscient healers, 253–54; and poisoning
patient's descent into madness,
262–68, 269; and police brutality
victim, 268–71; and transference,
251, 252–53, 256–61, 272–73n2.
See also *Bloodletting & Miraculous
Cures*

Coyote: as god, 53, 54, 56, 57–58; possession by, 51, 59, 63–64, 66, 68n2,
71n25; as spectral figure, 51–53,
55, 57–58, 59–60, 66; as symbol of
colonial violence/guilt, 53, 63–64;
as trickster, 53, 57

Crémazie, Octave, 17

Crosbie, Lynn, xviii

Crummey, Michael. See *River Thieves*

The Cure for Death by Lightning
(Anderson-Dargatz), xviii, 51–54,
58–67; abjection in, 63–66, 71n24;
Aboriginal assimilation in, 65–66;
Aboriginal "disappearance" in,
64–65; and Aboriginal land claims,
62, 66; Aboriginal lesbian as out-
sider/threat in, 59–61, 63, 64–65,
67; and Christianity vs. Aboriginal
spirituality, 59, 65, 66–67; Coyote
as spectral figure in, 51, 59–60, 66;
Coyote as symbol of colonial vio-
lence/guilt in, 63–64; expulsion
and sacrifice in, 64–65, 67; "freak-
ish" women in, 63–64; houses in,
61–62, 66; incest in, 59, 61, 62; les-

bian relationship in, 59–65, 67;
misogyny/racism in, 64; patriarchy
in, 59, 60, 61, 62–63, 65–66; and
possession by Coyote, 51, 59,
63–64, 66, 68n2, 71n25; and possession of land/property, 58, 66;
sacrifice and redemption in, 66, 67,
71n25; settler–Aboriginal tensions
in, 58–59, 60; and symbolism of
winter house, 61–62, 66; "unsettledness" in, 57–58, 66; wartime
setting of, 58, 60; "white"
Aboriginal saviour of, 65–66

Davies, Robertson, xiii, xiv, xvii, 211

De Guise, Charles. See *Le Cap au diable*

Delgamuukw v. British Columbia
(Supreme Court case), 68n5

Derrida, Jacques, vii, xiv, xvi, 97, 136,
271; on ghosts, 102–3, 163

"domestic Gothic," 4–5, 18n5. *See also*
feminist postcolonial Gothic

The Double Hook (Watson), x, xiv,
51–58, 59, 65, 66, 67, 208;
Aboriginal "disappearance" in,
69n13; and Aboriginal land claims,
52–54, 55, 56; birth and redemption in, 57–58, 67; burning of
house in, 57, 66; and Christianity
vs. Aboriginal spirituality, 53, 54,
56, 57–58, 69n12, 69–70n14; and
concluding image of Aboriginal
resistance, 57–58, 66; Coyote as
god in, 53, 54, 56, 57–58, 69n12;
Coyote as spectral figure in, 51–52,
55, 57–58; Coyote as symbol of
colonial violence/guilt in, 53;
Coyote's last word in, 57–58, 66;
expulsion and sacrifice in, 54–55,
56, 58; incestuous overtones in, 55,
68n9; occulted female in, 56; old

passion play re-enactment in,
184–85, 193; pleasure and pain in,
180, 183–84, 185–86, 196; and
postcolonialism, 188–89; ritualized
repetition in, 189–93; sexual abuse
in, 179, 181, 182–83, 185–94,
202n21; and sexual abuse–homosexuality connection, 187–94;
sexual violence in, 194, 196–97,
201–2n20, 202n21. *See also* residential schools
Kogawa, Joy: *Itsuka*, 85. See also
Obasan
Kostash, Myrna: *The Doomed
Bridegroom*, 168–69
Kristeva, Julia, 75, 87; on abjection,
131–33
Kroetsch, Robert, xviii
Kulyk Keefer, Janice: *The Ladies'
Lending Library*, 169. See also *The
Green Library*

Lai, Larissa: *When Fox Is a Thousand*,
xviii
Lam, Vincent, 253, 262. See also
Bloodletting & Miraculous Cures
lands, Aboriginal: alleged "emptiness"
of, 76, 111–12, 234; in Australia,
76, 77–78, 88, 89, 90–91, 93n19;
claims to, 52–54, 55, 56, 62, 66,
68n5, 70n15, 106, 225n6; and
geography of trauma/haunting,
106–7, 108, 213–14, 217–18,
221–22, 242; as haunted because
stolen, 242; ownership of, 38–39,
52–53, 111–12, 234, 242. *See also*
wilderness landscape
Lareau, Edmond, 1, 11, 13
Lawson, Alan, viii, ix, xv–xvi
Lee, SKY: *Disappearing Moon Café*,
xviii

lesbian relationships: in *The Cure for
Death by Lightning*, 59–65, 67; in
Fall on Your Knees, 130, 138–39,
144. *See also* homosexuality
Lewis, Matthew Gregory, 7, 18n7, 181
London, Jack, 24
Luckhurst, Roger, xvi, 99, 101, 121n1
Lysenko, Vera, 157; *Yellow Boots*, 168

*Mabo and Others v. Queensland (No.
2)* (Australian High Court decision), 76, 77–78, 88, 89, 90–91
MacDonald, Ann-Marie. See *Fall on
Your Knees*
MacLulich, T.D., 23–24
madness: in *Bloodletting & Miraculous
Cures*, 262–68, 269; in *Le Cap au
diable*, 1, 3–4; in *River Thieves*,
239–41
March, Mary (Demasduit): capture of,
231, 237–39, 240; death of, and
return of body, 231, 233, 240; and
husband's murder, 233, 238
McFarlane, Scott, 75, 88–89, 93n16
meta-narrative. *See* Canadian meta-
narrative, of settler-invader society;
"indigenization" meta-narrative
Miki, Roy, viii, 78, 79, 80–82
Monkey Beach (Robinson), xix, 97,
105, 205–25, 255; abjection in,
214–16; and beach as gothic setting in, 217–18, 219, 221–22; and
British/European Gothic, 177–78,
206, 207; Castricano on, 177–78,
206, 207, 216, 255; closed/inacces-
sible setting of, 213–14, 222; and
danger/disorder of non-Native
world, 212–13; domesticization of
fear and violence in, 119–20,
215–16, 217, 224; domesticization
of supernatural in, 109, 112–13,

212, 213; and "domestic violence" as perpetrated by state, 119–20, 212–13, 214–16, 223, 224; and exoticization/colonization of Other, 111; and geography of trauma/haunting, 106–7, 108, 213–14, 217–18, 221–22; Haisla culture in, 112–13, 177, 206, 208, 213, 216–23; monsters in, xix, 112–13, 212, 213, 214, 216, 217–22, 224–25; Native activism/"warrior" spirit in, 217, 218–20; as rejecting white concepts of "Otherness," 212, 214–16, 217–18, 219–20, 223–25; residential school system/abuses in, 108, 120, 213, 215–16, 217, 218, 223, 224; Sasquatch (B'gwus) in, 112, 214, 216, 217–18, 221; sexual abuse in, 108, 120, 215–16, 218, 222, 223, 224; shape-shifters in, 109, 110, 112, 217; and supernatural as women's power, 109, 112–13, 206, 214, 216–22; wilderness/natural world in, 212, 213, 219, 224

Monkey Beach, Lisamarie as heroine/ narrator of: and brother's disappearance/death, 107, 208, 213–14, 220, 221–22; and contact with spirits/monsters, 206, 216, 218–19, 220, 221–22; and discovery of sexual abuse, 215–16; and dreams of death, 214, 220, 221; flight to city by, 212, 220; and grandmother as supportive figure/source of wisdom, 109, 113, 217–18, 221, 222; and Haisla culture/heritage, 206, 208, 216–23; and mourning for dead, 220, 222; name of, 214; and repatriation of monsters, 112–13, 218, 220–21; and Sasquatch (B'gwus), 112, 214, 216, 217–18,

221; as shape-shifter, 109, 112; supernatural powers of, 109, 112, 214, 216–22; and T'sonoqua, 112–13, 221 and Uncle Josh as sexual abuser, 215–16, 221–22, 223, 224; and Uncle Mick as supportive figure/source of wisdom, 217, 218–20, 222

monsters, vii, viii–ix, x, xi, xii, xiii–xvii, xx; in *Le Cap au diable*, 5; in *Frankenstein*, 33, 77; of French/ English revolutions, 8; oppressors as, in *Obasan*, 83–84, 87, 89, 90–91; psychological, 270, 272; as symbols of Others, 77–78, 87, 217–18; and Wacousta as monstrous figure, xii, 210–12

monsters, as depicted in *Monkey Beach*, xix, 112–13, 214, 217–22, 224–25; as benevolent/non-destructive, 212, 213, 218–20; Lisamarie's contact with, 206, 216, 218–19, 220, 221–22; repatriation of, 112–13, 218, 220–21; Sasquatch (B'gwus), 112, 214, 216, 217–18, 221; T'sonoqua, 112–13, 221

Moodie, Susanna, xii, xiii, xiv, 30, 100–101

Morrison, Toni: *Beloved*, 101–2

Moses, Daniel David, xx

Moss, John, 24

Moss, Laura: *Is Canada Postcolonial?*, x, 17

mourning: and abjection, 150; and Canadian meta-narrative, 151n4; for dead, 220, 222; and ghosts, 128, 144–51, 220, 222; and mnemonic narrative (*Fall on Your Knees*), 128, 144–51

Mowat, Farley: on Aboriginal assimilation, 28–30; and adventure story

disruption of Canadian meta-narrative, 78–79, 80–82, 88–89; and domesticization of oppression, 84–85; on fragility of human rights, 82–83; gothic settings/landscape of, 83–85; identity/self-definition in, 79–80; and language of minority vs. language of oppressor, 79–80; and land stolen from Other, 78; and memory as gothic space, 84–85; mother's ghost in, 85–86; as narrative of minority, 78–79, 81; oppressors as monsters in, 83–84, 87, 89, 90–91; and redress to Japanese Canadians, 75, 89–91, 93–94n19; silences in, 79, 80, 85–86; as uncanny text, 75–91; and wartime treatment of Japanese Canadians, 75, 78, 81–85, 87–88

Old World, gothic fiction and poetry of. *See* British/European Gothic

Orientalism, vii–viii; and Aboriginal "Other," 90; and Catholicism, 15, 181; and criticism of redress to Japanese Canadians, 90; and imperial subject/colonized object, 164; Said on, vii–viii, 15, 26; in settler-invader context, 26

Osler, William, 252, 262, 263

Other: Aboriginal/racialized, and abjection of, 63–66, 71n24, 130–33, 136, 141, 150, 214–16; in Canadian meta-narrative, 127–28, 136–37; colonization/enslavement of, 102–5, 114–16; exoticization/colonization of, 108, 111, 137–41; land stolen from, 78, 242; monster, as symbol of, 77–78, 87, 217–18; settler-invader society's fear of, 76–77; white concepts of, as rejected in *Monkey Beach*, 212, 214–16, 217–18, 219–20, 223–25

Paluk, William, 157

"para-colonial," concept of, 53, 68n8

Paravisini-Gebert, Lizabeth, xv, 233

Poe, Edgar Allan, 66, 151n2, 237

postcolonial Gothic, in Canada, vii–xxi; and Aboriginal peoples, viii, xi, xvii, xviii–xx; and absence of Gothic tradition, ix, xii–xiii; and British/European Gothic, xi, xvi; and Canada as postcolonial society, x; and Canadian national identity, xvii–xviii, xxi; and challenge to dominant socio-cultural narratives, xviii–xix; evolution of, xvii; examples of, x, xii; feminist, xv, xxi; ghosts/haunting in, vii–ix, x, xi, xiii–xvii; imperial/hegemonic legacies of, vii–x; monsters in, vii, viii–ix, x, xi, xii, xiii–xvii; and national meta-narratives, xviii; and settler-invader context, viii, ix–x, xi, xiv, xvi; and suppression/marginalization of cultures/races, viii, xiv, xvii; and uncanny, vii, ix, xvi; and "unhomely," vii, viii, ix, xvii; and wilderness landscape, ix, xi–xii. *See also* Canadian Gothic; *see also specific topics*

post-traumatic stress disorder (PTSD), 142, 152n12

Punter, David, xv, 127, 257; on "domestic Gothic," 4, 18n5; on Gothic and modernism/contemporary ideas, 57, 98–100; on "paranoiac fiction," 258

Punter, David, and Glennis Byron, 229, 241–43, 246

Pyper, Andrew, xviii

Radcliffe, Ann, 2–3, 7, 8, 18n7, 55, 109, 181, 209; *The Mysteries of Udolpho*, 3, 55